Join the Recommended Country Inns® Travelers' Club and Save!

The Recommended Country Inns® guides are the preeminent guidebooks to the finest country inns in the United States. Authors personally visit and recommend each establishment listed in the guides, and **no fees are solicited or accepted for inclusion in the books.**

Now the Recommended Country Inns® guides offer a special new way for travelers to enjoy extra savings: through the Recommended Country Inns® Travelers' Club. Member benefits include savings such as:

- Discounts on accommodations
- Discounts on food
- Discounts on local attractions

How to Save: Read the profile for each inn to see if it offers an incentive to members. For participating establishments, look for information at the end of the inn's profile or in the index at the end of the book. Simply mention that you are a member of the Recommended Country Inns® Travelers' Club when making reservations, and show your membership card when you check in. All offers are subject to availability.

How to Join: If you wish to become a member of the Recommended Country Inns® Travelers' Club, simply fill out the attached form and send it by mail to:

Recommended Country Inns® Travelers' Club
c/o The Globe Pequot Press
PO Box 833
Old Saybrook, CT 06475
Or fax to: 860–395–2855

A membership card will be mailed to you upon receipt of the form. Please allow 4-6 weeks for delivery.

**Sign up today and start saving as a Recommended Country Inns®
Travelers' Club member!**

(All offers from participating inns expire November 30, 1998, unless otherwise mentioned.)

Recommended Country Inns® Travelers' Club
Membership Form

Name: _____

Address: _____

City _____ State _____ Zip _____

Phone _____ Fax _____ E-mail _____

Age: 18–35 _____;   36–50_____;   over 50_____

Sex: Male ____   Female ____   Marital Status: Single _____   Married_____

Annual Household Income:
   under $35,000 _____; $35,000–$75,0000 _____;   over $75,000_____

Credit cards: Mastercard_____; Visa _____; Amex _____; Discover _____; Other _____

Book purchased at: Store Name: _____; City _____, State _____

Mail completed form to:
Recommended Country Inns® Travelers' Club
c/o The Globe Pequot Press
PO Box 833
Old Saybrook, CT 06475
Or fax to: 860–395–2855

MW

Recommended
Country Inns®
THE MIDWEST

"The top of the . . . crop for a getaway splurge."
—*Chicago Sun-Times*

"A delightful writer, Puhala gets into history and description which enhances the reader's pleasure . . . lets you know what's available as far as facilities and activities . . . [and] lists things nearby each inn that are worth seeing or doing."
—*Ohioana Quarterly*

"Suggests . . . outstanding inns for quality, unique features, and value."
—*Chevron USA Odyssey*

"Puhala has opened a door to a Midwestern treasure house of travel gems—a spectrum of places not to be missed. One can almost smell the morning muffins and feel the sunshine."
—Wisconsin Division of Tourism

"Puhala has captured the essence of the inns: welcoming and warm as a fire's glow."
—*Detroit Free Press*

Recommended Country Inns® Series

"These guides are a marvelous start to planning the leisurely trek, romantic getaway, or time-off for reflection."
—*Internet Book Review*

The Recommended Country Inns® series is designed for the discriminating traveler who seeks the best in unique accommodations away from home.

From hundreds of inns personally visited and evaluated by the author, only the finest are described here. The inclusion of an inn is purely a personal decision on the part of the author; no one can pay or be paid to be in a Globe Pequot inn guide.

Organized for easy reference, these guides point you to just the kind of accommodations you are looking for: Comprehensive indexes by category provide listings of inns for romantic getaways, inns for the sports-minded, inns that serve gourmet meals, inns for the business traveler . . . and more. State maps help you pinpoint the location of each inn, and detailed driving directions tell you how to get there.

Use these guidebooks with confidence. Allow each author to share his or her selections with you and then discover for yourself the country inn experience.

Editions available:
Recommended Country Inns®
New England • Mid-Atlantic and Chesapeake Region
The South • The Midwest • West Coast
The Southwest • Rocky Mountain Region
also
Recommended Romantic Inns
Recommended Island Inns

Recommended Country Inns®

THE MIDWEST

Illinois ❧ Indiana ❧ Iowa ❧ Michigan
❧ Minnesota ❧ Missouri ❧ Nebraska
❧ Ohio ❧ Wisconsin

Sixth Edition

by Bob Puhala
illustrated by Bill Taylor Jr.

A *Voyager* Book

The Globe Pequot Press

Old Saybrook, Connecticut

To Kate, Dayne, Debbie, Ma, Pa, and Mark.
We did it again, guys! You are my blessings.

ISBN 0-7627-0001-7
ISSN 1078-5507 ·

Cover photo: Stuart Avenue Inn, Kalamazoo, MI p. 154

Cover design: Mullen & Katz
Map design: Nancy Freeborn
Text design: Saralyn D'Amato-Twomey

Manufactured in the United States of America
Sixth Edition/First Printing

Contents

Indexes

A Few Words about Visiting Midwestern Inns

I have a "magic number," just like all those sports teams closing in on a championship.

It's 1,000.

I figure that sometime in 1997, I'll step into my 1,000th country inn looking for the best overnights in the Midwest that can then be shared with you.

One thousand heartland inns, bed and breakfasts, historic hotels, guest ranches, farmsteads, and upscale retreats, all personally visited by me—and hundreds wth wife Debbie, daughters Kate and Dayne, brother Mark, even grandma and grandpa in tow so that I can offer you the cream of the crop: 209 fabulous nights away from home in the sixth edition of *Recommended Country Inns: The Midwest.*

You can already tell I like numbers. Here's another one. Since I started this gig with the book's first edition in 1987, I've rambled over more than 17,000 miles of Midwest roads to discover these gems.

That's lots of traveling. But there's no other way to do it. No other way to evaluate inns without seeing them with my own professional traveler's discerning eye; talking to the innkeepers; probing guests for insights, impressions, and anecdotes; tasting the food; sleeping in the beds (or covered wagons or under the stars, whatever the case may be); walking the grounds; exploring the cities, villages, hamlets, and cowtowns. In good weather and bad. Below-zero temperatures and searing heat. In high season and low season.

Let's see—209 inns out of nearly 1,000: That means only about one inn for every five I've visited made the cut. And there's only one reason I do it. So I can feel confident of recommending only the best Midwest inns to my readers.

I get plenty of rewards for my hard work. For this edition, I visted historic lighthouses transformed into inns on Michigan's Upper Peninsula in the waning days of winter. Of course, in the Upper Peninsula, winter takes a lot longer to wane than in more southern climes of the Midwest.

Even in April, massive piles of snow reached the second-story windows of some homes. Also remaining were beautiful 14-foot-high snow caves, nature's handicraft sculpted along the Lake Superior shoreline.

And I'll never forget that ever hopeful town-name sign along a lonely Upper Peninsula road that was virtually buried under a white blanket of the fluffy stuff: the town's name—FLORIDA.

There are other perks, too. Rivertown inns perched atop high bluffs afford magnificient views of the heartland's mighty rivers: the Mississippi, the Missouri, the Ohio.

Elegant Victorian mansions charm me with sparkling woodwork, master craftsmanship, and opulent furnishings. Turn-of-the-century summer houses, transformed into spectacular retreats, boast the fiery glow of Great Lakes sunrises and sunsets.

Log cabins located in North Woods and Ozark Mountain wilderness are steeped in pristine tranquillity. Some inns nestle on rivers with world-class white-water rapids; others, on historic estates and manors tucked deep in the rolling hills of Appalachia, offer genteel Southern hospitality.

And with Nebraska under my "Midwest" umbrella, some "inns" are rooted on cattle ranches and rangelands, which often stretch for thousands of acres over prime pasture.

Then there are the innkeepers—no two are alike. Some have fled big-city corporate life to pursue a dream. Others are ex-soldiers, homemakers, teachers, lawyers, farmers, engineers. They each graciously tackle the day-to-day task of running a hostelry mostly for the pleasure of making travelers feel as though there's a little bit of home waiting for them no matter where they go.

They have to love their innkeeper role; the work's too hard to make sense for any other reason.

You're part of the fun, too. Inn-goers seem to be more friendly, interesting, and involved with the world around them, possessing a special drive to experience new things, explore the past, or relive a little part of history.

Let's not forget our animal surprises. I've made so many furry friends (with everything from a horse named Firmy to a llama called Dali) while on the road that I could start up my own ranch. And I had some other interesting animal adventures, too. Let's see . . . there was the black bear standing in the middle of the road in a remote corner of northwest Wisconsin that looked me right in the eye before scurrying back into the brush. I saw eagles soar over bluff tops and dive into icy waters for a wintertime meal, foxes slink through the woods, deer stand frozen in my headlights, hawks, coyotes. . . .

Oh, yes—and those rattlesnakes that did a "shake, rattle, and roll" at Nebraska's Ash Hollow State Historical Park, on the Oregon Trail. I would've felt a whole lot better if I had had a six-gun strapped on my shootin' hip.

Of course, there are some glitches. Unlike the East Coast, where traditional country inns (a full-service restaurant with lodging accommodations for travelers) were a part of the landscape from Colonial times, the Midwest's definition of a "country inn" is pretty elastic. Here your choices include everything from historic log cabins and ranch bunkhouses to re-created Victorian resort hotels and small bed-and-breakfast inns.

You'll still have a great time, as long as you have an authoritative travel guidebook whose author has personally visited all the "inns" recommended to you.

A trusted guidebook with an excellent track record of directing people to those very kinds of establishments is one of the most important tools in planning a getaway. A trusted guidebook like this one. Just ask veteran inn-goers . . . and innkeepers, too.

So after more than a decade of "traveling together," I ask you to join me yet again and discover the Midwest's best country inns. Each has something special and exciting to offer: atmosphere, charm, romance, history, architecture, location, feeling. Maybe even a little soul.

I'm still surprised by how many of you I meet while out on the road. And how you've had my book in hand while telling me that you never realized there were so many "fabulous places" in the Midwest until you read about them in these pages. That means a lot to me. Thanks.

Several others have written to second my choices. Some have offered me anecdotes about their stays. A few of you have even added "innside" information about places you'd like to see in the book. Again, thanks.

No doubt I'll bump into more of you somewhere down the line. It might be in some little cowtown in Nebraska or some upscale whirlpool and fireplace wonderland where romance is the only currency.

Either way, be sure to stop and say, "Hey!"

About the Author

Bob Puhala is an award-winning journalist whose syndicated travel column for the *Chicago Sun-Times* is in its fifteenth year. He is also a regular columnist for *Home & Away* magazine and regularly appears on radio and television talking about travel. His articles have appeared in other newspapers and national magazines, including *USA Today, Travel & Leisure, Travel-Holiday,* *Discovery, Columbia Journalism Review,* and *Consumers Digest.*

Puhala has written 14 books and is a member of both The Authors Guild and the Society of American Travel Writers. He lives in the Chicago area with his wife, daughters, and family.

How to Use This Inn Guide

Country inns, historic hotels, and outstanding B&Bs are listed state by state and alphabetically by city, town, and village within each state. You'll find them in the following order: Illinois, Indiana, Iowa, Michigan, Minnesota, Missouri, Nebraska, Ohio, and Wisconsin. Preceding each state grouping is a map guide and handy index. There's also a complete alphabetical index at the end of the book.

Helpful guidebook features are the special inn indexes. These list particularly noteworthy inn activities, amenities, and features. They will help you select the inn that's right for you.

There is no charge of any kind for an inn to be included in this guidebook. I have chosen inns based on my professional experience and personal standards. I offer readers a choice among the finest, most interesting, and most historic accommodations available in the Midwest. I thank those of you who have written me in the past, and I continue to welcome comments, questions, and information about your favorite inn—whether or not it's included in my selections—or newly opened and soon-to-be-opened inns. Please address all correspondence to Bob Puhala, *Recommended Country Inns: The Midwest*, The Globe Pequot Press, P.O. Box 833, Old Saybrook, Connecticut 06475.

Rates: Inns often change rates without notice. The high/low prices I have quoted are meant to be used *only as guidelines*. They'll give you a reasonable idea of what a room might cost. For the most part, I haven't included tax rates or service charges, which add to your bill; neither have I described tipping suggestions. Inquire upon making reservations.

Menu Abbreviations: The following abbreviations are used:

EP: European Plan—room without meals.
EPB: European Plan—room with full breakfast.
AP: American Plan—room with all meals.
MAP: Modified American Plan—room with breakfast and dinner.
BYOB: Bring Your Own Bottle.

Note that meal plans change often. An inn offering certain quoted specialties may change chefs and, thus, their entire entree list. Other inns constantly adjust breakfast policies, some offering full breakfasts one season, then continental or buffet-style breakfasts the next. There are several inns offering lunch and dinner specials by reservation or request; this is noted under "Facilities and activities" in each inn description. Remember that it is always best to call ahead so that you know what to expect.

Innkeepers: Some inns remain in the same family for decades. Others change ownership more frequently. This might result in wholesale revisions of previous inn policies. Or inns might completely close their doors to the public as they convert to private residences. Be sure to call ahead to ensure that the inn of your choice still welcomes travelers.

Reservations and Deposits: Many inns maintain such a sterling reputation of excellence and service that they require reservations made months in advance. Even on average it's advisable to call at least one month in advance at most inns, especially if you're planning to visit during the high-volume travel season (usually summer). Smaller establishments may require even more advance notice. And if you wish to stay at inns during annual town festivals, call *right now*.

On the other hand, it's always possible that you'll be able to make spur-of-the-moment reservations—possible, but not always likely.

As for deposits, this is such a common requirement that I do not mention specific inn policies. Assume that, with few exceptions, you'll be required to pay a deposit to reserve a room, using a personal check or a credit card. Be sure to inquire about refund policies.

Credit Cards: Visa and MasterCard are accepted unless otherwise stated. Many inns accept additional credit cards, too. Others accept only cash or personal checks. Call ahead to be sure.

Business Travel: Establishments listed in the "Inns for Business Travelers" category are especially sensitive to the needs of the burgeoning class of business travelers. At a minimum, these inns, historic hotels, and bed and breakfasts offer corporate rates, meeting/conference rooms, and fax machines.

They also provide writing desks, reading lamps, and telephones in guest rooms, and they may be able to arrange photocopying, computer access, or other business-related services.

Entries in this category also geographically place the inn in context to the city's or town's primary business district.

Children: Inns that offer special rates for children are duly noted. Several inns do not publicly advertise kid discounts, so ask about them. Also note that some inns specialize in quiet getaway weekends for couples; others are antique-filled treasures. I still cringe when my kids get close to my baseball trophies; imagine how innkeepers might feel if your little ones were steamrolling toward a precious Ming vase. My wife and I are used to all types of kid-related noises (at all hours of the night), but some people are not. I guess what I'm trying to say is—please use your discretion when choosing an inn. Make sure it's one that the kids will enjoy. (See the "Inns Especially Good for Kids" index for some help.) As we and thousands of other parents have discovered, traveling with children is often a joy, but it's also tough work.

Pets: Spot usually won't be allowed inside. The rule: No pets unless otherwise stated.

Minimum Stay: Two-night minimums on weekends and even three nights during holidays are requirements at several inns, as noted. This is a frequently changing policy.

Bed Size: Inns may use three-quarter beds, twins, doubles, queens, or kings. While a few historic selections may offer antique rope beds or other fanciful contraptions, exotica is usually not a worry. If you have a preference, make it known in advance.

Television, Telephones, and Air Conditioning: Are you the type of person who loves to travel deep into the heart of the wilderness but still must get a nightly fix of David Letterman? Were you born to live in air-conditioned rooms? I've noted which inns offer the above amenities in guest rooms. (Other inns offer these amenities in common rooms only.)

Food for Thought: A number of B&Bs are included in my selections. Oftentimes, innkeepers will have area restaurant dinner menus for guests to look over. At the least, the innkeeper should inquire about your food preferences and suggest an appropriate local restaurant. Most of the time, choices range from casual to fine dining. If you have any special dietary requirements,

you should realize that such requests often are considered by inn restaurants. If you're not a red-meat eater, you'll usually find seafood and fowl entree selections. Therefore, if I do not mention restaurants as part of my inn descriptions, be assured that your hosts can advise you.

Wheelchair Access: Inns that have wheelchair access are noted in each "Rooms" listing; there is also a special "Inns with Wheelchair Access" index at the back of the book. Wheelchair access to restaurants and dining rooms only is listed under "Facilities and activities."

Bad Habits: More inns than ever prohibit smoking in guest rooms or common areas. You will find a special "No Smoking Inns" index at the back of the book.

Recommended Country Inns® Travelers' Club: I state the discount, free night's stay, or other value offered by inns welcoming club members. Note that all discounts listed refer to room rates only, not to meals, and that a number of offers are subject to availability.

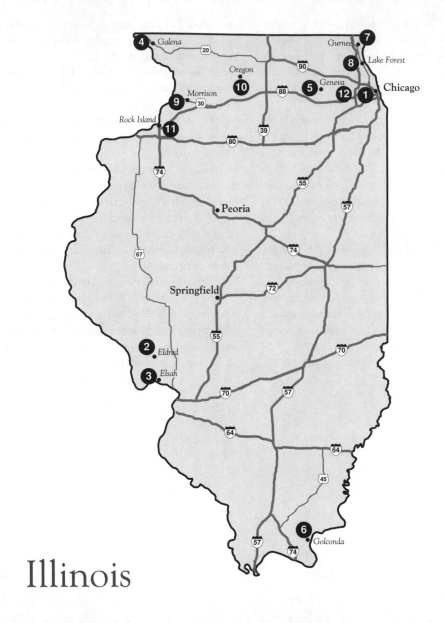

Illinois

Illinois

Numbers on map refer to towns numbered below.

The Gold Coast Guest House
CHICAGO, ILLINOIS 60610

I finally found a magnificent bed and breakfast in Chicago—right near the "Magnificent Mile."

It's located in the very heart of the Gold Coast, one of Chicago's most exclusive neighborhoods. And give Sally credit for her preservation efforts; she restored this stately 1873 brick townhouse, one of five historic buildings that used to line this portion of Elm Street. Now only three are left.

"When I bought the house, it was decorated very '60s," Sally said. "Like mirror squares on all the walls in the living rooms going up to and across the ceiling. Not quite my style."

Sally's style is a very contemporary *House Beautiful* look with some fine antiques spicing the classic design—along with decorating surprises.

For example, note the "four seasons" cherubs hanging on the exposed brick wall upon entering the inn. And did you spot those cute angel cherubs all the way at the top of the gathering room's "wall of windows" that stretches almost to the apex of the building?

Guest rooms offer the best of both classic and contemporary design. Bedchambers on the second floor, reached by a winding spiral staircase, are among my favorite, especially one graced with a big bay window overlooking the street, along with its art deco armoire and original brick fireplace.

And both second-floor rooms claim the inn's in-room whirlpools, too.

There's also an extra whirlpool bath on the first floor. Let Sally explain.

"That's for my guest from England who might have a room without a tub. The English must have their bath."

Sally should know. She lived in London for a year while working as a tour hostess for a major travel company. And Sally continues to tour the world via her guests, some of whom have come from as far away as India, Australia, and Guam. She keeps a stickpin map in the entryway, keeping track of her guests' homelands—as well as pictures of them!

Breakfasts are taken in the second-floor dining room that hangs like a balcony overlooking the gathering room below. Fresh bagels, English muffins, cold cereals, yogurt, juices, and more are part of the morning treats.

Then, if Mother Nature cooperates, relax in the private garden, ablaze with seasonal color; there's plenty of holly and evergreens for winter hues, too.

Now you should be ready to explore Chicago. Let's see, first I'll hit the Art Institute, got to go to Niketown, browse Water Tower Place, maybe dinner at a nearby sidewalk cafe, then it's off to the theater for an evening performance of . . .

How to get there: From the Kennedy Expressway (I–94) take the Ohio Street exit and continue down Ohio to Dearborn; turn left and proceed to Elm; turn left and continue to the inn.

Innkeeper: Sally Baker

Address/Telephone: 113 West Elm Street; (312) 337–0361, fax (312) 337 0362

Rooms: 4; all with private bath, 2 with whirlpool, 1 extra bath with whirlpool tub. No smoking inn.

Rates: $95 to $135, single; $105 to $150, double; continental breakfast and welcoming beverages.

Open: All year.

Facilities and activities: Gathering room looking out into private garden, with chairs and barbecue in summer. Nearby: five-minute walk to shops on "Magnificent Mile" (North Michigan Avenue); including Bloomingdale's, Niketown, Water Tower Place (with Marshall Field's), Burberry's, and lots more tony shops. Also walk to "Loop" live theater, upscale boutiques on Oak Street. Short drive to Field Museum, Museum of Natural History, Adler Planetarium, Art Institute, Soldier Field (home of the Chicago Bears), Shedd Aquarium, Oak Street Beach.

Hobson's Bluffdale
ELDRED, ILLINOIS 62027

"I'm a city girl," Lindy said. "Never set foot on a farm until I met Bill when we were both students at the University of Illinois." Bill stepped right in with a zinger. "That's right. She saw giraffes and zebras at the city zoo long before she ever saw any of my farm animals."

Bluffdale is a 320-acre farm (soybeans, corn, wheat, and a few pigs) run by the Hobsons; it's been in Bill's family since 1828. It was named by his great-great-grandfather for bluffs that run through the property.

Lindy took me into the original stone farmhouse, which still stands. It's cooking headquarters and also contains some of Bill's priceless family heirlooms, including a four-volume family history written by his great-great-grandfather.

Bill added: "Charles Dickens was one of his friends and visited here in the 1840s. They had to pick up Dickens at the train in a spring wagon and bring him to the farm."

Bluffdale is a spectacular getaway for anyone—but especially for city slickers and kids. Bill and Lindy encourage everyone to help with regular farm chores—feeding the chickens and pigs, gathering eggs, moving geese, bottle-feeding calves, picking fresh blackberries, harvesting vegetables from Bill's two-acre garden, and more.

Lindy is the cook who takes all this delicious farm-fresh food and whips up great feasts. Family-style meals include eggs, French toast or pancakes, fruits, and home-baked breads for breakfast; maybe a picnic lunch packed for a trek through the woods; and supper-table specials like fried chicken, baked ham, pot roast, or barbecued pork chops, topped off with oven-fresh sweets and homemade ice cream.

Overnight rooms are comfortable enough, done in bandana red and blues with brass lanterns and wide-plank floors. There's also a new Log Cabin in the Woods, a private getaway that transforms the "ranch" into your secluded playground.

But you don't come to Bluffdale for roomside splendor; there's far too much to do. The flexible schedule includes archaeological digs (this is historic Indian country), Saturday-night square dances, Sunday ice-cream socials, Monday ball games, Friday-night bonfire sing-alongs, and Tuesday-afternoon cookout picnics at Greenfield Lake.

How to get there: From St. Louis, take Missouri 367 north to Alton, Illinois. Continue north on U.S. 67, then head north on Illinois 267. Turn west at Illinois 208 and continue to Eldred. At Eldred–Hillview Road (at the bottom of a hill, opposite the Standard gas station), turn north, and proceed just over 3½ miles to the farm.

Innkeepers: Bill and Lindy Hobson

Address/Telephone: Hillview Road; (217) 983–2854

Rooms: 8, with 3 two-room suites, plus 1 cottage; all with private bath and air conditioning.

Rates: $65 to $82 per person; $43 for children ages 9 to 14, $36 for kids 4 to 8, $25 under age 4; AP. $375 adults, sliding scale for children, for weekly farm vacations; includes all activities and recreation. Three-night minimum Memorial Day, July 4, and Labor Day. Two-night minimum all other weekends, June through September.

Open: All year for B&B; farm vacations, March through November.

Facilities and activities: Horseback riding and trail rides, cart rides, swimming in heated pool, hot tub, canoe day trips, hiking through private wooded bluffs, arrowhead hunting, wild blackberry picking, fishing in private pond or Illinois River, pontoon boat rides, hayrides, square dancing, ice-cream socials, bonfire roasts, workshops in forestry, archaeology, pottery, ceramics, wildlife, and more. Nearby: water park.

Green Tree Inn
ELSAH, ILLINOIS 62028

I found it hard to believe that this 1850s-style river-town building is only about a decade old. "We designed it to convey nineteenth-century charm," Mary Ann said. "And since the entire town is on the National Register of Historic Places, we had to be very exact in matching the spirit of this building with its authentic nineteenth-century surroundings."

Guests at the Green Tree Inn are greeted with a complimentary carafe of chilled Catawba. Then it's off to one of the inn's charming guest rooms, each individually decorated.

My favorite is the Federal Room, done in Federal blues, boasting a canopy bed that copies 1850s Mississippi style. Bedposts are draped with linens made in Lao Ping province in China. "It's interesting that the linens are handmade in China but are copies of American nineteenth-century lace," Mary Ann said. Austrian and Swedish lace also grace windows. The Federal theme is carried through with two wing chairs and handsome wall portraits.

In the Victorian Room, an antique iron-rail scroll bed and Austrian lace curtains create an absolutely charming atmosphere. A quaint Country Room is equally stylish, with a casual and relaxed nature.

Or sample the elegant Governor's Suite, named for John Sevier, Tennessee's first chief executive in 1897 and Mary Ann's great-great-

great-grandfather. It's done in family-heirloom antiques (including a Victorian high-post cherry bed and Chippendale sofa) and has two private balconies.

A charming gathering room in the building's basement is a picture of country quaint. Red-checked tablecloths cover tables and chairs specially made by local craftspeople for the inn. Mary Ann serves breakfast here—everything from tasty omelets and homemade strawberry-tinged French toast or biscuits and gravy to pastries from the renowned local bakery.

The innkeeper also runs monthly workshops at the inn, featuring everything from planting nineteenth-century spring and woodland gardens to a Victorian tea luncheon that includes a workshop on daylilies. Of course, white gloves are required for this one.

For dinner I'd recommend Elsah's Landing and Alton Riverwalk for fine dining. Or try Finn Inn, a unique seafood restaurant in nearby Grafton, where huge aquariums filled with Mississippi River marine life (mainly turtles, carp, catfish) front dinner booths. Besides the lively setting, the inn offers specialties like turtle soup, white perch and spoonbill fillets, a sixteen-ounce whole catfish, fried turtle, and desserts like chocolate meringue and Kentucky Derby pie.

How to get there: From St. Louis, take Missouri 367 north to U.S. 67 and continue into Illinois. At Illinois 3, turn west and proceed to Elsah. There are only two major streets in the town, Mill and LaSalle.

Innkeepers: Michael and Mary Ann Pitchford

Address/Telephone: 15 Mill Street; (618) 374-2821

Rooms: 9, including 1 suite; all with private bath and air conditioning, phone on request.

Rates: $69 to $85, single or double; $105, suite; EPB.

Open: All year.

Facilities and activities: Dining room, gathering room, private balconies; nineteenth-century-style mercantile store featuring fine arts and crafts; paddle wheeler offering riverboat excursions. In the heart of historic Elsah. Short walk to Mississippi River. Jogging or biking on Great River Road. Nearby is 16-mile-long Vadalabene bike trail. About 40 antiques shops within 15 minutes' drive. Bald eagles winter along the river in great numbers from December through March. About 40 minutes from St. Louis.

Maple Leaf Cottage Inn
ELSAH, ILLINOIS 62028

Imagine stepping back into the steamboat era of the nineteenth century in a little Illinois village that appears much as it did in pre–Civil War days. It is a peaceful, easy feeling I get when driving into Elsah, on my way to Patty and Jerry's historic inn.

This cozy country inn occupies an entire village block, surrounded by blazing colors of a handsome English garden and facing the spectacular limestone bluffs that run down to the Mississippi River.

The rooms can be overwhelming, fashioned with seemingly every country accent and craft imaginable and available. Yet I found them to be some of the most relaxing and enjoyable lodgings

I've encountered since I began inn-hopping years ago.

The Wash House is a charming cottage (the first ever of the Maple Leaf Inn, which has been open to travelers for four decades). In 1891 it was the Maple's summer kitchen, but after a fire it became the family washhouse. Patty has carried this theme through to perfection, with quaint country decor that showcases an 1888 wooden washing machine, old-fashioned scrub boards, and even a clothesline. A wonderful rail bed adds to country charm. There are historic photos of the original Maples hanging on the walls. (And a feather bed is offered in the fall and winter!)

The most eye-catching decor in a guest

room called the Maples is artful white pickets, the only survivors from the original home, which front handsome silhouettes on the wall. The room also boasts white wicker furniture and colorful antique quilts.

Guests especially enjoy the wall silhouettes of Elsah's historic buildings, Patty said. "They give the feeling of looking out across the fence or down the road."

A handsome dining room features mapleleaf wall stencils, hand-traced and painted by Patty from maple trees on the inn grounds. Lace tablecloths add to country elegance.

Let's not forget Patty's incredible meals. Breakfasts might include a special recipe of heart-shaped French toast, tarragon eggs, fruit

cups, hot muffins, gourmet coffee and teas, and more; for dinner, consider boneless breast of chicken baked in herbs and butter, flounder stuffed with crab, Elsah Hills gravy, river-bluff rice with pecans, country green vegetables, and scrumptious garden-house cheesecake.

A cozy screened front porch, filled with wicker chairs and tables, is a great place to enjoy a peaceful evening in this town that time forgot.

How to get there: From St. Louis, take Missouri 367 north to U.S. 67 and continue into Illinois. At Illinois 3, turn west and proceed to Elsah. There are only two major streets in Elsah, Mill and LaSalle; Selma intersects both.

Innkeepers: Patty and Jerry Taetz

Address/Telephone: 38-40-42-44 LaSalle Street (mailing address: P.O. Box 156); (618) 374-1684

Rooms: 4; all with private bath, air conditioning, and TV; 1 with wheelchair access. Family cottage with 2 bedrooms and fireplace. No smoking inn.

Rates: $65, single; $80, double; EPB. Family cottage, $325 weekly.

Open: All year.

Facilities and activities: Restaurant, 7-course dinner ($25 per person); lecture/luncheons on Elsah history and architecture 5 days per month. English country garden, herb garden. Located in heart of historic Elsah, nineteenth-century Mississippi river town. Near Grant River Road, jogging and biking along the 16-mile Vadalabene bike trail. Nearly 40 antiques shops within a 15-minute drive. Bald eagles winter along river from December through March. About 40 minutes from St. Louis. Limo service to and from St. Louis Regional and Lambert International airports; will arrange for special trolley tours to St. Louis arch, Union Station, etc.; will arrange daily river and walking tours.

Aldrich Guest House
GALENA, ILLINOIS 61036

The Aldrich Guest House, an elegant 1853 Greek Revival mansion with Italianate touches, is part of the Galena legend of hometown-boy-made-good Ulysses S. Grant. Tales say that Grant mustered his Civil War troopers on the "green" next to the home. So I sat on the inn's screened porch, gazing at the expansive yard, trying hard to imagine the stoic figure of the bearded general drilling his ragtag army collection of Illinois farmboys, readying them for furious battle. Now you can also enjoy wonderful spring and summer blossoms, thanks to Sandy's green thumb; get set for an explosion of tulips, lilies, and other perennials.

Sandy's inn is a showcase for fine antiques.

You'll spot Victorian-era art, valuable porcelain, Dresden china, and lots of fancy crystal. And don't forget to notice the Chippendale furnishings in the dining room.

The innkeepers also love to celebrate the holidays in grand fashion. During Christmas guests can look forward to five Christmas trees, an extensive Santa Claus collection, and scores of other yuletide decorations. Really gets you in the mood to celebrate!

A broad fluted-oak banister heads the stairway leading to the second-floor guest rooms. The Tiffany Ann is a favorite, with its iron-rail bed, white wicker chair, and violet-bouquet wall coverings. "It looks like spring in here," Sandy said.

And the Sherrie Lee is another Victorian-style beauty, complete with canopy bed, bay window—and a water closet featuring a claw-footed bathtub and old-fashioned pull-chain commode, adding a feel of authenticity to the historic house.

Breakfast here is a treat. There was lots of chatter among couples from the Chicago area, Brooklynites, and a doctor and his family from Rhode Island, all gathered around a long dining-room table. Fresh flowers, balloon-style draperies, and fancy china place settings all harken back to a more elegant era.

Then comes the food: delicious *stratas*, soufflés, French toast, fruits, and more. And Sandy's home-baked pastries make you forget about your waistline. She also will recommend restaurants to suit your dinner tastes; I found Bubba's to be a Galena favorite. But other crowd pleasers are Silver Annie's, The Log Cabin, and Cafe Italia, one of my favorites.

Also check out 20 West, a great live-entertainment club with cozy couches and stuffed chairs instead of saloon stools. It's certainly easier to enjoy the cool jazz this way.

And here are some future plans for the Aldrich Guest House: Whirlpool baths and fireplaces in guest rooms are soon to come!

How to get there: Take U.S. 20 (across the bridge toward U. S. Grant's house) to Third Street. Turn left and go to the end of the block to the inn.

Innkeepers: Sandy and Herb Larson
Address/Telephone: 900 Third Street; (815) 777-3323
Rooms: 5; all with private bath and air conditioning.
Rates: Weekdays: $75 to $90; weekends: $80 to $110; EPB.
Open: All year.
Facilities and activities: Double parlor, screened porch, gardens. Walk or drive to restaurants and historic attractions of the old lead-mining town of Galena, including U. S. Grant home and scores of antiques, specialty, and art shops; museums, historic homes.
Recommended Country Inns® Travelers' Club Benefit: 10 percent discount, January–February, two-night-minimum stay.

Brierwreath Manor Bed and Breakfast

GALENA, ILLINOIS 61036

A homey atmosphere with soft sofas, comfy guest rooms, and a great wraparound porch perfect for people-watching in this historic lead-mining town—that's Brierwreath Manor. And it's only a half block from all the shops lining Galena's Main Street.

"People love our porch," Lyn said. "They do some sightseeing, come back and relax on the swing to recharge batteries, then go right back out again."

The 1884 home belonged to a local butcher who fought in the Civil War. "It's a simple, big house built to hold his wife, five kids, and mother-in-law," Lyn said. "He didn't include a lot of elaborate decorations. It's just a comfortable house."

Lyn and Mike, who are from the Chicago suburbs, fell in love with this home after working for a year at Lyn's sister's Galena guest house outside of town. They've furnished it with relaxation in mind—not many delicate antiques or Victorian finery to worry about—and I felt right at home.

The Mayor's Room (named for the previous owner, who happened to be Galena's top honcho) offers lace curtains, a queen-sized bed, a shower big enough for two, and a gas-log fireplace. An antique pedestal sink and the inn's other guest-room fireplace grace the Country Charms Suite. My favorite is the Heirloom Suite, which has the inn's finest antiques, including an

Eastlake dresser, armoire, and claw-footed bath-tub. (Lyn supplies the bubble bath.)

A typical breakfast might include pecan French toast, ham, watermelon slices, and more. For early birds an upstairs buffet features a variety of teas and coffees that should hold you until breakfast. And Galena is graced with several fine restaurants: the fun-filled Bubba's; super pork chops at Silver Annie's; and fine fettucine Alfredo at the Cafe Italia.

How to get there: From Chicago, take the Northwest Tollway (I–90) north to U.S. 20; then go west to Galena. Turn north on Main Street, west on Franklin, and south on Bench Street to the inn.

Innkeepers: Mike and Lyn Cook

Address/Telephone: 216 North Bench Street; (815) 777–0608

URL: http://www.galenalink.com/brierwreath

Rooms: 3, including 2 suites; all with private bath and air conditioning.

Rates: $85, single; $90, double; EPB. Two-night minimum on weekends, holidays. Special packages, off-season rates available.

Open: All year.

Facilities and activities: Sitting room, upstairs breakfast buffet; wraparound porch. Nearby: historic sites, art galleries, antiques shops, restaurants. Short ride to Mississippi Palisades State Park; riverboat rides, riverboat museum, and other attractions in Dubuque, Iowa.

Recommended Country Inns® Travelers' Club Benefit: $10 off on second night of two-night stay, Monday–Thursday.

DeSoto House
GALENA, ILLINOIS 61036

General Ulysses S. Grant stood in front of the grand DeSoto House. He was unmistakable in his heavy navy-blue Union Army greatcoat, wide-brimmed hat, full beard, and ever-present cigar.

I walked up to him, aimed my camera, said, "Smile," and clicked the shutter. The general wasn't even startled. In fact, he said, "You need another shot? I'll strike my presidential pose for ya." Now I was the one who was quite surprised.

I didn't expect to find Grant at the DeSoto House, even though he made it headquarters for his 1868 presidential bid. But Galena is full of surprises.

Of course, "Grant" turned out to be local actor Paul LeGreco, who portrays the general at special functions, including breakfast, dinner, and meetings at the hotel. The likeness is striking. And it's a stroke of advertising genius for the hotel.

Not that the massive 1855 structure—opened during the period when unprecedented lead-mining profits transformed Galena into a trade and commerce center rivaling Chicago—needs any gimmicks. More than $8 million was poured into the restoration project. That kind of money is reflected in the elegance evident throughout the building, which was once billed as "the largest hotel in the West."

On my way to the guest rooms, I passed

through an enclosed courtyard with high skylight windows that sent a rush of sun toward diners enjoying an elegant alfresco buffet in its open space. The guest rooms are decorated in various shades of soothing blues and beiges. Some of the furnishings include high-back chairs, dressers, and writing desks. Even the inside rooms have views, with windows overlooking the Grand Court.

The hotel offers breakfast and lunch in its indoor courtyard; or try a down-home country meal at the Steakburger Inn, a local breakfast favorite.

For elegant formal dining, the hotel's General Dining Room, located on the lower level; it's a romantic showplace with exposed brick walls and original ceiling beams. Menu choices include the finest steaks and seafood.

Or sample the French, Spanish, and Mediterranean delicacies at the Kingston Inn. Others choose Cafe Italia for wonderful pasta dishes.

And how can you pass up a chance to relax in the hotel's Einsweiler Library with a cognac nightcap in front of a roaring fire—an elegant way to end a day.

By the way, nine presidents have stayed at the DeSoto House, as well as the likes of Mark Twain, Ralph Waldo Emerson, Susan B. Anthony, and Horace Greeley. So a stay here puts you in pretty distinguished company.

How to get there: Take U.S. 20 to Galena. Turn north on South Main Street. The DeSoto House is halfway up the block, at the corner of Main and Grand.

Innkeeper: Dominique Cross
Address/Telephone: 230 South Main Street; (815) 777–0090
Rooms: 55, with 4 suites; all with private bath, air conditioning, TV, and phone. Wheelchair access.
Rates: Weekdays: $80 to $125, rooms; $110 to $185, suites; EP. Special weekend packages.
Open: All year.
Facilities and activities: Three full-service restaurants, tavern, indoor courtyard, courtyard specialty shops, free parking. On Main Street in historic Galena. Nearby: home of U. S. Grant; preserved Civil War architecture; specialty shops and museums.
Business travel: Located about 20 miles east of Dubuque. Corporate rates, conference rooms, fax.

DeZoya House Bed and Breakfast
GALENA, ILLINOIS 61036

If you want to stay overnight in one of Galena's more historic settings, try the DeZoya House. Built before 1830 by a local financier, the 4,000-square-foot structure is "the largest stone residence in Jo Daviess County."

It's significant because it remains the only Virginia-style Federal home in Galena. And unlike most homes around here, it was built wholly at one time. There are no later additions.

Fred and Jim are from Wicker Park in Chicago (my old neighborhood), so we talked like old pals. Fred told me that the two guest rooms on the second floor feature unusual cypress floors (probably brought up the Mississippi River from New Orleans by river-

boat) in addition to hand-carved four-poster beds. Two third-floor rooms, both with original plank floors, boast a sleigh bed (my favorite) and a pine cannonball bed.

The home rests on two acres, with Muddy Hollow Creek gurgling somewhere down the bluff. A screened porch is the center of conversation and games during summer months; guests also enjoy a small balcony that overlooks the property.

Breakfasts are real treats here. They might include a fancy fruit compote, quiche, strata, tomato tarts, home-baked breads, and more.

If you'd like even more privacy, check out the inn's cottage, built in 1835. Furnished in country pine, it boasts two bedrooms, sitting room, and a screened wicker porch.

How to get there: From Dubuque, take U.S. 20 east to Third Street, turn right, and continue all the way down the block to the inn.

Innkeepers: Fred Tuttle and James Zalewski

Address/Telephone: 1203 Third Street; (815) 777–1203

Rooms: 4; all with private bath and air conditioning.

Rates: $85, single or double; cottage: $125, one couple; $195 two couples; EPB.
Two-night minimum on weekends if Saturday night is included.

Open: All year.

Facilities and activities: Sitting room, library, screened porch, lawn activities, garden.
Short walk to Main Street shops and restaurants. Nearby: skiing, golf, fishing, river boat rides, historical attractions, state park.

Recommended Country Inns® Travelers' Club Benefit: 25 percent off in house, 33 percent off in cottage, for fourth and subsequent nights.

Hellman Guest House
GALENA, ILLINOIS 61036

Some of the best views of Galena can be enjoyed from the Hellman Guest House, built on Quality Hill with views of Horseshoe Mound and overlooking church steeples, gingerbread turrets, turn-of-the-century merchant buildings, and surrounding bluffs. Just one glimpse of the spectacular views convinced me that the entire town had actually been suspended in time.

Merilyn fell in love with the house as soon as she laid eyes on it in 1986. The sun-filled attic, with its turret room, inspired the painter in her; she is converting it into her private art studio.

The 1895 home, built by a wealthy local merchant, has a magnificent interior. I can't remember being more impressed by what appears from the outside to be a modest home; the inside offers cherry and oak woodwork, stained and leaded glass, and an incredibly opulent foyer—complete with its own fireplace.

A huge window in the formal parlor reveals spectacular views of Galena. For a closer peek I fixed my eye to the brass telescope, a 1942 U.S. military surveyor's tool that brought the town within arm's reach.

Guest rooms are equally distinctive. The Hellman is the original master bedroom of the home. Besides Victorian antiques and a queen-sized brass bed, it boasts a tower alcove with more incredible views.

Other rooms are named for Hellman's

daughters: Pauline offers a queen-sized iron-and-brass bed; Irene features a Victorian oak bed and sapphire-tinted accents; and Eleanor is a great afternoon sunroom, with a Victorian bath that includes a claw-footed bathtub. And get ready for the inn's next treat, which may already be a reality by the time you read this: a new luxury suite, complete with fireplace and whirlpool bath.

Yes, Merilyn allows guests to luxuriate in the spectacular view from the house's main tower. Get your camera ready; you won't want to miss this shot.

And breakfast treats . . . consider a fancy fruit plate, blueberry buttermilk pancakes, quiche, strata, even hobo hash. Of course, there are always oatmeal cookies for afternoon snacks.

How to get there: Although the house is located on Hill Street, guest parking is on High Street. From Dubuque, take U.S. 20 east into Galena and turn left on High Street (up the steep hill) to the inn's parking area (marked with a sign).

Innkeeper: Merilyn Tommaro

Address/Telephone: 318 Hill Street; (815) 777–3638

Rooms: 4; all with private bath and air conditioning.

Rates: $84 to $144, single; $89 to $149, double; EPB. Two-night minimum weekends and holidays.

Open: All year.

Facilities and activities: Parlor, library, porch, patio, and gardens. Nearby: Main Street shops, antiques, restaurants, historic attractions. Short drive to Dubuque's riverboat rides, museums, Mississippi River.

Recommended Country Inns® Travelers' Club Benefit: 5 percent discount, Sunday–Thursday, excluding holidays.

$\mathcal{L}$og Cabin Guest House
GALENA, ILLINOIS 61036

It's not often that Midwesterners get to step inside an authentic log cabin. Most have been destroyed by "progress." The few that remain usually belong to local historical societies, and most of these can be viewed only from the outside. That's why these cabins are so special.

One was built in 1865 by a Civil War veteran who came to the booming lead-mine frontier town of Galena to carve a fortune out of the ground. Two other cabins, dating from 1850 to 1860, were found north of Plattville, Wisconsin, dismantled there, and then reassembled and restored on this historic homestead.

I pulled open the old latch door to the soldier's cabin and found a room dominated by a huge stone hearth, with a massive stone floor covered by a braided rug. A large antique spinning wheel sat in one corner, and black kettles hanging from iron rails hovered over the remains of a toasty fire in the hearth.

The logs are whitewashed inside to give the quarters a bright, airy look, with cheery tieback curtains on the small windows. An antique spindle bed is tucked into the far corner of the room.

Upstairs is a sleeping loft, furnished with two three-quarter-sized rope beds—real pioneer spirit, here. I tried one out, and it actually felt quite comfortable. (Jon explained that it's all in how the ropes are strung.) A small corner crib adds more sleeping space for babies. Two other cabins are ideal romantic retreats that each accommodate one couple. Their stone fireplaces add to the coziness; so do the upstairs whirlpools.

And one cabin, which is just one story, is completely wheelchair accessible.

The Coach House was built on the property between 1832 and 1834 by the father of Civil War general Augustus Chetlain, one of nine Galena native sons who reached that rank in the Union Army's war against the South.

Inside the Coach House, I liked the original plank floors, spindle beds adorned with quilts, lace curtains on the windows, and floral-print wallpaper. A kitchenette, electricity, and indoor plumbing are the only bows to the twentieth century.

No breakfast or dinner is served here, but Jon recommends the Farmers' Home Hotel for hearty, reasonably priced morning meals. I like Bubba's for evening feasts. Both are located downtown, a short drive away, and the innkeeper will give you directions.

How to get there: Take U.S. 20 west through Galena to Chetlain Lane and turn left. Go ¼ mile and you'll find the farmstead on the left.

Innkeeper: Jon Allen

Address/Telephone: 11661 West Chetlain Lane; (815) 777–2845

Rooms: 5 authentic 1800s log cabins; historic Coach House; all with double whirlpool bath, wood-burning fireplace, air conditioning, TV, VCR, CD, and wet bar; 1 with wheelchair access.

Rates: Sunday through Thursday, $125 single; $150 double; Friday and Saturday, $150 single, $175 double; EP.

Facilities and activities: Coffeepots, minirefrigerators in rooms. Nearby: historic barn, fields, woods. Short drive to historic attractions, specialty shops, museums, and restaurants of Galena.

Park Avenue Guest House
GALENA, ILLINOIS 61036

Besides the imposing architecture of this 1893 Queen Anne home, the first thing I noticed were the "porch people"—wrought-iron chairs fashioned into likenesses of an entire family.

"They're dressed for all the holidays," Sharon said. "Halloween costumes, Uncle Sams on the Fourth of July, you name it."

As you have probably guessed, holidays play an important part at the Park Avenue, especially Christmas, when each room has its own decorated tree and the house is festooned with more than 200 feet of garlands, 1,400 holiday lights, and 27 window candles.

Guest rooms are charming. The Miriam Room, named for the original owner's daughter

(who still lives in town, as of this writing, at age ninety-plus), offers Victorian furniture, including a gray iron-rail bed. The Lucille Room is bright and cheery, with a queen-sized iron-rail bed and an Eastlake dresser. Sunlight lovers should choose the Anna Suite, boasting six huge windows, Victorian and Eastlake antiques, and an extra trundle bed.

Sharon's very proud of her newest room. It's huge, gobbling up the entire back of this spacious house, and lavished with Victorian furnishings, a gas fireplace, and five sunny windows that overlook the inn's fabulous gazebo.

That gazebo, by the way, always elicits questions from guests. "People, especially from

Chicago, seem to feel its ornate iron filigree design is familiar," Sharon said.

Maybe that's because the gazebo is constructed from cast-iron elevator doors salvaged from the historic Marquette Building in the Windy City.

Count on breakfast in the home's formal dining room or on the wraparound (and partially screened) porch. It might include fresh fruit, homemade breads and muffins, cereal, and more.

And ask the innkeepers to tell you about Admiral Bias Sampson, the home's first owner.

He is believed to have been aboard the battleship USS *Maine* prior to the Spanish-American War.

Or inquire about the inn's fabulous Christmas decorations, which include NINE TREES! One boasts only Santa Claus ornaments. Must be a sight to see!

How to get there: From Dubuque, take U.S. 20 east to Park Avenue, turn left, and continue to the inn.

Innkeepers: Sharon and John Fallbacher

Address/Telephone: 208 Park Avenue; (815) 777–1075

Rooms: 4, including 1 suite; all with private bath and air conditioning, 3 with gas-log fireplaces.

Rates: $85 to $95, single or double; $105, suite; continental breakfast. Two-night minimum on weekends. Midweek discounts, off-season rates available.

Open: All year.

Facilities and activities: Two parlors, screened porch, gazebo, and Victorian garden. Short walk to Galena historic attractions, shops, and restaurants. Short drive to Dubuque riverboat rides, bluff scenery, Mississippi River.

Recommended Country Inns® Travelers' Club Benefit: $10 off per night, Monday–Thursday, not valid with any other deductions.

$\mathcal{P}$ine Hollow Inn
GALENA, ILLINOIS 61036

This inn may be one of the best-kept secrets of northwestern Illinois. Located on a 110-acre Christmas-tree farm in the heart of Galena's historic lead-mining district, it is a gold mine for travelers who want to enjoy the splendor of country living while having Galena's treats only a three-minute drive away down Main Street.

My pa and I turned up Pine Hollow's long driveway, crossed Hughlett's Branch (creek), and stopped near a patch of black walnut trees that surround a picture-perfect country inn.

Andy and Molly, a pair of golden retrievers, greeted us with wagging tails.

"Samuel Hughlett owned this valley in Galena's lead-mining heyday," Sally explained, "and you can still find some 'sucker holes' in the ground." One old mining hole is now used as a den by coyotes.

In fact, this valley used to be called "Hughlett's Bottom," and Sally contemplated that as the name for the inn. "But I decided there'd be too much explaining to do," she said with a chuckle.

Sally and Larry planted 9,000 evergreen trees that are ready for the "U-chop" Christmas season (selections include beautifully shaped Scotch and white pines). They originally had planned to build a shed for tree sales, then changed that to a warming hut, and finally settled on a country inn. "I still don't have that shed," Sally said.

This is a landscape and wildlife wonderland, with wild turkeys galore, blue heron, deer, and howling coyotes. Hike the bluffs for panoramic views of the countryside. Or poke around the valley for mining artifacts; an archaeological dig a few years ago turned up a few historic items.

I prefer a guided tour with Andy, who beckoned me to follow him up a hill. "Guests have told me he's such a good leader, we should hang up a sign reading GUIDE DOG TOURS EVERY HOUR," Sally said.

Most country-charming guest rooms are huge, with four-poster canopy beds and wood-burning fireplaces. I like Number 3, which also has two skylights. Number 5 offers a beamed ceiling and a claw-footed tub, while Number 2's allure is a large whirlpool bath.

Sally's hearty country breakfast might include blueberry pancakes and sausage, sticky buns, and more.

How to get there: From Dubuque, take U.S. 20 east to Main Street and proceed 1½ miles north (Main Street changes into Dewey) to reach Pine Hollow. Turn left at the sign and continue up the driveway to the inn.

Innkeepers: Sally and Larry Priske

Address/Telephone: 3700 North Council Hill Road; (815) 777–1071

Rooms: 5; all with private bath and air conditioning. No smoking inn.

Rates: Weekdays: $75 to $85, single or double; weekends, $95 to $110, single or double; continental breakfast. Two-night minimum on weekends.

Open: All year.

Facilities and activities: Picnic-basket lunches available. Dining room, porches. Hiking, birding, wildlife watching. Nearby: Galena Main Street shops, restaurants, historic attractions. Drive to Dubuque for riverboat rides on Mississippi, fishing, museums.

Queen Anne Guest House
GALENA, ILLINOIS 61036

Tucked away on a quiet corner in a residential neighborhood, this gingerbread-crazy showplace is impossible to ignore.

Its elaborate turrets, knobs, fretworks, and overhangs combine to create a graceful snapshot of past elegance. Built in 1891 by William Ridd, an Englishman who became a prominent Galena merchant selling window, sash, and door treatments, it served as his showpiece. It seems he put extras everywhere to impress his customers.

A century later Diane and Frank's "customers" are still impressed. The house is a genuine "Painted Lady," boasting five different colors on its impressive gingerbread. Inside, stained, leaded, and beveled glass is everywhere, oak floors and woodwork lend more elegance, and the home has a very comfortable and relaxing atmosphere—thanks to the two friendly and gracious innkeepers.

Guest rooms are furnished with handsome antiques collected by Diane and Frank. "We like to think of the decor as country Victorian," Diane said. Make no mistake—she knows her stuff, as evidenced by her past work in the architectural salvage business.

One guest room has a magnificent Rice four-poster bed and three tall windows. Others feature everything from walnut dressers and Victorian settees to stained-glass lamps and marble-topped chests.

My favorite room claims the home's tower. Or maybe you'd like quarters with a claw-footed tub and pedestal sink?

The innkeepers also collect lots of antique clocks. Diane's favorite is a tall grandfather's clock that dates back to 1760.

An "expanded" continental breakfast is served in the dining room atop a long antique farmer's harvest table that was handmade in Dubuque. But it's not just *any* continental breakfast—this one is served by candlelight. Count on home-baked muffins and breads, fresh-fruit plates, juice, coffee, and more.

Galena nights mean fine dining. Cafe Italia offers up great Chicago-style Italian specialties; The Log Cabin, a favorite of locals, serves great steaks; and Bubba's is a fun, new seafood place.

Did I forget to mention the latest inn honors: the only Galena inn whose picture is featured in the state's "Discover Illinois" tourism campaign; or the three-diamond rating from triple AAA. And did you see that unique Victorian bike rack out back? Diane made it herself. Nice work!

How to get there: From Chicago, take the Northwest Tollway (I 90) north to U.S. 20 and go west to Galena. Turn right on Park Avenue (the street before the bridge) and continue to the corner of Park and Adams to the inn.

Innkeepers: Diane Thompson and Frank Checchin
Address/Telephone: 200 Park Avenue; (815) 777–3849
Rooms: 4; all with private bath and air conditioning. No smoking inn.
Rates: $75 to $95, single or double, weekdays; $85 to $100, weekends; continental breakfast. Special multinight and midweek discounts.
Open: All year.
Facilities and activities: Double parlor, library, video, entertainment room. Short walk to Grant City Park, Main Street shops and restaurants. Nearby: hiking, biking, state park, riverboat rides, horseback riding, skiing, golf.

The Victorian Mansion
GALENA, ILLINOIS 61036

Robert led me into his twenty-three-room 1861 Italianate mansion, long a prestigious address for entertaining important guests in this former boomtown along the Fever (Galena) River.

We sat down in the library to chat about this incredible inn, furnished and preserved with museum-quality antiques so authentically displayed that it's as if a photograph of the home in the 1860s had come to life.

I noticed soldiers' boots standing next to a tall coatrack and Civil War–era Union Army greatcoats slung over the high backs of elegant chairs in the dining room. That's not surprising, because General Ulysses S. Grant was a confi-

dant of the home's original owner, wealthy smelter Augustus Estey; and a group of the general's cronies often gathered to discuss political issues of the day with the cigar-chomping soldier in the very library where Robert and I were sitting.

"See that black grate above you?" Robert asked, pointing to the ceiling. "Estey had that built into his library ceiling to suck cigar smoke out of the air."

The house is immaculate. Walking through the front door, I passed a beautiful 10-foot-high Victorian oil painting depicting the wife of the first mayor of Princeton, Illinois. What especially intrigued me was the hallway's unusual chandelier, which has four graceful swan figurines supporting a large glass shade. But even these wonderful items are overshadowed by a grand oval staircase that spirals all the way up to the third floor.

Second-floor guest rooms exhibit exquisite antique furnishings. My favorite is the Grant Room, with its invitingly huge walnut bedframe, marble-topped bureau, and deeply colored floral-print carpeting. Robert's collection of antique *Harper's* political caricatures sniping at General Grant hang on the walls.

I found elegance everywhere in this magnif-

icent showplace. Plank floors are covered by handsome oriental-style carpets, some original to the home. Pocket doors (which slide unobtrusively into walls) separate many of the rooms. Historically correct wallpaper, four marble fireplaces, and opulent chandeliers are just a few of the extras.

How to get there: Take U.S. 20 west to High Street and turn left. Go all the way to the top of a steep hill to the mansion, which stands on the left side of the street.

Innkeeper: Robert George McClellan
Address/Telephone: 301 High Street; (815) 777–0675
Rooms: 8; all with private bath. No smoking inn.
Rates: $87.20, single or double, continental breakfast. Midwinter discount of 20 percent.
Open: All year.
Facilities and activities: Library, dining room, card room with TV. Nearby: historic attractions of Galena, U. S. Grant home, tours of historic houses; art, antiques, and specialty stores.

The Herrington
GENEVA, ILLINOIS 60134

"Papa, it's right on the water," Kate said.

"Can we swim in the river, Papa?" asked Dayne.

"Let's go fishing," Kate added.

"Do they have canoes?" Dayne wondered.

I guess the girls liked the location of The Herrington, a handsome inn nestled on the banks of the Fox River. Housed in the restored Geneva Rock Springs Creamery, where milk was kept and chilled along the swift waters of the river in the 1870s, the Herrington is a luxurious day-in-the-country getaway only about one hour west of Chicago's stress-filled hubbub.

Named for Geneva's first permanent white European settlers (the town sits on a site that the Potowatomie Indians called Big Springs), the inn combines its historic architecture with elegant modern-day fineries.

Walk inside double doors crested by Palladian windows to a luxurious sitting room, with a fireplace, wing-back chairs, and nooks and crannies perfect for late-night whispers. An old-fashioned bar climbs the wall on the far end of the room; you can lounge here until your table is ready for gourmet meals prepared by the inn chef.

Some guest rooms have riverside views; others have courtyard vistas (with glimpses of the rushing waters). If you choose to be on the river, your balcony literally hangs over the water, a great treat for landlocked Midwesterners.

While each guest room is individually decorated, they all allow guests to revel in an understated elegance that includes gracious pampering. We especially liked "our room," as our daughters called it, which featured scrolled brass beds adorned with eyelet lace coverlets, fireplace, ceiling fan, marble-tiled bathroom, and a big whirlpool tub that the kids couldn't wait to try out.

Another treat that the girls really looked forward to: At the end of the day, the inn staff will deliver milk and cookies to your room.

And that glass-enclosed riverside gazebo sitting in the middle of the courtyard sports another extra: a large whirlpool tub that allows you to take its soothing waters under the stars.

Geneva is one of the most historic little towns in the Chicago exurban area. So if you want to overnight at The Herrington during the town's annual festivals (April's Historic Geneva Days, June's Swedish Days, September's Festival of the Vine, the Riverwalk Octoberfest, and December's Christmas House Walk), be sure to make your reservations far in advance.

How to get there: From Chicago, take the Eisenhower Expressway (I–290) west to I–88 Aurora, exiting at Farnsworth Avenue; go north to Route 38 to the first left past the Fox River Bridge (River Lane).

Innkeeper: Dan Harrington, general manager
Address/Telephone: 15 South River Lane; (708) 208–7433
Rooms: 40; all with private bath, whirlpool bath, fireplace, and private balcony or patio.
Rates: $135 to $205, single or double, continental breakfast. Special package rates available.
Open: All year.
Facilities and activities: Full-service dining room, high tea, sitting room, bar, riverside spa, outdoor gazebo-enclosed whirlpool tub. Nearby: walk to historic town, shops, boutiques, riverwalk; rent bikes for river trail rides.
Business travel: Located about 1 hour from downtown Chicago. Corporate rates, conference room, fax. Rooms with phone.

The Mansion of Golconda
GOLCONDA, ILLINOIS 62938

I wandered down to southern Illinois' Ohio River country, some of the most beautiful scenery in the Midwest. This historic corner of the state is also rich in legend, from the trailblazing George Rogers Clark expedition to the Ohio River pirates of the 1790s who preyed on flatboats from infamous Cave-In-Rock.

Right in the heart of a small river town is The Mansion of Golconda. I was surprised to find that one of the innkeepers of this 1895 mansion was from my old neighborhood back in Chicago.

Don and Marilyn have established a tradition of fine dining and hospitality. The rose, gold, and blue dining rooms, furnished largely with period antiques, set the mood for what Marilyn proudly called "The Mansion's dining experience." In fact, former Illinois governor Jim Thompson dined here several times. "I had a chance to do some show-off cooking," Marilyn said. Current governor Jim Edgar has also enjoyed the inn cooking. And many others drive more than 100 miles just to eat here.

Dinner means candlelight and elaborate meals. Selections include sautéed chicken livers, honey-crisp chicken, steaks, and fresh seafood. I recommend catfish Camille, a spicy, grilled touch of heaven; or the shrimp stuffed with cold crabmeat. Marilyn serves dinners on antique china platters, and loaves of steaming-hot bread on rough-hewn breadboards add to the home-style "flavor" of the meal.

But hold on! You can't walk away without trying one of The Mansion's homemade desserts, which are prepared daily. The favorite of the moment: Almond Joy Pie—all custard, milk chocolate, and, of course, almonds.

Marilyn knows that sometimes travel-weary inn hoppers "want the breakfast to be good" at a country inn. So she caters to both light and hearty eaters. Juice, fruit, toast, and croissants satisfy some; eggs over easy, spicy southern Illinois pork sausage, and biscuits and gravy sate hungrier guests.

Did I forget to mention lunch on the back porch? How about red snapper with cream sauce or chicken with tomato-wine sauce?

Original stained-glass windows, six fireplaces, fine woodwork, and pocket doors are all architectural features of the inn. The guest bedrooms on the second floor contain Victorian and other antiques dating from the 1880s to the 1920s.

The Camellia room boasts a 7-foot-high, hand-carved Victorian mahogany headboard draped in lace curtains. "It's our fantasy room," Marilyn said. Azalea has two canopied four-poster beds. Most popular is Begonia, with its 1892 iron stove warming a two-person whirlpool tub.

More good news: The Mansion has received a "historic buildings" grant that will return its exterior to "showplace quality," Marilyn said.

How to get there: From north, east, and west, follow Illinois 146 into Golconda and turn right after the courthouse.

Innkeepers: Don and Marilyn Kunz
Address/Telephone: Columbus Avenue (mailing address: P.O. Box 339); (618) 683–4400
Rooms: 3, plus 1 cottage; all with private bath and air conditioning.
Rates: $85 to $110, single or double, EPB.
Open: All year except Christmas Eve and Day.
Facilities and activities: Full-service restaurant with wheelchair access. Lounge with TV, sitting room; patio, gardens. Nearby: a short walk to Ohio River, levee. A short drive to Shawnee National Forest, park, fishing, marina, houseboat and pontoon boat rental. Horseback riding, hiking; cross-country skiing in area during winter.

Sweet Basil Hill Farm
GURNEE, ILLINOIS 60031

"You're the most colorful guests that have visited my sheep in more than two years," Bob said to Kate and Dayne as they headed to the barn in their neon-colored ski jackets for a visit with his forty-head flock.

That's why Sweet Basil Hill Farm is one of my girls' favorite getaways—where else can they fuss over lovable barnyard creatures so close to our Chicago home?

Nestled on a hilltop amid seven and a half wooded acres, just 6 miles west of Lake Michigan and halfway between Chicago and Milwaukee, the inn is a wonderful retreat from big-city hassles.

Teri, a photographer, herb lover, and wool spinner, personally greets guests at the door. Step inside and you're in a world of handsome English and American country antiques, gleaming wood floors, 8-foot-tall cupboards and armoires, and wicker rockers and Shaker chairs.

Debbie, my wife, loved our two-room suite, with its Laura Ashley linens, European feather comforters, and antique knickknacks. Daughter Kate found a crystal ball and told our fortunes before we could unpack the suitcases.

The downstairs Basil Room is another favorite with its Shaker-style pencil-post canopy bed and Amish quilt.

Breakfast in the knotty-pine dining room is like dining inside a North Woods cabin. Seated at a long harvest table, we feasted on chicken, cheese, and broccoli pastry puffs; cinnamon and cranberry rolls; fresh juices; and warm apple-cinnamon dumplings for dessert. Then we hiked the back acres to visit with sheep, chickens, and llamas.

Get Bob to tell you the sheep's names (including Johann Sebastian Baa) and the story of how Half Jack got his moniker.

Those llamas (Fernando and Dali) love to rub noses with guests. Kate didn't hesitate going nose-to-nose with Fernando. Dayne waited until she saw that Kate didn't lose anything in the bargain.

Bob, a successful commercial actor, revels in giving tours of the place. That includes hikes to

the inn's "hugging tree." "Hug it and you'll have seven years' good luck. Feel silly about it, and you get eleven years."

And the newest inn addition: a two-bedroom English cottage with its own stone fireplace and a flower garden out front. What a way to enjoy a day.

How to get there: From Chicago, take the Tri-State Tollway (I–94) north to the Illinois 132 (Grand Avenue) exit; proceed to Illinois 21, then turn right. Go to Washington Street, turn right, and continue about a half mile. The inn is on the left.

Innkeepers: Bob and Teri Jones
Address/Telephone: 15397 West Washington Street; (847) 244–3333 or (800) 228–HERB
Rooms: 3, including 2 suites, plus 1 cottage; all with private bath and air conditioning.
Rates: $85 to $175, single or double, EPB. No smoking inn.
Open: All year.
Facilities and activities: Large parlor, herb garden, hiking trails. Nearby: Gurnee Mills, Six Flags Great America. A short drive to Lake Michigan, Chain O'Lakes and Illinois Beach state parks, Long Grove Historic District, Temple Farms Lipizzans Horse Show, Wauconda Orchards, charter fishing, hike and bike trails, tennis, golf, dog and horse racing, and winter sports.

Deer Path Inn
LAKE FOREST, ILLINOIS 60045

Though there's been a Deer Path Inn since 1854, the current building made its debut in 1929. It immediately became a hit with Chicago's movers and shakers (who built impressive mansions on the North Shore) and their visiting guests.

Certainly, the inn (located in the Historic Market District of Chicago's toniest suburb) makes a statement with its architecture. In fact, L. C. Jones was sent overseas to study English inn designs; when he returned he re-created the ornate Elizabethan style of a fifteenth-century manor house in Chiddingstone, Kent, complete with its unusual three-gable roofline. You can see a print of the original Chiddingstone in the inn's foyer.

The inn's ambience is quiet and sedate, much like that of a select, old-money European hotel. Fine English period furnishings, antiques, and artifacts (including pewter chandeliers suspended from heavily timbered ceilings), shining dark woods, stone fireplaces, leaded windows, and rough-plastered walls elicit a baronial feel of a country manor.

Many of the guest rooms (all named after properties of the National Trust of England) are oversized, and several are graced with fireplaces. The inn's signature room, the Cliveden Suite, also has an antique four-poster bed and whirlpool bath.

The English Room, which looks out onto a

formal garden ablaze with blossoms in spring and summer, offers wonderful gourmet dining, with several constantly changing specialties. Among my favorites is beef Wellington (done in a puff pastry with bordelaise sauce) and tournedos Dijonais (medallions of beef topped with mustard brown sauce).

Sunday's champagne brunch is an institution in Lake Forest. It includes choices like eggs Benedict, oysters Rockefeller, and ham with asparagus rolls in Mornay sauce. Let's not forget the English trifles and profiteroles.

How to get there: From Chicago, take I–94 north to U.S. 41; continue north and exit east on Deerpath Road; at Green Bay Road, turn south, go to Illinois Road, and turn east to the inn.

Innkeeper: Michel Lama, general manager

Address/Telephone: 255 East Illinois Road; (847) 234–2280 or (800) 788–9480, fax (847) 234–3352

Rooms: 53, including 32 suites; all with private bath.

Rates: $110 to $120, rooms; $170 to $320, suites; single or double; EPB. Special packages available.

Open: All year.

Facilities and activities: Fine dining, Sunday champagne brunch in the English Room; the Hunt Room, an English-style pub, features jazz pianist entertainment, outdoor garden. Nearby: walk to Market Square, the first planned shopping center in the country; walking tours of Historic District. A short drive to Lake Forest beach, Ravinia Park, Chicago Botanical Garden (in Glencoe), Six Flags Great America, Arlington International Racecourse.

Hillendale Bed & Breakfast Inn
MORRISON, ILLINOIS 61061

For a moment, let's just forget about Mike and Barb Winandy's 1891 bed and breakfast inn called Hillendale, an architectural wonder with twenty-nine rooms and seventeen baths.

Oh, sure, it might be one of the Midwest's most intriguing accommodations. Exotic woods such as ebony, rosewood, and walnut are everywhere. Guest bedchambers are exquisite, and fireplaces abound. Huge whirlpool tubs beckon to romance. Breakfasts are delightful.

But it's the innkeepers, themselves, who transform Hillendale into one of the Midwest's most magical getaways. They've traveled the world looking for adventure: Kilimanjaro, Machu Picchu, New Guinea rain forests.

They have photos to prove it: roaming the African veldt, embracing tribal headhunters, scaling glaciers.

And artifacts include museum-quality treasures, including miniature *mois* from Easter Island, necklaces from pygmy peoples, and woodcarvings from Stone Age tribes.

Many of the Winandys' artifacts come from travels twenty to thirty years ago, when native people literally pushed objects into their hands before they left adventure behind.

Like the 4-foot-tall woodcarving from headhunters in New Guinea, with whom Mike lived for a few months. "I had admired work of one of the tribal artisans. Before I left, he gifted me with the statue."

One problem. Mike had to travel almost eight weeks over river in a small dugout canoe just to reach the nearest village, then tramp through miles of jungle before arriving at his final destination.

"I just couldn't take it with me on the jungle trek," Mike said. "So I asked one of my guides if he'd get it back to town and send it to me."

Months passed after Mike returned home to the states, but still no woodcarving. "I never thought I'd see it again," he said.

Imagine Mike's shock when the woodcarving finally arrived at the doorstep of his house—two years later!

The Winandys share their world-travel bounties by displaying many of their artifacts and photographs in Hillendale's guest rooms. Each allows the visitor to "explore" a different part of the globe.

The Jumbo Room recalls the earthy tones of Africa, and includes a zebra-drum nightstand.

Another guest room, the Failte, has the feeling of the lush Irish countryside, offering photos from the Winandy's trip around the Ring of Kerry and visits to famous Irish castles.

In the Outback Cottage, behind the main house, Mike displays boomerangs he used to catch game in the desolate Outback regions of Australia.

Warm-weather visitors receive a bonus—a chance to relax at Hillendale's Japanese Teahouse, built by immigrant Sino artisans in the 1930s. The water garden in front of the teahouse contains the inn's Japanese koi collection—colorful Japanese "carp" as big as a muskie, and each potentially worth thousands of dollars.

How to get there: From Chicago, take I–88 west to exit 36 (Clinton—Route 30). Go 11½ miles on Illinois 30 (also known as Lincolnway in Morrison) to Olive Street in the town. Turn right, then the semicircle driveway will be on your left.

Innkeeper: Mike and Barb Winandy
Address/Telephone: 600 West Lincolnway; (815) 772–3454 or (800) 349–7702
Rooms: 10; all with private bath. No smoking inn.
Rates: $50 to $140, single or double, EPB.
Open: All year.
Facilities and activities: Dining room, gathering room, billiard room, fitness room, outdoor koi pool, Japanese Teahouse. Nearby: Heritage Canyon (Fulton); Blackhawk Chocolate Trail; Whiteside County antiques; Morrison Rockwood State Park; Albany Indian Burial Mounds; riverboat gambling; Timber Lake Playhouse; Lock and Dam #13.
Recommended Country Inns® Travelers' Club Benefit: 10 percent discount, Sunday–Thursday.

$\mathscr{P}$inehill Bed & Breakfast Inn

OREGON, ILLINOIS 61061

My pa couldn't resist Sharon's banana nut muffins, whose scrumptious aroma filled this mansion atop Jackson Hill. He ate two, then walked off his bounty on the inn's handsome three acres of manicured lawns.

Later we explored the 1874 house, built by one of the first merchants in Oregon. I imagined how the home's tall tower once offered panoramic views of the lush Rock River Valley, a prime location for autumn colors.

Walking through the house's huge front doors is like traveling back into the nineteenth century. Floor-to-ceiling windows grace the sitting room; the music room boasts a grand piano engulfed by sheet music and fine-arts books covering ballet and modern dance; French silk wallcoverings provide another touch of elegance; and a staircase leading to guest rooms is highlighted by ostentatious wheel windows with delicate blown glass.

"A way for the original owners to show off their money, I guess," Sharon said.

Guest rooms are delightful. The Somerset Maugham Room is named for that man of letters, who often visited Pinehill in the 1930s; he probably enjoyed the wood-burning marble fireplace on chilly nights, though I doubt that the whirlpool tub was around back then.

The Emma Lytle Room, named for a former owner, offers a marble fireplace and a Jenny Lind dressing table. It has an unusual cannonball four-poster bed that my girls, on a subsequent stay at this charming inn, found impossible not to bounce on. A family favorite is the two-room Lincoln Suite; kids love to sink into its European double feather bed.

But most popular is the Fischer Room, former servants' quarters now graced with an antique Victorian queen bed—and the best outside view of any room in the house.

Did I mention Sharon's delicious breakfasts, which might feature freshly baked muffins and crumpets, eggs, breakfast meats, juice, fresh fruits, and two Pinehill specialties—granola pancakes and hazelnut creme coffee?

Finally, this is a super inn for kids: Consider weeklong Easter egg hunts, teddy bear teas, ice-cream socials, chocolate teas (for adults, too!), storytelling, and more. Adults will enjoy "Artistic Porch" events, featuring working craftspeople and artists demonstrating their talents. And don't go home without some of Sharon's Pinehill Gourmet Fudge Collection, an Illinois-homemade selection of exotic delights featuring flavors like Seattle cappuccino (cinnamon, spices, and espresso) and Mississippi mud (white, milk, and dark chocolate with roasted peanuts). Yummy!

How to get there: From Chicago, take Illinois 64 west into Oregon; then turn right on Mix Street and go up the hill to the house.

Innkeeper: Sharon Burdick

Address/Telephone: 400 Mix Street; (815) 732–2061

Rooms: 5, including 1 suite; all with private full or half bath and air conditioning. No smoking inn.

Rates: $75 to $195, single or double, EPB.

Open: All year.

Facilities and activities: Year-round afternoon tea and tea parties; Sunday ice-cream social; picnic-basket lunches and dinners available. Sitting room, music room, screened and open porches. Croquet, bocce ball, badminton. Nearby: biking, cross-country skiing, golf, horseback riding, kids' playground, Rock River water activities—fishing, boating, water skiing, water slide. A short drive to 3 state parks, John Deere Historic Site, Sinissippi Christmas Tree Farm.

Recommended Country Inns® Travelers' Club Benefit: Stay 2 nights, get third free, subject to availability.

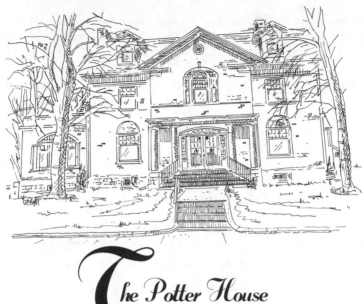

The Potter House
ROCK ISLAND, ILLINOIS 61201

This exceptional inn is a real sleeper. Built in 1907 with elaborate Colonial Revival flourishes, its stucco exterior may appear somewhat ordinary at first glance.

But don't be fooled. Inside is an elegant world of stained-glass windows, embossed leather wall covering, and Steuben glass shades; elaborate scrolls, scallops, and filigree; handsome mahogany hardwood; half a dozen fireplaces; even twenty-four-carat-gold "dots" that enhance the inn's huge beveled-glass entry doors.

Now that you know, any visit to the Quad Cities should include an overnight at The Potter House, or you'll miss out on some special pampering.

Frank and Maribeth, who were innkeepers in historic Gettysburg, Pennsylvania for seven years before coming here, have lovingly restored this home, which is on the National Register of Historic Places. Guest rooms are particularly beguiling. A huge fireplace is the focal point of Mrs. Potter's Room, the original master bedroom.

But Debbie and I stayed in Marguerite's Room, charming quarters featuring unique hand-painted, rag-rolled walls done by Maribeth herself. We loved the huge antique brass bed. And we both were surprised to find an unusual "hat cupboard" inside the closet. Marguerite, who lived in this room for nearly fifty years, was very fond of her bonnet collection, we were told.

The innkeepers both lavish attention on guests at breakfast in the handsome dining room, a grand setting with its rich mahogany paneling.

It might include an egg dish, breakfast meats, French toast, pancakes, and more. And be sure to take a peek at the former caretaker's house, now availabel for cozy overnights; the 1890s structure has handsome Mission-style furniture and its own living room, dining room, and full kitchen.

After breakfast explore Rock Island's Broadway Historic Area—or just make yourself at home in front of the living room's cozy fireplace, kick back, and relax.

How to get there: From the east or west, take I–280 to Illinois 92; go northeast toward downtown Rock Island. (Note that the Mississippi River here runs east and west.) Take the 18th Avenue exit; go east to a five-point intersection (18th, 17th, and 20th streets); turn left on the far side of the stone bell tower onto 20th Street; continue to 7th Avenue, turn left, and continue to the inn.

Innkeepers: Frank and Maribeth Skradski

Address/Telephone: 1906 7th Avenue; (800) 747–0339 or (309) 788–1906

Rooms: 5, including 1 suite, plus 1 cottage; all with private bath, air conditioning, cable TV, phone. No smoking inn.

Rates: Weekdays, $50 to $80, single or double; weekends, $80 to $95; $100, cottage (for 1–3 days); EPB. Two-night minimum on certain weekends.

Open: All year.

Facilities and activities: Parlor, sitting room, solarium. Horse-drawn carriage rides from inn door. Antique trolley to downtown entertainment and arts "District." Nearby: Circa 21 Dinner Theatre, Comedy Sportz club, murder mystery; 6 blocks to the Boatworks, on the Mississippi River, which includes river museum, restaurant on restored tug, and docks for *Casino Rock Island* high-stakes gambling boat. A short drive to quaint village of East Davenport; a few miles to Iowa low-stakes riverboat gambling ships.

Recommended Country Inns® Travelers' Club Benefit: 10 percent discount, Monday–Thursday.

The Wheaton Inn
WHEATON, ILLINOIS 60187

I enjoy The Wheaton Inn because it weaves so well today's sophistication with yesterday's elegance. The inn, completed in 1987, relies on opulence in the Colonial Williamsburg tradition for its distinctive flair.

Guest rooms are named after famous Wheaton citizens. Eleven have gas fireplaces, many boast Jacuzzi tubs, and each has an elegantly distinctive personality. All have European towel warmers in their bathrooms—another thoughtful touch, especially for travelers who venture out in Chicago winters.

Rooms have oversized styles often found in European concierge hotels. The Woodward Room is one of my favorites, with its Jacuzzi situated in front of a large bay window that overlooks the inn's gardens. The fireplace marble came from the face of Marshall Field's department store in downtown Chicago. (By the way, the room's namesake, Judge Alfred Woodward, is the father of newspaperman Bob Woodward, who broke the Watergate scandal for the *Washington Post* along with Carl Bernstein.)

Vaulted ceilings in the third-floor McCormick Room, along with its huge four-poster bed and windows overlooking the garden, make this another guest favorite. In fact, the mayor of Nairobi, Kenya, chose to stay in this room on a visit to the Chicago area. Another charmer is the Morton Room, with its alcoved ceiling, cozy fireplace, and 4½-foot-deep Jacuzzi, perfect for guests who yearn for a relaxing soak.

Especially romantic nights can be yours in the Rice Room, where a Jacuzzi sits almost in the middle of the room, in front of a fireplace, and two skylights let you gaze at the stars above.

Only the Ottoson Room, named after the inn architect, departs from the Williamsburg theme. A brass-topped, black iron-rail bed is dwarfed by cathedral ceilings that harbor a skylight.

In a cheery, window-lit breakfast room, guests enjoy the innkeeper's European-style buffet of imported coffee and teas, hot egg dishes, seasonal fruits, and delicious pastries and muffins. Personal service is a trademark here, so expect amenities like afternoon cheese and crackers, freshly baked cookies and milk, twenty-four-hour coffee, and bedtime turndown service with chocolate treats left on your pillow.

How to get there: From Chicago, take I–294 to Roosevelt Road, then go west to the inn.

Innkeeper: Dennis Stevens

Address/Telephone: 301 West Roosevelt Road; (708) 690–2600

Rooms: 16; all with private bath and air conditioning, some with Jacuzzi. Wheelchair access.

Rates: $99 to $195, single or double, EPB. Weekend packages.

Open: All year.

Facilities and activities: Patio, lawn area with croquet course and gardens, sitting room, dining area. Nearby: McCormick's Cantigny war museum, Prairie Path hike and bike trail; Herrick Lake paddle boating and fishing; Wheaton Water Park; Fox River and Geneva famous shopping districts; horseback riding; Morton Arboretum; Wheaton College's Billy Graham Center; golf courses; tennis courts; polo grounds. Also a short drive to Drury Lane Theatres.

Business travel: Located about 30 miles west of Chicago. Corporate rates, conference rooms, fax.

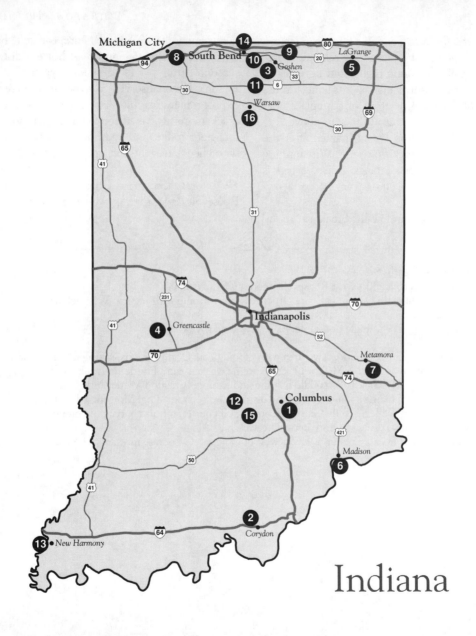

Michigan City

South Bend

LaGrange

Goshen

Warsaw

Greencastle

Indianapolis

Metamora

Columbus

Madison

Corydon

New Harmony

Indiana

Indiana

Numbers on map refer to towns numbered below.

The Columbus Inn
COLUMBUS, INDIANA 47201

Don't fight city hall. Just sleep in it.

This huge 1895 Romanesque brick building with its tall bell tower served as the city's seat of government for almost one hundred years. When it fell deserted, it seemed too august to simply demolish.

A Pittsburgh-based development company that specializes in historic preservation and restoration purchased the building in 1985—and the result is one of the most unusual and elegant inns around. In fact, *Time* magazine said that "A sense of quality has rubbed off all over Columbus."

Just stepping into the long entry hall is like entering an earlier era of elegance and gentility.

Ornately embossed tin ceilings, hand-carved oak woodwork, and original Victorian terra-cotta floors are graced with Victorian and Gothic love seats, huge brass chandeliers, and mahogany claw-footed banquet tables.

Guest rooms are magnificently furnished, with handsome teal or peach wall coverings and American Empire antique reproductions fashioned in France. I especially like the cherrywood sleigh beds and second-floor rooms with floor-to-ceiling windows.

Most spectacular is the Charles Sparrell Suite (named for the architect of the old city hall), a stunning 1,200-square-foot chamber that you reach by ascending twenty-seven steps. It has 21-foot ceilings, 12-foot-tall windows, a sleeping loft (that's seventeen more steps), a second bedroom on the lower level hidden by mirrored French doors, and two and a half baths.

I forgot to mention the large Victorian parlor furnished in fine antiques.

Breakfast in the handsomely restored lower level means a stylized buffet that might include fresh fruits and juices, homemade pumpkin bread, English muffins, apple and cherry strudel, egg casseroles with meat and cheeses, fresh vegetables, and New Orleans–style bread pudding served piping hot.

The inn offers English-style afternoon tea daily from 11:00 A.M. to 6:00 P.M. But High Tea, beginning at 4:00 P.M., is the most special treat with its authentic scones and other goodies.

If you still have an appetite for dinner, Paul or his staff will recommend several good restaurants.

How to get there: From Indianapolis, follow U.S. 31 south into Columbus and turn south on Washington Street. At Fourth Street, turn west, then go north on Franklin Street to the inn.

Innkeeper: Paul Staublin

Address/Telephone: 445 Fifth Street; (812) 378–4289

Rooms: 34, including 5 suites; all with private bath, air conditioning, TV, and phone. Wheelchair access.

Rates: $86, single; $96, double; $110 to $190, suites; EPB.

Open: All year.

Facilities and activities: Afternoon teas and sumptuous buffet breakfasts. Columbus is self-proclaimed "architectural showplace of America." Fifty significant contemporary works in one of the richest, most concentrated collections anywhere—a Who's Who of contemporary architects, designers, and sculptors. Horse-and-buggy tours of town stop at inn's front door. Historic-district tour map provided upon arrival. City's Visitor Center across the street. Walk or drive to restaurants.

Recommended Country Inns® Travelers' Club Benefit: Stay two nights, get third night free, weekends only, subject to availability. Alternative: Stay two nights double occupancy, get two dinners, all for $200, all costs included, subject to availability.

Kinter House Inn
CORYDON, INDIANA 47112

In 1837 Jacob Kinter opened the doors of the Kinter House as Corydon's finest hotel. Today it remains the historic village's best hostelry and one of the most handsome inns in the Midwest.

Old-fashioned hospitality is the hallmark of this carefully restored National Historic Landmark. From the rockers on the front porch to the fine period antiques gracing guest rooms named after historic Corydon figures, you're treated in first-class style.

Many guest-room antiques are museum quality. The Josiah Lincoln Suite (named for Abe's uncle, who was a frequent guest here) boasts an 8-foot walnut headboard from circa 1800 and a marble-topped walnut dresser hand-carved in an elaborate grapevine design.

In the Governor's Room (named for Jonathan Jennings, the state's first chief executive, who toiled for an annual salary of $1,000), an 1850 four-poster walnut-and-mahogany bed with intricate leaf hand carvings is magnificent.

Yet my two favorites remain the huge Squire Boone Room (Squire Boone was an early Indian explorer and brother of Daniel), with its pencil-post cherry beds, plank floor, and exquisite inlaid star-pattern game table; and the President William Henry Harrison Room (Harrison, a one-time landowner here, was personally known by every citizen of early Corydon), with its 1880 hand-carved mahogany grapevine dresser that looks as though it belongs in the Smithsonian. (The claw-footed mahogany shaving stand would also be mighty handy for trimming mustaches like mine.)

Third-floor guest rooms reflect an Early American theme, with plank floors, brass beds, and antique quilts.

The inn's homemade breakfast treats are legion. The meal might include goodies like ham-and-egg puffs, sausage cheese grits, cocoa banana bread, and Sock-It-to-Me Cake (a house specialty).

How to get there: From Indianapolis, take I–65 south to I–64, go west to Indiana 135 (exit 105), then south to Indiana 62; turn east on Indiana 62, following that road to the inn at Capitol Avenue and Columbus Street.

Innkeeper: Mary Jane Bridgewater

Address/Telephone: 201 South Capitol Avenue; (812) 738–2020

Rooms: 15, with 4 suites; all with private bath, air conditioning, and phone. No smoking inn.

Rates: $49 to $89, single or double, Friday and Saturday; $39 to $69, Sunday through Thursday; July through October, add $10 to all rates; EPB.

Open: All year.

Facilities and activities: Parlor, sitting room, porch. Nearby: Old Capitol building, Old Capitol Square antiques and crafts shops, art galleries, restaurants, Hayswood Theatre. Short drive to historic buildings, Battle of Corydon Civil War Site, historic Branham Tavern, Squire Boone Caverns and Village, Blue River canoeing, Marengo Cave Park, Wyandotte Caves, and Harrison-Crawford State Forest.

The Checkerberry Inn
GOSHEN, INDIANA 46526

"We wanted to create a European feel to the inn," Susan said. "After all, being surrounded on all sides by Amish farmlands is more than enough country ambience."

The fine appointments of this northern Indiana inn do remind me of intimate, elegant European hotels I've stayed at. In fact, the handsome photographs adorning the inn walls were taken by John during his travels in the French Bordeaux region.

Amish straw hats hang over beds, lending a nice regional touch to luxurious guest rooms that boast fine-arts prints, furniture with definite European flair, wide windows that allow views of the rolling countryside, and amenities like Swiss goat's milk soap in the baths. Rooms are named for flowers; my favorite is Foxglove, with its whirlpool bath, sitting-room fireplace, and six windows.

Queen Anne's Lace is another handsome room; its most interesting feature is a primitive secretary, made in the 1850s. It consists of 1,200 individual pieces, and it took three years to complete. Its geometric designs put that craftsman far ahead of his time.

The inn's restaurant leans toward country-French and contemporary cuisine. Four-course meals begin with a fresh garden salad, followed by a fresh fruit sorbet, entree, and dessert. An inn specialty is double duck breast sautéed and served over sweet onions, topped with an orange and port wine sauce, accompanied by *pommes Anna* and a bouquet of fresh vegetables. The vegetables, herbs, and spices are grown specially for the inn. Other favorites include chicken basil, veal medallions, and rack of lamb served off the bone with herb cream-and-garlic cheese.

The inn sits on one hundred acres, so there's plenty of quiet and relaxation. It's just a walk through French doors to the swimming pool, and the woods contain numerous hiking trails. And the inn provides Indiana's only professional croquet course. So now is the time to perfect your game.

How to get there: From Chicago, take the Indiana Toll Road (I–80/90) to the Middlebury exit (#107). Go south on Indiana 13, turn west on Indiana 4, then go south on County Road 37 to the inn. It's 14 miles from the toll-road exit to the inn.

Innkeepers: John and Susan Graff, owners; Sheila Reed, manager
Address/Telephone: 62644 County Road 37; (219) 642–4445
Rooms: 13, including 3 suites; all with private bath and air conditioning. Wheelchair access.
Rates: Sunday through Thursday, $80 to $275; Friday and Saturday, $100 to $325; single or double, continental breakfast.
Open: May through December; limited time February through April; closed January.
Facilities and activities: Full-service dining room, swimming pool, arbor, croquet course, tennis court, hiking trails, cross-country ski area. In the midst of Amish farmlands; offers horse-drawn buggy tours of Amish surroundings, sleigh rides in winter. Near Shipshewana auctions, Middlebury festivals.
Recommended Country Inns® Travelers' Club Benefit: 10 percent discount, subject to availability.

$\mathcal{W}$alden Inn
GREENCASTLE, INDIANA 46135

"The inn doesn't have a lake, or pond, or anything like that," Matt said. "All we have is our integrity of service and cuisine." I can tell you that both are excellent.

From Dublin, Ireland, Matt is a classically trained European chef who doubles as the innkeeper. The meals he now prepares have "roots in indigenous American regional cooking" but also reflect touches of his classical continental background.

He is especially proud of his Cape scallops, which he calls "absolutely the world's finest," served in cream-and-saffron sauce or sautéed with dill or raspberry butter. Another specialty is loin of lamb, wrapped in a puff pastry with dux-elles of mushrooms and spinach. Then there's Chicken Pecan—a boneless chicken breast breaded with Dijon mustard, coated with chopped pecans, and sautéed—served with della nonna sauce and a rainbow of vegetables.

Matt's appetizers are equally appealing. The game pâté is served with pistachios and truffles and wrapped in a puff pastry, and the puree-of-lobster-and-scallop soup features julienne of smoked salmon.

Dessert? Try the Fair Queen Chocolate Pie, with brandied raisins and orange zest, or the strawberries with caramel-and-bourbon sauce.

Is it any wonder people drive hours on end to dine at Matt's table?

Guest rooms are bright and comfortable, featuring furnishings with simple Queen Anne lines built by Amish craftsmen of northern Ohio. Bedspreads are handmade by Wisconsin craftswomen. There's also a flower box outside almost every window. One of my favorite rooms is in the Cole Porter Suite, which has a sitting-room fireplace and canopy bed.

The inn library is another handsome attraction, with its salmon-colored tile fireplace that endlessly crackles with a fire during winter, large Palladian window, and Queen Anne antiques and reproductions. Or repair to the inn's bar, the Fluttering Duck, for a nightcap.

How to get there: From Indianapolis, take I–70 west to U.S. 231. Go north into Greencastle. At Seminary Street (a green sign signals directions to DePauw University), turn left and go 4 blocks to the inn.

Innkeeper: Matthew O'Neil

Address/Telephone: 2 Seminary Square; (317) 653–2761

Rooms: 55, with 3 suites; all with private bath, air conditioning, phone, and TV. Wheelchair access.

Rates: $70 to $85, single; $80 to $95, double; $89 to $130, suites; EP. Two-night minimum on DePauw University parents' weekend, graduation weekend, and other special-events weekends.

Open: All year except Christmas Day.

Facilities and activities: Full-service restaurant, handsome sitting room and library, bar; short walk to DePauw University events, attractions.

The 1886 Inn
LAGRANGE, INDIANA 46761

We'd just come from the Shipshewana auction, a weekly event in the heart of Indiana's Amish country that offers all kinds of treasures, from hand-stitched Amish quilts and faceless Amish dolls to wood furniture hand-carved by Amish craftsmen.

Our daughters clutched their new dolls (you're not surprised, are you?) as we drove up to this inn, a massive red-brick Italianate mansion built in its namesake year. It's surrounded by a handsome cobbled-brick sidewalk and a wrought-iron fence. Three beautiful wrought-iron balconies recall the building's gracious past.

Duane told me that the home was built by a Civil War veteran who became a prominent LaGrange County politician. The mansion bespeaks the politician's station in the community. Ceilings soar—even the second-floor ceiling is 13 feet high—and there are arched doorways and handcarved ash woodwork.

And it's difficult to remember a more elegant staircase newel post, its intricate handiwork an indication of the meticulous care put into crafting this house.

Duane said that after the owner's death in 1916, the home stood vacant for more than 50 years. Hard to believe all this beauty survived its years as the town's "haunted house."

"It was boarded up after the death of the owner, Samuel Shepardson," Duane added.

"Incredibly, many of the furnishings remained in the house.

"When it was finally opened up, it looked like a time capsule."

A crew of Amish craftsmen came in to complete restoration work. Their skill is showcased throughout the house, including the guest rooms, which have fine woodwork, brass beds, tall arched windows, lovely chandeliers, antique furnishings, and those soaring ceilings. Several even have their own balcony.

Breakfasts include cereals, home-baked muffins, fresh fruit, juices, and other beverages. Then it's time to go out and explore the county. LaGrange's population is at least one-third Amish, and their shops and markets are scattered over the landscape.

How to get there: From Elkhart, take U.S. 20 west into LaGrange; at Detroit Street, turn north, then continue 2 blocks past the courthouse square to Factory Street and the inn. (It's located 1 block north and 2 blocks west of the courthouse square.)

Innkeeper: Duane Billman
Address/Telephone: 212 Factory Street; (219) 463–4227
Rooms: 5, including 1 suite; all with private bath.
Rates: $49, single; $89, double; continental breakfast.
Open: All year.
Facilities and activities: Sitting room, dining room, outside sitting area. Nearby: antiques and crafts shops, Amish markets, Shipshewana Flea Market, Pigeon River Fish and Game Preserve, Menno-Hof, LaGrange County parks for hiking, biking.

Cliff House
MADISON, INDIANA 47259

I stood on the inn's second-story veranda overlooking the great bend of the Ohio River and was swept away by thoughts of pioneers in keelboats floating to frontier settlements. How exciting (and dangerous) that must have been.

I also realized that the Cliff House might have the most spectacular big-river vista of any Midwest inn.

Before I discuss the inn, you must know a bit about the town. Nestled in a valley surrounded by 500-foot-high, tree-studded hills and limestone cliffs overlooking the Ohio River, Madison is deeply rooted in its past. Perhaps the greatest legacy of its 170-plus years is well-preserved architecture, with 133 city blocks listed on the National Register of Historic Places.

Pick a street at random and you'll find stately turn-of-the-century buildings in a variety of styles, ranging from Federal and Gothic to Greek Revival and Italianate.

You must tour the Lanier Mansion, a grand estate on the Ohio that emanates Southern gentility. It may have the most spectacular location of any similar landmark building in the region.

Talking about location, from the Cliff House's perch on the ridge of the hill, you can see much of Madison and the Ohio. Built in 1885, this large antebellum-style home with tall white pillars facing the river resembles plantation houses of the South.

Guest rooms on the second and third floors include the Pink Room, with a four-poster full tester bed (complete with horsehair mattress) and a nice view of the river; the Yellow Room, with *all* windows facing the river; and my favorite, the Red Room, a romantic retreat with a queen-sized, four-poster canopy bed and a panoramic view of the Ohio from bay windows.

Breakfast is served in the formal dining room on antique Haviland china accompanied by pearl-handled flatware. It might include homemade muffins, breads and morning cakes, croissants, juices, and coffee.

Maybe you can get Lynda to tell you about the love affair between the home's original owner and James Whitcomb Riley.

How to get there: From Indianapolis, take I–74 south to U.S. 421 and continue south into Madison. Turn right on Milton and follow it as it turns into Michigan Road. Watch for Fairmont, turn right up the hill, and follow the gravel pathway to the inn.

Innkeeper: Lynda Jae Brierweister
Address/Telephone: 122 Fairmont Drive; (812) 265–5272
Rooms: 6; all with private bath and air conditioning.
Rates: $58.30, single; $96.25, double; continental breakfast.
Open: All year.
Facilities and activities: Sitting room, music room, veranda. Nearby: a short drive to historic downtown buildings; crafts, antiques, and specialty shops; restaurants; Lanier Mansion State Historic Site; tours of historic homes (September); Chautauqua; Ohio River scenic road.

Main Street B & B

MADISON, INDIANA 47250

Be prepared to be pampered.

This Federal-style home, located in the heart of the Historic District, was built between 1843 and 1846 and has always been a private residence. Its size is deceiving—from the street, it doesn't look as though it could contain 5,000 square feet of space.

But all that room has been put to good use. In fact, the historic house, complete with "recent" ornamentations added in 1870, was featured in *Colonial Homes* magazine in October 1988.

Classical music wafted through the house as I sat in the living room, resplendent with its wood-plank floors, manteled fireplace, and com-

fortable sofas and chairs. Pampered, indeed.

Guest rooms are upstairs, and one glance made it easy to understand why *Colonial Homes* so liked this inn. English country antiques and reproductions including four-poster beds, poplar plank floors, wing chairs, and handsome ceiling borders ensure that visitors enjoy classy and cozy surroundings; there's also a fine collection of dhurrie and oriental rugs.

Mary's homemade breakfasts are real treats; consider whole-wheat breads, muesli, coffee cake smothered in strawberry glaze, fresh fruit, baked eggs and bacon, sliced tomatoes on toast rounds . . . Yum! Here's even more pampering: On request, Mary will bring a wake-up coffee tray to your room before breakfast. And she provides turndown service—of course.

How to get there: From Indianapolis, take I–74 south to U.S. 421 and continue south to Madison. Proceed to Main Street and turn right, traveling through town to the inn.

Innkeepers: Mark and Mary Balph

Address/Telephone: 739 West Main Street; (812) 265–3539 or (800) 362–6246

Rooms: 3, including 1 suite; all with private bath and air conditioning.

Rates: $89, single or double, EPB.

Open: All year.

Facilities and activities: Sitting room, parlor, enclosed porch. Nearby: historic buildings, antiques and specialty shops, restaurants. A short drive to historic homes, riverboat rides, Ohio River scenic road.

Recommended Country Inns® Travelers' Club Benefit: Stay two nights, get third night free, Monday–Thursday, subject to availability.

The Thorp House
METAMORA, INDIANA 47030

This historic 1838 canal town looks much as it did more than 150 years ago, with clapboard-covered buildings, log cabins, and general stores lining the narrow Whitewater Canal, which originally stretched 76 miles from Hagerstown through the village to Lawrenceburg.

I couldn't resist a ride on the *Ben Franklin III*, the town's horse-drawn canal boat, which carried me over the only operating aqueduct in the country to an authentic canal lock. I also couldn't resist giving the horses, Tony and Rex, a pat on their muzzles for a job well done.

Eventually I crossed the canal footbridge and came to The Thorp House, an original 1840 canal home transformed into a delightful inn by Mike and Jean. (A unique treat: Arrive in Metamora via the scenic route aboard the steam-powered Whitewater Valley Railroad, and the innkeepers will pick you up in a horse and buggy for a ride back to the inn.)

"Though Thorp didn't build the house, he moved here in 1856 after bringing his family from Pennsylvania via the canal system," Jean said.

The innkeepers did most of the restoration work, uncovering fancy cast hinges on the front door and original pine and poplar plank floors. Five guest rooms (all named for the innkeepers' first paternal Indiana settler ancestors) are country-cozy—dotted with crafts, dried flower bouquets, and antiques.

My favorites: the William Rose Room, with stenciled walls, country quilt on the bed, and a window view of the canal; and Shedric Owens, boasting an antique pie-safe dresser.

The inn's recently added suite is already popular with guests. Its two spacious rooms are graced with the heirloom furniture used by Jean's grandmother when she set up housekeeping more than seventy years ago.

Breakfast is an all-you-can-eat affair, with selections from the inn's regular menu. "We just fill up the plates, and if you want more, we'll fill 'em up again and again," Jean said. That's quite generous, considering that selections might include everything from homemade biscuits and sausage gravy, and egg and cheese casseroles to French toast, Belgian waffles, black raspberry pie, and sourdough pecan rolls.

How to get there: From Indianapolis, take I–74 east to the Batesville exit; then proceed north on Indiana 229 to Metamora. Cross the canal footbridge to Clayborne and the inn.

Innkeepers: Mike and Jean Owens
Address/Telephone: Clayborne Street; (317) 647–5425 or (317) 932–2365
Rooms: 5, including 1 suite; all with private bath.
Rates: $70, single or double; $125, suite; EPB.
Open: April through mid-December.
Facilities and activities: Full-service restaurant and 5 craft shops on first floor. Nearby: more than 100 fine-arts, crafts, and specialty stores; historic houses; old gristmill; canal boat rides; excursions on the Whitewater Valley Railroad.
Recommended Country Inns® Travelers' Club Benefit: 10 percent discount, Monday–Thursday, or stay 2 nights, get third night free. subject to availability.

Creekwood Inn
MICHIGAN CITY, INDIANA 46360

The Creekwood Inn is nestled amid thirty-three acres of walnut, oak, and pine trees near a fork in tiny Walnut Creek. The winding wooded roadway leading to the inn is breathtaking, especially in the fall, when nature paints the trees in glorious colors.

Done in English Cottage design, the inn is warm, cozy, and classically gracious. Massive hand-hewn wooden ceiling beams on the main floor were taken from an old area toll bridge by the original owner, who built the home in the 1930s. The parlor has a large fireplace, surrounded by comfortable sofas and chairs—a perfect setting for afternoon tea or intimate midnight conversation. Wood planking makes up the floors. And you can gaze out a bay window that overlooks the estate's lovely grounds.

Mary Lou said she wanted to combine the ambience of a country inn with the modern amenities that people have come to expect. She has done better than that; she has established a first-class retreat. Twelve large guest rooms and a suite are tastefully decorated in a mixture of styles; some have fireplaces and terraces. All have huge beds, overstuffed chairs, and mini-refrigerators.

And the Conservatory, overlooking the inn's pond and gardens, offers both a comfy spot to enjoy nature and a chance to luxuriate in the whirlpool or hit the exercise room.

Mary Lou visited Oxford, England, and was inspired to plant an English perennial garden on the east side of the inn. Things just keep getting better.

One winter my wife and I stayed here during an especially snowy stretch. We simply walked out the front door, slipped on our touring skis, and beat a path to the inn's private cross-country trails, which wind through deep woods and past Lake Spencer, the inn's private lake. Average skiers, we completed the loops in about twenty minutes, returning with a hearty breakfast appetite. Mary Lou serves a tasty continental breakfast of freshly baked breads, pastries, fruit, and coffee.

Late-afternoon tea in the parlor offers cookies and some delicious pastries. You may even have a cup of hot chocolate at bedtime on a blustery winter night, stretching before the fire and toasting your toes.

Mary Lou now serves dinner every night at the inn's American Grille. Be prepared for treats from chef Kathy deFuniak, who came from Ambria's in Chicago's Lincoln Park. These might include New Zealand lamb loin with basil whipped potatoes and summer tomato salad, crispy soft-shell crab with citrus vinaigrette, portabello mushroom lasagna, herb-roasted chicken with sweet corn and garlic polenta, and much more.

Desserts might include anything from simple fresh-fruit tarts to "gooey chocolate" treats—her husband's favorite.

How to get there: Heading northeast to Michigan City on I–94, take exit 40B. Then take an immediate left turn onto 600W, and turn into the first drive on the left. The inn is at Route 20/35, just off the interstate.

Innkeeper: Mary Lou Linnen
Address/Telephone: Route 20/35 at Interstate 94; (219) 872–8357
Rooms: 13, including 1 suite; all with private bath and air conditioning. Wheelchair access.
Rates: $112 to $156, double; $104 to $149, single; $166, suite; continental breakfast.
Open: All year except 2 weeks in mid-March and Christmas Day.
Facilities and activities: A short drive to southeastern shore of Lake Michigan, Indiana Dunes State Park, Warren Dunes State Park in Michigan. Charter fishing, swimming, boating. Antiquing in nearby lakeside communities. Area winery tours. Old Lighthouse Museum. "Fruit Belt" for fruit and vegetable farms.

Essenhaus Country Inn
MIDDLEBURY, INDIANA 46540

This handsome inn resembles a large Amish farmhouse—no coincidence, since it's located in the heart of Indiana's Amish country. I saw black buggies pulled by horses clip-clopping down main highways, little girls with long black dresses and prayer bonnets, and boys wearing the familiar broad-brimmed hats.

Up and down side roads of the Crystal Valley you're likely to find Amish quilt shops, bakeries, and crafts stores. Best bet for sightseers: a package deal that includes three-hour guided tours of Indiana's rich Amish heritage; you'll visit a cheese factory, buggy shop, Amish furniture factory, and hardware store and learn about the new Menno Hof Center in Shipshewana.

So it's great to have the Essenhaus Country Inn as a base to explore Amish life. The inn has pure country styling, with handcrafted pine furniture specially made by craftsmen in nearby Nappanee, another heavily Amish settlement.

The main floor resembles a huge great room that's open to the rafters high above. It boasts all kinds of high-back sofas, rocking chairs, game tables, and sitting areas that truly have the feel of home. I also enjoy gazing about the fine country crafts and antiques that decorate the room.

I especially like the silver-plated potbelly stove, a decorative gadget that my kids loved to snuggle next to.

The second floor resembles a country meadow. A white picket fence corrals the second-floor balcony; and a white clapboard, one-room country schoolhouse, complete with desks and strewn with handsome country crafts, adds to the charm. It's a great spot for kids.

Guest rooms are elegantly country, with their handcrafted pine furnishings. I'm always hooked by four-poster beds, as comfortable to lie in as to look at. Rosalie made all the attractive country drapes. Quilts and spreads were done by local artisans.

For a real treat, try the Heritage Country Suite, with its cathedral ceilings, antique lamps, and whirlpool tub.

As inn guests you may make dinner reservations at Das Dutchman Essenhaus, the popular Amish-style restaurant that normally seats on a first-come, first-served basis. (A wait in line often stretches toward thirty minutes.) Count on delicious family-style fare, with heartland meats, potatoes, dressing, heaping bowls of vegetables, and steaming loaves of homemade bread. Dessert includes tasty old-fashioned apple dumplings, my favorite.

How to get there: From South Bend, take U.S. 20 east to the inn in Middlebury.

Innkeepers: Bob and Sue Miller, owners; Wilbur and Rosalie Bontrager, managers
Address/Telephone: 240 U.S. 20; (219) 825–9447
Rooms: 33, including 5 suites and the Dawdy House; all with private bath, air conditioning, phone, and TV. Wheelchair access.
Rates: $65, single; $85, double; $105 to $135, suites; continental breakfast at the Dawdy House only. Children under 13 free; cribs and cots available.
Open: All year.
Facilities and activities: Large enclosed porch, game room, kids' playground. Renowned restaurant, Das Dutchman Essenhaus, also owned by the Millers, nearby. Villagelike setting, specialty and country stores a short walk away. Located in heart of Indiana Amish country. Amish quilt-and-crafts shops throughout Crystal Valley. Near Shipshewana, where numerous festivals are celebrated.

The Beiger Mansion
MISHAWAKA, INDIANA 46554

"Hey, Pa," shouted Dayne. "A gift shop."

"Yesss!" chimed in her sister, Kate.

My girls seem to have inherited a specific trait from wife Debbie: the ability, need, and craving to shop.

That's okay. It's fun for me, too. And it keeps those folks happy at American Express.

Actually, the Beiger Mansion doesn't have a "shop." It boasts a gallery with scores of wonderful handcrafted pieces showcasing Indiana artists.

The inn is unique, too. The four-level neoclassical limestone home took six years to build. It was finally completed in 1909, all 22,000 square feet of it, for Martin V. Beiger, Mishawaka's first self-made millionaire.

Stop inside and you'll see why his opulent home reminded society mavens of digs in famed Newport, Rhode Island. (Actually, it was built to resemble those fantastic mansions, the desire of Beiger's wife, Susie, to have a home similar to her friends from that Rhode Island retreat of the fantastically rich.)

Ornate rooms, complicated wall treatments and handpainted murals, natural woods, and a grand staircase transformed the home into one of local society's favorite soirée spots in the early 1900s.

Guest rooms are fanciful. Room 1 offers a handsome sleigh bed and original stenciled tub. The Honeymoon Suite features its own "solarium." Room 2 boasts a wood-burning fireplace, and Room 7 registers a four-poster bed with lace canopy, wood-burning fireplace, and original chandelier.

Beiger is also known for its kitchen. Consider these delicious and eclectic choices on one Saturday evening: an appetizer of crab Rangoon (Dungeness crab meat with Chinese cabbage, bok choy, yellow sweet peppers, and cheddar cheese) baked in a pastry shell; mush-room with hazelnut soup; and for an entree, rosemary lamb chops—the house specialty. Unless you'd rather have Mediterranean eggplant cassoulet.

How to get there: From South Bed, take U.S. 33 east to Mishawaka, which is Lincoln Way in town, and continue to the inn. Or exit the Indiana Toll Road at the Mishawaka exit.

Innkeepers: Ron Montandon and Phil Robinson
Address/Telephone: 317 Lincoln Way East; (219) 256–0365; fax (219) 259–2622
Rooms: 7, with 1 suite; all with private bath and air conditioning. No smoking inn.
Rates: $70 to $95, single or double; $195, suite; EPB. Corporate rates available.
Open: All year.
Facilities and activities: Dining room, gallery. Minutes from University of Notre Dame, St. Mary's College.
Recommended Country Inns® Travelers' Club Benefit: Stay two nights, get third night free, subject to availability.

The Victorian Guest House
NAPPANEE, INDIANA 46550

"When I saw a FOR SALE sign on this beautiful house, I had to think for a second," Vickie said. "After all, I'd worked in computers for 14 years. Was this for me?

"Then I decided it might really be interesting to take a 'Victorian plunge' into innkeeping.

"And you know what! I *love* it!"

So do her guests.

Vickie has done quite a job on the old Coppes House, completed in 1893 after taking five years to build. That patience is evident in the craftsmanship used to turn the home into Nappanee's showplace. (It's also the only building in town listed on the National Register of Historic Places.)

The front door, graced with lace curtains in the style of the period, opens to an etched-glass entryway. Original brass hardware shines everywhere, while rich panels of golden oak, cherry, and sycamore, found throughout the home, add to its luster.

"Lamb" stained glass, once made locally and of a high value, is found everywhere. I love the rose pattern set against a royal-blue background in the master bath of the Coppes Suite; more handsome stained-glass windows grace the front-hall stairway in a spectacular display of elegance.

The Coppes Suite is the guests' favorite. Its most unusual attraction is a custom-made, free-standing bathtub, built for the 6'3"-tall original owner. It looks like a huge trough, but it's beautiful. So big that it holds fifty gallons of water; so big that the innkeeper had to run a second set of pipes to fill it up in a reasonable amount of time.

The Wicker Room, with brass bed and lots of white lace, boasts its own balcony; while the Loft (old servant's quarters) features a tub that fills "from the bottom up." The water comes out from where you'd expect the drain to be. It fascinates guests.

An elegant continental breakfast is served in the imposing dining room (look for the servant call-button under the rug); count on treats like quiche, homemade muffins, fresh fruit, tea, juices, and more. I suggest the Country Table, downtown, for good Amish-cooked dinners.

How to get there: From South Bend, take U.S. 31 south, then turn east on U.S. 6. Continue into Nappanee to the inn.

Innkeeper: Vickie Hunsberger
Address/Telephone: 302 East Market Street; (219) 773–4383 or 773–7034
Rooms: 6; all with private bath.
Rates: $49 to $84, single or double, EPB. $15 for extra person.
Open: All year.
Facilities and activities: Formal tea monthly. In heart of Indiana Amish country. Nearby: restaurants, Amish Acres, Amish quilt shops, specialty stores, antiques, Borkholder Dutch Village. Near Shipshewana, famous for auctions of antiques and livestock and flea markets with more than 900 vendors. Numerous festivals throughout the year.

The Allison House Inn
NASHVILLE, INDIANA 47448

Tammy has added quaint touches to her country-charmed inn, nestled in the rolling hills of southern Indiana and just a stone's throw from Nashville's boutiques.

For example, her Victorian dollhouse near the sitting-room fireplace has decor that changes with the seasons. (Tammy pointed out that the miniature painting in one of the dollhouse's rooms is an original called *Bluebird in Sumac*, done by the same artist that executed the handsome paintings hanging in guest rooms.)

Then there's the folk-art rendering of the Allison House, done by a local artist, which depicts the entire Galm family—including Allison, the inn's dog.

I found the inn delightful. It was built in 1883, and the original owners had one of the first automobiles in Nashville. "Of course, no one in that family knew how to drive," Tammy said, "so they had to hire someone to tool them around town."

Guest rooms are named for the wildlife paintings that grace each of them. Some of my favorites: Eagle, with its iron-rail beds, quilt wall hanging, and Brown County crafts; Bluebird in Dogwood, with its sandpiper ceiling-borders; Moor Hen, featuring an authentic, World War I military field desk; and Bluebird in Sumac, with a lovely, full-sized quilt wall hanging fashioned by Bob's great-grandmother in the 1800s.

You can take breakfast in the dining room and share some of your town adventures with other guests; or you can sun on the large deck, where colorful flowers add to the country charm. Besides the usual fare, Tammy serves a caramel-nut roll that will make your mouth water. There are several restaurants that serve down-home family-style dinners; the innkeepers can recommend one that's right for you.

Be sure to explore Nashville, one of the Midwest's most famous folk-art-and-crafts colonies. Scores of galleries and boutiques line downtown streets. Or obtain a map and take a driving tour of Brown County's many log homes, several dating from the 1880s.

And for some of the best rolling-hill panoramas in the region, visit nearby Brown County State Park. Its fall colors are spectacular.

How to get there: From Indianapolis, take I–65 south to Indiana 46. Go west to Nashville. Turn north at Indiana 135 and proceed to Franklin Street. Turn left, go to Jefferson Street, and turn right to the inn.

Innkeepers: Bob and Tammy Galm

Address/Telephone: 90 South Jefferson Street (mailing address: P.O. Box 546); (812) 988–0814

Rooms: 5; all with private bath. No smoking inn.

Rates: $85, single or double, EPB. Two-night minimum. No credit cards.

Open: All year.

Facilities and activities: Sitting room, porch. Walk to restaurants, specialty shops, craft stores, and boutiques. Summer theater. Brown County State Park a short drive away.

Recommended Country Inns® Travelers' Club Benefit: 10 percent discount, two-night minimum, Sunday–Thursday.

The New Harmony Inn
NEW HARMONY, INDIANA 47631

As I drove across a bridge leading from southern Illinois into Indiana, a scripted sign arching high above the steel girders proclaimed NEW HARMONY, IND. Now I know why the town elders make that announcement. Driving into quiet New Harmony can lead to culture shock.

Amid historic structures that are a reminder of a long-ago utopian religious community stands The New Harmony Inn, blending harmoniously with its cultural surroundings. It's all dark brick, and its simple lines immediately call to mind Shaker stylings. Surrounded by tall trees, it looks unbelievably peaceful.

I talked with Nancy in her office across the street before I entered the inn. She said that the New Harmony's goal is to provide "simple rest and relaxation" for its guests. That's exactly what I experienced.

Like all guests, I walked into the Entry House, a welcoming area that features a large open sitting area, a high balcony, and a chapel intended for meditation. Rooms are located in buildings (referred to as "dormitories") across expansive lawns.

My favorites are the rooms with a wood-burning fireplace and sleeping loft reached by a spiral staircase. Others have a kitchenette and exterior balcony overlooking the grounds.

The spartan furniture reflects the strong influence of Shaker design. Rocking chairs, simple oak tables, some sofa beds, and area rugs on hardwood floors complete the decor.

I immediately headed for the "greenhouse" swimming pool, which is open all year. It's just a short walk from the rooms and a great way to relax after a long drive; there's also a recently completed health spa, with whirlpool, sauna, tennis courts, and Nautilus exercise equipment.

The inn's Bayou Grill serves breakfast in the coffee shop. Nancy recommends the nearby Red Geranium for wholesome dinner delicacies. You can choose from down-home dishes like baked chicken, grilled ham steak, and braised brisket of beef with vegetables.

Then wander around this tranquil town. And I dare you to find your way through the town's historic hedge maze.

How to get there: New Harmony is located at the point where Indiana 66 meets the Wabash River, 7 miles from I–64. In Indiana, take the Poseyville exit; in Illinois, take the Grayville exit.

Innkeeper: Nancy McIntire
Address/Telephone: North Street; (812) 682–4491
Rooms: 90; all with private bath and air conditioning. Wheelchair access.
Rates: $65, single; $75, double; EP. Children under 12 free; 12 and over, $10. Special winter packages.
Open: All year.
Facilities and activities: Entry House, indoor swimming pool. Located in historic town renowned for early nineteenth-century utopian society community. Modernistic visitor center distributes information on historic buildings that dot settlement and conducts audiovisual presentations and walking tours. Nearby: specialty shops, fine restaurants.

Queen Anne Inn
SOUTH BEND, INDIANA 46601

Bob is a former Marine Corps officer who now sports a handlebar mustache; Pauline was a college professor of education. Both delight in revealing the history of their wonderful inn.

The seventeen-room Queen Anne Victorian was built in 1893 by Sam Good, a South Bend contractor who became wealthy in the California gold rush. Bob said Good was friends with famed architect Frank Lloyd Wright, who built the nearby Wright house. (Well, of course!)

"A result of that friendship is this," Bob said, as he led me into the library, revealing an exquisite leaded-glass bookcase designed by Wright.

There are other elegant touches here: Silk wall coverings, crystal chandeliers, leaded glass, and a carved oak staircase with an ornate newel post imported from Italy all offer glimpses into the house's masterful craftsmanship.

Also surviving is a porte-cochère, with handsome fluted columns, which was used for guests arriving in coach and buggy.

It's hard to believe that the house, at one time called the best example of Queen Anne neoclassical architecture within 100 miles, was once traded for a single Commodore computer! Get Bob to tell you *that* story. Or how the house was moved 7 blocks to save it from the wrecker's ball; it is the largest and heaviest house (350 tons) ever to be moved in the county.

Bob said that there are ten kinds of oak used throughout the house, and the dining room is done in solid mahogany. The crystal chandelier in the music room is original to the home. "Didn't know what we had until I went up there to polish it," Bob said. "Turned out to be solid sterling silver."

Guest rooms, named for common birds of the area, are attractive and filled with period antiques and reproductions. A few favorites: Scarlet Tanager Room, with its twin sleigh beds and bed quilt made by Pauline; Cardinal Suite, with a fireplace, cozy window seat, and queen-sized brass-and-pewter bed; and the Hummingbird Room, with its huge Jenny Lind bed graced with eyelet-lace covers.

Pauline is a great chef, and her baking fills the air with a scrumptious aroma. A full breakfast may include blueberry pancakes, Texas French toast, bran muffins, fruit, juice, beverages, coffee cake, and more.

And here's something more: afternoon high tea (also open to the public) featuring English scones, sweets, and tea breads.

How to get there: From Chicago, take I–94 east to U.S. 20, then continue east. At U.S. 31, exit north into South Bend. Go to Washington, turn left, and continue to the inn.

Innkeepers: Pauline and Bob Medhurst
Address/Telephone: 420 West Washington; (219) 234–5959
Rooms: 5, with 1 suite; all with private bath, air conditioning, TV, and phone.
Rates: $65 to $100, single; $75 to $105, double; EPB. Two-night minimum on Notre Dame football and graduation weekends.
Open: All year.
Facilities and activities: Afternoon high tea available. Parlor, library, porch. Open House first Sunday in December. Located in West Washington Historic District. Nearby: Century Center, Tippecanoe Place, Covelski Stadium, Studebaker Auto Museum, Copshalom, Oliver House Museum. A short drive to restaurants and Notre Dame campus and its events and activities.
Recommended Country Inns® Travelers' Club Benefit: 10 percent discount, Monday–Thursday.

Story Inn
STORY, INDIANA 47448

Now I'm gonna tell you the story about Story.

My wife and I had driven from Nashville, down twisting backroads and through dense forest in search of the Story Inn. We finally came to a T in the road, and there was Story, Indiana—a tumbledown old mill, a few cottages, and a tin-sided general store that looked like something straight out of "The Beverly Hillbillies."

That general store was the Story Inn. It even had two old American Oil gas pumps on its front porch, their red-and-gold glass crowns lighted and shining, along with a collection of broken stoves and other geegaws.

We fought the urge to flee and walked inside. Fresh flowers graced tables in an expansive dining room, whose ceilings, walls, and timbers are crammed with antiques, kerosene lamps, patent medicine bottles that promise cures for the grippe, and all kinds of gadgets. A big wood-burning stove sits in the center of the room. And the menu reads like a gourmet's wish list.

There's been a general store here since the 1850s, although this building went up in 1916. During the 1920s Studebaker chassis were assembled on the second floor. Upstairs, workers used to slide them out from the loft to the ground below.

Food. That's the real story. Gustatory delights change weekly. Maybe you'd enjoy steak *au poivre* (an eleven-ounce rib eye marinated in wine, garlic, and pepper, and deglazed in brandy); *poulet printemps* (chicken breast breaded in pecan meal, sautéed and finished in rhubarb, rosé wine, and savory sauce); or medallions of baked pork stuffed with apricots, currants, pine nuts, herb bread crumbs, and marinated mustard seed, glazed with maple syrup and honey mustard and topped with orange sauce.

Many vegetables and herbs come from the inn's garden. And the restaurant offers a selection of California, French, and Australian wines. The house dessert is Turtle Cheese Cake, tinged with coffee liqueur and topped with toffee, crushed pecans, and chocolate.

I don't think I ever want to leave here.

How to get there: From Nashville, take Indiana 46 east, then Indiana 135 south into Story. You can't miss the inn.

Innkeepers: Bob and Gretchen Haddix, owners; Robin Smith and Suzanne Kelley, managers

Address/Telephone: State Road 135 South (mailing address: P.O. Box 64); (812) 988–2273

Rooms: 12, including 4 cottages with suites; all with private bath and air conditioning, some with TV. No smoking inn.

Rates: $76.25, single; $87.25, double; $98.25 to $109.25, cottages; EPB.

Open: All year.

Facilities and activities: Gourmet restaurant serves breakfast to public every day except Monday; dinner, Tuesday through Sunday. Tea time (including homemade desserts) 2:00 to 5:00 P.M. daily. Nearby: Edges Brown County State Park for hiking, biking, relaxing. Nashville, with scores of specialty stores, antiques shops, and art galleries, is 14 miles north.

White Hill Manor
WARSAW, INDIANA 46580

This elegant English Tudor mansion, built in 1934, has been called "the finest hotel I have ever had the pleasure of staying in" by guests from all around the world.

It's a testament to a time when $7,000 of mortgage money could buy crown moldings, hand-hewn oak beams, arched entryways, mullioned windows, and a slate roof.

Situated on the highest land in Warsaw and surrounded by whispering trees, the inn is a retreat into the elegance of yesteryear. In the singularly English common room, I literally sank into one of the twin burgundy leather sofas that front a roaring fire, sorely needed therapy after a punishing day on snowy roads.

Soon afternoon tea was served in a garden room sprinkled with white wicker chairs and glass-topped tables.

Then it was time for guests to retreat to their handsome rooms. A favorite is the Windsor Suite, with its thoroughly English decor, sitting-room windows overlooking the courtyard, and a luxurious spa bath (two-person whirlpool) that has provided plenty of adventurous nights for honeymooners and romantics alike.

I also like the Buttery, formerly part of the home's original kitchen. It boasts specially designed stained-glass windows and an antique claw-footed tub.

And don't pass up a chance to overnight in

the Library. The arched door to this room looks like something out of an English manor house. Step inside and you'll see hand-hewn oak ceiling beams that add to the British ambience, along with a king-sized brass bed.

Breakfasts on the porch, itself a handsome room that has more hand-hewn beams and the original slate floor, might include fresh fruits, stuffed eggs, cinnamon-spiked French toast, and hot coffee.

And here's one for you trivia buffs: Did you know that more ducks are raised here in Kosciusko County than anywhere else in the world?

How to get there: From the west, take U.S. 30 into Warsaw; turn south on Parker Street, then east on Center Street to the inn. From the east, take U.S. 30 into Warsaw, turn west on Center Street to the inn.

Innkeeper: Carm Zoyla Henderson
Address/Telephone: 2513 East Center Street; (219) 269–6933
Rooms: 8, including 1 suite; all with private bath, air conditioning, TV, and phone. Wheelchair access.
Rates: $70 to $120, single or double, EPB.
Open: All year.
Facilities and activities: Afternoon tea and evening snacks. Lunch and dinner can be arranged for inn guests. Porch, common room. Next door to Wagon Wheel Dinner Theatre and Restaurant. Nearby: exercise spa and racquet club; a short drive to nearly 100 lakes for all kinds of water sports, golf, skiing, camping, summer festivals, bike trails, quaint shopping, and sights in northeastern Indiana's Amish country.
Business travel: Located about 40 miles southeast of South Bend, 40 miles northwest of Fort Wayne. Corporate rates, meeting room, fax.
Recommended Country Inns® Travelers' Club Benefit: 10 percent discount, Monday–Thursday, or 25 percent discount when staying four or more nights, subject to availability.

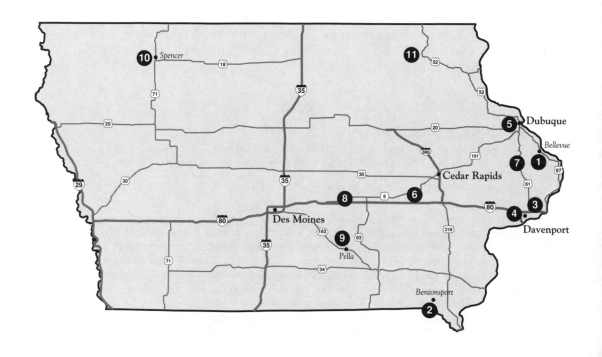

Iowa

Iowa

Numbers on map refer to towns numbered below.

ont Rest Victorian House of Bellevue

BELLEVUE, IOWA 52031

"This house was once lost in a poker game," Christine said.

That was in 1896, just three years after Seth Baker built Mont Rest, a nine-acre estate nestled halfway up a wooded bluff affording one of Iowa's most panoramic views of the Mississippi River.

Locals nicknamed the imposing white house, with its round white tower protruding like a periscope from the home's belly, Baker's Castle—a moniker that has stuck into the 1990s. Today Mont Rest stands as the river town's most notable "Painted Lady."

I cannot overemphasize that the inn's vista of the Mississippi is truly breathtaking.

The Bellevue Room is the inn's largest

sleeping quarters and has a great view of both the river and the quaint town. It has a 9-foot headboard on the bed and matching furniture with pink marble tops. The room's a favorite for honeymoon and anniversary couples.

Another favorite is the Great River Room, all done in delicate blues with print ceiling borders, a pinwheel-style bed quilt, and a marble-topped dresser; it's a terrific spot from which to gaze out endlessly over the mighty "Miss'sip."

Eagle's Nest, a charming room with hand-stenciled hardwood floors and an iron-rail bed, is also one of my favorites. Sometimes you can see eagles making their nests in the trees.

The Baker Room, located in the building's

tall tower, offers one of the Midwest's best river vistas, but, Christine said, "It's not for the faint of heart." Wicker antiques, hooked rugs, and a roof garden boasting a gingerbread deck are some additional perks.

A full country breakfast awaits overnight guests. Imagine country-style eggs with green peppers and cheese, smoked sausage, homemade banana nut bread and coffee cake, fresh fruit, orange juice, and beverages. Dine at Potter's Mill, built in 1843 on the edge of Big Mill Creek and now carefully restored and transformed into a unique restaurant; it serves some of the best prime rib and pork loin in these parts. Not to mention catfish and trout from local rivers and streams.

And listen to this: The Snyders' latest plans include renovation of a historic general store, transforming it into an "animatronic, special effects, 'haunted' bed and breakfast inn, complete with 'ghosts' and other gulp-inducing treats. "My brother's a Hollywood SFX man," Christine explained.

How to get there: From Dubuque, take U.S. 52 south into Bellevue. Turn right on Spring Street and continue to the inn.

Innkeepers: Tom and Christine Snyder

Address/Telephone: 300 Spring Street; (319) 872–4220

Rooms: 6; 3 share 3 baths, 2 with private half bath; all with air conditioning. No smoking inn.

Rates: $64 to $94, single or double, EPB. $175 for special Murder Mystery Weekends that include room and gourmet dinner for two.

Open: All year except Christmas Eve and Day.

Facilities and activities: Sitting room with fireplace, gourmet meals, therapeutic massage, panoramic views of Mississippi River due to inn's bluff-top location. Situated in one of the most picturesque river towns in Iowa. Nearby: nine parks (several with great bluff-top river views), trout streams, 9-hole golf course, Young Museum, tours of Lock and Dam No. 12, butterfly garden, antiques shops, hiking, biking, Indian cave. Fests include Fourth of July Heritage Days and Tom Sawyer Days in August.

Mason House Inn

BENTONSPORT, IOWA 52565

If you look upstream from the 1882 bridge in this historic riverfront village, you'll see ripples on the water marking the site of the old dam. It's a reminder of the days when the Des Moines River teemed with riverboat traffic, mills lined the winding banks, and nearly 1,500 people lived in the town. Today the year-round population numbers 31.

The Mason House Inn was built in 1846 by Mormon craftsmen who stayed in Bentonsport for one year while making their famous trek to Utah. It mainly served steamboat passengers traveling from St. Louis to Des Moines.

No wonder the inn still stands sturdy, its cozy Georgian stylings providing a warm welcome for big-city visitors who want to experience a quiet and restful stay.

Many of the rooms appear as they did in their heyday, with several original furnishings. Especially interesting is a memorial hair wreath measuring 3 feet by 4 feet that hangs in the parlor. Here you can also pump and play tunes on an 1882 Estey organ.

William (a former pastor for the Christian Church) and Sheral (who holds a degree in hotel and restaurant management) did extensive remodeling in 1990, connecting the inn with the old railroad station; now it boasts two extra rooms: the Wash House and Old Country Store, each with period furnishings.

Other guest quarters include the Wild Rose Room, with its 9-foot-high walnut headboard, and the Mason Room, with matching bedroom set, 9-foot French mirror, fainting couch, and wood-burning stove—all original to the inn.

I especially like the Steamboat Room, with its burl walnut bedroom set and windows offering a good view of the river. And don't miss the copper-lined "Murphy" bathtub, which unfolds from the Keeping Room wall cabinet. The innkeepers claim that it's the only one of its kind in Iowa.

The country breakfast, served in the Keeping Room next to the 1803 cookstove, is a special event. How do eggs and sausage, blueberry waffles, peach crisp, and Mason House sticky pecan rolls sound? Sheral serves dinner,

including dishes like smoked brisket of beef, orange roughy filet, and roasted chicken breast, with advance reservations.

There's now an antiques shop out back, called the Outback Antique Shop—what else? And get the innkeepers to tell you how the Mason House was saved from that tragic "Flood of the Century" a few years back. Hint: lots of help and love from neighbors—and 31,000 sandbags!

How to get there: Bentonsport is in the southeast corner of Iowa's Van Buren County between Keosauqua and Bonaparte on J40, a paved county road. Take Iowa 1 south through Keosauqua, cross the river, and go uphill to J40. Then go east to Bentonsport. Turn right on any village road toward the river. The inn is along the bank.

Innkeepers: Dr. William and Sheral McDermet

Address/Telephone: Rural Route 2, Box 237, Bentonsport, Keosauqua, Iowa 52565; (319) 592-3133

Rooms: 9; 5 with private bath. No smoking inn.

Rates: $44 to $64, single; $54 to $74, double; EPB. No credit cards.

Open: All year.

Facilities and activities: Located in village declared National Historic District in 1972. Walk to shops (open April through November, daily) that include native crafts, antiques, blacksmith, weaver, and potter. Nearby: bike, hike, canoe on Des Moines River. A short drive to restaurants, Shimek State Forest, cross-country skiing.

Recommended Country Inns® Travelers' Club Benefit: 20 percent discount, subject to availability.

The Abbey Hotel
BETTENDORF, IOWA 52722

It wouldn't be any exaggeration to describe a night at the Abbey Hotel as "heavenly."

That's because this landmark Bettendorf building was originally opened in 1917 as a convent for the Sisters of Our Lady of Mount Carmel. And it continues to display many trappings of its former life: There's a statue of an angel blowing a trumpet perched on one of the roofs, and stained-glass windows contain prayers scribed in Latin.

Even a spectacular Gothic chapel remains, still used for masses and weddings by the Anglican Church. Its domed exterior replicates the grand cathedrals of Europe; inside, you'll find an altar imported from turn-of-the-century Belgium and beautiful stained-glass windows depicting Christ, Mary, saints, and nuns.

Since its conversion to a hotel in 1982, the Abbey has achieved all kinds of awards. As many as five of the original nuns' "cells" have been combined for a spacious and luxurious guest room. Ours featured an imported marble bath, a mahogany armoire with cable television, a sitting area with two overstuffed chairs and couch, and several tall windows offering spectacular views of the Mississippi and the Quad Cities.

The room also had a second entry door, which opened onto a long veranda overlooking a lovely courtyard. This is where the sisters often walked for contemplation; today a corner of the courtyard is filled by the hotel's in-ground swimming pool. (Incidentally, the pool was added by the Franciscan Brothers, who took over the building as a monastery in 1978 after the nuns moved to a smaller outpost in Eldridge, about 10 miles north of here.)

For a peek at how the monastery appeared before its luxurious makeover, head to the third-floor museum. One cell has been maintained in its original size and configuration. Note the nun's habit, sandals, and Bible; these were among the few possessions that sisters were allowed to keep during their lifetime of sacrifice and prayer here. And that simple bed is just a board covered with straw.

How to get there: From Rock Island, take I–74 across the Mississippi River into Iowa; get off at the first exit past the river, Highway 67 (signs may say STATE STREET, GRANT STREET, RIVER-FRONT EXIT). Follow that exit road, which turns into 14th Street. Then continue on 14th Street, up the hill, to the hotel.

Innkeepers: Joseph and Joan Lemon and Joseph Lemon Jr., owners; Theresa Lemon, manager
Address/Telephone: 1401 Central Avenue; (319) 355–0291 or (800) 438–7535, fax (319) 355–7647
Rooms: 19, with 1 suite; all with private bath. No smoking inn.
Rates: $75 to $125, single or double; $149, suite; continental breakfast.
Open: All year.
Facilities and activities: Dinner, room service available. Breakfast room, banquet rooms, verandas with Mississippi River views, courtyard, Gothic chapel, outdoor swimming pool. Nearby: a short drive to President Riverboat Casino, Adler Theater and River Center, Casino Rock Island Riverboat, Rock Island Arsenal, Quad City Downs Harness Race Track, PGA Championship Golf Course.
Business travel: Located 5 minutes from downtown Bettendorf, 8 minutes from downtown Davenport. Corporate rates, meeting rooms, fax.

Jumer's Castle Lodge
BETTENDORF, IOWA 52722

If you'd like to experience a bigger-than-life European getaway, walk into this eastern Iowa hostelry that's earned national recognition.

Centuries-old traditions of European innkeeping are evident everywhere as you step through heavy beveled-glass doors into a grand lobby. Like the other common rooms, the lobby has magnificent tapestries hanging on walls, regal statuary, sleek bronzes, and what the hotel likes to call "a veritable pageant of precious artwork."

And see if you can spot the three-bears hand-carved umbrella stand; it is quite unusual.

"There's definitely a baronial feel to this place," said my brother, Mark. You bet. I mean, even the elevators contain floral European-style wall coverings and elegant mirrors.

And if there's a hotel library more elegant than this one, I'd like to see it. Bookshelves soar to incredible heights as a giant hearth roars with a warming blaze, surrounded by two high-back handcarved walnut chairs and other luxurious appointments. Makes you want to settle down in a comfy chair with a good book and not come out for a day or two.

One of my favorite guest-room styles is the loft, with an iron spiral staircase leading to upstairs bedchambers. Perhaps you'd prefer a spacious suite, complete with its own four-poster canopy bed, fireplace, and antique oil paintings.

Dining is another Jumer's experience not to be missed. It's an award-winning kitchen that serves up authentic German house specialties like wursts, sausages, spaetzle, and sauerkraut. Savor the flavors of the restaurant's fresh-baked rolls and breads. And desserts, ranging from tortes and strudels to creamy cheesecakes, are heavenly.

How to get there: From the (Quad Cities) Moline Airport, exit at Spruce Hills Drive, and continue to the hotel.

Innkeeper: Dan Conners, general manager

Address/Telephone: I–74 at Spruce Hills Drive; (319) 359–7141 or (800) 285–8637

Rooms: 210 rooms, lofts, and suites; all with private bath and air conditioning, some with fireplace, whirlpool bath, wet bar, and other amenities. Wheelchair access.

Rates: Regular rooms: $78 to $88, single, $87 to $99, double; suites: $90 to $110, single, $97 to $119, double; lofts: $118 to $133, single, $127 to $142, double; EP. Special seasonal packages available.

Open: All year.

Facilities and activities: Full-service restaurant, Bavarian dining room, room service, Schwarzer Bar lounge and Library Bar, indoor and outdoor swimming pools, sauna, exercise room, game court, putting green, limousine service, antiques shop, gift shop. Nearby: riverboat casinos.

Business travel: Located about five minutes from downtown Bettendorf and downtown Davenport. Corporate rates, meeting and conference rooms, fax.

Bishop's House Inn
DAVENPORT, IOWA 52803

"It sure beats a room at the parish rectory," I told my brother, Mark, as we walked into the Bishop's House Inn, an 1871 landmark Italianate mansion that was once the personal residence of Roman Catholic Bishop John L. Davis.

Oak woodworks, six marble fireplaces, parquet floors, stained glass, ceiling medallions, hand-painted and -stenciled walls are just some of the many spectacular features of this nineteenth-century architectural gem, which is as impressive today as it was when the bishop roamed the house.

Inside, innkeeper Sandy presides over a Victorian showplace. Take my word that the common rooms are elegant; let's get right to guest rooms.

Most opulent is the Davis Suite, a huge Victorian bedchamber that includes hand-printed Bradbury and Bradbury wall coverings, a massive oak bedroom set adorned with a huge featherbed, and a woodburning fireplace (circa 1890) whose mantel shows off unusual spindles, tiles, and beveled mirrors.

I especially like the suite's bath, clad in Vermont marble and featuring an oval whirlpool tub.

Another spectacular room is the Rohlman Chamber, named for Bishop Henry P. Rohlman, the second Catholic clergyman to occupy the home. The bedchamber was originally part of the bishop's sitting room; now it has an Eastlake walnut bedroom set, wood-burning fireplace, feath-erbed—and an unusual marble shower stall added especially for the priest.

Other guest rooms are equally gracious, including the Housekeeper's Chamber, which features the house's original bathroom (yep, that's the bishop's claw-footed tub).

Take if from me; you're going to like it here.

How to get there: From I–80, exit at U.S. 61 (which turns into Brady Street in Davenport); go south and continue to the inn, located at the intersection of Brady and Kirkwood Boulevard.

Innkeeper: Sandy Krueger
Address/Telephone: 1527 Brady Street; (319) 322–8303
Rooms: 6, including 1 suite; all with private bath, air conditioning, and ceiling fan.
Rates: $65 to $115, single or double; $140, suite; EPB. $10 room-rate discount
      Monday through Thursday.
Open: All year.
Facilities and activities: Formal parlor, sitting room, dining room, second-floor guest parlor.
      Nearby: a short drive to riverboat casinos, The Children's Museum, Wildcat Den
      State Park, Buffalo Bill's family homestead in LeClaire, Rock Island Arsenal and
      Museum.

The Hancock House

DUBUQUE, IOWA 52001-4644

Here is a triple treat: a magnificent bluff-top setting, an exquisite Queen Anne mansion, and spectacular views of the Mississippi River.

I know those are many superlatives, but it would take a thesaurusful of adjectives to do justice to The Hancock House.

"You can see sixteen church steeples from any guest room," the innkeepers told me. I challenge guests to find them all. Of course, I think you have to be a native Dubuquer to get the tough one.

Chuck and Susan have continued to meticulously restore this twenty-seven-room mansion built in 1891 by Charles Hancock, owner of the largest wholesale grocery in the Midwest at that time. Everything is larger than life. You really must experience the 28-by-18-foot dining room—completely done in quarter-sawn oak, with coffered and beamed ceiling and elegant fireplace—to appreciate it.

Speaking of fireplaces, the one in the sitting room, with its elaborate gingerbread detailing, took first place in design competition at the 1893 Columbian Exposition in Chicago.

Guest rooms are fabulous. I like the North Bedroom, with its magnificent half-tester bed, original marble bath with handsome mosaic floor, marble coal-burning fireplace (which includes a coal-powered footwarmer), and Bradley & Howard–signed table lamp.

Maybe you'd rather try the East Bedroom. It has a white iron-rail bed, marble sink, claw-footed tub, and four huge windows.

You get spectacular views of the Mississippi. At night you can see the yellow running lights of double-decked river paddleboats. In the summer you see scores of sailboats.

The innkeepers told me: "Then there are the church bells that ring on Sunday mornings. The sound is heavenly. But one day a guest asked me which church played 'Blue Moon.' Those are the bank chimes."

Newer rooms include the original servant's bedroom, with great river vistas, and the Doll Room, a third-floor aerie that claims both the house's turret and a whirlpool tub. For a real touch of elegance, sample the inn's huge suite. Its 900 square feet include a large living/sitting room brightened by the light from seven win-dows; a wet bar located in the old nursemaid's pantry; an inviting whirlpool bath for two; and a bedroom with a white iron-rail bed and handsome stained-glass window.

And in one of the inn's spectacular sitting rooms, with its incredible views, you can see three states at once—Iowa, Illinois, and Wisconsin.

Finally, something new planned for this year: a restored cottage across the street from the main inn. More good times for the Hancock House.

How to get there: From Illinois, take the Julien Dubuque Bridge to Locust Street, turn north on Locust, and continue. At Twelfth Street, turn left, and then take another left on Grove Terrace to the inn.

Innkeepers: Chuck and Susan Huntley

Address/Telephone: 1105 Grove Terrace; (319) 557–8989

Rooms: 9, including 1 suite; all with private bath and air conditioning, 4 with whirlpool tubs, TV and phone on request. No smoking inn.

Rates: $75 to $150, single or double, EPB and complimentary beverages.

Open: All year.

Facilities and activities: Sitting rooms, porch. Located in the heart of historic Mississippi River town, with magnificent river views. Nearby: restaurants, cable-car elevator, riverboat rides, Woodward Riverboat Museum, Ham House Museum. Brilliant fall colors, hiking, biking, cross-country and downhill skiing.

Business travel: Located a few minutes from downtown Dubuque. Corporate rates, conference room, fax.

Recommended Country Inns® Travelers' Club Benefit: 25 percent discount, Monday–Thursday.

Juniper Hill Farm Bed & Breakfast
DUBUQUE, IOWA 52002

"See that hawk up over the tree," Bill said. I squinted my eyes, and in the distance I spotted him, soaring on thermals.

After I calmed down, Bill said, "You should be here in spring and fall. That's when we get lots of bald eagles."

Don't worry. I'll be back.

Juniper Hill Farm sits next to Sundown ski area, tucked high in the magnificent bluff country that rolls away from the banks of the Mississippi River, just 8 miles away.

Bill led me to one of the inn's picture windows for another thrilling view—a panorama that overlooks a 28-mile valley surrounded by hills, woods, and nature in abundance.

I could see all the way to Wisconsin!

Bill and Ruth have fashioned a warm and cozy getaway up in these hills. The building, constructed in 1940 as a Scottish cottage, is elegant and gracious in its country stylings. I especially liked the Gathering Room, finished completely in knotty pine—floor, walls, ceiling, everything.

Three guest suites offer the finest country getaway imaginable. My favorite might be the Garden View Suite. Besides handmade quilts "done by Mennonite ladies in western Iowa," a two-poster bed, and white wicker furniture, the room offers a double whirlpool bath that's especially popular with honeymooners and romantics.

From one of the windows, Bill pointed out an old stagecoach trail that ran through these parts in the 1870s. "You can still see wheel ruts in the ground after the snow melts each spring," Bill said.

Ruth's breakfasts are another treat. Served in the dining room, they include pancakes, sausage, country ham, blueberry syrup, peach sauce, baked apples, and more.

Did I mention that guests are welcome to fish in the farm's private pond? Bill stocks it with large mouth bass. And this may be the only Midwest inn where downhill skiers can schuss right to their front door!

How to get there: From Chicago and Dubuque, take Highway 20 west through Dubuque to Northwest Arterial. Turn north (right), and continue to Asbury Road (second intersection on Northwest Arterial). Then go west on Asbury about 3¾ miles to Budd Road. Turn right, and continue less than a half mile to Juniper Hill.

Innkeepers: Bill and Ruth McEllhiney
Address/Telephone: 15325 Budd Road; (800) 572–1449 or (319) 582–4405
Rooms: 3 suites; all with private bath and air conditioning.
E-mail: jhbandb@aol.com
Rates: $70 to $140, single or double, EPB and evening snacks and beverages. Two-night minimum on weekends.
Open: All year.
Facilities and activities: Parlor, atrium room, outdoor hot tub, stocked fishing pond, hiking trails, cross-country ski trails, access to adjacent Sundown downhill ski area. A short drive to Dubuque (casino riverboat gambling, riverboat museums, shopping, dining, Greyhound Park); Dyersville, Iowa, site of the *Field of Dreams* baseball field; and Galena, Illinois, home to historic architecture, quaint shops, and art galleries.

The Mandolin
DUBUQUE, IOWA 52001

One glance inside and I saw that the home had been built for someone special—and incredibly wealthy. Imagine stained-glass windows, parquet floors, hand-painted canvas wall coverings. You get the idea.

In fact, this 1908 Queen Anne mansion was the home of Nicholas Schrup, Dubuque's leading financial figure at the turn of the century. Apparently he spared no expense, and luckily most of his special touches have survived through the years.

The foyer is massive, graced with tall oak columns and an inlaid wood parquet floor. I immediately noticed the stained-glass window on a stairway landing, fashioned with the likeness of St. Cecilia, patron saint of musicians. She's clutching a mandolin, hence the name of the inn.

Imagine cypress woodwork in the parlor, probably brought up the Mississippi in a riverboat. The usual sheen of the wood changes with movement. It has almost an iridescence to it.

The Music Room boasts original hand-painted murals on the north wall. And the dining room! It's engulfed by oak paneling, a floor-to-ceiling beveled-glass china cupboard, and an Italian fireplace. My favorite touch: the original hand-painted wall mural that makes it appear as if you're in the middle of a dark Victorian forest.

Rooms are equally impressive. Holly Marie

boasts a seven-piece French walnut furniture set, complete with huge armoire, marble-topped dresser, and full-length dressing mirror.

I especially like Grand Tour, graced with American walnut pieces and an Irish rose lace bedspread, as well as an antique Irish pitcher and bowl brought back from Ireland by Jan herself.

In fact, the touches of "auld sod" would sit quite well with my Irish mom, whose ancestral relatives hail from County Armagh.

Jan's breakfasts are three-course gourmet affairs that include everything from stuffed French toast to tropical-fruit breads and hazelnut coffee. You'll need to walk around historic Dubuque to work off the goodies.

Several Schrups still live in the Dubuque area—can you believe that they still consider this their house of humble beginnings? Humble beginnings? This is a palace.

How to get there: From Galena, take U.S. 20 west across the bridge into Dubuque, turn right on Locust Street, proceed to Loras Street (14th Street); turn right and continue 1 block to Main Street, then turn left and continue to the inn.

Innkeeper: Jan Oswald
Address/Telephone: 199 Loras; (319) 556–0069, fax (319) 556–0587
Rooms: 8; 4 with private bath, all with air conditioning. No smoking inn.
Rates: $65 to $110, single or double, EPB.
Open: All year.
Facilities and activities: Sitting room, music room. Wraparound veranda. Nearby: restaurants, riverboat rides on the Mississippi, museums, Cable Car Square, Fenelon Place Elevator, Sundown ski area, hiking, dog racing.

The Redstone Inn
DUBUQUE, IOWA 52001

If you ever had dreams of piloting a paddle wheeler down the mighty Mississippi, you can get the next best thing in Dubuque. In this historic river town, you can ply the waters on the stern-wheeler *Spirit of Dubuque*, walk the decks of the side-wheeler *William M. Black*, and immerse yourself in the exhibits of the F. W. Woodward Riverboat Museum.

And there's no better way of continuing a "living history" visit than by staying at The Redstone Inn, an 1894 Victorian mansion restored to all its original splendor.

I registered in a rich, oak-paneled hallway on a first floor that retains much of the home's original ambience. The mauve, deep blue, green,

and burgundy colors are used to complement the Redstone's many original stained-glass windows.

Because no two guest rooms are alike, you can select your favorite from a color-photo portfolio kept at the reception area.

I'm in good shape, so the almost forty steps it takes to get to the third-floor rooms were no problem. (In fact, I enjoyed the exercise.) My room was like many offered at the inn—antique furnishings with walnut beds, balloon curtains, period lighting fixtures, muted floral wallpapers, and bed quilts. Mine also had a whirlpool bath, which I headed for immediately; some also have fireplaces, with free logs.

Breakfast is served in your room or downstairs in the small dining room. Starched white table linens and fresh flowers adorn the tables. I munched on chewy homemade caramel rolls, croissants, and bagels.

Afternoon teas feature a variety of English teas, dainty finger sandwiches, tarts, biscuits—and maybe gingerbread cherry pie, an inn specialty. Count on English truffles, too. I recommend the "225" and its *nouvelle cuisine* delights for romantic dinners; it's just a short drive away.

Be sure to peek at the inn's parlor, an exquisite example of Victorian elegance. It took me a

few minutes to get comfortable in this very formal room with its ornate furniture, oriental-style rugs, and tile fireplace with elaborate mantel. The gas chandelier is original to the home. So are the cherub figurines that gaze down from the plaster-cast ceiling; yes, they are gold leaf.

How to get there: Whether entering Dubuque from the west via U.S. 151 or east on U.S. 20, pick up Locust Street at the bridge and proceed to University. Turn left and drive to Bluff; then turn left again. The inn is on the street's left side.

Innkeeper: Chris Wackerly, manager

Address/Telephone: 504 Bluff Street; (319) 582–1894, fax (319) 582–1893

Rooms: 15, with 6 suites; all with private bath, air conditioning, phone, and TV.

Rates: Rooms: weekends: $75 to $98, single or double; weekdays: $60 to $75, single or double; $115 to $175, suites; continental breakfast.

Open: All year.

Facilities and activities: Afternoon teas (Tuesday through Sunday, 2:00 to 6:00 P.M.). Walk to restaurants. Dubuque attractions include Sundown downhill ski area, Mississippi riverboat cruises, riverboat museum, Cable Car Square (specialty shops in a historic location), scenic railcar climbing 189-foot bluff with view of 3 states.

Business travel: Located in the heart of downtown Dubuque. Corporate rates, meeting rooms, fax.

Die Heimat Country Inn
HOMESTEAD, IOWA 52236

Homestead is a peaceful little village off a busy interstate in the historic Amana Colonies, settled in the 1840s by German immigrants seeking religious freedom and a communal lifestyle. As soon as I turned off the highway to reach Die Heimat Country Inn, I became absorbed in the quiet of this century-and-a-half-old agricultural community.

Whatever pressures might have been building inside me during the long drive to Iowa disappeared once I stepped inside. Jacki greeted me at the desk, full of good cheer and chatter. The charming lobby is generously decorated with nationally famous Amana furniture (the sofas are original to the 1854 inn) and a large walnut Amana grandfather's clock ticking softly in the corner of the room.

Soothing German zither music wafted through the inn, and I immediately began to feel at home. (*Die Heimat* is German for "the homestead" or "the home place.") On the way to my room, Jacki pointed out the cross-stitched hangings on the walls; they're German house blessings, many brought from the old country.

My room was small and cozy, with sturdy Amana furniture, an electric kerosene lamp, writing desk, rocking chair, and brass-lantern ceiling lamp. It's so quiet that you'll probably wake up in the morning to the sound of chirping birds, as I did.

Other rooms might feature handsome Amana four-poster walnut beds graced with lace canopies, handmade Amana quilts, handmade Colonies crafts, and rocking chairs.

Breakfast includes French toast, eggs, fruit soup, and home-baked goodies.

After breakfast I explored the thrumming communities of the seven Amana Colonies villages, with all kinds of historical and commercial attractions, including fabulous bakery goods and meat shops. The innkeepers can point out the "can't miss" stops.

Bill Zuber's restaurant, just down the street from the inn, was one of her recommendations. Zuber was a pitcher for the New York Yankees, a hometown boy discovered by scouts when he was seen tossing cabbages during a local harvest. I liked the menus in the shapes of baseballs, and the home-style cooking, from historic recipes used by the Amana Colonies' old communal kitchens, was scrumptious. My baked chicken with fried potatoes, veggies, and green peas in thick gravy would be hard to beat. Also served are Amana ham, pork, and baked steaks.

How to get there: Take I–80 to exit 225 (151 north), and go about 5 miles. At the intersection of Highways 6 and 49, turn left past Bill Zuber's restaurant to the inn just down the block.

Innkeepers: Warren and Jacki Lock

Address/Telephone: Main Street; (319) 622–3937

Rooms: 19, including 8 deluxe; all with private bath, air conditioning, and TV. Well-behaved pets OK.

Rates: $43.95 to $66, single or double, EPB. Special weekday winter rates.

Open: All year.

Facilities and activities: Sitting room. Shaded yard with Amana wooden gliders. Walk to restaurant, nature trail. Short drive to 7 historic Amana Colonies villages, with antiques, crafts, and specialty stores, museums, bakeries, Amana furniture shops. Also nearby: winery, summer theater, golf, biking, cross-country skiing in Lake Macbride State Park, Palisades Kepler State Park.

Squiers Manor
MAQUOKETA, IOWA 52060

Nothing prepares you for the splendor of this 1882 house, listed on the National Register of Historic Places.

The handsome Queen Anne home boasts fine wood everywhere. There's a walnut parlor, a cherry dining room, and butternut throughout the rest of the house.

Fine antiques are everywhere, too; some, like the 1820s Federal four-poster mahogany bed in the Harriet Squiers Room, are of museum quality.

That's not surprising, since Cathy and Virl also own a nationally renowned antiques store just a few miles out of town.

I especially liked the Jeannie Mitchel Bridal Suite. Its canopied brass bed stands more than 7 feet tall. (Note the mother-of-pearl on the footboard.) And the Victorian Renaissance dresser with marble top is another treasure.

Did I mention that the suite has a double whirlpool bath?

So does the J. E. Squiers Room; there a verde (green) marble floor creates a path leading to a cozy corner whirlpool for two.

Opal's Parlor (named after a longtime resident of the manor when its rooms were rented as apartments) features not only 1860s antiques and hand-crocheted bedspreads but also a Swiss shower that acts "like a human car wash," said Cathy.

Every common room bespeaks luxury and splendor. The parlor's fireplace, with tiles depicting characters in Roman mythology, is unusual. Look at the fabulous hand-carved cherry buffet in the dining room. The dining room's 10-foot-tall, hand-carved jewelers' clock is another conversation starter.

And the library, an enclave done entirely in butternut paneling and graced with its original fireplace, is flat-out gorgeous.

Not only do you get great atmosphere; Cathy's breakfasts are terrific, too. Consider pumpkin pecan muffins, black-walnut bread, eggs Katrina, pecan-stuffed French toast, seafood quiches, apple pudding, and more.

Another wrinkle is "candlelight evening desserts." Imagine nibbling on Cathy's chocolate bourbon pecan pie, delicious tortes, or Grandma Annie's bread pudding, a guest favorite.

And there are two fantastic new suites reclaimed from the home's grand ballroom. The Loft boasts a gas-log fireplace for instant romance, a 6-by-4-foot whirlpool tub, wicker sitting room—with breakfast delivered to your bedchamber.

The Ballroom (that's the other suite's name) is an incredible 1,100 square feet of luxury, with a whirlpool tub nestled in a "garden" setting, king-sized bed, cathedral ceiling, massive sitting room, reading nook, and lots more surprises.

How to get there: From Dubuque, take U.S. 61 south to U.S. 64, then turn east into town. One block past the second stoplight, turn right, then go 1 block to the inn.

Innkeepers: Cathy and Virl Banowetz
Address/Telephone: 418 West Pleasant Street; (319) 652–6961
Rooms: 8, including 3 suites; all with private bath and air conditioning.
Rates: $75 to $100, single or double; $150 to $185, suites; EPB.
Open: All year.
Facilities and activities: Library, parlor, porch. A short drive to Mississippi River towns; Dubuque, site of low-stakes riverboat casino gambling; and Galena, Illinois, a Civil War–era architectural wonderland.
Recommended Country Inns® Travelers' Club Benefit: Stay two nights, get third night free, Sunday–Thursday, excluding holiday weeks.

$\mathcal{L}$a Corsette Maison Inn
NEWTON, IOWA 50208

My wife, Debbie, and I sat in front of a roaring fire in an elegant parlor, enjoying a romantic gourmet-style breakfast.

First Kay brought us a delightful fresh fruit compote of pink grapefruit, mandarin orange slices, grapes, and kiwi. Her home-baked apple muffins with strudel were next. (We could have eaten four apiece, they were so delicious.)

We sipped on raspberry and orange juice, which washed down authentic English scones, another of Kay's specialties. Then came a wonderful frittata with two cheeses—and some special La Corsette French bread.

It was one of the ultimate bed-and-breakfast breakfast experiences.

No wonder food at Kay's inn has received a 4½-star rating from the *Des Moines Register* and has been hailed as a "gleaming jewel in the crown of fine restaurants."

The mansion itself is a 1909 Mission-style masterpiece built by an early Iowa state senator. Not much has changed in the intervening years. Gleaming mission oak woodwork, Art Nouveau stained-glass windows, and other turn-of-the-century architectural flourishes make La Corsette a special place.

We overnighted in the Windsor Hunt Suite; the massive bedchamber has a huge four-poster bed (you use a stepstool to reach the high mattress), and the sitting room boasts its own fireplace—which we used for a romantic end to the day—as well as a two-person whirlpool bath.

Other rooms are imbued with their own particular charms. The Penthouse bedchambers, for instance, are located in the tower and surrounded by beveled-glass windows.

The innkeeper gives house tours before dinner each evening. One of her anecdotes reveals that Fred Maytag, of washing-machine fame, got his seed money from La Corsette's owner to start his company. Another tells that Fred personally used a "one-minute brand" washer made by another company in town. His own Maytag "chewed up" his clothes.

Kay's five-course, gourmet-style dinners, prepared by both herself and a new chef (a graduate of the Culinary Institute of America, by the way), are renowned. The first person to make reservations for the evening sets the night's menu. Choices include the likes of French veal in cream, broccoli-stuffed game hen with Mornay sauce, and roast loin of pork with prune chutney.

Maybe you'd rather have a basket dinner delivered to your door during weekday visits. This three-course treat might included stuffed pork chops, fancy veggies, home-baked breads, and more.

Or choose to stay at the 100-year-old Sister Inn next door. Here Kay features double whirlpools and antique soaking tubs. Looks like fun.

How to get there: From the Quad Cities, take I–80 to Newton (exit 164), and go north until the second light (Highway 6); then turn right and continue 7 blocks to the inn.

Innkeeper: Kay Owen

Address/Telephone: 629 1st Avenue; (515) 792–6833

Rooms: 5, including 2 suites; all with private bath and air conditioning. No smoking inn.

Rates: $65 to $80, single or double; $75 to $170, suites; Sister Inn, 2 bedchambers, $145 and $170; EPB. Multinight minimum during Pella, Iowa, Tulip Festival and some other special events. Pets allowed by prearrangement.

Open: All year.

Facilities and activities: Gourmet 5-course dinners. Two sitting rooms with fireplace; porch. Nearby: Maytag Company tours, tennis courts, golf courses, horseback riding, cross-country skiing. A short drive to Trainland, U.S.A.; Prairie Meadows Horse Track; Krumm Nature Preserve.

Strawtown Inn
PELLA, IOWA 50219

I visited the Strawtown Inn during the spring, when thousands of blooming tulips planted along walkways and in gardens create swirls of rainbow colors and fragrant scents for lucky guests. (They're replaced by bright red geraniums in summer.)

This is just one way the inn honors its ethnic heritage. Another is the inn's name: Mid-1800s Dutch settlers built huts on this corner of the then-tiny village from long slough grass and covered them with straw woven into a stick frame.

The guest rooms are delightful. Each *kamer* (room) is artfully decorated and has its own personality. The *Bedstee kamer*, with Dutch prints,

pastel floral wallpaper, and Dutch beds built into the wall, is one of my favorites. Stenciling fans will love the *Pannigen kamer*, with its Dutch border stencils on walls and ceilings.

And the *Juliana kamer* is a long room with a slanted ceiling, skylight windows, walnut antique reproductions, and a photograph of former Netherlands Queen Juliana hanging on the wall. It was named for the queen to commemorate her May 1942 visit to Pella. The queen, howwever, didn't get to enjoy the Jacuzzi tub that now beckons guests.

I cannot think of a better place to enjoy a Dutch breakfast than in the inn's bright morning room. Ladder-back chairs, rich oak woodwork, cheery pastel colors, and scatter rugs covering plank floors add to the old-world ambience. A cold-meat tray is a real treat, along with Dutch cheeses, breads, rolls, beverages, and hard-boiled eggs.

Five antiques-laden rooms host inn lunches and dinners; one even has double Dutch ovens. The food is celebrated, having received recommendations from such diverse publications as the *Des Moines Register*, the *New Yorker*, *Travel Holiday*, and the *Saturday Evening Post*. I was especially intrigued by stuffed pork chops with apple walnut dressing and mushroom sauce,

Dutch spiced beef, and pheasant under glass carved tableside.

The inn also holds special international gourmet-dinner weekends throughout the year.

Be sure to take time and wander around this quaint town. Many of Pella's stores have Dutch fronts; you can see wooden shoes being carved at the Historical Village, and authentic Dutch street organs pipe happy tunes for visitors.

How to get there: Pella is reached off Iowa 163. Follow that to Washington Street. The inn is on the west side of town.

Innkeeper: Sue Vanderschaaf
Address/Telephone: 1111 Washington Street; (515) 628–2681
Rooms: 17, with 5 suites; all with private bath and wheelchair access.
Rates: Rooms: Weekdays: $60 to $85, single; $85 to $95, double; weekends: $82.50 to
$92.50, single or double; suites, $120 to $147.50; EPB.
Open: All year.
Facilities and activities: Full-service restaurant with 5 dining rooms; a third-story barroom.
Hot-tub area with sunroom. Gift, antiques, and country-store shops next door.
Surrounding town has many old-world Dutch-front buildings; thousands of planted
tulip beds. Massive *klokkenspel* (several Dutch figures performing to the accompaniment of a carillon) at Franklin Place. Annual Tulip Time festival in May.
Business travel: Located about 43 miles southeast of Des Moines. Corporate rates, meeting rooms.

Hannah Marie Country Inn
SPENCER, IOWA 51301

Mary may be the most cheerful innkeeper I've ever met.

"I want you to feel right at home, so it's okay to open the door and shout, 'I'm here, Mom.'"

Mary's historic farmhouse was built in 1910. "It took talented craftsmen two years to restore the building," she said. A San Francisco expert on Victorian paints was called in to custom-mix turn-of-the-century colors for the inn. "That accounts for our special glow," Mary added.

Everything is special about the Hannah Marie, named for Mary's mother. Consider the guest rooms. Beda, named for her aunt, is the "tomboy" room. It has walnut furniture, soft apricot and forest-green colors, queen bed, and whirlpool bath. "It's delightfully cuddly," Mary said. "You get a great feeling of being wrapped in a cocoon."

Elisabeth, the "genteel woman" room, boasts lots of bird's-eye maple and has an antique white iron tub. "I tell people to relax here," Mary said. "That's why all baths come with yellow rubber duckies. We also have the best bubbles around. So many guests just soak in their tub immersed in their bubble baths. Even lots of the men."

Louella is the inn's smallest room but features a red acrylic claw-footed tub. "When the sun shines through the lace curtains and falls on the tub, it's really beautiful," Mary said.

Elegant breakfasts include fresh fruit and juice, strata, homemade scones and muffins, strudel, and tortes. Afternoon tea luncheons (also served to the public) can be three-course affairs. The special "Tea with the Mad Hatter" takes its theme from *Alice in Wonderland*, with guidelines provided by the Alice Shops of Oxford, England, and the Lewis Carroll Society. "Near the afternoon's end, everyone gets to celebrate their un-birthday," Mary said, "complete with un-birthday candles."

Her top-hat scones are also special, receiving rave reviews from veteran England vacationers. Hors d'oeuvres are served daily between 5:00 and 7:00 P.M.

"I also provide parasols and walking sticks for farm strolls," Mary said. She can't wait for a croquet course to be constructed on her "farm lawns." In the meantime, Mary moved a country Victorian-vintage home 6 miles from the middle of town to her property. The Carl Gustav dining room hosts afternoon tea luncheons, gourmet cooking classes, evening dinner, and more. And upstairs are two luxury rooms with double whirlpool baths.

How to get there: From Minnesota, take U.S. 71 south to Spencer (in northwest Iowa), then continue south 4 miles; the inn is on the east side of the road.

Innkeeper: Mary Nichols

Address/Telephone: U.S. 71 (mailing address: R. R. 1); (712) 262–1286

Rooms: 5; all with private bath, whirlpools, and air conditioning. No smoking inn.

Rates: $70 to $105, single or double; $15 extra person; EPB and afternoon hors d'oeuvres. Special packages.

Open: April through December.

Facilities and activities: Lunch, afternoon high tea, and evening hors d'oeuvres available. Located on 200-acre corn-and-soybean farm; hammock, rocking chairs, and country swing on porch; rope swing on old farm tree; croquet. Nearby: a short drive to restaurants. Boating, fishing, and swimming in Iowa's great lakes 20 miles away. Lots of antiques shops, arts and crafts nearby.

Recommended Country Inns® Travelers' Club Benefit: 10 percent discount, Monday–Thursday, April–May and October–mid-December, subject to availability.

Old World Inn
SPILLVILLE, IOWA 52168

All the food is homemade, from scratch. It's Czech-style, with Pilsner Urquell Czech beer to go along with the meal. Need I say more?

This 1871 general store, a two-story limestone building just a stone's throw from the Turkey River, was restored by Ed in 1987 and transformed into this specialty restaurant and lodging. If you're wondering about the Czech influence, let me add a little more history.

The quiet village is where famed composer Antonin Dvořák stayed during the summer of 1893. Its landscape so reminded him of the Czechoslovakian countryside that he was inspired to write the *New World Symphony* here.

Now Linda features hearty Czech food in her restaurant, in a dining room that offers huge merchant's windows, red-checked tablecloths, and country and Old World crafts, all of which provide a homey decor.

During my last visit I just missed a Czech film crew that stayed at the inn while filming a documentary about Dvořák's time here.

Ask Linda about the tunnels in the basement, and how bootleggers used them to transport illegal hooch to "blind pigs" during Prohibition days.

I checked the menu, filled with dishes like Czech ham, sauerkraut and dumplings, roast duck, braised Viennese pork roast, beef cabbage soup, and desserts featuring prune and apricot *kolaches*, poppyseed cake, and *bublania* (sponge-cake base with baked-in fruit, served in warm whipped cream). It was tough to make a decision.

Country-charming guest rooms include Victorian dressing tables, quilt wall hangings, wall borders, high-back chairs, and old merchant globe ceiling lamps.

And a full Czech breakfast might include eggs and dumplings, *Jitrnice* (pork and barley sausage with garlic), rye toast, fruit, and more.

How to get there: From Dubuque, take U.S. 52 north to Iowa 325. Turn west and follow into Spillville. This road leads right to a T and the inn.

Innkeepers: Linda and Ed Klimesh
Address/Telephone: 331 South Main Street; (319) 562–3739
Rooms: 4, including 1 suite; all with private bath.
Rates: $50, single; $60, double; $75, suite; EPB.
Open: All year.
Facilities and activities: Renowned Czech restaurant downstairs, featuring home cooking and daily specials. Nearby: walk to the Bily Clocks museum and the Antonin Dvořák exhibit.

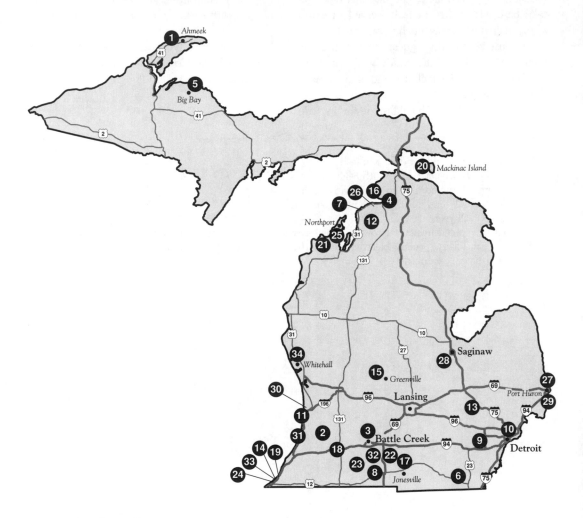

Michigan

Michigan

Numbers on map refer to towns numbered below.

Sand Hills Lighthouse Inn

AHMEEK, MICHIGAN 49901

Nestled on Five Mile Point, the Sand Hills Lighthouse was the last named lighthouse, specially built in 1917, to house *three* lightkeepers and their families. So it's huge and has been restored to Victorian splendor by Bill and Eve.

In fact, they bought the lighthouse thirty-five years ago with the intention of someday transforming this bit of maritime history into a retreat for travelers. "It was in a shambles from years of neglect," Bill said. "So we started from the ground up." What you now see is the result of five years' restoration work—much of it done by Bill and Eve themselves.

Look at their handicraft—ornate crown moldings, hand-tooled walls, a spectacular stair-

case balustrade that's original to the house, rich hardwoods (I love the English paneling in the Gathering Room)—it's a Victorian paradise with many updated luxuries, too.

Sand Hills boasts eight guest rooms, all offering private baths, several with a whirlpool. My favorites might be the balcony rooms, whose private aeries open onto Lake Superior for vistas of spectacular sunrises and sunsets.

Bill encourages guests to climb up the lighthouse tower for more panoramic views of the shoreline and surrounding wilderness. (He calls it a 100-step lighthouse—there are 100 steps from entering the front door to reaching the tower room, which housed the lens that signaled ships and led them away from a dangerous, rocky shore.)

There's also a half-mile of lakeshore to explore and thirty-five acres of woods and trails, which explode with spring wildflowers. Let's face it—this is a serious and special get-away-from-it-all place.

A final note: I mentioned that sunrises and sunsets over Lake Superior are incredible. But did I tell you about nature's other sky show—the northern lights dancing under nighttime's canopy of stars?

How to get there: Located about 25 miles northeast of Houghton. Follow U.S. 41 along the Keweenaw Peninsula's shoreline to the tiny village of Ahmeek; turn left at the first street. Immediately upon turning, you'll see signs directing you to Five Mile Point Road, where you'll continue 8 miles to the lighthouse.

Innkeepers: Bill and Eve Frabotta
Address/Telephone: Five Mile Point Road (mailing address: P.O. Box 414); (906) 337–1744
Rooms: 8; all with private bath
Rates: $115 to $175, single or double, EPB.
Open: All year.
Facilities and activities: Spectacular sunrises from breakfast dining room, half-mile of private shoreline. Nearby: short drive to Brockway Mountain Drive, perhaps the most incredible views of autumn foliage in the Midwest; antiquing in small towns along the shore.

DeLano Inn

ALLEGAN, MICHIGAN 49010

Bob and Jean are former Chicagoans, so we got along famously. Their handsome inn, built between 1863 and 1865 by a Civil War veteran, is an ornate Italian Provincial mansion that is the crown jewel of this quiet historic neighborhood.

I asked Bob how Chicagoans got their hands on one of the most renowned buildings in Allegan. "We have family in town, and we always drove by the house when we came up here on visits," Bob explained. "Then one time we saw a FOR SALE sign. We bought the house in one day."

It took seven months to restore the home, however, even though it was in remarkably good condition for its age. "That's because only four families had owned it previously," Bob said. "In fact, it was in one family's hands for more than one hundred years."

I really like bright homes, and three huge 9-foot-tall windows in the common room illuminate the inn from dawn to dusk. The house also boasts fine Italian-marble fireplaces, ornate ceiling crowns and moldings, original leaded-glass windows, and more.

Guest rooms do not lack their own attractions. My favorite is the Ashley Room, offering a huge four-poster bed with Dutch eyelet-lace canopy. There is a three-step stool to reach the bed's topside; that's because at least four mattresses are required to fill the Victorian bedframe and reach the base of its tall headboard.

The Doyle Room contains a large brass bed that one can get lost in—because it's a European feather bed. Other rooms offer period furnishings, such as stenciled beds and handsome Victorian marble-topped dressers, and boast original plank floors.

All guest quarters afford scenic views.

The silver service used to serve breakfast is original to the house. Antiques lovers should also like the dining room's 8-by-9-foot oak side-board, which displays the innkeepers' beautiful china and crystal collection.

The large front porch with antique wicker furniture and rockers is delightful for relaxing. DeLano Inn evenings also include complimentary cheesecake (it's made in Chicago and is delicious) and coffee, as well as time to talk with new friends.

How to get there: Allegan is located just off I–94 from the Paw Paw exit 60. Then take Michigan 40 north into town.

Innkeepers: Robert and Jean Ashley
Address/Telephone: 302 Cutler Street; (616) 673–2609
Rooms: 5 share separate men's and women's baths down the hall; all with air conditioning.
Rates: $60 to $85, single or double, EPB. Special winter rates available.
Open: All year.
Facilities and activities: Walk to antiques shops, museums, riverfront. Nearby: historic-home tours, water sports, winter sports, dinner cruises, train rides, snowmobiling, cross-country and downhill skiing, Todd Farm. Specialty shops of Saugatuck beach community about 20 miles northwest.

The Old Lamp-Lighter's Homestay
BATTLE CREEK, MICHIGAN 49017

A local architect once called this 1912 mansion "flagrantly medieval." It has also been cited by a national architectural association as "one of the purest Arts and Crafts–style houses" existing today.

Whatever they call it, I say The Old Lamp-Lighter's Homestay is quite special.

Let me list a few of the home's outstanding features: The dining room is a showplace. You enter by walking through intricate stained-glass French doors that depict a Victorian forest, and you are confronted by four hand-painted, original canvas wall murals portraying another forested landscape—an almost mythological scene that quickly grabs your attention. That's not all.

Over a long dining-room table where guests eat breakfast hangs a massive Steuben chandelier so breathtaking that it looks as if it belongs in the Metropolitan Museum of Art. In the living room a large stone fireplace is flanked by two of the thirteen stained-glass windows that grace the home. Add a French Aubusson rug and fine Victorian furnishings to the tally. Honduran mahogany and oak woodwork are everywhere.

Originally the home of Seirn Cole, a prominent Battle Creek builder, this is now home to Tracy and Cheryl and their lucky guests.

Guest rooms boast their own antique finery. Consider the Kellogg Room, with its 1912 Circassian walnut bedroom set; the Rich Room, with its heirloom hand-hooked rug; and the McCamly Room, which is great for families—it sleeps six and offers period tables and chairs for fun and games.

The atmosphere remains very Gothic here. The inn is private and quiet, and even on sunny days it can be quite dark, due to its stylings. But the opportunity to enjoy these one-of-a-kind surroundings makes it a sunny day for travelers.

How to get there: From east or west, take I–94 to Battle Creek, exit north on Michigan 66. Follow Michigan 66, which turns into Division and the Capital Avenue Northeast, to the inn.

Innkeepers: Tracy Greenman and Cheryl Pearce

Address/Telephone: 276 Capital Avenue, Northeast; (616) 963–2603

Rooms: 7; all with private bath, air conditioning, and TV. No smoking inn.

Rates: $60 to $85, single; $75 to $100, double; EPB. Cross-country skiing and golf packages available.

Open: All year.

Facilities and activities: Sitting room, parlor, dining room, library, antiques shop. Nearby: fitness center, parks, McCamly Place (Saturday night concerts), Civic Theater, shops, restaurants, jogging, biking.

The Terrace Inn
BAY VIEW, MICHIGAN 49770

Entering The Terrace Inn is like walking into the past. That's because the 1911 inn, located on a quiet street among tall beech, oak, and maple trees, is part of the historic Bay View community.

The entire town is listed on the National Register of Historic Places. There are more than four hundred Victorian summer homes here, built between 1875 and the turn of the century. If you're a fan of Victorian homes and like lots of gingerbread, you'll go crazy.

I spent lots of time walking along gently curving streets lined with buildings graced with intricate gingerbread finery. It's as if the entire town is a frozen snapshot, stopped still in the 1890s.

The inn, built by W. J. DeVol in 1910, sits high on a terrace off Little Traverse Bay. It's one of the last buildings constructed by a group of Methodists who established the Bay View Association in 1875 as part of its traveling Chautauqua arts series. That dedication to the arts continues here today.

There's a great fireplace in the parlor that warms guests on chilly summer nights. And rocking chairs are everywhere.

Guest rooms have iron-rail beds; cheery, bright quilts; oak dressers; and high ceilings. I especially liked the transom windows; I could relax on my bed while gazing out at the sky.

In the off-season, Denise serves guests a continental breakfast next to that great inn fireplace. Dinners in the turn-of-the-century eating hall, during the summer season only, feature scrumptious feasts. An inn specialty is planked whitefish served with *duchesse* potatoes and freshly baked bread.

How to get there: From the south, take U.S. 31 east through Petoskey. Upon leaving the city limits and entering Bay View, the road jogs to the right and crosses a railroad track. Turn right at the first road after the track (the main entrance to Bay View). Turn right again at the first street (Lakeview) and turn left at the Glendale Street stop sign. The rear entrance to the inn is ¼ mile down Glendale on the left. From the north, take U.S. 31 south. The main entrance to Bay View is the second street past the pedestrian overpass. Then follow the above directions.

Innkeepers: Tom and Denise Erhart

Address/Telephone: 216 Fairview; (616) 347–2410

E-mail/URL: terracei@freeway.net / http://www.freeway.net/terracei

Rooms: 44; all with private bath, 8 with air conditioning.

Rates: $69 to $99, single or double, continental breakfast. Winter ski packages, specialty packages, and winter rates available.

Open: All year.

Facilities and activities: BYOB. Dining and sitting rooms, ice-cream parlor, porch. Within walking distance of weekly chamber music concerts, Sunday evening vespers program, drama and musical theater productions. Nearby: hiking trails on 165 acres of virgin forest; tennis; swimming at private beach; Saturday-evening movies at the Auditorium. Gaslight Shopping District 5 minutes away. Near town of Harbor Springs, with boutiques, golf, horseback riding, sailing, fishing. Mackinac Island about a 45-minute drive north of Bay View.

Recommended Country Inns® Travelers' Club Benefit: 10 percent discount, Monday–Thursday.

$\mathcal{B}$ig $\mathcal{B}$ay $\mathcal{P}$oint $\mathcal{L}$ighthouse
BIG BAY, MICHIGAN 49808

I visited here in the waning months of winter. But winter dies slowly in Michigan's Upper Peninsula. There was still nearly a foot of snow on the ground around the lighthouse. And snow caves on Lake Superior soared more than 14 feet into the air.

The lighthouse sits atop a high cliff jutting out into the deep waters of Lake Superior. It's one of the few surviving lighthouses in the country that offer visitors a chance to relive the days of the keepers by staying overnight in its historic quarters.

Built in 1896 on a half-mile of shoreline and surrounded by 50 pristine acres filled with deer, foxes, wild turkey, and other creatures that feed near the lighthouse's meadow at daybreak, the inn still sends out a warning beam of light to sailors on the lake; however, an automated signal replaced the original light in 1941.

You can see the 1,500-pound, third-order Fresnel lens (second largest ever used on the Great Lakes); and make sure you hike stairs to the top of the lighthouse lantern—its tower rises more than 120 feet above the water's surface.

Guest rooms are very comfortable, decorated in Victorian style. One of my favorites, the Lake View Suite, might be the inn's best spot to watch sunrises over the water. The Tower Room, formerly the head keeper's office, also boasts a nice view of the lake.

And for those of you who love sunsets, the Sunset Suite offers that view over both the lake and Huron Mountains.

Did I mention the resident inn ghost? Noooooo? Well, get Linda to tell you about this apparition, thought to be a former lighthouse keeper—who was found mysteriously hanging from a tree less than a mile from the lighthouse.

Sweet dreams!

How to get there: From Marquette, take Highway 550 north into the town of Bog Bay (about 30 miles north of Marquette); then follow the lighthouse signs for 3½ miles to the point and the inn. Roads remain clear throughout the year.

Innkeepers: John Gale, Jeff and Linda Gamble
Address/Telephone: 3 Lighthouse Road; (906) 345–9957
Rooms: 7; all with private bath. No smoking inn.
Rates: May through October: $115 to $155, single or double; November through April: $85 to $125; EPB. Two-night minimum on weekends, July 1–Oct. 31.
Open: All year.
Facilities and activities: Great Room, sauna in tower, half-mile of shoreline. Nearby: half-day treks to waterfalls and mountaintops by Huron Mountain Outfitters; North Country Outfitters for boats, hunting, fishing equipment and ski rentals; North Shores Treasures features works of local artists; Lumberjack Inn, used in film *Anatomy of a Murder*. Thirty minutes to Marquette, Presque Isle Park, the Ore Docks, Superior Dome stadium, Marquette Golf Club.

Hiram D. Ellis Inn

BLISSFIELD, MICHIGAN 49228

One of the first things I noticed was a sign hanging in the bathroom. It simply said, ENJOY THE SOFT WATER. A typically quaint touch in this comfortable inn.

The fine red-brick home was built in 1883 by its namesake, a Scots-Irish harness-and-hardware store operator. Walk around the northwest side of the home and you'll see the cornerstone confirming that date.

I tinkered with the piano that rests in the downstairs sitting room. But my playing could set dogs howling; my wife, Debbie, just groans.

All rooms are tastefully furnished with period antiques and reproductions. I especially liked the Hervey Bliss Room, named after the village's founder, and the Hiram D. Ellis room boasts a Victorian headboard at least 6 feet high. Soft wild-flower-print wallpaper adds a soothing touch, as do Dutch lace curtains that hang on the room's three tall windows.

The continental breakfast is a simple one: freshly baked breads, muffins, homemade jellies and jams, juices, and other beverages.

Be sure you save room for the daily buffets offered by the Hathaway House, just across the street. This is an eighteen-room 1851 Greek Revival–style mansion that was once called the finest home between Buffalo and Toledo; you can see the architect's 1850 charcoal sketch of the home in the foyer. The Sunday buffet includes roast round of beef, baked ham carved at the board, country-fried chicken and shrimp, potatoes, vegetables, and a choice of six home-made dressings for your salad.

How to get there: From Detroit, take I–75 south to U.S. 223. Then go west into Blissfield. U.S. 223 is called Adrian Street in Blissfield.

Innkeepers: Christine and Frank Seely

Address/Telephone: 415 West Adrian Street; (517) 486–3155

Rooms: 4; all with private bath, air conditioning, TV, and phone.

Rates: $81 to $102.20, single or double, continental breakfast.

Open: All year.

Facilities and activities: Two sitting rooms. Part of the Hathaway House "village" of restaurants and specialty shops. Nearby: Main Street Stable and Tavern, Croswell Opera House, Lenawee Historical Museum, Michigan International Speedway. Seventy minutes southwest of Detroit, 20 minutes northwest of Toledo.

The Bridge Street Inn
CHARLEVOIX, MICHIGAN 49720

The home (once called the Baker Cottage and intended as the personal residence of the namesake family who built the grand Beach Hotel, long since demolished) has a terrific view of Lake Michigan, Lake Charlevoix, and the downtown drawbridge.

Vera has created a whimsical world of antique attractions inside this magnificent building with its spiky gables, leaded- and stained-glass windows, and long wraparound porch. The decor reflects a gentle English cottage look, with original maple floors covered with oriental area rugs, Waverly print fabrics on loveseats, and blue-checked wing chairs.

Both living and dining rooms are graced with English, German, and Chinese antiques, and a baby grand piano invites guests to play some of the old tunes charted on scores of sheet music.

Nine guest rooms are warm and friendly, with hardwood plank floors dashed with antique floral rugs. Vera adds a special touch with fresh flowers in each of the rooms, which are individually decorated with more antiques.

In the Autumn Leaves Room are a quarter-sized cigar-store Indian and a genuine humpback steamer trunk. The Harbor Rose Room has oak and cherry furnishings and a view of the lake. But I'll take Evening Glow, where I had a spectacular view of Charlevoix's great sunsets.

Breakfast is served in the dining room, with its handsome woodwork and rose-colored Victorian print carpeting; or you might open the French doors and take your meal to a cozy sitting area. Vera's choices include homemade Belgian waffles with fresh fruit, home-baked scones with fresh marmalade, strawberry bread with cream cheese, plum and apple tarts, sour cream coffee cake, and more.

I like the nearby Grey Gables Inn for dinners, especially their Lake Superior whitefish. The innkeepers also recommend Tapawingo and Rowe Inne, gourmet restaurants that are among the most highly rated in Michigan. Or just stroll to the channel; there the Weathervane restaurant features fine food—and you can sit at a window table and watch the boats go by.

How to get there: From Chicago, take I–94 north to I–196 and continue north. At U.S. 131, go north; then at Michigan 66, turn northwest. At U.S. 31, go north into downtown Charlevoix. Here the road is also called Michigan Avenue. Take U.S. 31 1 block north of the drawbridge to Dixon and the inn.

Innkeepers: John and Vera McKown

Address/Telephone: 113 Michigan Avenue; (616) 547–6606

Rooms: 9; 3 with private bath. No smoking inn.

Rates: $59 to $115, single or double, continental breakfast. Two-night minimum on holiday and summer weekends. Off-season rates available.

Open: All year.

Facilities and activities: Charlevoix is a colorful harbor town on Lake Michigan. Nearby: huge marina, fleet, pleasure boating, and charter fishing; restaurants, specialty, and antiques shops. Swimming and picnicking on Lake Michigan and Lake Charlevoix beaches. Ferry boats to Beaver Island; July Venetian Festival; August Art Fair; Fall Color Cruises.

Chicago Pike Inn
COLDWATER, MICHIGAN 49036

One glance at the Chicago Pike Inn, and my pa and I realized we were about to experience something special.

This spectacular house was built in 1903 by Morris Clarke; owners Jane and Harold Schultz, along with daughters Becky and Jody, have carefully restored it to reflect early 1900s grandeur. I admired the magnificent reception room, with its double-manteled cherrywood fireplace adorned by Staffordshire dogs, and with a sweeping cherry staircase that leads to upstairs guest rooms.

"Local legend says that the wood came from Morris Clarke's own cherry orchard," my tour guide, Jane, said.

The rest of the inn reflects Jane's impeccable taste in antiques and fine fabrics. Leaded Bradley and Hubbard lamps, Schumacher and Waverly wall coverings, fluted cherrywood columns, hand-carved antique furniture, stained-glass windows, parquet floors—the list is seemingly endless.

What results from all this attention to the smallest details (guests are supplied with thick terrycloth robes, and Jane's Victorian candy stand in the library is always stocked with fine goodies) is a feeling of luxury and comfort that's difficult to match.

We headed to the library, with its unusual whitewood woodwork. My pa settled in a wing chair next to a roaring fire and immersed himself in his reading. I complimented Jane on a spectacular restoration. "It's such a grand old house," she said. "Restoring it is kind of our legacy to the community."

Guest quarters are exquisite. I stayed in Ned's Room, its bold red-and-paisley wall coverings, huge brass bed, and green leather wing chair giving it the feel of an exclusive gentlemen's club. My pa opted for Charles' Room, reflecting the Victorians' fascination with period Chinese and boasting a handsome sleigh bed framed by a wall canopy.

My daughters would love the Grandchildren's Room, all pink with two twin iron-and-brass beds, white Victorian wicker, and eleven antique portraits of darling little girls.

Then there's Miss Sophia's Suite, two rooms fairly bursting with a hand-carved antique bed,

an oak-manteled fireplace, a velvet-covered period sofa, a Martha Washington chair—and even its own private balcony.

Another addition is the Carriage House, a two-room beauty whose rooms feature amenities like whirlpool baths, balconies, and canopy beds. Add Becky's scrumptious breakfasts and her delightful hospitality, and you have all the ingredients for one of the best Midwest inns.

And how about this for distinction? The Chicago Pike Inn was named "Inn of the Year" by a noteworthy publication. Congrats!

How to get there: The inn is located on U.S. 12 (the old Chicago Pike), midway between Detroit and Chicago, just minutes south of I–94.

Innkeeper: Rebecca A. Schultz
Address/Telephone: 215 East Chicago Street; (517) 279-8744
Rooms: 8, including 2 suites; all with private bath, TV, and phone on request.
Rates: $80 to $165, single or double, EPB.
Open: All year.
Facilities and activities: Parlor, library, dining room, wraparound front porch, gardens, gazebo. Walk to downtown shops. Nearby: antiquing; golf; boating, fishing, and swimming at Morrison, Randall, Marble, and Coldwater lakes; cross-country skiing; orchards; nature trails. Turkeyville Dinner Theatre; museums; wineries; historic architecture.

The Dearborn Inn
DEARBORN, MICHIGAN 48124

My wife, Debbie, and I drove up the sweeping circular driveway that leads to the graceful porticoed entrance of the Dearborn Inn. It reminded me of a grand mansion of a wealthy Colonial landowner.

Listed on the National Trust (recognized for its stately Georgian architecture), the hotel was built in 1931 by Henry Ford. It served as the nation's first "airport hotel" (a small landing field was located across the street) and housed visitors to the Henry Ford Museum and Greenfield Village just down the road.

It has become an elegant showplace, showered with opulent appointments. I easily recognized Ford's love for early America carried out in the hotel's decor. Our suite in the main building exhibited handsome Colonial fashions, with four-poster beds, wing and Windsor chairs, polished wooden chests, and brass lamps. We easily surrendered to this kind of luxury.

Particularly fun is a small Colonial "village on the green," with five historic-home replicas of famous Americans; you'll feel like a houseguest of Edgar Allan Poe, Patrick Henry, Barbara Fritchie, Walt Whitman, or Revolutionary War hero Oliver Wolcott.

My favorite remains the Poe Cottage, a little white clapboard house that often serves as a honeymoon suite. A delightfully devilish touch: the black iron raven hovering above the doorway.

Dining here is a gustatory delight. The Early American Room, romantic with glittering chandeliers, crisp white linen, and fresh flowers on tables, pampers food lovers. We dined on rock Cornish game hen Madeira and country pork-loin applejack while a tuxedo-clad, three-piece combo provided music for evening dancing.

After a delightful meal we headed to the Snug, a lounge where liquor bottles are still kept out of sight, underneath the copper-topped bar, in deference to Ford's lifelong opposition to alcohol.

How to get there: From Detroit Metro Airport, go north on Merriman Road to I–94 East. Follow I–94 about 5 miles to Southfield Freeway; then go north 3 miles to Oakwood Boulevard. Finally, go west 2 miles to the inn.

Innkeeper: Yves Robin, general manager

Address/Telephone: 20301 Oakwood Boulevard; (313) 271–2700 or (800) 228–9290

Rooms: 222, including 20 suites, plus 5 reproduced historic homes; all with private bath, air conditioning, TV, radio, and phone.

Rates: $92 to $109, weekends; $139 to $175 weekdays, single or double; EP. Special weekend and B&B packages available.

Open: All year.

Facilities and activities: Two full-service restaurants, lounge, sitting room, concierge, room service, gift shop, newsstand; baby-sitting service on request. Also gardens, patio, outdoor swimming pool, tennis courts, fitness center. Nearby: Henry Ford Museum, Greenfield Village, professional sports, Fairlane Town Shopping Center, Dearborn Historical Museum, Henry Ford Estate, Northville Downs, golf, and Windsor, Ontario.

Business travel: Located about 30 minutes from downtown Detroit. Corporate rates, meeting rooms, fax.

The Blanche House
DETROIT, MICHIGAN 48214

"Wow!" my pa said. "This place looks like a mini-White House."

We laughed upon discovering that, historically speaking, this 1905 Colonial Revival home is known as the "Little White House." It also keeps good company, nestled in the historic Berry subdivision of Detroit, just a block from the Detroit River and close to the Mayor's Residence.

Just pull up to the curb and you'll realize how this house got its nickname: 20-foot-tall Corinthian porch pillars support a portico entrance that will have you straining to see Bill and Hillary walking around inside. Ten-foot entrance doors adorned with etched glass herald

the elegance about to greet visitors within.

Inside, classically handcrafted plasterwork includes ornate moldings, medallions, and rosettes; restored oak woodwork sparkles throughout the house; and there's even a smattering of Pewabic tiling, which is native to Michigan.

Mary Jean gave us a tour of her 10,000-square-foot house, noting that the inn was Detroit's first bed and breakfast establishment.

"In the 1920s the Blanche House [and the Castle, an adjoining house] also served as a private school for boys," she said. "In fact, Henry Ford II attended school here."

Guest rooms are lovely snapshots of period

charm, filled as they are with antique furnishings, like four-poster beds, embroidered coverlets, and handmade quilts. Among my favorites are those bedchambers near the back of the manse, which provide vistas of the Detroit River and the Stanton Canal.

You might even see geese lounging on the water and get a peek at Canada's horizon.

Other favorites are the inn's three suites, spacious bedchambers offering a welcoming whirlpool bath for coosome twosomes. The finest might be the Lee Stanton Canal Suite, with its art deco antique fireplace, queen-size sleigh bed, whirlpool, and private balcony complete with porch swing—all overlooking its namesake canal.

Mary Jean's breakfasts offer more delights. Goodies might include fresh fruit, cheese strudels, home-baked breads and muffins, even eggs Benedict on weekends.

And here's a note especially for women travelers: The Blanche House offers a unique service for its female guests, one that you just don't regularly find at bed and breakfasts: spa service. A special overnight rate includes everything from a massage and facial to a manicure and pedicure.

How to get there: From the south, take I–75 north into Detroit, then exit at I–375 and go south. Proceed about 1 mile to East Jefferson Avenue, then turn east (left) and continue to Parkview. There you'll see a sign directing you to the inn.

Innkeepers: Mary Jean Shannon and Sean Shannon
Address/Telephone: 506 Parkview; (313) 822–7090
Rooms: 13, including 3 suites; all with private bath. No smoking inn.
Rates: $60 to $115, single, $65 to $115, double; $125, suites (weekend rate only); EPB.
Open: All year.
Facilities and activities: Sitting room, dining room. Nearby: minutes to downtown Detroit and its attractions: Renaissance Center, Greektown, Detroit Institute of Arts, Tiger Stadium, Detroit Historical Museum, Museum of African American History, Children's Museum, Detroit Science Center. A short drive to Henry Ford Museum, Greenfield Village, Cranbrook Institute of Science, auto barons' homes, Belle Isle.
Recommended Country Inns® Travelers' Club Benefit: 10 percent discount, Sunday–Thursday, subject to availability. Romantic Getaway Package: hot tub room with champagne; dinner for two at the Harlequin Café and full breakfast in the morning, $145 plus tax.

The Kirby House
DOUGLAS, MICHIGAN 49453

The grand Kirby House is an irresistible Victorian pleasure. It just jumped out at me with its turrets, gables, leaded- and stained-glass windows, and a quaint peach-colored picket fence surrounding the grounds.

Marsha and Loren have preserved elegant Victorian interiors that really impressed me. Especially fetching are leaded-prism windows that fling shards of sunlight on original hardwood floors. I was particularly taken with the parlor fireplace (one of four in the house). Marsha told me that it was of an unusual cast-iron design.

The home was built in 1890 by Sarah Kirby, who made her considerable fortune from farming ginseng. She wanted to be rid of troublesome pitchers and wash basins, so she replaced them with corner sinks in the bedrooms; some remain to this day.

In 1932 the home became a community hospital and operated in that capacity for thirty years. In fact, the old hospital operating room is now named for Jackie Onassis. Ask Marsha to explain that one.

I almost lost my head over the Anne Boleyn Room. Marsha surmised that it was the maid's room in older times, because a dumbwaiter was located in the corner. Now it's bright and airy, with a fabulous oak sleigh bed and pleasant period pieces.

Breakfast means croissants, cheese Danish, old-fashioned sticky buns, fresh fruit, sausage, bacon, eggs, quiches, and juices, all served buffet-style. By early morning many of the guests were already enjoying the inn's backyard deck, where lounge chairs, hot tub, and swimming pool await.

A town sensation is the nearby Checquers, an English-flavored restaurant boasting shepherd's pie, Chicken Cornu with curried yogurt sauce, and bubble and squeak (sirloin chucks wrapped in cabbage with hot brown sauce).

Also browse in the shops of downtown Saugatuck and visit the innkeepers' newest venture—Village Green Mercantile; besides great merchandise, two one-bedroom apartments above the store feature whirlpool baths, fireplaces, queen-sized beds, televisions, VCRs . . . wow!

How to get there: From Chicago, take I–94 north to I–196 north and go to exit 36. Go north on Blue Star Highway into Douglas. Turn left at the only traffic light and you're there.

Innkeepers: Marsha and Loren Konto
Address/Telephone: Center Street and Blue Star Highway (mailing address: P.O. Box 1174, Saugatuck, Michigan 49453); (616) 857–2904
Rooms: 8; 6 with private bath, 3 with air conditioning.
Rates: Weekdays: $75 shared bath, $100 private bath; weekends: $100 shared bath, $115 private bath; EPB. Special weekday package.
Open: All year.
Facilities and activities: BYOB. Common room, swimming pool, hot tub. Walk to Lake Michigan beach. Nearby: restaurants; art colony in Saugatuck; Allegan Forest; Grand Rapids antiques markets; Holland's ethnic Dutch villages, museums, specialty shops. Cross-country skiing close by.

The Rosemont Inn
DOUGLAS, MICHIGAN 49406

The last time I spoke to Joe and Marilyn, they'd just completed their newest addition to the inn—a Victorian gazebo on the front lawn facing Lake Michigan. "We've already had our first gazebo wedding, too," noted Marilyn.

It's certainly the perfect spot for any kind of celebration or weekend getaway. Winds rustle tall trees, which shade the inn's landscaped grounds from a bright sun. Waves crash on the lakeshore, just across the tiny road and down a steep bluff. And an expansive wraparound porch invites peace and relaxation.

In fact, the Rosemont Inn stands like an inviting friend, a turn-of-the-century Queen Anne Victorian that got its start as an 1886 tourist hotel. Enter through French doors opening onto a formal sitting room; the handsome antique hardwood fireplace signals the elegance you will find throughout the inn.

Joe and Marilyn continue to improve this already wonderful place. Relax on the enclosed front porch, overlooking the lake. I love the Garden Room, perhaps my favorite inn spot out back; it's bright and sunny, with cathedral ceilings and a ceiling-to-floor glass wall that looks out over the gardens and swimming pool. There are also a sauna and whirlpool in the back, overlooking the pool.

Check out the fireplace here, great for warming up guests on cool spring and autumn nights, to say nothing of Michigan winters. Of course, the inn is perfect headquarters for cross-country ski adventurers.

And the deck, with its colorful umbrella tables, is another addition that's become a favorite guest hangout.

The Garden Room serves as the location of the innkeepers' buffet-style continental breakfasts. Count on juices, croissants, muffins, delicious quiches, bagels, cereals, and more. Marilyn and Joseph can also suggest some fine dinner spots in nearby Saugatuck.

Country Victorian antiques and reproductions fill the delightful guest rooms, each unique in design; nine have gas fireplaces, which add a cozy touch. I especially liked our room, with its brass bed adorned with a charming crazy quilt, a pinch of colorful pizzazz. Some rooms have a view of the lake through the tall maples that ring the grounds.

Two of three common areas also feature wet bars.

One summer Debbie, Kate, and I, along with some relatives, spent a glorious long weekend at the inn. Especially inviting was the swimming pool, where the kids splashed and played endlessly. It made for good memories. Especially when we were blessed with Dayne about nine months after our stay here!

How to get there: From Chicago, take I–94 north to I–196 north. At exit 36, near Douglas, take Ferry Street north to Center Street. Turn west on Center Street and go to Lakeshore Drive; then turn north to the inn.

Innkeepers: Joseph and Marilyn Sajdak
Address/Telephone: 83 Lakeshore Drive (mailing address: P. O. Box 214, Saugatuck, 49453); (616) 857–2637 or (800) 721–2637
Rooms: 14; all with private bath and air conditioning, 10 with gas fireplace. Wheelchair access. No smoking inn.
Rates: May through mid-June and mid-September through October, $70 to $115, single; $80 to $145, double; mid-June through mid-September, $125 to $175, single or double; November through April, $60 to $95, single; $70 to $125, double. Continental breakfast. Off-season rates available.
Open: All year.
Facilities and activities: Garden room, swimming pool, screened porch, Victorian gazebo. Across the road from Lake Michigan. Nearby: charter fishing, boating, scenic supper cruises; golf, hiking the Lake Michigan dunes, dune rides; summer theater; cross-country skiing in winter. Fine restaurants, art galleries, antiques shops, boutiques.

The House on the Hill
ELLSWORTH, MICHIGAN 49729

Buster and Julie are from Texas. Didn't take a genius to figure that one out, what with their delightful Texas twang and the Lone Star State flag flying high from a pole in the backyard.

Buster grabbed my hand and gave me a welcoming whomp on the back. "We specialize in old-time Southern hospitality," he told me. I soon discovered there couldn't be two more gracious hosts around.

Their century-old renovated farmhouse is perched atop a high hill, overlooking St. Clair Lake like an imposing sentinel. "It's part of a chain of lakes," Buster said. "You can hop from one to another all day."

The Arnims decided to become innkeepers after touring a number of inns during a swing through New England. A relative in Indiana told them about this home. After doing research on the area (while still in Texas), the Houston natives put a down payment on the house without ever setting foot in Michigan!

The guest rooms are a mixture of elegance and charm, with antique furnishings and country crafts set about in lively combinations.

The Rose Room, bright and cheery, boasts a view of the lake. The Pine Room features a cathedral ceiling and a four-poster bed covered in white lace. But my favorite may be the Birch Suite, with its panoramic vista of the water down the hill.

Meals at the inn are bountiful. "We serve a

good Texas breakfast," Buster said. "I don't let anyone go away hungry." Get ready for fresh fruit, ham, sausage, eggs, homemade breads, and Julie's delicious strudels.

"One of the reasons we decided on this location is that we're right between two gourmet restaurants that may be the finest the state has to offer," Buster said. The Rowe Inn and Tapawingo are landmarks that draw crowds from miles away. Gourmet delights include rhubarb-strawberry soup, spinach-and-Montrachet tart, breast of pheasant *chasseur*, and white-chocolate mousse with raspberry sauce.

After dinner, come back to the inn and relax on the veranda. The long gingerbread-laced wraparound porch, from which you can view the lake far down the hill, has comfy wicker rockers. Maybe Pooker, the inn's new Lhasa apso pooch, will join you.

And did I mention the inn's newest addition—the "Red Barn," three additional rooms with decks offering vistas of meadows, hills, and woods, and maybe even a deer or two.

How to get there: From Grand Rapids, take U.S. 131 north to Michigan 66. Turn west, and near East Jordan, go west on County 48 to the inn. Or take I–75 north to Michigan 32, go west to County 48, and then turn west again to the inn.

Innkeepers: Buster and Julie Arnim
Address/Telephone: Box 206, Lake Street; (616) 588–6304
Rooms: 7, including 1 suite; all with private bath and air conditioning. No smoking inn.
Rates: $115 to $125, single or double, EPB.
Open: All year.
Facilities and activities: Turreted veranda overlooking St. Clair Lake. Inn access to lake and dock. Nearby: golf, boating, fishing, swimming, two gourmet restaurants (Tapawingo and The Rowe Inn). Lake Michigan is 5 miles away.

Pine Ridge Inn
FENTON, MICHIGAN 48430

If ever there was a setting for privacy and romance, this is it.

Secluded in a very private forty acres amid swaying pine trees and rolling hills, the Pine Ridge Inn is an exclusive hideaway. No phones. No pets. Just you and your honey for a luxurious and romantic interlude.

Guest rooms are elegant and huge, with lovey-dovey relaxation kept in mind. Those king-sized beds are actually firm waterbeds. Whirlpools are massive, measuring 7 by 7 feet. And a romantic fire in the hearth is only a fingertip away, thanks to gas-log fireplaces that light up the room with a very romantic glow.

They say you "never have to leave your room" at the Pine Ridge. Sure enough. A gourment snack tray is delivered to your bedchamber each evening. And a delicious continental breakfast tray will be found at your door come morning.

For those who do venture outside, walk along a cozy forest path marked with red hearts. Or gaze longingly at the inn's pond. Winter visitors might cross-country ski on a blanket of newly fallen snow.

But when your guest room has all of the above, plus stereo and remote-control television, why bother ever leaving until it's time to leave?

How to get there: From east or west, take I–96 to U.S. 23. Turn north and continue to White Lake Road exit; turn left, then turn left immediately onto Old U.S. 23, and continue to inn.

Innkeeper: Jim and Val Soldan

Address/Telephone: N-10345 Old U.S. 23; (810) 629–8911 or (800) 353–8911

Rooms: 4; all with private bath, whirlpool tub, and fireplace.

Rates: $145, single or double, Monday through Thursday; $195, single or double, Friday through Sunday and holidays; continental breakfast.

Open: All year.

Facilities and activities: Walking paths through forest and by pond. Less than an hour's drive to Pontiac Silverdome, Henry Ford Museum and Greenfield Village, and metro Detroit.

Tall Oaks Inn
GRAND BEACH, MICHIGAN 49117

My wife pointed out that the welcoming goose statues flanking the inn door were sporting red-vinyl rainhats. It was a temporary but whimsical touch at an inn that is quiet and comfortable—but above all elegant.

The inn was built in 1914 as a summer retreat for employees of a Midwest box-making company. Later it became part of a complex that included the largest frame hotel ever seen in these parts; yes, bigger than the Grand Hotel on Mackinac Island. That hotel, with its own 70-meter ski jump, cross-country trails, huge pier, and twenty-seven-hole golf course (which still is part of Grand Beach), burned down during the winter of 1939.

Enough history. Tall Oaks is the story today, and it is fabulous. Guest rooms are named for North American wildflowers and are so attractive that you'll have a hard time deciding on a favorite.

Suites are huge. Typical is the Prairie Clover, which I like very much. Its spindle bed, tall Victorian dresser, 8-foot armoire, and wood-burning fireplace would seem to be enough to entice any traveler. But there are also a sitting room, a two-person whirlpool bath, and a private deck looking out over the handsome grounds, which were blooming in trillium and dogwood during my visit.

I'll bet you never saw a single room as gracious as the Wild Rose. It boasts a full-sized German antique bed that's split in the middle so that it might be divided if the occupants are not married, a traditional Old World touch. It also has its own whirlpool bath, solid-pine plank floors, and a private deck.

Guest common rooms are uncommonly elegant. The living room is dominated by a 10-foot-wide fieldstone fireplace that crackles with a fire on most summer nights (it can get nippy by the lake) and throughout the day during winters. I counted thirty-nine windows in the Garden Room; they make up three entire walls. It's a great place to relax, play games, read a book by the potbellied stove, or watch the inn's only television—a big-screen giant.

Julia's full breakfast might include delicious egg casseroles, French toast or waffles, homemade muffins, fresh juices, coffee, and more.

How to get there: From Chicago, take I–94 to U.S. 12 (second New Buffalo exit). Go south to the Grand Beach sign, cross the railroad tracks, turn left through arches, and continue to the Y in the road. Bear left (on Station Road) and continue to Crescent Road and the inn.

Innkeeper: Julia Mead

Address/Telephone: Station and Crescent Roads; (616) 469–0097

Rooms: 10, including 9 suites; all with private bath and air conditioning. Wheelchair access.

Rates: $65 to $165, single or double, EPB. Reduced rates on off-season weekdays. Two-night minimum on weekends June through October.

Open: All year.

Facilities and activities: Living room, garden room. BYOB. Five acres of heavily wooded grounds. Private beach, cross-country ski trails. Inn has 12 pairs of cross-country skis for guest use; also 8 bicycles. A short drive to restaurants, New Buffalo's antiques and specialty shops; Lake Michigan dunes, Warren Dunes State Park, orchards, wineries.

Winter Inn
GREENVILLE, MICHIGAN 48838

The Winter Inn is an unusual find, tucked on a busy commercial street of this small town. It seems that lumbermen who worked the Big Woods would come to the "city" for some rest and relaxation. They'd take stagecoaches from the city train station to the hotel on "Main Street."

The 1902 inn was one of Greenville's two first-class hotels. I could see lots of evidence for that claim. For example, the lounge contains one of my favorite inn antiques: an immense Brunswick oak-and-mahogany bar made in the 1880s, complete with a long brass footrail. With the lounge's pressed-tin ceiling, oak floor, and a collection of antique prints, oil lamps, and mem-

orabilia, it made me feel as though I had just stepped into an authentic Victorian pub.

The dining room boasts more handsome surroundings. Tables are cast with the warm glow of light filtered through stained-glass windows, and there's lots of greenery. A light breakfast of fresh fruit, danish, and coffee comes with your stay. And dinner fare is all-American small-town good, featuring seafood, home-baked chicken, and tasty steaks.

The lobby is filled with more antiques. Handsome nineteenth-century Victorian couches and chairs, cut and stained glass, magnificent tapestries, and ceiling-high hallway mirrors celebrate the inn's heritage. There's a pub, with dancing, in the basement. It's also fun to browse among the inn's historic photos (located on the second floor), which depict a long-ago era.

Guest rooms are furnished in contemporary style and remain comfortable and cozy. All have extra-long beds, especially attractive to someone like me who stands 6'2".

How to get there: From Chicago, take I–94 north to I–196 and continue north to U.S. 131. Go north to Michigan 57 and turn east, continuing to Greenville. The road turns into Lafayette Street in the city.

Innkeepers: Wade and Becky Thornton
Address/Telephone: 100 North Lafayette Street; (616) 754–3132 or 754–7108
Rooms: 14; all with private bath, air conditioning, phone, and TV.
Rates: $45.58, single; $50.88, double; continental breakfast.
Open: All year.
Facilities and activities: Full-service restaurant and bar. A short drive to several ski areas, Grand Rapids historical district, and Gerald R. Ford Presidential Museum.

Kimberly Country Estate

HARBOR SPRINGS, MICHIGAN 49740

Ronn and Billie's inn could be a showcase for *House Beautiful.*

That's not surprising, I guess; Ronn, an interior designer, has transformed this Southern plantation–style home into an elegant retreat that offers some of the most extraordinarily luxurious inn surroundings possible.

My brother, Mark, and I got the red-carpet treatment (literally) as we mounted steps to the house, set atop a gentle hill and surrounded by fields and farms.

Inside, Chippendale and Queen Anne furniture, Battenburg linens, Laura Ashley fabrics, and exquisite antiques collected by the innkeepers over forty years add to the elegance.

The Lexington Suite is the epitome of romanticism, with its four-poster bed and Battenburg linens lending touches of sophistication; this room also has its own sitting area, wood-burning fireplace, and Jacuzzi.

Le Soleil is another of my favorites, with its walls of windows, sunny yellow color, and hand stenciling. And four of the rooms open onto a shaded veranda overlooking the inn's 22-by-40-foot swimming pool.

The library is a most stunning common room. It's entirely paneled with North Carolina black walnut—milled on the spot as the house was built, Billie told me.

Pampering is legion here. Guests find a

decanter of sherry in their rooms upon arrival, with an invitation to join Ronn and Billie for afternoon tea and hors d'oeuvres—sometimes at poolside in good weather. At night they return to their rooms to discover beds turned down and chocolate truffles on the pillows.

Weekend breakfasts are another Southern-tinged plantation treat. Billie might serve fresh fruit compote, scrambled eggs, smoked turkey sausage, home-baked muffins, and more.

If you want to experience the "estate of the art" in country inn living, make your reservations now.

How to get there: From Petoskey, take U.S. 31 north to Michigan 119, continue north toward Harbor Springs; turn right at Emmet Heights Road, then left on Bester Road, and continue to the inn.

Innkeepers: Ronn and Billie Serba
Address/Telephone: 2287 Bester Road; (616) 526–7646 or 526–9502
Rooms: 6, including 3 suites; all with private bath. Wheelchair access.
Rates: $135 to $250, single or double, EPB and afternoon tea. Two-night minimum on weekends. Special packages. No smoking inn.
Open: All year.
Facilities and activities: Living room, library, lower-level entertainment room, terrace, swimming pool. Nearby: golf, biking, hiking; sailing and other water activities on Little Traverse Bay. A short drive to chic shops in Harbor Springs, downhill skiing at Boyne Highlands and Nubs Nob.

The Munro House
JONESVILLE, MICHIGAN 49250

This handsome pre–Civil War home, started in 1832, was the first brick house built in Hillsdale County. In fact, it took seven years to complete, and the bricks were hauled here by ox and cart from 10 miles away.

The Munro House also was part of the Underground Railroad. The innkeepers showed me the hidden room that housed runaway slaves, located above the ceiling of what is now one of the guest baths. Slaves were moved at night, along a route through Detroit to Windsor, Ontario, in Canada—to freedom.

This is a gracious house, with ten Italian marble fireplaces, 12-foot ceilings, and guest rooms furnished with fine period antiques. The Munro Room, named after the Civil War general whose family occupied the home for more than one hundred years, has original poplar plank floors, a handsome American Empire–style sleigh bed, fireplace, crystal chandelier, and its own porch. There are also vintage period linens on the bed, double stack pillows, and a cozy down comforter.

If you stay in the Sauk Trail Room, you'll be living history. That's because Wild Bill Hickok, who was from Ohio, slept in these antique four-poster cannonball beds.

I also like the Shaker Room, resplendent in its simplicity. More plank floors, with a trundle bed, ladderback chairs, and utilitarian wooden peg rack in true Shaker style. There's also a Shaker "hired man's bed" made especially for this room.

During summer you can take coffee on the porch, or you can walk among Joyce's fragrant perennial and herb gardens. In winter you might head to the cozy warmth of the library's fireplace.

Breakfast is a treat. Joyce's orange-vanilla French toast is her specialty, and she also may be serving morning meats, fresh fruit, juices, freshly baked sweets, and beverages. She'll be happy to recommend a nearby restaurant to suit your dinner tastes, whatever they may be.

Remember that Joyce is only the sixth owner of the home since 1832! Get her to show you the original shutters that fold up, hidden in the window frames. They are of the type invented by Thomas Jefferson.

Or maybe you'd rather see the two new Jacuzzi rooms. Now Thomas Jefferson did *not* invent those whirlpool jets, that's for sure.

How to get there: From Detroit, take I–94 west to U.S. 127. Go south to U.S. 12, then turn west and continue into Jonesville. The inn is at the corner of that highway and Maumee Street.

Innkeeper: Joyce Yarde

Address/Telephone: 202 Maumee Street; (517) 849–9292

Rooms: 7; all with private bath, 3 with fireplace.

Rates: $70 to $150, single or double, EPB. Lower rates on weekdays.

Open: All year.

Facilities and activities: Evening coffee with homemade dessert. Gift shop, sitting parlor, gardens. Nearby: walk to Grosvenor House Museum. Mill Race golf course, restaurants, 2 arboretums, biking, canoeing, and cross-country skiing. More than 50 antiques shops located minutes away in Allen, antiques capital of the state. Professional summer theater in Coldwater.

Recommended Country Inns® Travelers' Club Benefit: Stay two nights, get third night free, subject to availability.

Hall House
KALAMAZOO, MICHIGAN 49007

As I walked through the dining room on one visit here, the innkeeper pulled me to a window. "There's one of our guests you haven't met yet," he said, pointing to a woman walking out front, wearing a down-to-the-ankles English day dress. "That's Lady Wedgwood. She and her secretary are staying here while she's taking part in the Western Michigan Medieval Festival."

While I didn't expect to meet lords and ladies at the Hall House, I wasn't really surprised. This Georgian Revival red-brick home, built in 1923, is fit for a king. The foyer is graced with Pewabic tile, and common rooms boast handsome ceiling moldings and mahogany woodwork. It is beautiful.

Bob and Liz caught the innkeeping bug while in Europe. "We frequented so many bed and breakfasts over there that we felt as if we were already running an inn," Liz joked. "Now we want our guests to enjoy the experience as much as we did."

The guest rooms are named for previous owners of the house. The Vander Horst Room, a bow to the home's builder, has a tile fireplace, four-poster canopy bed, custom cedar closets, and a large bath (including a Swiss shower) done in tile made at Detroit's own Pewabic pottery site. Every piece of tile is still handmade and glazed. (By the way, *Pewabic* is an Indian word meaning "clay with a copper color." Pewabic's founders used copper ore in many of their glazes, giving them a characteristic verdigris color. The Hall House is the only identified residential building in southwestern Michigan with original Pewabic tile installations.)

Lady Wedgwood stayed in the Borgman Room, with its queen-sized brass bed. One guest remembers sitting with her at breakfast one morning while she instructed her in the fine art of mating parakeets! And the Rutherford Room has an elegant shower that features seven shower heads.

The two newest rooms are the Finn Library and Costello Penthouse; the Penthouse is an apartment-sized suite complete with a "workout loft" outfitted with an exercise bike "so you can work off your breakfast."

With advance notice, you can enjoy breakfast in your room. Or head down to the sun room for fresh croissants, egg dishes, muffins, fruit breads, juice, and home-baked scones. The innkeepers can match your dinner tastes to several fine area restaurants.

And I challenge you to find two secret hiding places that apparently held the family jewels in earlier times.

How to get there: From Detroit or Chicago, take I–94 to U.S. 131 north (exit 74). Go north to Michigan 43 east (West Main Street, exit 38). Turn east and continue for about 3 miles. As you start down a hill, look for the inn almost at the bottom, on the southwest corner of Thompson Street.

Innkeepers: Liz and Bob Costello, owners; Mike and Cyndi Johnson, managers

Address/Telephone: 106 Thompson Street; (616) 343–2500

Rooms. 4, with 2 suites; all with private bath, air conditioning, and TV. No smoking inn.

Rates: $79, single; $85 to $95, double; EPB on weekends, continental breakfast on weekdays. Two-night minimum on selected weekends.

Open: All year.

Facilities and activities: Kalamazoo is a city of festivals, with some event virtually every weekend. Nearby: parks, Kalamazoo Museum, Institute of Arts, Air Zoo, Timber Ridge downhill-ski area, tours of General Motors plant, year-round theater, 2 universities with music, sports, and other events. Also antiques stores, winery tours, restaurants, dinner train.

Stuart Avenue Inn

KALAMAZOO, MICHIGAN 49007

Bill and Andy often say that their goal is to provide travelers with a pleasant experience in an elegant, friendly home. They've succeeded, having chosen some of the most wonderfully Victorian houses and lovingly restored them with well-appointed (and comfortable) antique furnishings.

I stayed at the Bartlett-Upjohn House, a magnificent example of 1886 Victorian, Queen Anne, and Eastlake architecture, with several pointy gables and lots of exterior gingerbread. (Look up and you can see the unusual gold roof ornament high on the home's imposing tower.)

Walk into the house and you're overwhelmed by Victorian excess. There's even a fireplace located in the handsome foyer, which opens onto two parlors, a music room, and the dining room. Those rooms are paneled in oak and cherry, and the hand-painted wall coverings are authentic restorations. The main staircase leading to second-floor guest rooms is itself an elegant touch, with unusual straight spindles.

Then there's a massive stained-glass window on the staircase landing that often washes the foyer in jagged slashes of color.

My guest room had a great view of the historic neighborhood, with floor-to-ceiling windows, Belgian lace curtains, elaborate woodwork, Chippendale sofa, and one of the most comfortable beds I've ever slept in. "We've been restoring old homes for many years," Andy said. "And one thing we've learned is that a good bed is most appreciated by guests."

Breakfast is served in the handsome dining room, which overlooks woods and the McDuffee Gardens—an acre of trees, greenery, and flowers where guests may stroll, picnic (in the gazebo), or watch goldfish frolic in the lily-graced pond. "This type of garden is common in England but rare in the United States," Andy said.

The 1902 Chappell House next door is another part of the Casteels' yesteryear complex. It holds seven rooms, with elaborate VIP suites that boast double Jacuzzis and wet bars; several also have a fireplace.

Or you can low-key your visit with an overnight in the 1886 Carriage House.

Andy and Bill will prepare elegant gourmet suppers for inn guests upon request. Two favorite specialties include marinated roast pork tenderloin and whitefish Grenoble.

And you can top off your romantic dinner with a little bit of chocolate decadence— Magnifico's Amaretti Torte.

On one of my visits here, our then-infant daughter, Dayne, was the centerpiece of mealtime conversation. Guests buzzed around her, amid clattering dishes, hearty exchanges, and lots of laughter. Dayne, of course, slept through the entire commotion.

How to get there: From Chicago, take I–94 east to northbound U.S. 131 exit. Go north to Michigan 43 (exit 38A), turn east, and continue for 3 miles to Stuart Avenue. Then turn left to the inn.

Innkeepers: Bill and Andrea Casteel

Address/Telephone: 229 Stuart Avenue; (616) 342–0230

Rooms: 7 in the Bartlett-Upjohn House, 8 in the Chapell House, 2 in the Carriage
House; all with private bath, air conditioning, phone, and TV. No smoking inn.

Rates: $49 to $69, single; $59 to $79, double; $100 to $130, suites; continental breakfast.

Open: All year.

Facilities and activities: Dinner available; 2 parlors, music room, and dining room. Located
in the Stuart Avenue Historic District. Nearby: Western Michigan University,
Kalamazoo College, and the schools' many sports facilities, and downtown. Many
citywide festivals, antiques stores. Less than an hour's drive to Lake Michigan
beaches and water activities.

The Pebble House
LAKESIDE, MICHIGAN 49116

I like this inn for its peaceful, laid-back ambience. It's as comfortable as your favorite easy chair, a good place to wind down and relax. And it's located in the heart of Michigan's dune-swept Harbor Country, with Lake Michigan just across the road.

"We call it a European-style inn," Jean said, "because of our Scandinavian breakfast." That's a special treat, with European breads, imported cheeses, smoked sausages, herring, and Jean's fresh muffins and home-baked pastries.

There's a daily hot dish, too; it might include anything from Swedish pancakes to Danish brunch eggs.

The main building, constructed in 1912, is located in a tranquil village with rolling country-side noted for its farms, orchards, and vineyards. I could see the lake from the porch and from some of the guest-room windows and decks.

One of my favorite spots is an enclosed porch with a large fireplace, perfect for nighttime reading by a crackling fire. The inn also has a large collection of oversized Mission-style furniture, giving it one of the most distinctive looks around.

Guest rooms have self-descriptive names. The Rose Room boasts lace curtains, rose borders, and an Art Nouveau rocker in front of a floor-to-ceiling etched-glass window that overlooks Lake Michigan.

Trek through the inn grounds on board-walks that pass among wildflower gardens and manicured lawns to reach the Coach House and Blueberry House, whose suites make guests feel like owners of this lakeside estate. I especially enjoy the Coach House's Garden Room, done in Arts and Crafts style and graced by a leaded-glass window and a deck facing the lake.

Not surprisingly, Jean and Ed are leaders in the Midwest Arts and Crafts movement. They travel extensively to search for antiques and to learn more about the origins of that movement; in fact, the inn offers special weekends for those who share similar interests.

Try Miller's for formal *nouvelle cuisine* dining that draws many media types from Chicago; Hannah's offers fine dining, too. Escape to Beyond the Sea Crab House or Red Arrow Road House for less glitzy surroundings but great food. For gourmet cuisine head to Jenny's.

I also sugggest the Harbert Swedish Bakery, in Harbert on Red Arrow Highway. The freshly baked Danish butter-pecan sweet rolls, pineapple bran muffins, pecan brownies, and elephant ears are a delight to anyone with a sweet tooth.

How to get there: Take I–94 to the Union Pier (exit 6). At the bottom of the ramp, turn left if coming from Chicago, or right if coming from Detroit or the west to Lakeside Road. Continue on Lakeside Road, crossing Red Arrow Highway, until you reach the stop sign at Lakeshore Road. Turn left and continue for ½ mile. The Pebble House is on the left.

Innkeepers: Jean and Ed Lawrence

Address/Telephone: 15093 Lakeshore Road; (616) 469–1416

Rooms: 6, plus 3 suites and 1 house; all with deck or balcony, private bath, and air condi-tioning. Wheelchair access.

Rates: $80 to $93, single; $90 to $103, double; $106 to $130, single suite; $116 to $140, double suite; $220, house; EPB.

Open: All year.

Facilities and activities: Private tennis court, screen house with hammocks. Access to beach across road. Nearby: hiking, boating, fishing, charter fishing for chinook salmon and coho, sailing, golf, biking, horseback riding, downhill and cross-country skiing, snowmobiling, tobogganing. Warren Dunes State Park nearby. A short drive to restaurants, antiques shops, art galleries, winery tours, pick-your own fruit farms. Hang gliding in Warren Dunes.

Recommended Country Inns® Travelers' Club Benefit: 10 percent discount or stay two nights, get third night free, Monday–Thursday.

$\mathcal{G}$rand Hotel
MACKINAC ISLAND, MICHIGAN 49757

The Grand Hotel, built in 1887, has been called one of the great hotels of the railroad and Great Lakes steamer era. Its location high on an island bluff provides magnificent vistas over the Straits of Mackinac waters.

Its incredible, many-columned veranda is 660 feet long (it claims to be the longest in the world) and is decorated with huge American flags snapping in the wind, bright yellow awnings that catch the color of the sun, and colorful red geraniums hanging everywhere. Many guests simply sit in generous rockers, sip on a drink, relax, and enjoy cooling lake breezes. I also like to admire the hotel's acres of woodland and lawns, finely manicured with exquisite flower gardens and greenery arrangements.

At the Grand Hotel, I feel immersed in a long-ago era of luxury and elegance. Even the attire of hotel attendants is impressive; they're dressed in long red coats and black bow ties. Once I rode the hotel's elegant horse-drawn carriage (the driver wore a black top hat and formal "pink" hunting jacket) from the ferry docks, up the long hill, to the grand portico.

Inside, the hotel is all greens, yellows, and whites, with balloon draperies on the windows, high-back chairs and sofas everywhere in numerous public rooms, and a healthy dash of yesteryear memorabilia hanging on hallway walls. One 1889 breakfast menu especially caught my eye, listing an extraordinary selection of foods, including lamb chops, lake fish, stewed potatoes in cream, and sweetbreads.

Special services are legion and include complimentary morning coffee, concerts during afternoon tea, horse-drawn-carriage island tours, dinner dances, and much more. It seems as if the pampering never stops.

Many of the guest rooms have spectacular lake views. Rates include breakfast and dinner, with Lake Superior whitefish an evening specialty. A dessert treat—the Grand pecan ball with hot fudge sauce—almost made me melt.

How to get there: From either Mackinaw City from the Lower Peninsula or from St. Ignace on the Upper Peninsula, a thirty-minute ferry ride brings you to Mackinac Island. Dock porters will greet your boat. There's an island airstrip for chartered flights and private planes.

Innkeeper: R. D. Musser III, corporation president

Address/Telephone: Mackinac Island; (906) 847–3331 or (800) 334–7263 (reservations)

Rooms: 324; all with private bath.

Rates: $145 to $275, per person, May through mid-June; $170 to $275 mid-June through late October. Children in same room with 2 persons, $35 to $99 per child; MAP. Special packages available.

Open: Mid-May to late October.

Facilities and activities: Main dining room, Geranium Bar, Grand Stand (food and drink), Audubon Bar, Carleton's Tea Store, pool grill. Magnificent swimming pool, private golf course, bike rentals, saddle horses, tennis courts, exercise trail. Carriage tours, dancing, movies. Expansive grounds, spectacular veranda with wonderful lake vistas. Nearby: museums, historic Fort Mackinac, Mackinac Island State Park, and other sites, guided tours; specialty shops. There are no motor vehicles allowed on historic Mackinac Island; visitors walk or rent horses, horse-drawn carriages and taxis, and bicycles.

Haan's 1830 Inn
MACKINAC ISLAND, MICHIGAN 49757

Haan's 1830 Inn is easily one of my favorite Mackinac Island hideaways. A stately Greek Revival design with tall white columns, it dates all the way back to ... surprise—1830. That's the time when the island was still operating as a fur-trading center.

The home, listed on the National Register of Historic Places as one of the oldest examples of Greek Revival architecture in the old Northwest Territory, was once owned by Colonel William Preston, the last physician at the historic English settlement of Fort Mackinac and the first mayor of the island. I never pass up a chance to tour this historic fort, which stands sentinel atop the island overlooking the straits.

The exterior is a gem. Once a frontier log cabin (it's actually built on the foundations of a trader cabin brought over from the mainland during the American Revolution), the main house's Greek Revival features date back to 1830, and the west wing was added in 1847. I could see original tongue-and-groove walls and the wavy paned leaded windows made in the early 1800s.

Guest rooms are furnished in striking authentic period antiques, beautiful pieces that call to mind the island's rich legacy. Such historic items as Colonel Preston's original desk and bed grace the premises.

Rooms are named after significant island figures. The Lafayette Davis Room has a cherry four-poster bed with a hand-tied canopy. It also has fine English prints. Old newspapers, dating from March and April of 1847, were found inside the walls during restoration. They were used as a crude insulation against the frigid winter wind.

The John Jacob Astor Room has a hand-crafted antique burled-walnut double bed with English bedspreads and a rare butternut chest; a screened-in porch offers a view of the garden of neighboring St. Anne's Church. (The church, whose congregation began worship here in 1695, was the first one dedicated in this part of the country.)

Haan's has added a private suite with post-and-beam construction, 1790 cannonball beds, sunroom, and whirlpool bath. Try it!

Breakfast is taken in the dining room on a handsome 12-foot-long farm harvest table. It includes home-baked spice breads, muffins, coffee cakes, juice, and other beverages. The innkeepers will recommend one of the island's many restaurants for dinner fare.

Did I mention that no cars are allowed on the island? You must walk, or you can rent a horse or horse-drawn carriage, hansom (horse-drawn taxi), or bicycle. There are miles of rugged lakeshore to explore.

How to get there: Catch a ferryboat from the Upper or Lower Peninsula, off I–75, at St. Ignace or Mackinaw City. Once on the island, walk a few blocks east down Huron (Main) Street, around Hennepin Harbor, to the inn.

Innkeepers: Nicholas and Nancy Haan
Address/Telephone: P.O. Box 123; (906) 847–6244 (winter number: 708–526–2662)
Rooms: 7, with 1 suite; 5 with private bath.
Rates: $80 to $120, single or double; $130 to $145, suite; continental breakfast. Most of May through early June and September, 20 percent discount; October, 25 percent discount. No credit cards.
Open: Mid-May to mid-October.
Facilities and activities: Located off Front Street, main street of Mackinac Island, one of the Midwest's most famous summer resort communities. Short walk or drive to historic sites, specialty shops, restaurants, golf course, ferryboats, other attractions.

$\mathcal{M}$etivier Inn

MACKINAC ISLAND, MICHIGAN 49757

This handsome 1877 building, situated on one of the most history-laden streets of historic Mackinac Island, borrows heavily from the Colonial English and French influences that saturated the region in the 1700s and 1800s.

Most of the furniture is from the Ethan Allen English pine collection. It's perfectly suited to the inn's styling. There also are a number of original antiques gracing both common and guest rooms.

The guest rooms are enchanting, especially if you want to enjoy country-inn ambience without sacrificing modern conveniences. Each room is named for a historic island figure. The John Jacob Astor Room (a building used as one of his historic fur-trading offices is located just down Market Street; it's now a preserved historic home) has a four-poster bed, wicker chairs, and soothing rose-colored wallpaper. A special touch: I could see the bay waters from a romantic turret alcove.

Other rooms have antique headboards and iron-rail beds, marble-topped dressers, tulip lamps, padded rockers, and more.

Four rooms and an entire tower have been added recently. Owner Jane has decorated in more of a "Victorian, Mackinac Island style," with antique wicker dominating the rooms warmed by light peach and yellow floral colors.

I enjoyed relaxing in a wicker rocker on the

expansive front porch and watching the parade of island visitors pass by. You might want to explore the island's 6 square miles of unique beauty. Just walk, rent a horse or horse-drawn carriage, or rent a bicycle. There are no motorized vehicles allowed on the island. Staying overnight on Mackinac Island is like stepping into a long-ago world, filled with history and surprises.

Breakfast fare includes fresh fruit, croissants, delicious coffee cakes, juice, and other beverages.

For dinner I put on my best dinner jacket and headed for the famous Grand Hotel. Its luxurious formal dining room offers a wonderful Mackinac whitefish and a score of more traditional gourmet feasts.

How to get there: Take a ferryboat to Mackinac Island. Ferries run from both the Upper and Lower peninsulas, off I-75. From the Sheppler ferry dock, follow the road leading up the hill; turn right on Market Street to the inn.

Innkeepers: Mike and Jane Bacon, Ken and Diane Neyer, owners
Address/Telephone: Market Street (mailing address: Box 285); (906) 847-6234
Rooms: 22; all with private bath.
Rates: $145 to $235, single or double, continental breakfast. Spring and fall discount packages and off-season rates available. Cribs and cots available.
Open: May through October.
Facilities and activities: Short walk from main street on Mackinac Island. No motor vehicles allowed—only horses, carriages, bicycles. Nearby: restaurants, many specialty shops, historic island sites, horseback riding, swimming, golf, tennis.

$\mathcal{L}$eelanau Country Inn
MAPLE CITY, MICHIGAN 49664

This gabled clapboard house has all the comforts needed for a restful stay in the country, including front and side porches that boast comfy chairs. Tall trees shade the grounds, and seasonal flowers burst in rainbow colors everywhere. I found Linda in the garden doing yet more planting.

The house is an old farmstead that was built in 1891. Pictures of the then newly built structure hang on inn walls. Linda pointed out photos of all the families that have lived here. And she said that the granddaughter of the original owners now lives right across the street.

The inn began serving traveling families from Chicago. Linda has an early-1900s guest register. "Some deal," she laughed. "Guests paid $1 per day for a room and three meals."

While the prices have changed, I found the same kind of warm hospitality that must have welcomed turn-of-the-century guests to this charming country retreat.

Although there are three dining rooms, my favorite one is on the long enclosed porch; it's done in lively colors and offers a view of the flowers and grounds out front. The inn specializes in seafood, which John has flown in fresh from Boston. Another inn specialty is homemade pasta. Favorites like blackfish Provençal and chicken with pecan sauce are served regularly. So is the delicious prime rib. And don't pass up desserts like the inn specialty—Peanut Butter Pie drenched in fudge topping.

Linda has fashioned guest rooms that are simple, quaint, and charming. The plank floors made me feel as though I were back at my aunt's Wisconsin farm. Fancy bedspreads and wall wreaths add attractive splashes of color, and the old-fashioned rocking chairs are fun.

Breakfast includes fresh fruit, freshly made croissants, rolls, coffee, and tea.

One final note: Maybe I didn't emphasize strongly enough how wonderful the food is here at the inn. Well, in a local newspaper poll, Leelanau Country Inn has been voted the best restaurant in Leelanau County, with the best Sunday brunch, the best country setting, and the best service; it was also voted the best place to go for a drive and have a meal. I get hungry just writing about it!

How to get there: From Chicago, take I–94 north to I–196 north. Continue to U.S. 31 north. Turn north on Michigan 22 and continue north just past County Road 667. Turn right into the inn's driveway.

Innkeepers: John and Linda Sisson
Address/Telephone: 149 East Harbor Highway; (616) 228–5060
Rooms: 6 share 2 baths.
Rates: $35 to $45, single or double, in off-season; $45 to $55, single or double, Memorial Day through Labor Day; continental breakfast.
Open: All year.
Facilities and activities: Full service dining room with wheelchair access; sitting area, porch. Area winery tours. Nearby: Sleeping Bear Dunes National Lakeshore; Glen Lake; Lake Michigan; historic Leland "Fishtown" with crafts, art, and specialty shops.

McCarthy's Bear Creek Inn
MARSHALL, MICHIGAN 49068

The first things I noticed as I pulled up to this imposing home, perched atop a knoll overlooking Bear Creek, were the fieldstone fences. They were hand-built by the home's original owner in the 1940s and meander about the grounds, surrounding the main house, outbuildings, more than century-old tall burr oaks, sugar maples, and stately spruces.

This is country living at its finest, with fourteen acres of farm fields to wander through and explore and a twisting creek gurgling outside the windows of inn rooms.

Two children and a dog were cavorting on the creek's edge as I stood and let the beauty of the landscape absorb me. The mutt's yipping and

their laughter pretty much characterized good times here.

The handsome Williamsburg-style Cape Cod main house, which brings to mind an English country estate, is comfortable country. Note the handsome cupola; like much of the inn's elegant furniture, it was designed and built by Mike and Beth.

A sitting room has a fireplace with a stuffed black teddy bear sitting on the mantel. One first-floor guest room has a four-poster cherry bed, soothing green-and-rose floral wall coverings, wing chairs, and a large bay window overlooking the fields. Upstairs, rooms feature iron-rail, brass, and Jenny Lind beds, high-back chairs, and private porches that provide great views of the grounds.

Seven rooms have recently been fashioned out of an historic outbuilding called the Creek House just behind the main inn. In fact, you'll feel that it's possible to reach out and scoop up chilly creek water in your hands. Here rooms are more elegantly country, and the Sunset Room's large arched window offers spectacular sunset vistas.

French doors open from the sitting room onto an enclosed porch with fieldstone floors and more spectacular views of outbuildings and farm fields. The extensive continental breakfast buffet served in the dining room includes breads for toasting, fresh fruit, cereals, egg dishes, home-baked goodies, and beverages. (Hard to believe this feast is called "continental," isn't it?) I'd recommend Win Schuler's restaurant for very good family-style dinnertime meals. The innkeepers will arrange dinner reservations for you there or at any other of Marshall's eating establishments.

How to get there: From Lansing, take I–69 south to Michigan Avenue, and turn west. Then turn south on 15 Mile Road, then a quick right (west) on C Drive North to the inn.

Innkeepers: Mike and Beth McCarthy

Address/Telephone: 15230 C Drive North; (616) 781–8383

Rooms: 14; all with private bath and air conditioning, some with wheelchair access and balcony.

Rates: $65 to $98, single or double, expansive continental breakfast. Sunday-night discount available for $59.

Open: All year except December 24 and 25.

Facilities and activities: Cross-country skiing, hiking, and fishing on grounds. Nearby: scores of fine Victorian homes throughout town, with 12 national historic sites and 35 state historic sites. Museums, including Honolulu House; numerous antiques stores. Local theater. Boating, swimming, fishing, natural-habitat zoo. Monthly town events and celebrations.

The National House Inn
MARSHALL, MICHIGAN 49068

Stepping into The National House Inn is like entering a way station on frontier back roads of the nineteenth-century: Rough plank wood floors, hand-hewn timbers, and a massive brick open-hearth fireplace with a 13-foot single-timber mantelpiece bring back visions of the frontier.

And why not? The house was built in 1835 as a stagecoach stop. It's the oldest operating inn in Michigan.

More history? Barbara told me that the inn is reputed to have been part of the Underground Railroad and once also functioned as a wagon factory. Now it provides a glimpse into the past for travelers and is furnished with antiques and Victorian finery.

The rooms are named after local historical figures. "Color schemes are authentic to the early 1800s," Barbara said. So you'll see muted salmons, blues, and greens—all copied "from original milk-paint colors that were made from wild berries to achieve their hue."

The elegant Ketchum Suite is formal Victorian, with a high bedstead and a tall dresser with a marble top. Other rooms reveal iron- and brass-rail beds, elaborate rockers, and balloon period curtains.

I was overwhelmed by the huge armoire in the Charles Gorham Room; it must stand 9 feet high. Still more rooms evoke pure country charm, with bright quilts that complement pine, maple, and oak furniture, and folk-art portraits that grace the walls.

Breakfast in the nineteenth century–styled dining room features five different home-baked pastries (including bran muffins, bundt cake, and nut breads), boiled eggs, fruit, cereal, applesauce, juice, and other beverages.

Ask the innkeeper to suggest an area restaurant; there are several good ones nearby. I love touring the town, which is teeming with all sorts of Victorian-era homes, histories, and legends.

How to get there: From Detroit, take I–94 west to Marshall (exit 110). At the Fountain Circle, jog right and follow the road around to the inn.

Innkeeper: Barbara Bradley, manager

Address/Telephone: 102 South Parkview; (616) 781–7374

Rooms: 16, including 2 suites; all with private bath and air conditioning. Wheelchair access.

Rates: $65 to $120, single; $67 to $130, double; EPB.

Open: All year except Christmas Eve and Christmas Day.

Facilities and activities: Sitting room, dining room, The Tin Whistle Gift Shoppe. Nearby: many fine examples of historic Victorian homes throughout town, with 12 national historic sites and 35 state historic sites. Museums, including the Honolulu House. Antiques stores. Stage productions at local theaters. Boating, fishing, swimming at nearby lakes. Winter cross-country skiing. Monthly town events and annual celebrations.

Business travel: Located about 10 miles east of Battle Creek. Corporate rates, meeting rooms, fax.

The 1873 Mendon Country Inn

MENDON, MICHIGAN 49072

The 1873 Mendon Country Inn is everything I imagine a country inn should be. Others must feel the same way: It's been featured in *Country Living* magazine, *Country Home*, *Country*—the accolades just keep coming.

Like all newcomers, I was welcomed in the Indian Room, a gathering place on the first floor with Native American artifacts strewn about. Here Dick provides guests with area maps that identify local points of interest—restaurants, specialty stores, historical attractions—just about everything needed to enjoy a stay in this quaint town.

He told me that the inn was built as a frontier hotel in the 1840s, then rebuilt with locally kilned St. Joseph River clay bricks in 1873. It was called The Wakeman House, a name the locals still use for the inn today.

Guest rooms are decorated thematically, though several exhibit interiors done in the grand style so popular after the Civil War. The Amish Room has a beautiful antique Amish quilt. The Nautical Room features country-pine furnishings, with a swag of fishermen's netting used for the bed canopy; it also has a creekside porch. But my favorite is the Wakeman Room, of elegant post–Civil War design, including 8-foot-tall windows, a 12-foot-high ceiling, and fine oversized country Empire furnishings.

The best bargain is the Hired Man Room, a

small space in country-style decor with a three-quarter bed and a shower across the hall, for only $50. That includes a breakfast of juice, rolls, and coffee.

The inn's Roof Top Garden affords another view of the creek and is great for sunbathing or private late-night moon gazing. "We're the only country inn around with its own treehouse," Dick told me. Not to mention the stage out back that serves as a centerpiece for folk, dulcimer, and other music concerts and special entertainment.

Dick and Dolly's most recent inn addition, the Creekside Lodge, is fashioned in Native American stylings; but I doubt if early Indian inhabitants of the area enjoyed whirlpool suites with fireplaces, full cedar saunas, and covered decks overlooking water and wildlife areas.

There's lots more to enjoy. The innkeepers' Sanctuary at Wildwood, about 20 miles west of the inn (near Jones) is a 95-acre private retreat with five Jacuzzi and fireplace suites, two deer herds, and almost 5 miles of cross-country ski trails. The stained-glass window in the gathering room is a real knockout. What a beautiful and very private getaway!

How to get there: From Chicago, take the Dan Ryan expressway south to the Indiana toll road (I–80/90), and go west past Elkhart to U.S. 131. Then go north to Michigan 60/66. Head east into Mendon. M–60/66 is called Main Street once in town; follow it to the inn.

Innkeepers: Dick and Dolly Buerkle
Address/Telephone: 440 West Main Street; (616) 496–8132, fax (616) 496 8403
Rooms: 18, including 9 suites with Jacuzzi and fireplace; all with private bath, 17 with air conditioning. Wheelchair access.
Rates: $50 to $129, single or double; $139 to $159, suites; continental breakfast.
Open: All year.
Facilities and activities: Rooftop garden with view of creek. Continuous special inn weekend events like Country Fair, featuring the work of more than 30 craftspeople; Halloween night, with spooky magic, ghost stories, and goblin's brew; Saturday-night summer concerts; winter "Tavern" dinners; Valentine's Day special; Thanksgiving in the Country; and family Christmas weekends, an old-fashioned celebration. Tandem bikes and canoes available for guests. Special "courting canoes," $50 per couple packages. Nearby: antiques market and Shipshewana, Indiana, Auction and Flea Market; local Amish settlement. Restaurants, golf, tennis, fishing, boating, museums, winery tours.

$\mathcal{B}$auhaus on $\mathcal{B}$arton
NEW BUFFALO, MICHIGAN 49117

Hey, daddy-o, Maynard G. Crebbs would dig Bauhaus on Barton, a 1950s-style bed and breakfast that is the hippest place to stay in Harbor Country. Walk through the streamlined marble entryway of this sleek, pink stucco, Bauhaus-style building into an era, as owner Roger Harvey says, "when coffee tables and your mom were still blonde: or "when dishware was durable enough to survive a thermonuclear attack."

Rooms, named for 1950s television shows, are decorated with period furniture. Imagine giant lamps with weirdly shaped shades and fins resembling classic Cadillacs; Sputnik chandeliers; and chenille bedspreads—Hey, that's my grandma's old house! They also sport '50s vintage radios (usually no FM) and magazines from the era.

The coolest room might be the two-bedroom suite on the second floor. It includes the Jetsons, a large, sunny skypad furnished with '50s "atomic" bedroom furniture, and a rug that traces comet patterns in far outer space; and saluting traditions of the TV show, the Ozzie and Harriet portion of the suite sports two twin beds (they're made by Heywood Wakefield for you '50s collectors out there).

And you'll think that John Beresford Tipton tapped you on the shoulder, presenting you with a check for a cool million once you're snuggled inside the Millionaire Suite, 600-square feet of pure '50s glamour.

For all the kitsch, the ambience is sophisticated. But there are house rules:

- Beehives and pompadours must meet federal doorway-clearance regulations.
- Angst-ridden, sneering teens a la James Dean will be misunderstood at all times while on the premises.
- Party dolls, prom queens, and debutantes are not allowed to monopolize the deluxe cootie-free bathroom facilities.
- Patrons named Troy, Tab, Fabian, or Tammy will not be given preferential treatment.

Hot diggity! This is one swell, snazzy place to visit.

How to get there: Take I–94 to exit 1; go north to the first traffic light and turn left on Red Arrow Highway (Route 12); turn right at the next street, which is Barton. The inn is at the corner.

Innkeepers: Beverly and Roger Harvey
Address/Telephone: 33 North Barton Street; (616) 469–6419
Rooms: 4, with 3 suites; all with private bath. No smoking inn.
Rates: Weekends: $95, single or double; $130 to $230, suites; weekdays: $85, single or double; $110 to $200, suites; EPB. Off-season rates available.
Open: All year except January.
Facilities and activities: Fireplace in guest common room, porches, decks, gazebo in back-yard. Walk to Lake Michigan, antiques shops, art galleries, boutiques, marina. Short drive to Lighthouse Place, Warren Dunes State Park.

North Shore Inn
NORTHPORT, MICHIGAN 49670

It's hard to imagine a more beautiful setting for a country inn.

This handsome Colonial-influenced retreat nestles on the shore of Northport Bay in northwest Michigan, the landscape that Ernest Hemingway roamed as a boy. Picture windows are everywhere, allowing spectacular vistas of the water (as well as the vast bayside panorama of maple, birch, and pine forests) from all rooms.

My brother, Mark, an avid boatman, was captivated by the waterside setting. "The water is crystal clear," Sue told us. "Great for swimming or sailing."

Sue serves glasses of local wine and spiced cakes each evening. "Guests often take it down to the water to enjoy a nightly parade of swans that swim by here," Sue said. Others walk through French doors to a screened porch where they can sit in comfortable wicker chairs and soak in the scenery.

Guest rooms are lovely, with country decor, hand-sewn quilts, and other special touches. Mark especially liked the Bayshore Room, with its own fireplace and glorious views of the water.

I opted for the huge Country Rose Room, with a pink marble fireplace, a queen-sized brass bed covered by a white eyelet quilt, and a private balcony where you can take breakfast in the morning or follow the moonglow across the water at night.

For breakfast Sue offers a gourmet selection that might include German apple pancake puffs with country sausage, home-baked cherry rolls, muffins and breakfast breads, and more.

How to get there: From Traverse City, take Michigan 22 north to Highway 201; follow that through town to County Road 640, then turn right and proceed to the inn.

Innkeeper: Susan Hammersley

Address/Telephone: 12794 County Road 640; (616) 386–7111

Rooms: 4; all with fireplace, private bath, and air conditioning. TV and phone upon request. No smoking inn.

Rates: $140, single or double (July through August); $135 rest of year; EPB, afternoon snacks and evening aperitifs. Two-night minimum on summer weekends.

Open: May through October; other weekends by special arrangement.

Facilities and activities: Common room with fireplace; kitchen. Sandy beach just steps outside the door. Nearby: sports, fishing in Grand Traverse Bay; hiking, cross-country ski trails at Leelanau State Park; biking along quiet country roads; historic lighthouse; golf; quaint shops, galleries in Northport and surrounding towns.

Stafford's Bay View Inn
PETOSKEY, MICHIGAN 49770

Stafford's Bay View Inn, overlooking Little Traverse Bay, calls itself a "Grand Old Dame of the Victorian resort era." It's certainly steeped in rich Victorian traditions; in fact, it sits next to a village whose treasure of Victorian gingerbread architecture may be unmatched anywhere.

Built in 1886, this elegant white clapboard inn has served North Country hospitality to four generations of discerning travelers. It's a classic summer house, in the sense that it offers cool breezes due to its bayside location, all kinds of outdoor activities, and an ambitious community program of music, drama, and art. There's great shopping nearby, too. Chic boutiques in nearby Harbor Springs are just a short drive away.

A long sun porch, furnished with oversized wicker pieces, overlooks the bay. Guest rooms filled with antiques and reproductions from several famous Michigan furniture makers reflect the styles of the Victorian era. Room 3 has a four-poster bed so high that even I had to use a step-stool to climb atop it—and I'm 6'2".

You'll also find brass beds and sleigh beds, and inviting flower wreaths on room doors. Four new suites have fireplaces and whirlpool baths. And a library features television with video and book collections, including lots of special kids' stuff.

Several dining rooms serve food with a fine reputation, including fresh Great Lakes whitefish and local specialties such as honey mustard shrimp and Veal Louisiana in creole mustard sauce, which have been featured in *Gourmet* magazine.

A full breakfast ordered from the regular menu is included in the price of the rooms. That means choices like malted waffles or whole-wheat pancakes with Michigan maple syrup, biscuits with sausage gravy, even eggs Benedict and red-flannel hash.

Would you rather overnight in a hotel that Ernest Hemingway slept in? Then head to Stafford's other inn, the Perry Hotel, where the famed writer stayed in 1916 during a trout-fishing expedition; records show he paid 75¢ for a room.

The hotel retains its turn-of-the-century ambience, with tin-pressed ceilings, Victorian furnishings, elegant guest-rooms—even wicker chairs on the long veranda. Get a bayside room for views of the water from your private balcony. And the hotel's pub serves breakfast, lunch, and dinner, with entertainment on weekends.

Stafford's also offers food at three other nearby locations: One Water Street, on Lake Charlevoix in Boyne City, offers specialties like Trout Hemingway and cold black-cherry soup, as well as various game selections; Stafford's Pier Restaurant is in Harbor Springs, near one of Michigan's most scenic drives along Michigan 119, north from the village; another is the Weathervane, in Charlevoix.

How to get there: From any direction, the inn is right on U.S. 31, just outside Bay View.

Innkeepers: Stafford and Janice Smith; Reg Smith, manager
Address/Telephone: U.S. 31 (mailing address: P.O. Box 3); (616) 347–2771
Rooms: 31, with 10 suites; all with private bath and air conditioning. Wheelchair access
Rates: $88 to $160, single or double, but $128 to $195 in July; EPB except Sunday, when brunch is served. Special packages available.
Open: All year.
Facilities and activities: Full-service restaurant, sitting rooms, sun porch. Nearby: Bay View, a city whose Victorian architecture qualifies it as a National Historic Site; Petoskey's Gaslight Shopping District and ritzy Harbor Springs boutiques. Bay View Chautauqua programs feature concerts and lectures throughout summer. Biking in summer; cross-country skiing at Boyne Mountain, Nubs Nob, ice boating, snowmobiling in winter. Sailboat charters on Lake Michigan; golf.

The Victorian Inn
PORT HURON, MICHIGAN 48060

I heard about the Victorian Inn because of their food. In fact, it's probably safe to say that the establishment is far more famous for its superb kitchen than for its bed-and-breakfast offerings.

Consider this dinner menu, from which I chose during my visit in April. First there is filet mignon with béarnaise sauce; accompany this with a 1993 Haywood Cabernet, and you've got a winning dinner combination.

Not in the mood for steak? How about grilled swordfish with Dijon lime-ginger sauce? Or pecan chicken, dipped in a honey-mustard glaze, pressed into chopped pecans, and roasted?

Or maybe barbecue-spiced sea scallops with roasted tomato butter is more your mood toady? That "tomato butter" sauce is concocted from roasted plum tomatoes, chilies, chicken stock, fresh cilantro, and lime juice.

Yum!

And wait until you see the dessert tray.

The green-clapboard building was constructed in 1896 for Scottish immigrant John Davidson, who became a successful local dry-goods dealer. When the innkeepers restored the house in 1983, they used the original plans and drawing supplied by the home's architect, Issac Erb. Because of this good fortune (and lots of long hours and hard work), preservation and restoration took place within six months.

The four guest rooms are charming. The Victorian Room boasts a bird's-eye maple headboard. Another favorite appointment: a handsome four-poster bed graces the Edward Room, along with a marble-topped dresser and original brass-and-blown-glass chandelier.

Oh, and I need some advice. Is it polite to eat dinner twice in one day?

How to get there: From Flint, take 69 west into Port Huron; turn left on Seventh Street and proceed to the intersection of Seventh and Union—and the inn.

Innkeepers: Ed and Vicki Peterson; Lew and Lynne Secory
Address/Telephone: 1229 Seventh Street; (810) 984–1437
Rooms: 4; 2 with private bath.
Rates: $65 to $75, single or double, continental breakfast.
Open: All year.
Facilities and activities: Dining room. Short drive to Bluewater Bridge (to Canada), Pine Grove Park, St. Clair River, Edison Depot, Fort Gratiot Lighthouse, Military Street Historic Home District. An hour's drive to metro Detroit.

St. Clair Inn
ST. CLAIR, MICHIGAN 48079

The St. Clair Inn hugs fast to the shore of its namesake river overlooking Canada, just across the channel. Built on the site of a historic sawmill in 1926, the inn luxuriates in its English Tudor architecture while providing a comfortable vantage point for viewing a constant parade of merchant ships and tankers that ply these waters leading to Great Lakes ports.

Inside heavy oak doors, note massive pillars supporting a rough-hewn beamed ceiling, calling to mind the spine of a sailing ship. Two massive stone hearths flank windows looking out over the river; each has high-back chairs nearby for cozy conversations or serious reading.

On my last stay here, I ran to the inn's dock (sometimes referred to as "the world's longest freshwater boardwalk") upon hearing the blast of a foghorn. A massive freighter, seemingly an arm's length away. almost scraped both shorelines as it moved through the mist-shrouded channel. I waved to a sailor standing on the high aft deck. He tipped his cap and waved back.

I like all the guest chambers, especially the north wing's river-view rooms, with their own private balcony looking out over the water. Then there's the Captain's House, with its sunken lounge, fireplace, sunporch, Jacuzzi, and wet bar. And the Annex rooms have their own riverfront docks.

Even the indoor swimming pool boasts more spectacular river views.

The inn menu owes much to its proximity to Lake Huron. It includes northern Canadian walleye, lake perch, and more. The pork chops are an inn specialty, and a fresh strawberry pie is served in a sea of whipped cream.

How to get there: Follow I–94 east to exit 257. Turn right (east) onto Fred Moore Highway and follow it to Clinton Avenue. Then turn right to North Riverside. Turn left and proceed to the inn.

Innkeeper: Ves Calvert

Address/Telephone: 500 North Riverside; (313) 963–5735

Rooms: 92, with 20 suites; all with private bath.

Rates: $75 to $135, single or double; $225, Jacuzzi suites; EP. Wheelchair access.

Open: All year.

Facilities and activities: Breakfast, lunch, and dinner available in six dining rooms. River lounge, indoor swimming pool and whirlpool, riverfront boardwalk. Nearby: Winter cross-country skiing; summer water sports, charter fishing, hiking, golf, and tennis. Antiques and specialty stores across the street.

Business travelers: Meeting rooms, fax, conference calling, electronic copy boards, corporate rates.

Montague Inn
SAGINAW, MICHIGAN 48601

After driving nearly sixteen hours with my wife and baby Dayne, then six months old, I made an evening call to the Montague Inn, searching for a room. It was answered by one of the owners, Norm Kinney, who told me he had had a cancellation, so he'd be expecting us. Turns out we got the last room.

We were lucky in several ways, since the Montague Inn quickly became one of our favorite stopovers. It's an elegant Georgian mansion, built in 1929 by its namesake, a prosperous businessman who made products from Saginaw's sugar-beet crop.

The inn has the ambience of a fine, intimate European hotel, with elegant classical Georgian antiques, oriental and Persian rugs, formal flower and herb gardens, private "park," and lakeside location all adding to its clublike atmosphere.

It also boasts six fireplaces, a dining room overlooking Lake Linton, and a library that contains a swinging shelf to reveal a small hidden room.

Our quarters, the third-floor Goodridge Room, was a cozy bedchamber tucked beneath a gable, with three alcove windows overlooking the grounds, two twin beds, and a cedar-lined bath.

Most inn rooms are far more spacious; some offer marble fireplaces, art deco–tiled baths, pegged oak floors, and views of the lake or park.

Dining is also a treat. Formal servers wear what closely resemble butlers' uniforms. Entrees include shrimp sautéed in hazelnut oil and finished with strawberry puree and ground hazelnuts; Norwegian salmon served with Brie in a puff pastry; and grilled medallions of tenderloin sauced with Dijon and *demiglace*. Even lunch offers selections like grilled tenderloin tips and smoked turkey salad.

Especially noteworthy are the wild-game dinners offered to adventuresome gourmands by the inn. Consider marinated venison with rabbit sausage, and you get the idea.

Norm's wife, Kathryn, conducts tours and offers samples of the inn's herb garden, relating the history and myths of herbs; later, a special luncheon features herb-rich delicacies.

How to get there: From Detroit, take I–75 north into Saginaw. Exit on Michigan 46 and go west to Remington. Follow Remington northwest to Washington and turn left. Continue to the inn.

Innkeepers: Norm and Kathryn Kinney, owners; Janet Hoffmann, manager
Address/Telephone: 1581 South Washington Avenue; (517) 752–3939
Rooms: 18, including 1 suite; 15 with private bath, all with air conditioning, TV, and
    phone.
Rates: $66 to $154, single; $77 to $165, double; continental breakfast. Add $10 for third
    person or child in room; kids under 10 free.
Open: All year.
Facilities and activities: Full-service restaurant (lunch, dinner Tuesday through Saturday by
    reservation). Nestled on 8 beautifully landscaped acres, formal flower gardens, herb
    garden; cooking classes in summer, elegant picnic lunches provided guests for after-
    noons spent at Lake Linton, just behind inn. Nearby: walk to Japanese Garden and
    Teahouse, children's zoo, Hoyt Park, Old West Side business district. Health club,
    summer and winter sports activities available to guests.
Recommended Country Inns® Travelers' Club Benefit: 10 percent discount, Monday–
    Thursday.

Kemah Guest House Bed and Breakfast on the Hill

SAUGATUCK, MICHIGAN 49453

The Kemah Guest House is one of the most intriguing residences in the lakeside village of Saugatuck. It reminds me of traditional European homes and combines an Old World German flair with touches of art deco—and Frank Lloyd Wright!

Built by a German sea captain, the home is named for its site on a breezy hill. (*Kemah* is a Potawatomi Indian word meaning "teeth of the wind.") Cindi said that the captain, ever a superstitious seaman, wanted to ensure that his sails would always billow with the winds, so he graced his home with a good-luck moniker.

It was remodeled in 1926 by William Springer, a Chicago Board of Trade member. You can see his initials carved everywhere—from wood panels in the rathskeller to the massive wrought-iron arched doorway.

There are so many highlights:

Stained- and leaded-glass windows depict sailing scenes.

Hand-carved wooden landscapes on the solarium paneling recount the house's various appearances through the decades.

A bricked, semicircular solarium with a running fountain was designed by T. E. Tallmadge, a disciple of Frank Lloyd Wright, and captures the master's Prairie School architectural style.

Beamed ceilings, cornice boards, and a fireplace (of Pewabic tile) recall the art deco era.

Have a drink in a genuine rathskeller, displaying the home's original wine casks, wall stencils, and leather-strap and wood-frame chairs hand-carved in Colorado in the 1930s.

Can you find the secret panel that hid whiskey and spirits during Prohibition days? A hint: Look at the windows near the arched door and kitchen.

There's a cave on the grounds and an Indian grave on the side of the hill.

Cindi has fashioned charming guest rooms in rich individual styles. One is done in fine imported Dutch lace; another recalls a gentleman's room, with its oak furniture and a 6-foot-tall Victorian headboard on the bed.

My favorite room features an eleven-piece bedroom set made in 1918, one of only two like it ever made. It's all walnut, of gorgeous craftsmanship. Look for the secret jewelry drawer in the dresser.

There are rolls, danish, fresh fruit, juices, and coffee for breakfast; sometimes you'll also be treated to French toast, quiche, and more. If you wish, the innkeepers will recommend one of many good area restaurants, too.

How to get there: From Chicago, take I–94 north to I–196. Take exit 36 just south of Douglas, merge onto Blue Star Highway, and go north to Lake Street. Turn left (west), go ½ mile, and turn right on Allegan; proceed to the top of the hill (Allegan and Pleasant).

Innkeepers: Terry and Cindi Tatsch, owners; Dan Osborn, manager
Address/Telephone: 633 Allegan Street; (616) 857–2919
URL: http://www.bbonline.com/mi/kemah
Rooms: 6; 2 with private whirlpool bath, 2 with private bath down the hall.
Rates: May through October, $85 to $140, single or double, continental breakfast. Off-season rates available.
Open: All year.
Facilities and activities: Rathskeller (for guests only). Located on a quiet hill, high above the bustle of this lakeside Midwest art-colony village. Nearby: a short drive to restaurants, antiques and specialty shops, art galleries, beaches, swimming, boating, dunes exploring, and more.
Recommended Country Inns® Travelers' Club Benefit: Stay two nights, get third night free, Monday–Thursday, not valid with special offers/coupons or on holidays; mention discount when making reservation.

The Park House
SAUGATUCK, MICHIGAN 49453

When I arrived at The Park House, Lynda and Joe were muscling up railroad ties and timbers, landscaping their garden and grounds. Nobody else was working that hard on a hot Sunday afternoon in this fun-filled Lake Michigan resort town.

So it's not surprising that The Park House is a treasure. Built in 1857 by a local lumberman, the two-story clapboard home is Saugatuck's oldest historic residence. The innkeepers recently restored the historic wing of this handsome inn, which had been removed in the 1940s. Now the porch wraps around the house, is screened in, and overlooks pretty gardens.

Lynda told me a great story of how the inn got its name. Seems that a former owner fenced the home's almost eight acres and stocked the pasture with deer. Their grazing cropped the grass, giving the grounds a manicured look. People started calling it the "park" house.

Want more history? Susan B. Anthony stayed here for two weeks in the 1870s and helped form the county's first temperance society. In fact, Joe laughingly said, Anthony was responsible for closing down half the bars in Allegan County!

The house is built from original timbers that once stood on the property. Some special touches include the original wide-plank pine floors, pretty wall stencils done by Lynda, a wide fireplace, and antique furnishings throughout the home. French doors in the parlor open onto an herb garden. All in all, it's a real country charmer.

Each cozy guest room is distinctively decorated, and all have a queen-sized iron-rail bed and warm oak furniture. Six rooms also feature a fireplace.

For more elegant surroundings, repair to a Park House suite; each comes with a fireplace, two-person whirlpool bath, and a private balcony. Lynda will even serve you breakfast in bed.

Or rent one of the inn's cottages. The Rose Garden sits just west of the main inn house and has its own outdoor hot tub. The Mill House, complete with a Franklin stove, offers spectacular vistas from floor-to-ceiling windows that overlook the harbor. Indian Point features lots of cedar with a wall of glass overlooking the Kalamazoo River. And there are two more in nearby Douglas.

For main-house inn guests, Lynda serves a buffet-style breakfast at an antique oak table in a gathering room dotted with country crafts and antiques. Get ready for freshly baked muffins, granola, fruit, homemade jams, and the Pettys' own blend of coffee. They'll also suggest a few "can't miss" dinner spots.

The Park House is usually part of a spectacular Elizabethan Christmas feast and a February progressive dinner in which guests partake of each meal course at a historic Saugatuck inn; the holiday decorating ideas alone are worth the price of the meal.

How to get there: From Chicago, take I–94 north to I–196 and continue north to exit 41 (Blue Star Highway). Turn west and continue on Washington (where Blue Star turns left) to the inn. (Washington changes to Holland at the city limits.)

Innkeepers: Lynda and Joe Petty
Address/Telephone: 888 Holland; (616) 857–4535
URL: http://www.bbonline.com/mi/parkhouse
Rooms: 9, including 2 suites, plus 6 cottages; all with private bath and air conditioning. Wheelchair access.
Rates: $85 to $115, rooms; $150, suites; $115 to $225, cottages; continental breakfast.
Open: All year.
Facilities and activities: Gathering room, screened porch. Nearby: a short drive to restaurants, Lake Michigan beaches, swimming, boating, charter fishing, cross-country skiing, specialty stores, antiques shops, art galleries, sand-dune schooner rides, golf, hiking, hiking, lake cruises.
Recommended Country Inns® Travelers' Club Benefit: Stay two nights, get third night free, Monday–Thursday.

Twin Gables Country Inn
SAUGATUCK, MICHIGAN 49453

Denise explained that her inn originally stood on a hill across the Kalamazoo River. One winter it was moved across the frozen waters by mule team and log sled to Saugatuck.

She laughed. "After all that trouble, the owners thought they'd put it too close to a road. So they moved it again to its present location."

The inn is all that's left of a genuine Midwest ghost town. The old logging town of Singapore hugged a spot on the dune-filled eastern shores of Lake Michigan that is now occupied by Saugatuck. But when the trees had been cut down, lumber interests left, and the town was abandoned. Eventually the crumbling buildings were buried under tons of ever-shifting sand

dunes. Now the old town is just a historical footnote.

The 1865 inn is built from timbers cut in the old Singapore sawmill. And it was designed by the same architect who built the magnificent Grand Hotel on Mackinac Island.

It has a fascinating history, including stints as an icehouse for an 1860s brewery, a tanning factory, and boat-building works. Denise said that tugboats were constructed under this roof.

It's now named for the historic hotel that was established here in 1922.

I love the old pressed-tin ceilings, walls, and wainscoting. Add to that a common-room fireplace surrounded by comfy chairs, sofas, and rockers, and the atmosphere is just right for lazing away a weekend.

The inn's heated outdoor pool is a great haven, or you can take a dip in the large indoor hot tub.

The guest rooms are lovingly furnished, each distinctive and warm. The Bright Oak Room, of course, has lots of light oak furnishings, and is brightly decorated in shades of yellow—quite a sight on a sun-drenched morning—while the Cape Cod Room features beautifully crafted pine furniture made by Mike. (He also handcrafted the four-poster yellow pine bed in the Captain's Quarters.) But my favorite is the Dutch Room, all tulips and royal blue colors,

with 1914 furniture made in Gettysburg, Pennsylvania.

A buffet-style continental breakfast of fresh fruit, granola, sweet rolls, juice, and a privately blended coffee that's famous with guests is served in the dining room. Or you can eat out on the long porch and watch boats sail out of the village harbor. Good hearty dinners are served up in area restaurants; Denise can recommend the spot that's right for you.

How to get there: From Chicago, take I–94 north to I–196. Continue north to exit 36 and go north on Blue Star Highway. Turn left on Lake Street and continue to the inn.

Innkeepers: Mike and Denise Simcik

Address/Telephone: 900 Lake Street (mailing address: P.O. Box 881); (616) 857–4346

Rooms: 14, with 1 suite; all with private bath and air conditioning, some with wheelchair access; 3 cottages, 1 with fireplace.

Rates: May 1 through September, $68 to $88 weekdays; $88 to $98 weekends; continental breakfast. Two- to 7-day rates for cottages. Off-season rates available. Two-night minimum on weekends during summer season; 3-night minimum on holiday weekends.

Open: All year.

Facilities and activities: Sitting and dining rooms, great room with wood-burning fireplace. Heated swimming pool, indoor hot tub, garden terrace with pond. Short walk or drive to art galleries, specialty shops, antiques stores, beaches, swimming, boating, and more.

Wickwood Inn

SAUGATUCK, MICHIGAN 49453

Staying at the Wickwood Inn is almost like taking a mini–European vacation. That's because it was inspired by a visit to the grand Duke's Hotel in London.

The result is outstanding. All linens, wallpapers, and fabrics are from British designer Laura Ashley's collections. There are elegant pieces from Baker Furniture's "Historic Charleston" line. Complimentary soaps and shampoos by Crabtree & Evelyn of London are provided in every bathroom.

I discovered more British influences. The library/bar calls to mind an English gentlemen's club. One of my favorite gathering rooms is the sunken garden, with its vaulted beamed ceiling

and greenery everywhere.

These are some of the finest guest rooms I have ever seen. Exquisite walnut, pine, and cherry antique furnishings are outstanding. The Carrie Wicks Suite features a magnificent four-poster Rice bed. In the Master Suite I found a cherrywood canopy bed with an antique hand-crocheted canopy. Its sitting room contains an Empire-style couch, with finely carved swan heads gracing the arms.

For a more casual feel, try Sydney Alexander. This room, with its country French red-and-white Souleiado print, overlooks the inn courtyard; it "feels like a bit of Provence."

Men invariably like the Winter Room, with

its brawny king-sized bed and primitive nautical prints of early sailing ships.

Other rooms feature scalloped wallpaper borders, brass and hand-painted headboards, hand-rubbed paneling, primitive sailing-ship prints, braided rugs, and more.

Morning pampering begins upon awakening, with coffee and your favorite newspaper waiting at your door.

Then make your way down to the sun-dappled Garden Room, where breakfast awaits; it's fit for royalty, with the likes of country ham, cheese and herb *strata*, blueberry French toast, fresh-baked croissants, homemade scones and coffee cake; fruit salads; granola, juices, coffee, and more. It's an ever-changing menu—all prepared from the best-selling *Silver Palate* cookbook of author/innkeeper Julee.

After breakfast head for refreshing breezes at the inn's screened gazebo, which demands nothing of you except to relax in oversized California redwood furniture.

How to get there: From Chicago, take I–94 north to I–196. Continue north to exit 41; turn southwest on Blue Star Highway, just outside Saugatuck. At the fork in the road, take Holland Street (to the right) into town. Turn right at Lucy, then left at Butler to the inn.

Innkeepers: Julie Rosso-Miller and Bill Miller, owners; Corinne Roberts, manager
Address/Telephone: 510 Butler Street; (616) 857–1097
Rooms: 11, with 2 suites; all with private bath and air conditioning. Wheelchair access.
Rates: $155 to $185, single; $165 to $195, double; EPB and evening hors d'oeuvres.
    Off-season rates available.
Open: All year except December 24 and 25.
Facilities and activities: Weekend buffet brunch available. Sunken garden room,
    library/bar. Nearby: beaches of Lake Michigan. Saugatuck specialty stores, antiques
    shops, restaurants, golf, boating, fishing, cross-country skiing.
Business travel: Located about 45 miles west of Grand Rapids/Kent County Airport.
    Corporate rates, meeting room, fax.

Old Harbor Inn
SOUTH HAVEN, MICHIGAN 49090

The Old Harbor Inn sits on the banks of the Black River, in what resembles a re-created New England fishing village. I strolled along cobble-stoned walkways, on boardwalks that skirt the water, and through quaint shops that had names like Bahama Mama's and Flying Colors (both specializing in splashy beachwear).

I also walked to the village docks where charter fishing boats offer coho challenges on Lake Michigan; or you can take up more sedate pursuits, like leisurely sailboat cruises.

This is all part of the charm of South Haven, a lakeside village with an atmosphere that closely resembles that of a California beach town.

If you don't believe me, just go to North Beach during the height of the summer season. It teems with Hawaiian shirts, outrageous bikinis, volleyball games, Frisbee players, and remarkable tans.

I'd like to make the inn my headquarters for all the above fun. That's because guests relax in high South Haven style, enjoying the luxury of their elegant Old Harbor Inn hideaway.

By far my favorite room is Number 6. It's huge, with a handsome sitting area, a fine mix of antique reproductions and contemporary fur-nishings, queen-sized bed, white wicker settee, and a minikitchen.

It also has magnificent views of the Black

River from a long bank of windows on two walls; you can soak up river views while relaxing in a massive indoor hot tub that seems to assure romance.

There's even more: A blue-and-white ceramic-tile fireplace sits in the corner of the room, and French doors open to a walkout balcony facing the river.

Dinner is just a short walk away, aboard *Idler,* an authentic Mississippi riverboat that offers fine cuisine on the lower decks while a complete delicatessen and cocktail lounge occupy the upper deck. Try your luck aboard the famous *Captain Nichols Perch Fleet* sailing daily in season for one of the best-eating fish in the world.

Visit during Labor Day weekend and you'll be treated to the Venetian Festival's lighted-boat parade, with miles of brightly illuminated boats floating down the Black River.

How to get there: Exit I–196 at Phoenix Street. Continue for three stoplights, then turn right to the inn.

Innkeeper: Gwen DeBruyn, manager

Address/Telephone: 515 Williams Street; (616) 637–8480

Rooms: 36, including 6 suites; all with private bath and air conditioning, some with whirlpool bath and kitchenette. Wheelchair access.

Rates: Weekends: $110 to $150; suites, $175 to $205; weekdays: $98 to $125; suites, $160 to $185; EP. Children free when sharing same suite with adults. Two-night minimum on weekends. Off-season rates available.

Open: All year.

Facilities and activities: Indoor pool, hot tub, 22 quaint shops and eateries in village. Nearby: beaches, sailing, sailboarding, spectacular sunsets, U-pick farms, windswept sand dunes, biking, hiking, horseback riding, cross-country skiing, boutiques, art galleries.

Recommended Country Inns® Travelers' Club Benefit: 10 percent discount, Monday–Thursday, or 25 percent discount, Sunday–Thursday, January–March, subject to availability.

$\mathcal{Y}$elton $\mathcal{M}$anor
SOUTH HAVEN, MICHIGAN 49090

My wife, Debbie, and I consider South Haven's North Beach among the finest in the Midwest. In fact, a summer never passes without our bringing our daughters, Kate and Dayne, up to South Haven for a little sand-castle construction and a dip in the water.

Now that the inn has been lavishly restored to its historic *chalet de la mer* ("house of the sea") style, we may have to invent even more excuses for trips up this way.

Originally built in 1873 for two Chicago sisters, the handsome home is a delightful mix of country Victorian and luxury. Many of the furnishings were handcrafted—the pencil-post beds found in many guest rooms were fashioned by Amish craftsmen.

We stayed in the elegant Rose Room—a special treat—with slanted walls tucked under the house's gables, Dutch-lace curtains, and window views of the lake.

Snuggling is easy in the huge king-sized bed adorned with eight pillows and a down comforter, and a large Jacuzzi can be adventurous—without the kids. There's also a sitting room with television, but I've got the feeling it's not often used.

Other rooms offer their own delicate Victorian country stylings, fancy wall coverings, walnut chests, four-poster beds, and more.

Or opt for a room in the new guest house,

just opposite the main house; these luxury retreats have Jacuzzi, fireplace, television, VCR, and more.

A cozy common sitting room warmed by a fireplace is a good spot for conversation during winter months. In summer I especially like to breakfast on the enclosed porch. The meal might include ham soufflés with salsa, stuffed French toast with cream cheese, apple tortes with cheese filling, or homemade poppyseed cake.

And an open "refrigerator room" is always stocked with beverages, freshly baked goodies, and other treats.

This is one of the finest inns around.

How to get there: From the north or south, take I–196 to I–196 Business Loop (Phoenix Street), then turn right on Broadway; at the drawbridge, Broadway turns onto Dyckman; take Dyckman to the stop sign. The inn is located on the left corner of Dyckman and North Shore Drive.

Innkeepers: Elaine Herbert and Robert Kripaitis, owners; Glenda Corona, manager

Address/Telephone: 140 North Shore Drive; (616) 637–5220

Rooms: 17, including 2 suites and a guest house; all with private bath and air conditioning.

Rates: July and August: $125 to $200, single or double, EPB and hors d'oeuvres. Two-night minimum on weekends in high season. Special rates and packages and off-season rates available.

Open: All year.

Facilities and activities: Sitting rooms, enclosed porch-dining area. Nearby: walk to beach, specialty shops; Lake Michigan water activities, including salmon and trout charters; restaurants. U-pick fruit farms, winery tours, cider mills, golf, nature trails, biking, hiking, cross-country skiing, Todd Farm Goose Sanctuary.

The Victorian Villa Guest House
UNION CITY, MICHIGAN 49094

Steady yourself before entering The Victorian Villa for the first time. The grandeur of its elegant Victorian appointments is overwhelming. I could manage only a silly "Wow!"

This Italianate mansion, built in 1876 at the then-whopping cost of $12,000, is nestled in the quaint river village of Union City. Its formal Victorian decor makes it an absolutely perfect romantic hideaway.

The formal entrance hallway, with a winding staircase, is all dark woodwork, highlighted with hurricane lamps, red-velvet curtains, and gingerbread transoms. The "informal" parlor is absolutely elegant. Heavy red-velvet high-back chairs are placed around a marble fireplace. Tall

hurricane lamps and tulip-shaped chandeliers cast a warm glow over the room. One of my favorite touches is a massive gingerbread arch over the doorway.

Guest rooms are equally impressive. The 1890s Edwardian Bedchamber has a headboard almost 8 feet high, with antique quilts and pillows, dark-rose wallpaper, and a marble-topped dresser. The 1860s Rococo Bedchamber has a working fireplace, Tiffany-style lamps, an antique armoire, and a tall Victorian rocker.

Tower suites are decorated in country Victorian and separated by a small sitting room. I like the rough-hewn country feel, with iron-rail beds, exposed brick walls, and round tower windows. And the inn's Carriage House bedchambers are equally impressive. Try the Sherlock Holmes bedchamber, very English with its grand library. (The inn is becoming renowned for its Holmes and Dr. Watson weekends.)

Breakfast in a magnificent formal dining room includes special treats: breakfast meats; concoctions that offer heaping helpings of sausage, cheddar cheese, eggs, and onions; muffins; homemade preserves; Amish pastries; fresh fruits; imported teas; and more. Afternoon English tea also is part of Villa tradition, with scones, tea cookies, fresh pastries, and lots of other extras. And you'll find fancy chocolates on your bed pillows at turndown time.

How to get there: From east or west, take I–94 to I–69 and go south. Turn west on Michigan 60 (exit 25) and continue 7 miles to Union City. There Broadway Street is the town's main street.

Innkeepers: Ronald Gibson, owner; Cindy Shattuck, manager

Address/Telephone: 601 North Broadway Street; (517) 741–7383

Rooms: 10, including 4 suites; all with private bath, 5 with air conditioning. No smoking inn.

Rates: $70 to $140, single; $75 to $145, double; $110 to $145, suites; EPB and afternoon tea/refreshments.

Open: All year.

Facilities and activities: Seven-course nineteenth-century dinners available Friday and Saturday by reservation for $28.50 to $32.50 per person; 5-course picnic basket lunches available by reservation at $22.50 per person; luncheons and afternoon tea, too. Sitting room, parlor, Christmas & Sherlock Holmes gift shop. Gazebo is the site for classical music concerts. Specialty weekends include Victorian Summer Days, murder mysteries, Sherlock Holmes Days, Victorian dinner theater, and more. Nearby: about 500 quality antiques dealers within 25 miles. Six Victorian homes/museums, nineteenth-century historical walking tours, 3 summer stock theaters, country auctions, fishing, summer festivals, golf, cross-country skiing, biking (free tandems to guests).

The Inn at Union Pier
UNION PIER, MICHIGAN 49129

I cannot put out of my mind those cylindrical, ceiling-high, wood-burning Swedish stoves that grace most guest rooms. These colorful tile masterpieces are so difficult to assemble that the inn "imported" experts from Sweden to ensure that they were installed correctly.

But that's only one of the highlights of this elegant inn, located on the eastern shore of Lake Michigan. Just a walk from the sand castles and sweeps of the lake's beaches—only 200 steps from the front door—I enjoyed refined hospitality with all the comforts of a well-appointed country home.

The seventy-plus-year-old beach-resort house has been completely redone in spectacular finery by Mark and Joyce. Especially elegant touches are the huge terra-cotta-and-iron chandeliers in the gathering room. There are also beveled-glass windows casting prisms of sunlight on the pretty pastel colors used to decorate the inn. That massive pagoda-style oriental stove in the gathering room is another Swedish design.

Joyce's guest rooms, located in the Great house (the main building), Four Seasons quarters, and Pier House, are pictures of country elegance. From the polished hardwood floors and comfy country furnishings to those wonderful Swedish stoves and lacy window curtains, I felt like a country squire.

A long wood deck connects the main house

with the Four Seasons; just between them is an outdoor hot tub, a favorite gathering spot for guests.

Breakfast is served in a dining room whose many windows make the meal a bright and happy affair. Tables are adorned with white linen napkins and fresh flowers, some of the innkeepers' attentive touches. There are two courses: first comes fresh fruit, juices, and home-baked breads; then hearty entrees like blueberry pancakes, cinnamon bread—maybe even a Finnish eggs Florentine, a blend of eggs with spinach, cheeses, and sausage. In winter you might enjoy some old-fashioned baked apples, or "egg bakes" with fried tomatoes and all the trimmings, including homemade biscuits and muffins.

Especially mouth-watering are cinnamon butter and blueberry streusel muffins.

Snacks such as iced coffee, lemonade, and cookies are treats for summer guests. Chicken dumpling soup and hot chocolate are often offered at afternoon snacktimes during the cold season. For dinner, Mark and Joyce can recommend many fine area restaurants for dinners to suit your taste.

How to get there: From Chicago, take I–94 north to exit 6. Go north on Townline Road less than a mile to Red Arrow Highway. Turn right; then go a little more than ½ mile and turn left on Berrien. The inn is about 2 blocks ahead on the left side of the road.

Innkeepers: Mark and Joyce Pitts

Address/Telephone: 9708 Berrien (mailing address: P.O. Box 222); (616) 469–4700

Rooms: 16; all with private bath and air conditioning, 11 with Swedish wood-burning stove. Wheelchair access.

Rates: $115 to $185, single or double, EPB. Off-season rates and packages available.

Open: All year.

Facilities and activities: Sitting rooms, enclosed porch, deck and dining area; decktop hot tub, dry sauna. Located in southwestern Michigan's Harbor Country, where lakeshore communities hug Lake Michigan. Walk to breathtaking beaches; drive to antiques shops, U-pick fruit farms. Inn will arrange sailboarding, bicycling, fishing, canoeing, horseback riding, winery tours, cross-country skiing in winter.

Recommended Country Inns® Travelers' Club Benefit: 25 percent discount, Sunday–Thursday, October 1–May 23, excluding holidays and weekends.

*P*ine Garth Inn
UNION PIER, MICHIGAN 49129

When I first came to this stretch of shifting sands in southwestern Michigan almost 20 years ago, all I found was an empty Lake Michigan shoreline, sleepy towns, and small cottages.

How times have changed.

Now there's a huge marina crammed with massive cabin cruisers, luxury townhouses stacked one atop the other, and a small-town "Main Street" that's increasingly filled with tony shops to lure big-city spendthrifts.

And those small cottages—they're more likely to have four-bedroom summer mansions as next door neighbors than somebody's clapboard cabin.

Yet, Harbor Country, a 50-mile swath of white-sand beaches stretching from Michigan City, Indiana, to Harbert, Michigan (and beyond), somehow manages to retain its small-town charm and be a big attraction (especially for stressed-out Chicago folks) at the same time.

In fact, Harbor Country is now the cool weekend place to be, with a wave of lodgings, stores, and restaurants hitting the beaches and environs.

One of the best ways to enjoy the region is by staying at the Pine Garth Inn—the only bed and breakfast in Harbor Country nestled on the lakeshore. Located on a high bluff, six of the seven rooms in the 1905 inn offer breathtaking vistas of Lake Michigan and the hostelry's private white-sand beach below.

Rachel's Room, a favorite of my daughters Kate and Dayne, boasts flamingos perching on the headboard and an entire wall of windows overlooking Lake Michigan—and opening out to a private terrace.

Or go upstairs to Melissa's Room, done in Laura Ashley blues and yellows. Another favorite of the girls because "it's so romantic," it features a canopied bed and deck overlooking the lake. Even the bathroom boasts a lake view.

Of course, the girls love the private beach, reached by walking down a terrace of stairs clinging to the bluff. We looked for shells and ran around in the sand. Spending time with those girls—life can't get much better than that.

How to get there: Take the I–94 to Michigan exit 6, which is the Union Pier exit. Turn right (on Towline Road) and proceed west toward the lake and go to the flashing red light, which is Red Arrow Highway. *Do not turn.* Continue on Townline Road to the next stop sign, which is Lakeshore Road. Turn right and proceed about ¼ mile to the inn (it'll be on your left).

Innkeepers: Russ and Paula Bulin
Address/Telephone: 15790 Lakeshore Road (mailing address: P.O. Box 347);
   (616) 469–1642
Rooms: 7; all with private bath. No smoking inn.
Rates: $110 to $145, single or double, EPB.
Open: All year.
Facilities and activities: Gathering room, screened porch, five decks overlooking Lake
   Michigan, 200 feet of private sugar-sand beach with beach chairs. Short drive to
   New Buffalo arts and antiques stores, skiing, water sports, restaurants.
Recommended Country Inns® Travelers' Club Benefit: Stay two nights, get third night free,
   Sunday–Thursday, November–April, excluding holidays, subject to availability.

Michillinda Beach Lodge
WHITEHALL, MICHIGAN 49461

A few years ago, we spent one of our most enjoyable family weekends ever right here.

Without knowing much about the place, we booked a room at Michillinda Beach Lodge, perched high on a sandy bluff overlooking the Lake Michigan shore, just south of Whitehall/Montague.

Originally a turn-of-the-century country estate built by a Michigan lumber baron, the twenty-two-acre lodge combines spectacular lake vistas with hearty homemade meals. On first glance, it seemed like a perfect location for a relaxing getaway.

We were not disappointed. Our deluxe surf-side cottage unit included three rooms (plenty of roaming space for daughters Kate and Dayne). An entire wall of windows and balcony overlooked the water; we spent lots of time here watching passing sailboats and cargo ships, and the crashing surf.

But scenic Lake Michigan vistas aside, the test of a beachside resort is—the beach. Michillinda boasts a great kiddie beach; the sandy-bottomed shallow extends nearly 50 feet into the water without passing over an adult's waist.

It's perfect for kid water adventures that won't have parents stressed out with worries about possible dangers.

It's also great sandcastle-building and sunbathing territory, as we soon found out.

Kate and Dayne never wanted to leave this place.

The lodge's organized fun includes children's programs and family activities like Wednesday-night Western campfire hoedowns and Friday-night variety shows. Let's not forget the tennis courts, swimming pool, and miniature golf course on the grounds.

And while in the area, you cannot pass up the chance to roam the dunes on Mac Woods' dune rides, in nearby Mears. The souped-up four-wheelers dash passengers over tall sand dunes and past windblown landscape that looks more like the moon than Michigan. It's also a thrill when your kamikaze driver skims the surf at about fifty miles per hour, resulting in splashy thrills for all involved.

How to get there: From Muskegon, take U.S. 31 north and exit at White Lake Drive (Whitehall); go west to Whitehall Road and turn south (left); continue to Michillinda Road, then turn west (right) to the lodge on Lake Michigan's shoreline.

Innkeepers: Don and Sue Eilers
Address/Telephone: 5207 Scenic Drive; (616) 893–1895
Rooms: 49; all with private bath, 32 with lake views, 30 with balcony or deck.
Rates: $135 to $170 per couple, MAP. Weekly rates available. Also children's, extra person's rates.
Open: Mid-May through Labor Day.
Facilities and activities: Full-service dining room, private beach, swimming pool, wading pool, miniature golf, tennis, volleyball court, shuffleboard, basketball, kids' playground. Also bingo, Western campfire program, children's morning games, Friday evening staff variety show, daily coffee hours, Sunday morning meditations. Nearby: a short drive to Lake Michigan dune rides, golf, horseback riding, Michigan's largest water park.

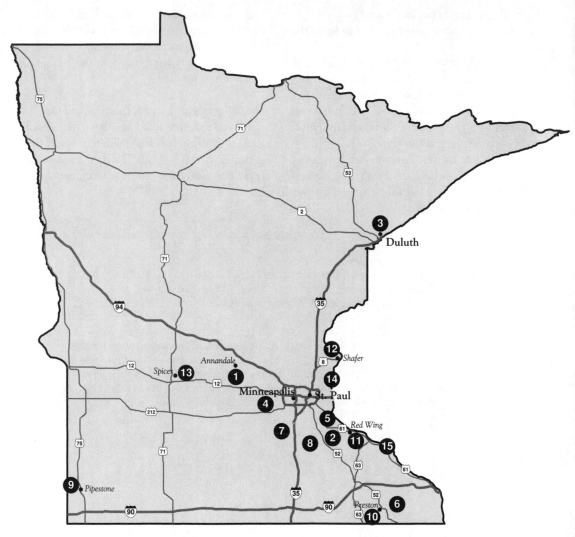

Minnesota

Minnesota

Numbers on map refer to towns numbered below.

Thayer Hotel
ANNANDALE, MINNESOTA 55302

There's something about pioneer hotels and country-Victorian charm that brings to mind tales of the Old West—probably because, like most little boys, I always wanted to be a cowboy.

This 1888 building was built to accommodate overnight passengers and crew of the Soo Line railroad at this turn-of-the-century resort town. (There are scores of lakes within an hour's drive of the hotel.)

Now I know why all the handsome glass transoms above the guest-room doors are etched with Soo Line themes—everything from massive locomotives to the line's attractive logo.

Guest rooms ooze country charm. Spotless and cheery, they're decorated to convey a turn-of-the-century feel. Some have canopy, four-poster, or iron-rail beds. Others have fancy Dutch lace curtains on windows that stretch almost from ceiling to floor. I love the brass clothes hooks and handmade quilts.

Some highlights: The Hunter's Room offers a big brass bed and masculine colors. Kitty's Room features, what else?—lots of cat-related accessories. And there are two whirlpool rooms, too.

Another bow to the twentieth century: There's a sauna on the third floor.

I think you'll agree that the dining room looks much like a frontier restaurant. The woodwork here is rare. It is made from tamarack-swamp trees. You don't find many swamps around here any more.

Sample the hotel's fresh-baked country chicken; it's "finger-licking good." Another mouth-watering delight is a six-ounce filet mignon; it's the hotel's specialty. But Sharon's four-course breakfast is another treat. Imagine a fruit compote with juices, home-baked bread, eggs Ostrich, cheese blintzes, and for sweet tooths—chocolate-covered strawberries.

Perhaps the most interesting new wrinkle at the hotel is the innkeeper herself. Sharon is a psychic, and she'll do readings for guests at their request. In fact, she even offers "psychic weekend" packages; you can spend a few days getting to know yourself better—maybe even peek into your own future.

How to get there: From Minneapolis, take Minnesota 55 northwest to Annandale. The hotel is located on 55, in the heart of the downtown area.

Innkeeper: Sharon Gammell
Address/Telephone: Downtown on Highway 55; (612) 274–8222
Rooms: 11; all with private bath and air conditioning, some with TV.
Rates: $89.95 to $135, single or double, EPB. Special picnic, theater, golf, and cross-country ski package rates.
Open: All year.
Facilities and activities: Full-service restaurant, lounge, sauna. Very good antiquing area.
Nearby: 25 lakes within 5 miles. Snowmobiling and skiing.

Quill and Quilt

CANNON FALLS, MINNESOTA 55009

The first thing I noticed was the oak and Italian-marble fireplace in the parlor. It had a double mantel, and on display were the innkeepers' collection of glass candlesticks and tiny cottages depicting a European village.

Then I wandered into the library—and found a haven that was difficult to leave. The reason: a huge collection of Agatha Christie novels, along with O. Henry short stories and a dollop of Sherlock Holmes.

I decided that the Quill and Quilt felt more like home with each passing minute.

The 1897 house, a delicate Colonial Revival, is country elegant. From its gracious daily social hour to dainty chocolates set on your pillow during evening's turndown time, you'll discover that James and Stacy have lots of pampering in mind.

The guest rooms are charming. The first-floor Quilter's Room has a classic gingerbread panel overhanging the pocket-door transom. Inside you'll enjoy a brass bed, a handmade sampler quilt and a wall hanging that closely matches it, and wood-planked floors. You'll also discover fluffy, color-coordinated bathrobes in your private bath down the hall.

Grandmother's Fan boasts early American hand stenciling on ceiling borders, around windows—the pattern even carries onto curtains. A four-poster bed also looks mighty inviting.

The Covill Suite is bright and dramatic, with seven windows, a lace-canopied, four-poster king-sized bed, and a double whirlpool bath. Relax on the private porch, and you may catch action on the baseball field out back.

Tracy's Room offers a queen-sized iron-and-brass bed, a handmade quilt, and an antique rocking chair.

And after a long day of bike riding, hiking, or just plain wandering around picturesque Cannon Falls, settle down in the Keystone Room for a classic movie.

Breakfast treats include French toast, quich-es, and breakfast meats; the specialty is a crab and asparagus quiche that's a guest favorite. And since James and Stacy are also antiques collectors and dealers, here's your chance to get your questions answered about restoring and collecting historic furniture.

How to get there: From the Twin Cities or Rochester, take U.S. 52 to the Cannon Falls exit (Minnesota 19); then turn east on Minnesota 19 to Seventh Street (about ½ mile), turn north on Seventh to Hoffman, and go east a half block to the inn.

Innkeepers: James and Stacy Smith
Address/Telephone: 615 West Hoffman Street; (507) 263–5507
Rooms: 4, with 1 suite; all with private bath and air conditioning.
Rates: $60 to $130, single or double, EPB. Midweek and holiday packages available.
Open: All year.
Facilities and activities: Social hour, sitting room, library, dining room, recreation room, coffeepots in all rooms, porches. Nearby: Cannon Valley trail (biking, hiking, cross-country skiing); antiques shops, boutiques, historic river towns; golfing, tennis, swimming, boating, canoeing, tubing, downhill skiing.
Recommended Country Inns® Travelers' Club Benefit: 5 percent discount, Monday–Thursday.

Fitger's Inn
DULUTH, MINNESOTA 55802

I sat on a chair in the courtyard on a sweltering summer day and toasted my good fortune. Lake Superior was throwing some cooling breezes over its cold waters. Colorful sailing boats crisscrossed choppy waves. In the distance a large tanker slowly passed across the horizon.

Fitger's Inn surely comes in handy during the dog days of August.

Actually, any time is the right time to visit this handsome hotel. It's located in a brick complex of ten buildings that overlook Lake Superior that housed the Fitger Brewing Company for 115 years until it closed its doors in 1972.

In 1984 major renovation and restoration began, and the results were so appealing that the inn won historical-renovation awards. Now the elegance of the ninenteenth century blends with brewery lore and modern amenities to create fashionable lodgings that are fun, too.

You can obtain walking-tour pamphlets that explain some of the secrets of Fitger's, so I'll only mention a few of the "shouldn't misses":

Start in the lobby. Imagine that exquisite leaded-glass skylight, dating to 1884, in a brewery!

The elegantly crafted, hand-wrought-iron registration desk is also original to the inn. This 1884 masterpiece used to be the brewery's cashier's cage.

Notice all the original oak woodwork, the

oak stairway, and the charcoal drawing of Gambrinus (mythical Flemish king and inventor of beer, naturally) done by a member of the Fitger family in Bremen, Germany.

That shiny copper planter used to be a tasting pot for the brewmaster.

There's a lot more brew lore, but let's head to the guest rooms. They're handsome and tasteful, with antique and reproduction furnishings, elegant wallpaper, and brass lamps.

My favorites are those with floor-to-ceiling windows overlooking the lake, which afford great views of the sunrise.

How to get there: From Minneapolis, take I–35 north to Duluth and follow the Superior Street exit to the inn.

Innkeeper: Donald James, general manager

Address/Telephone: 600 East Superior Street; (218) 722–8826 and Minnesota toll-free (800) 726–2982

Rooms: 60, including 18 suites; all with private bath, air conditioning, TV, and phone. Wheelchair access.

Rates: $82 to $114, single or double; $130 to $245, suites; rates mid-May through November; continental breakfast in lobby. Off-season rates available.

Open: All year.

Facilities and activities: Three restaurants, 2 lounges, and a nightclub. Expansive patio courtyard facing Lake Superior. Nearby: boat excursions, charter fishing, Lake Superior Zoological Gardens, Glensheen historic estate, sailboat rentals, The Depot (art museum), and more.

Business travel: Located a few minutes from downtown Duluth. Corporate rates, meeting rooms, fax.

The Mansion
DULUTH, MINNESOTA 55804

"It's kind of like a medieval castle," Susan said.

Sure is. The entryway Gallery is all massive plaster-cast walls sand-finished to resemble blocks in a great baronial hall, with heavy exposed beams adding to the Middle Ages styling. With its spiky iron wall sconces and floor-to-ceiling torchlights, I expected Sir Lancelot to clank down the hall in his shiny suit of armor.

Warren said that the majestic 1932 Tudor home took four years to build; it has twenty-five rooms, with ten guest rooms. This house made me feel special. An exquisite touch is the library, crafted in English hand-hewn white pine, with a 5-foot-wide fireplace and a tremendous selection of classic books. A cozy spot is a Swedish pine-paneled living room, with another fireplace, brass chandeliers, and leaded-glass windows. Just down the hallway is a large screened porch with arched windows.

Seven guest rooms have a view of Lake Superior. One of my favorites is the South Room, with its high walnut Victorian headboard and matching furnishings, which are at least 150 years old. There's also a working fireplace. Even from here I could hear the sound of crashing waves pounding the beach.

Would you like to have an entire floor of the fabulous mansion to yourself? The master suite offers windows overlooking the lake, including a big bay that's the setting for a king-sized bed, two dressing rooms, and an 18-foot-long black-and-white marble bath with a crystal chandelier.

Nobody goes hungry here. Susan whips up a handsome country breakfast of French toast, bacon, eggs, and sausage—and her special home-baked caramel rolls. Best bets for a Duluth dinner are at the Pickwick and Fitger's.

French doors off the Gallery lead to magnificent grounds fronting the lake. I walked down to the beach and skipped stones off the water.

How to get there: In Duluth, follow U.S. 61 (also called North Shore Drive and London Road). Follow this north and turn into the driveway leading to the mansion.

Innkeepers: Warren and Susan Monson
Address/Telephone: 3600 London Road; (218) 724–0739
Rooms: 11, with 1 suite; 7 with private bath. Wheelchair access.
Rates: $115 to $185, single or double; $195, suite; EPB. Off-season rates available.
Open: Memorial Day through mid-October; most weekends at other times of the year by special arrangement.
Facilities and activities: Sitting and dining rooms, library, screened porch. Six acres of grounds with 525 feet of gorgeous Lake Superior shoreline; lawns, woods, and gardens. An hour's drive from Apostle Islands National Lakeshore.

Christopher Inn
EXCELSIOR, MINNESOTA 55331

A huge white-and-yellow tent covered the expansive, sloping front lawn of the Christopher Inn. Chairs sat under the tent's shade, lined up in crisp rows. Howard busily explained to helpers what else was needed to prepare for a wedding, which was to take place on the front porch of the inn in just a few hours.

Still, amid all the frenetic hubbub, the Christopher Inn was a nice place to be.

It's a palace of Victorian gingerbread gone wild, built in 1887, whose front lawn once stretched 2 blocks to the scenic shore of Lake Minnetonka. Now it's on the National Register of Historic Places.

Guest rooms, graced with Laura Ashley decor, are named after Johnson family members. Peter (who had been helping his dad in the yard with last-second wedding chores), is furnished with a huge mahogany headboard that almost touches the ceiling. Ann has two Victorian Eastlake double beds and hardwood floors and is decorated in cheery country Victorian.

Chris is an explosion of all things blue—wallpaper, rug, curtains, even down to the stripes on chair fabrics.

Third-floor rooms are the largest (also the most modern), with ceilings sloping under the eaves.

The parlor, a favorite gathering spot for guests, is bright and cheerful; it would have to be, with its seven huge windows washing the room with sunlight. Victorian couches and chairs are comfy, and there's a piano for ivory ticklers.

"I always dreamed of having my own private grass tennis court," says Howard, a teaching tennis pro. Lucky for him the inn has one, an original feature of the 1887 home.

Breakfast may mean Joan's eggs Benedict, a fruit goblet (that day's featured melon, strawberries, kiwi, and grapes), peaches and cream, French toast, seafood *strata*, coffee cake, and rolls. You may have to drag your body from the table.

The innkeepers can recommend an in-town restaurant to suit your dinner tastes.

P.S.: Howard was last seen hosing down the front steps just hours before the wedding—not surprising, since the Christopher Inn hosts nearly fifty weddings annually for up to 300 guests. This just might make it the "wedding receptions king" of Midwest country inns.

How to get there: From Minneapolis, take Minnesota 7 west to Excelsior exit. Go to Mill Street (just past bridge) and turn left to the inn.

Innkeepers: Joan and Howard Johnson
Address/Telephone: 201 Mill Street; (612) 474–6816
Rooms: 7; all with private bath, air conditioning, and phone jacks, 2 with fireplace, 1
    with wheelchair access. No smoking inn.
Rates: $80 to $140, single or double, EPB. Midweek discounts up to 20 percent.
Open: All year.
Facilities and activities: Wimbledon-style grass tennis court. Complimentary bicycles.
    Horse-drawn carriage can take guests to dinner at area restaurants in all but winter
    months. Nearby: Old Log Theater, paddle-wheel-boat cruises, antiques stores, cross-
    country skiing, ice-house fishing.

ℛosewood Inn

This handsome Queen Anne, built in 1878, now houses one of the most romantic getaways imaginable. That's not really surprising, since Pam and Dick's other Hastings hideaway (the Thorwood Inn) reflects similar pampering-inspired luxuries.

As soon as you see Rebecca's Room, you'll get the idea. This is a stirring romantic retreat, with a marvelous all-marble bathroom highlighted by a double whirlpool bath resting in front of its own fireplace. There's a second fireplace opposite an inviting four-poster antique bed. And a four-season porch offers views of the inn's rose garden.

Or consider the Vermillion Room, with a see-through fireplace that warms both an ornate brass bed and a sunken double whirlpool bath.

If you want shameful opulence, try the Mississippi Room. As large as an apartment, it offers skylights over a sleigh bed, its own fireplace, baby grand piano, bathroom with both a copper tub and double whirlpool—and a meditation room where "people can either relax or be creative," said the innkeeper. "We've even had several guests do paintings here." A collection of some of those works are hanging about the room.

The breakfasts are added treats. And the mealtime flexibility is unusual: They'll serve whenever guests are hungry, between 6:00 and 11:00 A.M. Eat in one of the dining areas, on the porch, in your room, or in bed—the choice is yours.

The feast might include homemade breads and blueberry muffins, cheese *strata*, wild-rice gratiné, cherry strudel, raspberry coffee cake. . . . Aren't you hungry just thinking about all this food?

Another chance to feast: The inn offers gourmet dinners in the formal parlor—or in your own room. The meal might feature delights such as beef Wellington and a raspberry strudel with chocolate and vanilla sauce. The cost is $44.70 to $56.70 per couple.

The innkeepers are also happy to arrange an in-room "hat box" supper, or to package a delightful evening with dinner at one of the town's fine restaurants, including limousine service. And they occasionally arrange dinner at the inn featuring Minnesota-accented recipes accompanied by live chamber music.

How to get there: From the Twin Cities, take U.S. 61 south into Hastings and exit at Seventh Street; then turn left and proceed 1½ blocks to the inn.

Innkeepers: Pam and Dick Thorsen

Address/Telephone: Seventh and Ramsey; (612) 437–3297

Rooms: 8, with 4 suites; all with private bath and air conditioning; TV and phone upon request. No smoking inn.

Rates: $87 to $217, single or double, EPB. Two-night minimum on weekends. Special packages available.

Open: All year.

Facilities and activities: Dinner by reservation. Sitting room, parlor, library, porch. Nearby: historic river-town architecture, arts and crafts, stores, antiques shops, specialty boutiques, Mississippi River water activities, bluff touring on bikes and hikes, St. Croix Valley Nature Center, Alexis Bailly vineyard winery, downhill and cross-country skiing, snowshoeing, golf.

Thorwood Inn
HASTINGS, MINNESOTA 55033

"People seem to enjoy the morning breakfast baskets more than anything else," Pam told me as we sat in the parlor of her gracious inn. "It has grown into quite a tradition."

Once when she mentioned to a repeat couple that she'd been thinking of changing that practice, "They immediately spun around, with dismayed looks on their faces, and said, 'You wouldn't.' I knew right then we could never change."

Lucky for us. The breakfast basket, delivered to the door of your room, is stuffed with platters of fresh fruits, omelets or quiches, pull-apart pastries and rolls, home-baked breads, coffee, juice, and more. As Dick says, "Pace yourself."

It's all part of the pampering the innkeepers lavish on guests.

A complimentary bottle of wine from the local Alexis Bailly vineyards and snacks of fruits and pastries continue the Thorwood notion of caring for guests.

The home, fashioned in ornate Second Empire style and completed in 1880, is a testament to the innkeepers' restoration prowess. When I saw the marble fireplaces, ornate rosettes and plaster moldings on the ceilings, and elegant antiques and surroundings, it was difficult to imagine that the house had once been cut up into several apartments.

For fine detail, just look to the music room.

Pam said that maple instead of oak was used for flooring because it provided better resonance for live piano concerts, popular with society crowds at the turn of the century.

One of my favorite guest rooms is Captain Anthony's, named for the original owner's son-in-law, who operated a line of steamboats on the Mississippi. It has a canopied four-poster brass bed and Victorian rose-teal-and-blue Laura Ashley fabrics. The Lullaby Room (the house's historic nursery) has a double whirlpool bath. "Guests in this room feel like they're in the tree-tops," Pam said, as she looked out a tall window.

Maureen's Room is another popular choice, with its unusual rag-rug headboard, fireplace, country-quilted bed, and double whirlpool bath.

Or try Sarah's Room, with its bedroom-sized loft, window views of the Mississippi River Valley, and skylight over a queen-sized brass bed.

But perhaps the ultimate retreat is the Steeple Room, with its see-through fireplace and double whirlpool—set in the house's steeple. The steeple rises 23 feet above the tub and boasts a ball chandelier hanging from the pinnacle.

How to get there: From LaCrosse, take U.S. 61 north to Hastings; then turn left on Fourth Street and proceed to inn.

Innkeepers: Pam and Dick Thorsen

Address/Telephone: Fourth and Pine; (612) 437–3297

Rooms: 7; all with private bath and air conditioning. Wheelchair access. No smoking inn.

Rates: $87 to $157, single or double, EPB. Can arrange for pet-sitters. Special package rates available.

Open: All year.

Facilities and activities: "Hat box" dinners in your room. Nearby: walking tour of historical area just blocks away. Quaint Mississippi River town with specialty and antiques shops, several good restaurants. Parks and nature trails; also river, streams, lakes, and all sorts of summer and winter sports.

Mrs. B's Historic Lanesboro Inn
LANESBORO, MINNESOTA 55949

Imagine a five-course *nouvelle* meal featuring the likes of a delicious homemade soup made with parsnips, potato, and olive oil; salad with sun-dried tomatoes, fresh artichokes, and leafy greens; *spaetzle* (German dumplings); boneless turkey stuffed with wild rice and fresh vegetables; and desserts like triple chocolate cake with dark chocolate, coffee, and caramel garnish.

That's the kind of gustatory delights that Chef Allen Schleusener, who is classically trained in Heartland cuisine, has planned for visitors to this charming destination.

Historic Lanesboro is surrounded by high bluffs covered with tall hardwood trees. In fact, a 500-foot bluff, looming just beyond the inn,

almost blocks the town's main street.

The 1872 inn has a big canopy shading tall arched merchant windows facing the street. Anyone is welcome to play a tune on the sitting room's baby grand piano; there's also a big brick fireplace with comfy high-back chairs and sofa nearby.

The guest rooms are comfortable and cozy, with pine headboards and canopy beds, quilts, rose-floral-print wallpaper, writing desks, and other antique pine reproductions. One room has a headboard with two hand-carved dragon's heads on its posts. Some of them have outside balconies, and it's fun to sit out on a ladder-back rocking chair and look out over the Root River behind the inn to the high bluffs beyond. And new terraces have been added onto the back of the historic building.

I recommend a walk along a hiking trail that crosses the old bridge and faces the bluff. Then you'll really get a feel for the bluff country. It's probably also a good way to work off Allen's breakfasts, which include treats like blueberry buttermilk pancakes, Canadian shoulder bacon, and fresh fruits.

How to get there: Take Minnesota 16 to Lanesboro. In town, turn north on Parkway and proceed to the inn.

Innkeepers: Bill and Mimi Sermeus

Address/Telephone: 101 Parkway; (507) 467-2154

Rooms: 10; all with private bath and air conditioning. Wheelchair access. TV and phone on request.

Rates: $58 to $68, single or double, weekdays; $85 to $95, single or double, weekends; EPB. Lodging, MAP package available Wednesday through Sunday (5-course, 3-hour gourmet dinner, $22.95). No credit cards.

Open: All year.

Facilities and activities: Gourmet dinners; Friday tea time. Sitting room, porches. Nearby: bike and cross-country ski trails, antiques shops, bluffs, golf, tennis, fishing. In heart of state hardwood forest.

Schumacher's New Prague Hotel
NEW PRAGUE, MINNESOTA 56071

I stepped into Schumacher's New Prague Hotel through a hand-stenciled door and thought I'd somehow been caught in a time warp, ending up in old-time Bavaria.

John and Kathleen are very proud of their beautiful inn, and rightly so. It looks similar to many European country hotels I've stayed at. A peaceful air of rich handiwork, fine craftsmanship, wonderful imported Old World antiques, and a deep commitment to dining excellence are what make Schumacher's one of the best there is.

Built in 1898, the hotel has an ornate European-style lobby, with pressed-tin ceilings, rich floral wallpaper, fine European antiques, and oriental rugs that cover original maple hardwood floors. A wonderful front desk is original, too.

John commissioned renowned Bavarian folk artist Pipka to design the graceful stenciled scenes that enliven guest, lobby, and restaurant rooms.

Upstairs are eleven individually decorated guest rooms, named in German for the months of the year, and furnished with Old World trunks, chairs, beds, and wardrobes; several have fireplaces, and all boast double whirlpool baths. More authentic touches include eiderdown-filled pillows and comforters, and 100-percent-cotton bedding and tablecloths, which were purchased in Austria, Czechoslovakia, and Germany.

August is my favorite, with its king-sized

bed, primitive Bavarian folk art, and a red wild-flower theme carried out in stenciled hearts on the pine floor and on an ornately decorated wardrobe. You'll feel as if you've been transported to southern Germany.

And *Mai* has a high-canopied double bed, reached by a small ladder; the design inside the canopy features storybook-style figures from newlyweds to senior couples. John places a complimentary bottle of imported German wine and two glasses in each room, just one of the many thoughtful touches.

Guess who's the chef? John is a classically trained cooking-school graduate who specializes in excellent Old World cuisine—with a Czech flair. His extensive menu features more than fifty-five dinner entrees.

"What's your pleasure? I'll cook you a feast!" he said. A typical Central European meal includes *romacka* (cream of bean soup with dill) and Czech roast duck served with red cabbage, potato dumplings, and dressing, with apple strudel for dessert. Then you're ready to browse in the hotel's gift shop, which offers handmade gifts and glassware from Central Europe.

How to get there: From Minneapolis, take 35 W south; exit on County Road 2. Continue to Minnesota 13 and turn south; proceed directly into New Prague; the hotel is on the left.

Innkeepers: John and Kathleen Schumacher
Address/Telephone: 212 West Main Street; (612) 758–2133
Rooms: 11; all with private bath, air conditioning, and phone, some with gas fireplace and hair dryer.
Rates: $107 to $130, single or double, Sunday through Thursday; $132.50 to $165, single or double, Friday through Saturday; EP. Special packages and senior citizens' rates available. Personal checks from Minnesota only.
Open: All year except Christmas Eve and Christmas Day.
Facilities and activities: Full-service restaurant with wheelchair access. Bavarian bar, European gift shop, travel agency. Nearby: drive to cross-country and downhill skiing, swimming, golf, boating, fishing, biking, hiking, orchard, museums, racetrack, amusement park.

The Archer House
NORTHFIELD, MINNESOTA 55057

On my return to The Archer House, I once again realized that this is one charming hotel.

First let me tell you that The Archer House is just a short walk from the local bank that the Jesse James gang attempted to rob in 1876. Yep, the Great Northfield Raid was a desperado disaster that virtually ended Jesse's reign of terror on the frontier.

This is a terrific restoration job. Doors are left open to unoccupied rooms so that browsers can appreciate the rooms' turn-of-the-century charm. Each room reflects a personality of its own, with ruggedly elegant country warmth. I loved the hand-crafted pine furniture, some with rosemaling, and the brass beds, handmade quilts

done by local artisans, and embroidered samplers.

I stayed in the Manawa Room, done in a Dutch-country style, with blue floors, stencils on walls, a pine bed with blue-and-white-point star quilt, and a needlepoint sampler. I'm sure my room's Dutch hex sign has brought me good luck.

New suites all feature inviting whirlpool baths, and some have a lovely view of the Cannon River, which is sporting a new riverwalk.

The pace here is unhurried and casual, making it an ideal place to relax amid the homespun graciousness of this interesting and pretty Minnesota town.

Especially during September, when Jesse's gang "robs" the local bank in a colorful festival celebrating "The town that Defeated Jesse James."

How to get there: From the Twin Cities, take I–35 south to the Northfield exit. Follow Highway 19 east to the first stoplight. Go east for 2 blocks. Turn left onto Division Street and go 2 blocks.

The Archer House is on the left. From Rochester, take Highway 52 north to Cannon Falls. Then take Highway 19 west 11 miles to Northfield. Go straight onto Division Street. The Archer House is on the right.

Innkeeper: Bob Carel
Address/Telephone: 212 Division Street; (507) 645–5661 or Minnesota toll-free
  (800) 247–2235
Rooms: 36, with 19 suites; all with private bath, air conditioning, TV, and phone.
Rates: $45 to $150, single or double, EP.
Open: All year.
Facilities and activities: Tavern restaurant, deli, ice-cream and coffee shop, bookstore, specialty stores. Nearby: Carleton and St. Olaf colleges and Northfield Arts Guild offer programs of theater, art, concerts, films, and lectures. Hiking, biking, canoeing on Cannon River, tennis, swimming, cross-country skiing, ice skating (in season).

The Calumet

PIPESTONE, MINNESOTA 56164

The Calumet Hotel is located in the historic district of tiny Pipestone, a wisp of a town located in the heart of traditional lands of the Dakota Yankton–Sioux nation. I drove just outside of town and stood gazing over the "grass prairies," still a massively empty, windy landscape—the beginning of the Great Plains.

Native Americans mined pipestone at ancient quarries nearby. The soft stone, considered sacred, still is used for ceremonial pipes. Visitors can view the quarries and local Indians mining the stone as their ancestors did before them.

This pioneer legacy continues at the inn, a massive pink-and-red quartzite building made of hand-chiseled, locally quarried stone, completed in 1888. Easily its most outstanding feature is a four-story exposed red-stone wall that dominates the lobby.

Everything here seems larger than life. I walked up a magnificent four-story staircase of oak and maple to reach my room. A high skylight washed the stairs in warm sunlight. (I counted ninety-two steps. Don't worry, there's an elevator, too.)

My room was classically restored to Victorian elegance, with marble-topped dressers, a velvet-covered rocking chair, and two walnut beds sporting high headboards. Later I found out that antiques brokers were commissioned to seek out the nineteenth-century pieces. They searched old British estates, Colorado gold-rush mansions, Carolina plantations, and historic New England homes to uncover the splendid period pieces.

The rooms have names like Paradise Regained and Abigail's Dream. My favorite is the Choctaw Indian Walk, with a wall of exposed brick and Native American artifacts and designs.

Throughout the restored rooms I found fainting couches, chairs of golden oak built extra wide to accommodate ladies' Victorian-era bustles, claw-footed dressers, and antique prints and photos. The hotel quickly became one of my favorites. A photo album at the front desk helps you choose what style room most appeals to you.

The inn is enjoying a highly rated renaissance through its restoration efforts. Its restaurant was named one of the top fifty dining establishments in Minnesota. And make sure to wander on the edge of the Great Plains, where the nearby Pipestone National Monument (ancient Indian pipestone quarries a short drive away) is fascinating. I stayed there for hours.

How to get there: I-75 and Minnesota 30 and 23 lead into Pipestone, located in extreme southwestern Minnesota. Once in town, make your way to East Main Street and continue to the corner of Hiawatha and the hotel.

Innkeeper: Cheryl Kruse, manager

Address/Telephone: Corner of Main and Hiawatha; (507) 825–5871 or (800) 535 7610

Rooms: 38 (15 antique, 23 modern); all with private bath and air conditioning. Wheelchair access.

Rates. $46 to $90, single; $53 to $90, double; continental breakfast.

Open: All year.

Facilities and activities: Full-service dining room, lounge, pub, gift shop featuring Native American crafts. In Pipestone historic district; walk to other historic structures. Nearby: a short drive to Pipestone National Monument, Upper Midwest Indian Cultural Center, Pipestone County Museum, health club, Hole-in-the-Wall ski area.

Recommended Country Inns® Travelers' Club Benefit: 15 percent discount, subject to availability.

The Jail House
PRESTON, MINNESOTA 55965

"Slumber in Our Slammer."

That's how "wardens" Marc and Jeanne invite guests to enjoy their handsome inn, whose not yet fully restored exterior should in no way inhibit guests from luxuriating in lavish surroundings inside.

This was once the Fillmore County Jail, built in 1869 and housing unwilling guests until 1971. Get the innkeepers to tell you the story about prisoners who chiseled their way to freedom by using dinner spoons.

Once modern-day guests step inside, they won't want to leave. The innkeepers have done a magnificent job of transforming this historic building into one of the more ornate Minnesota inns, complete with authentic period antiques dating from 1860 to 1890.

Of course, Marc and Jeanne couldn't resist keeping one guest room looking much as it might have during its jail heyday. The Cell Block is all steel doors and iron bars—you even sleep behind bars. One big difference—you have the keys. And I doubt that prisoners had a walk-through shower leading to a double whirlpool tub, fluffy quilted beds, rocking chairs, and other decidedly un-convict niceties.

What's ironic is that this room looks like the innkeepers have done the least to it, but it caused the most backbreaking work.

Guest rooms are named for former sheriffs

who served at the jail. Among my favorites: the original courtroom now fashioned into a huge suite with a sitting room and double whirlpool; and the Drunk Tank, boasting Eastlake antiques and original wide-plank pine flooring.

Back to inn antiques: Consider an old china tub weighing nearly 1,000 pounds; an 1880s, spoon-carved, three-piece bedroom set; and an antique copper bath made in Chicago.

Breakfast is served in the skylit basement and might include baked egg casseroles, home-baked breads and muffins, and more—the "Cook's Choice" doesn't allow any "convict" to go away hungry.

One problem with this "jail house." As soon as "prisoners" are paroled and sent home, they begin to plot another caper that will land them back in the slammer!

How to get there: From the north, take Minnesota 52 south into Preston; turn right on County Road 12 and continue to Houston Street; then turn right to the inn.

Innkeepers: Marc and Jeanne Sather

Address/Telephone: 109 Houston 3 Northwest; (507) 765–2181

Rooms: 12, with 1 suite; all with private bath and air conditioning, TV and phone on request.

Rates: Weekdays: $40 to $115, single or double; weekends: $69 to $149; EPB weekends, continental breakfast weekdays.

Facilities and activities: Two common areas with stone fireplaces, parlor, basement dining room. Nearby: state parks, biking, hiking, cross-country skiing, Amish country tours, trout fishing, antiques and Amish crafts stores, cave tours, golf, historic sites, museums, canoeing, tubing, bird watching, local summer theater.

Pratt-Taber Inn
RED WING, MINNESOTA 55066

Garrison Keillor wrote, "When I search for a peaceful moment, I will think of sitting on the porch of the Pratt-Taber Inn." I couldn't agree more.

I opened the door of this elaborate Italianate mansion and walked into a world of old-time elegance. The thirteen-room mansion, built in 1876 by one of Red Wing's first bankers, has been restored to a special magnificence in this historic river town crested by high bluffs of the Mississippi River. I was impressed by the immense leaded-glass doors that open into a sitting room full of Victorian finery.

Inside, I admired fine details like feather-painted slate fireplaces and fancy gingerbread woodwork. Rich woods of butternut and walnut provide a graceful backdrop for priceless 1870s antique furnishings that the innkeepers have spent years collecting. And it's so peaceful here, I like to simply daydream on the porches or in front of a roaring fire.

Polly's Room might be the guest favorite. This elegant suite boasts fine Victorian furnishing (consider an 1870s marble-topped dresser, 1850s gentlman's chair and Chippendale desk) and a cozy foreplace that burns birch logs.

Gourmet breakfasts might include eggs benedict, quiches, sausage and ham roll-ups, and more. It's usually taken in the Victorian dining room, but just a note on the kitchen table the night before will fetch you breakfast in bed or on the inn's screened porch. Don't pass up the sumptuous seafood or steak dinners served in the elegant Victorian dining room at the St. James Hotel, in the heart of town.

I want you to try and spot the hidden Murphy bed in the library. But it's no fair asking Jim or Karen for hints. Find it yourself.

How to get there: Take U.S. 61 into Red Wing and proceed to Dakota. Turn west; then turn north on West Fourth to the home located at the corner of Fourth and Dakota.

Innkeepers: Jim and Karen Kleinfeldt

Address/Telephone: 706 West Fourth; (612) 388–5945

Rooms: 6, with 1 suite; 2 with private bath.

Rates: $97.46 to $120.45, single or double, EPB.

Open: All year.

Facilities and activities: Parlors, front porch, screened side porch, bikes for guests. Nearby: riverboat dinner excursions on Mississippi River, trolley-car rides, horse-and-buggy rides, cross-country and downhill skiing at Frontenac Ski Area and Welch Village, 5 golf courses, bingo on Prairie Island Indian Reservation. Also, Red Wing antiques shops, specialty shops, art galleries, T. B. Sheldon Auditorium, bluffs to drive and climb.

St. James Hotel
RED WING, MINNESOTA 55066

E. F. told me that the St. James Hotel was one of the first fine Victorian hotels in the Midwest. It was built in 1875, and its elegance reflected Red Wing's prosperity as the world's largest wheat market at the time.

Now Red Wing is just a historic Mississippi river town. But the St. James's tradition of refined Victorian tastes continues.

"Quiet elegance" is the phrase that best describes the guest rooms. Each is uniquely decorated; I especially like the fancily scrolled wall borders, so popular back in the hotel's heyday. In fact, they set the color tones for coordinated wallpapers and handmade quilts.

Authentic antiques and fine reproductions re-create a long-ago era of luxury. E. F. has a great collection of beds—massive four-poster beds, Jenny Lind spindles, shiny brass beds, and more. Unique gingerbread window treatments splash spiky shafts of sunlight into rooms.

In some rooms a view of the Mississippi River and surrounding high bluffs is a big treat.

You'll be spoiled after just one day at the St. James. A complimentary chilled bottle of wine welcomes you to your room, and there'll be a steaming pot of coffee and morning paper delivered to your door.

I like all the choices for dining because there is something for every mood and taste: a light snack at the Veranda Café, with alfresco dining on a porch overlooking the Mississippi; or dinners featuring fillet of Canadian walleye and other gustatory delights at the Port of Red Wing, decorated to recapture the adventure of the riverboat era.

Then it's up to Jimmy's, the hotel's English-style pub—a great way to end the day.

(*Note:* Ask for a historic room if that is your preference; there are several with modern decor.)

How to get there: Take U.S. 61 into Red Wing, where it becomes Main Street; the hotel's address is 406 Main Street.

Innkeeper: E. F. Foster
Address/Telephone: 406 Main Street; (612) 388–2846
Rooms: 60; all with private bath, air conditioning, TV, and phone, 10 with whirlpool bath. Wheelchair access.
Rates: $75 to $155, single or double, EP.
Open: All year.
Facilities and activities: Two dining areas, 13 specialty shops, two lounges. Nearby: walking and driving tours of historic riverfront town; antiques and specialty shops; Mississippi River water sports and activities.
Business travel: Located 44 miles south of downtown St. Paul, 55 miles south of downtown Minneapolis. Corporate rates, meeting rooms, fax.

Country Bed & Breakfast
SHAFER, MINNESOTA 55074

"I'm so tired from collecting sap, and I still have to boil it down today. Then I'll just go to sleep."

Poor Budd. I'd stopped by his thirty-five-acre country spread and caught him in the middle of his busy chores. But that didn't stop him or Lois from showcasing their overwhelming country hospitality. After a few minutes with them, I felt as if I'd returned home after a long journey away from this pretty farmstead.

Both Lois and Budd showed me around the place. Lois pointed to the chicken coop. "I'm so proud of my chickens," she said. "I got to have lots of them. You know, fresh eggs for breakfast."

Budd and I laughed. "Yeah, we give you an

$18 breakfast here for nothing," he said, "and you can eat as much as you want."

This is no mere boast. Country breakfast features Swedish egg-coffee; omelets with ham, sausage, or bacon—Budd's specialty; Lois's buttermilk pancakes with homemade maple syrup from their groves out back; and raspberries and strawberries from Budd's organic garden. "If you leave here hungry, it's your own fault," he joked. In the evening they suggest that guests take a short drive to Marine on St. Croix for delicious homemade dinners at Crabtree's Kitchen.

Their farmhouse is a quaint 1881 red-brick Victorian. Lois, who grew up here, pointed out original plank floors and a big wood-burning stove in a country kitchen. A comfortable sitting room has a sofa, chair, and television.

Guest rooms upstairs are pictures of farm-country charm. Lois has covered plank floors with scatter rugs; she also uses some white wicker chairs and other country antiques, sheer white curtains on tall windows that flood rooms with sunlight, and pretty print wallpapers.

The Country Estates room is especially inviting, with its antique double bed, jade green and rose colors, and a claw-foot tub.

I lazed part of the day away on the front porch—Budd, my dad, and I just "stirring up the pot" with our stories. There's also a back deck where you can just sit and breathe the fresh country air.

This is the perfect place to retreat to country solitude. And you couldn't find two kinder hosts. In fact, I already missed Budd and Lois five minutes after we left . . . and the dog and the ducks and the chickens and . . .

How to get there: Enter Shafer on County Road 21. Go through town 1 mile. Then turn left on Ranch Trail and proceed to the second farm on the left (the red-brick house).

Innkeepers: Lois and Budd Barott
Address/Telephone: 32030 Ranch Trail Road; (612) 257–4773
Rooms: 3; 2 with private bath, all with air conditioning. No smoking inn.
Rates: $55, single; $95, double; EPB. No credit cards.
Open: All year.
Facilities and activities: Porch. Spacious tree-shaded lawn. Maple groves. Walking in surrounding fields. Nearby: restaurants; Ki-Chi-Saga Lake; the Sunrise and St. Croix rivers with riverboat cruises, tubing, canoeing, swimming, fishing; 2 downhill ski resorts. Cross-country ski and nature trails at Wild River State Park. Also antiques, pottery shops in area. Five miles west of historic Taylors Falls.

Spicer Castle

SPICER, MINNESOTA 56288

"The house was built in 1893 by the grandfather of Allen and Marti," the inn's manager told me. "It was part of the Medayto Farm, where he experimented with new agricultural techniques."

What a gorgeous piece of country, too. Hugging the shore of huge Green Lake, Spicer Castle stands sentinel on a craggy bluff overlooking the blue water. I gazed out at the lake from the inn's back porch, watching a storm brew far out over the waves.

I asked how it got its name. "Fishermen used the house as a landmark to locate good fishing spots," I was told. "Before long, references to 'Spicer's Castle' began appearing on fishing maps

of the area. The name just stuck."

That's not surprising. It's an imposing house, sitting on five acres with a proud, Tudor-style profile that includes a tall tower resembling those found at ancient castles.

Inside, the parlor has a very masculine feel, with half-timbered ceilings, brick fireplace, tapestry rugs. It's hard to imagine, but all the furnishings are original to the home. Most of the oil paintings, watercolors, and charcoals were done by family members. I browsed through family photo albums. It's even family-member musicians who take up the violin or sit at the piano to provide tunes for dancing.

Guest rooms, comfortable and cozy, have

the same warm family feel to them. Mason's Room has a four-poster bed graced with a paisley quilt, the likes of which I hadn't seen before. Frances's Room boasts an iron-rail bed and a Victorian dresser. Jessie's sports a walnut Jenny Lind spindle bed.

Amy's Room and Ruth's Room have outside decks that overlook the water. And families might be interested in the log cabin or cottage that rest on the handsome grounds.

But the most spectacular room (one of the most popular with guests, anyway), is the newly refurbished Eunice's Room; it's bright and sunny, with fourteen windows, natural woodwork, a turn-of-the-century swinging bed, and a two-person whirlpool tub. Ooh-la-la!

Mornings are great fun because they mean breakfast on the dining porch overlooking the lake. You may enjoy Belgian waffles, eggs Benedict, homemade muffins, juice, and coffee. Ginger said that guests sometimes receive morning salutes from captains passing in their boats.

Now that Spicer's has its own pontoon boat, it offers dinner cruises on Green Lake. What a great way to enjoy the sunset.

How to get there: From Minneapolis, take U.S. 12 west to Minnesota 23 and turn north into Spicer. Turn right on County 95 (Indian Beach Road, which is the lake road) and follow to the sign that tells you where to turn onto the access road reaching the castle.

Innkeepers: Allen and Marti Latham, owners; Mary Swanson, manager
Address/Telephone: Off Minnesota 23 on Green Lake (mailing address: P. O. Box 307); (612) 796-5870
Rooms: 8, plus 1 cottage and 1 cabin; all with private bath.
Rates: $50 to $120, single; $60 to $130, double; EPB.
Open: All year, but weekends only mid-September through mid-May.
Facilities and activities: Afternoon tea, sitting room. Located on beautiful Green Lake. Spacious porch and grounds. Nearby: restaurants, sandy beach, fishing, hiking, golf, cross-country skiing.

The Lowell Inn
STILLWATER, MINNESOTA 55082

I remember The Lowell Inn for its china cats.

That's right. I walked into my enormous French Provincial–style room only to find a little "kitty" curled up at the foot of my bed. Cats and kittens are in every guest room; Arthur and Maureen believe they add homey warmth to the elegant rooms.

It's not something I expected to find here. The inn, which opened on Christmas Day 1930, is built in a formal Colonial Williamsburg style. The huge veranda is supported by thirteen tall white pillars that represent the original thirteen colonies, and each bears a pole flying respective state flags.

Stepping inside, I saw an exquisite mixture of Colonial and French Provincial antiques. Many of the inn's gorgeous collectibles are part of the private collection of Nelle Palmer, wife of the original owner.

The dining rooms are handsome, dotted with Dresden china, Capodimonte porcelain, Sheffield silver, and more. They also exhibit a bit of a classy atmosphere. The George Washington Room is adorned with hand-crested Irish linen, authentic Williamsburg ladder-back chairs, and portraits of George and Martha. Still another surprise is an indoor trout pool in the Garden Room. You can select your dinner by pointing to the fish of your choice. Huge polished agate tables accentuate the earthy quality of the room.

Easily my favorite is the Matterhorn Room, all done in deep, rich woods and authentic Swiss wood carvings. The inn's showpiece, as far as I'm concerned, is a life-sized eagle hand-carved by a seventy-eight-year-old Swiss master wood carver.

Dinners here might begin with Swiss *escargots* (pure-white snails picked from vineyards in France and Switzerland), followed by a large chilled green salad with pickled relishes; and, for an entree, *fondue Bourguignonne* (beef or shrimp individually seasoned with six different sauces).

Guest rooms are individually decorated in a combination of Colonial and French Provincial styles, with soft colors, frills, mirrors, antiques, and goose-down comforters; four have inviting Jacuzzis. A complimentary bottle of wine in my room was a welcome surprise, another pampering touch that pleases guests.

How to get there: From Minneapolis–St. Paul, take State Road 36 east. It changes into Stillwater's Main Street. Turn left on Myrtle and go about a block to Second Street.

Innkeepers: Arthur and Maureen Palmer
Address/Telephone: 102 North Street; (612) 439–1100
Rooms: 21, including 2 suites; all with private bath, air conditioning, and phone.
Rates: Weekdays: $95 to $170, single or double, EP. Weekends: $219 to $299, single or double, AP.
Open: All year.
Facilities and activities: Full-service restaurant with wheelchair access. Nearby: many quality antiques, gift, and specialty shops; good town bakeries; cave tours. Not far from the Mississippi River. The inn can arrange River Run excursions May to September. Winter cross-country skiing at O'Brien State Park. Downhill skiing at 3 resorts.

The Rivertown Inn
STILLWATER, MINNESOTA 55082

I've had my eye on The Rivertown Inn for quite some time. The stately Victorian home, built in 1882 by a prominent local lumberman, sits on a hill high above Stillwater, a lovely town hugging the banks of the scenic St. Croix River.

But it wasn't until Judy and Chuck bought the historic home and completed much-needed restoration work that its turn-of-the-century charm emerged. Now I had to include it in my book.

Judy pointed out original brass chandeliers, which were once illuminated by gas. I marveled at the masterful dining room table that seemed to stretch out forever.

"This table came from a castle in England,"

she said. "I have four more leaves. It seats eighteen people."

Intricate gingerbread fretwork adorns many inn rooms. "It's all original to the house," Judy told me. "We found it stored in rows out back in the carriage house. It was quite a discovery."

As we talked, lovely violin music played. It was a perfect accompaniment for exploring the guest rooms.

My favorite is John O'Brien's Room, with its huge oak-manteled tile fireplace, tall walnut Victorian headboard and dresser, parquet floors, and splash of gingerbread. It has the feel of a room in an exclusive English men's club.

I also love its double whirlpool bath.

Faith's Room is another gem, with its own fireplace, marble-topped dresser, washstand, and sitting area. But special features here are an astounding 11-foot-high walnut headboard and a double whirlpool bath.

More highlights: There's a double whirlpool in Melissa's Room, which also boasts an antique brass tube bed; Julie's Room has a walnut bed, corner whirlpool, and view of the river; and Patricia's Room is done in golden oak, has a whirlpool tub, and looks out over Stillwater's many historic steeples.

Here's the newest addition: Cover Park Manor—an 1890s country Victorian home with four guest suites, all with whirlpool bath and gas fireplace.

Judy and Chuck will serve breakfast in the dining room, on the porch (if weather permits), or, if you prefer, in your room. Count on home-made pastries like caramel rolls, puffs, flans, home-baked breads, fresh fruit, and mouth-watering entrees.

How to get there: From Minneapolis, take Minnesota 36 east to Stillwater. Turn left on Olive Street; go up the hill to Fifth Street and the inn.

Innkeepers: Judy and Chuck Dougherty, owners; Janic Hrachovec, manager

Address/Telephone: 306 West Olive; (612) 430–2955 or (800) 562–3632

E-mail: rivertn@aol.com

Rooms: 12, including 4 suites; all with private bath and air conditioning, 9 with whirlpool bath and fireplace. No smoking inn.

Rates: $79 to $179, single or double, EPB.

Open: All year.

Facilities and activities: Lunch by arrangement, afternoon tea, hors d'oeuvres, dinner. Sitting room. Gazebo on grounds. Nearby: a short drive to scenic St. Croix river way; riverboat rides; art galleries, specialty shops, antiques stores; golf courses; apple orchards; biking, hiking, cross-country and downhill skiing, canoeing, swimming; tours of historic homes; restaurants.

Recommended Country Inns® Travelers' Club Benefit: 25 percent discount, Monday–Thursday, subject to availability.

The Anderson House
WABASHA, MINNESOTA 55981

The Anderson House has the most unusual selection of special inn services I've ever run across.

- Hot bricks wrapped in cotton warm your feet after a long day's journey.
- Shoes will be shined free of charge if you leave them outside your door before retiring for the evening.
- Mustard plasters will be conjured up to treat stuffy congestion and chest colds.
- Eleven cats are on daily call: You can rent one to help purr you to sleep and make you feel more at home. Aloysius and Morris are guest favorites.
- Pennsylvania Dutch specialties like scrapple and *fastnachts,* a meat dish with tasty doughnuts, are served for breakfast.

Now have I got your attention?

It's the oldest operating hotel in Minnesota, never having closed its doors since its opening day in 1856. The rambling red-brick inn, which takes up a block of the town's Main Street, traces its roots back to Pennsylvania Dutch country. In fact, Grandma Ida Anderson, who ran the hotel at the turn of the century, earned her reputation for scrumptious meals conjured up in the hotel's kitchen. The tradition continues under her great-grandson, John.

John has delightfully remodeled all the guest rooms. Most have floral-print wallpaper; antique maple, oak, and walnut beds and dressers; and handmade quilts and bedspreads. John said that the latter were made by two talented ladies from a nearby nursing home. Some rooms that share a bath have a sink. Other rooms afford you a glimpse of the Mississippi River, just across the street.

A favorite of mine is a room with an enchanting Dutch sleigh bed and matching chest; both are hand-stenciled with flowery patterns and fine handiwork. And a few rooms now have a whirlpool bath.

Get ready for a real dining treat. Unique inn offerings include cheese soup, chicken with Dutch dumplings, bacon-corn chowder, *kugel-hopf*, *limpa*, pork tenderloin medallions cooked in sauerkraut, and Dutch beer—and, if you're very lucky, sometimes sticky-sweet shoo-fly pie for dessert.

John's family marks the fourth generation of Anderson House ownership. That means a long-standing tradition of warm hospitality that's hard to beat.

How to get there: U.S. 61 and Minnesota 60 go right through town. The inn is located on North Main Street.

Innkeeper: John Hall

Address/Telephone: 333 North Main Street; (612) 565–4524 or Minnesota toll-free (800) 862–9702, other states toll-free (800) 325–2270

Rooms: 24, including 6 suites; 14 with private bath, all with air conditioning, some with TV. Pets OK in certain rooms.

Rates: $50, shared bath; $69 to $89, private bath; $99 to $125, suites; EP. Midweek and other packages available.

Open: All year; restaurant closed in January.

Facilities and activities: Full-service dining room with wheelchair access, ice-cream parlor. In winter, ice fishing, skating, boating. Nearby: about 30 miles from 3 ski resorts. Across the street from Mississippi River fishing, boating. Drive to antiques shops.

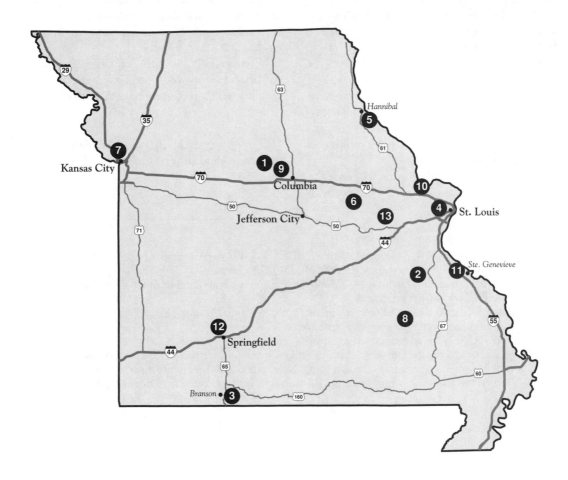

Missouri

Missouri

Numbers on map refer to towns numbered below.

Borgman's Bed and Breakfast
ARROW ROCK, MISSOURI 65320

Borgman's Bed and Breakfast has been called "one of the most enjoyable inns in the state." After my visit to this charming white clapboard home, I heartily agree.

Helen greeted me at the door of her little farmhouse, built between 1855 and 1865 in this tiny historic town. It's filled with country-style antiques and furnishings that put even the most harried guests at ease.

Helen's daughter, Kathy, designed the stenciled wall borders that adorn each of the guest-room ceilings. And the beautiful country quilts that add splashes of colors to the beds were handmade by Helen, of course.

Relaxation is the key here. I just sat on the porch, in the shade of tall trees, feeling the cool summer breeze. Helen wound up the old Victrola for a song. It's also fun to stop by the kitchen to visit with Helen when she's making her famous cinnamon buns fresh each morning for breakfast.

"It's gotten to the point where guests kind of expect me to serve them," Helen said. "I guess they feel it's a real treat." She also offers homemade breads, cereal, fruits, and beverages.

As Helen and I walked to the upstairs guest rooms, I could feel the country comfort soaking into my city bones. I saw tall Victorian headboards, exposed chimney brick, hurricane-style lamps, lacy window curtains, and rocking chairs in the handsome rooms. The only first-floor guest room has the original plank floor, a four-poster bed adorned with one of Helen's bright quilts, and another antique rocker. All the rooms are bright, cheery, and peaceful.

Kathy works at the Arrow Rock information center and can tell you all about the wonderful history and attractions the village offers. She'll also recommend restaurants that serve wholesome down-home dinner fare.

Area history is fascinating. Lewis and Clark noted the region during their historic explorations. Indians used local outcroppings of flint to point their arrows—hence the town name. Three forts were once located in the area; one was used during the War of 1812. A portion of the town was burned down during the Civil War.

In town, I toured a wonderful "pioneer" Main Street, lined with historic buildings that still have wooden-board sidewalks and rough-hewn stones forming crude street gutters. A guided historic walking tour is offered from April through October (sometimes on weekends only, so check ahead).

How to get there: From Kansas City or St. Louis, take I-70 to Route 41. Go north to Arrow Rock and turn right on Van Buren (the first road into Arrow Rock) to the inn about 2 blocks up the street.

Innkeepers: Kathy and Helen Borgman
Address/Telephone: Van Buren Street; (816) 837–3350
Rooms: 4 share 3 baths; all with air conditioning. No smoking inn.
Rates: $40, single; $50 to $55, double; continental breakfast. No credit cards.
Open: All year.
Facilities and activities: Sitting room. Porch with rockers. Nearby: walk to restaurants, state historical buildings and sites, archaeological digs, antiques and specialty shops, and The Lyceum Theatre, one of Missouri's oldest repertory companies. Guided walking tours of town also offered.

ℳansion Hill Country Inn
BONNE TERRE, MISSOURI 63628

Cathy always dreamed of owning a country inn. Little did she imagine that it would be a thirty-two-room mansion on a 130-acre estate atop the highest point in historic Bonne Terre.

But first, sit still—you have to know some history. This old mining town was once the richest lead district in the country. When mining ceased and water pumps were shut down, the 200-foot-deep mine shafts filled with water. So Cathy and Doug, in a stroke of genius, created a world-class scuba-diving center in the old Bonne Terre mine, with more than 17 miles of dive trails.

Now both divers and dedicated inn hoppers have an equally impressive place to stay

overnight. The early-1900s mansion, built as a home for the president of the St. Joe Lead Company, reflects the gracious living and prosperity of those lead-boom days.

I walked into a foyer gleaming with polished hardwood. Wandering into the library, with its massive brick fireplace, heavy-beamed ceiling, stately columns, and decidedly nautical themes (with model sailing ships and other "waterabilia"), I eavesdropped as a group of divers planned their next mine adventure.

Doug told me that he had done most of the inn's heavy-duty interior restoration, while Cathy spent hundreds of hours coordinating inn decor and searching out special antique items that bring the mansion to life. It shows.

We walked through French doors onto an enclosed porch overlooking an impressive courtyard, garden, and fountain on the first terrace level. The second level was designed for world-class lawn croquet, Doug told me. You also can see miles of Ozark Mountain foothills.

Guest rooms have a view of the surrounding estate grounds and are decorated in period pieces and reproductions, with four-poster beds among the furnishings. Cathy made many of the inn's floral-styled draperies, valances, and other appointments.

Other inn guest rooms are located in a historic turn-of-the-century railroad depot located at the bottom of the estate driveway (just down the hill).

Dining here is another nice treat: The plantation-style menu offers staples like baked chicken and thick, juicy steaks; for dessert, the Key lime pie is delicious. Relaxing in the wine and beer garden, surrounded by a white picket fence, is a nice way to wind down an evening. The garden is fitted with a new deck and an outdoor bar; a soothing mint julep is just a few steps away.

How to get there: From St. Louis, take I–55 south to U.S. 67. Continue south to Route 47. Go west into Bonne Terre. At Summit, turn left. At the top of the hill, turn left into a driveway marked by estate posts and inn signs. Proceed up the long road to the inn.

Innkeepers: Doug and Cathy Goergens
Address/Telephone: Mansion Hill Drive; (314) 358–5311
Rooms: 13; 10 with private bath and air conditioning.
Rates: $40 to $120, single or double, continental breakfast. Special packages can include scuba diving.
Open: All year; closed Sunday.
Facilities and activities: Full-service inn, bar, gift shop, gardens, deck. Situated on 130-acre estate, view of Ozark Mountain foothills. Nearby: cross-country skiing, nature trails, fishing; horse-drawn carriage tours of mining town. Short ride to Bonne Terre mine, with land tours at this National Historic Site. Also world-class scuba diving at mine.

The Branson House Bed & Breakfast Inn

BRANSON, MISSOURI 65616

Suddenly tiny Branson has become the live country-music capital of the world, boasting more than thirty music theaters featuring the likes of Glen Campbell, Louise Mandrell, Willie Nelson, Boxcar Willie, Jim Stafford, Johnny Cash, Mel Tillis, The Statler Brothers—and even Andy Williams, who is building his own Moon River Theater in this down-home hamlet.

"I ran into Mel Tillis the other day at the grocery store," one Branson resident told me. "He was pushing a cart just like everyone else."

Nestled in Ozark Mountain hill country, with its Southern-style friendliness and great weather, Branson is a great place for a B&B—like The Branson House, located near the heart of historic downtown. Done in 1920s Arts and Crafts stylings, the inn features beautiful stone and boulder masonry.

Opal treats guests like treasured country cousins. She serves specially prepared breakfasts of egg and meat casseroles, homemade coffeecake, fresh fruit, and beverages; in warm weather you can eat on the veranda overlooking downtown Branson and Lake Taneycomo.

Guests enjoy complimentary sherry or port from the buffet in the living room. And late-night snackers might weather a milk-and-cookie attack in the country kitchen.

"The first time I walked into this house as a little girl attending a party, I knew it was the only one I ever really wanted," Opal said.

Her seven guest rooms are individually decorated with antiques and collectibles from all over the country. The Honeymoon Suite features an 1830s four-poster spool bed found in California; its massive armoire, which Opal discovered in Arkansas, dates to the 1830s.

I also like the French Balcony room, with its fine French linens and private perch—perfect for Ozark summer days.

A homey parlor, with its own Arts and Crafts stone fireplace, is replete with books, magazines, and games. It's also a great place to swap stories on shows you've seen during your visit to Branson.

By the way, my pa and I can recommend any show starring Louise Mandrell. That's down-home entertainment!

How to get there: From Springfield, Missouri, or Harrison, Arkansas, take I–65 to Branson. Exit on Missouri 76 (its name changes to Main Street close to town); go west to Fourth Street, turn left, and proceed to the inn at the intersection of Fourth and Atlantic.

Innkeeper: Opal Kelly

Address/Telephone: 120 Fourth Street; (417) 334–0959

Rooms: 7, including 1 suite; all with private bath and air conditioning.

Rates: $65 to $90, single or double, EPB. No smoking inn.

Open: April 1 through December 15.

Facilities and activities: Parlor, front porch. Nearby: walk to Lake Taneycomo, historic downtown Branson. A short drive to 27 live country music theaters, Silver Dollar City, Shepherd of the Hills outdoor drama, lakes, water sports, fishing, antiques shops, and boutiques.

Seven Gables Inn
CLAYTON, MISSOURI 63105

I was surprised to find a luxurious European-style retreat in such surroundings—sleek skyscrapers and modern sculpture dominate the landscape of this tony St. Louis suburb.

The building itself is a masterpiece of sorts. It was built in 1918, and the architect based his design on Hawthorne's House of Seven Gables, which stands in Salem, Massachusetts.

This romantic continental getaway also provides great European-style dining experiences. Chez Louis—intimate, elegant, and serving classic continental gourmet cuisine—has received awards and rave reviews from the likes of the *New York Times* and the *St. Louis Post-Dispatch*. Bernard is reluctant to reveal much of the menu, since it changes weekly and sometimes daily. Seafood prepared in classical French style is always a good choice.

The restaurant also boasts a 320-item wine list featuring French, Italian, and Californian products.

Guest rooms are uniquely European, done in handsome country-French antiques and reproductions, some with brass and white iron-rail beds, writing desks, and comfortable chairs. Fresh flowers give rooms a sweet scent. Fluffy terrycloth robes are part of a luxurious bath. Even the soap is hand-milled in France.

Of course, there's turndown service, with chocolates left on your pillow. You had to wonder?

Head to the inn's other restaurant, Bernard's, for its upbeat, bistro-style tempo. May through September (weather permitting), the Garden Court, an expansive, cobbled patio with the feel of a European sidewalk cafe, is open for "lunch among the flowers or dinner under the stars."

The Seven Gables Inn has been included in the exclusive *Relais et Châteaux*, an organization listing some of the finest hotels in the world. (Only a few U.S. hotels are so honored. To give you an idea of their standards, the list includes the renowned Crillon in Paris.)

How to get there: From the airport, take I–170 south to the Ladue exit and go west into Clayton. This road will take you directly to the hotel.

Innkeeper: Dennis Fennedy
Address/Telephone: 26 North Meramec; (314) 863–8400
Rooms: 32, including 4 suites; all with private bath, air conditioning, TV, and phone. Wheelchair access.
Rates: $115, single; $130, double; $159, suites; EP.
Open: All year.
Facilities and activities: Two restaurants, bistro, garden court. A short drive to all St. Louis attractions: Busch Stadium, Union Station, the Arch, historic river district, and more.
Business travel: Located about 15 miles west of downtown St. Louis. Corporate rates, meeting rooms, fax.
Recommended Country Inns® Travelers' Club Benefit: 10 percent discount.

Garth Woodside Mansion
HANNIBAL, MISSOURI 63401

This is a historic country estate at its finest, a handsome Victorian home on thirty-nine acres of meadows and woodland, graced with noble old trees and a private fishing pond. (Guests can angle for bass and perch.) Built in 1871 as a summer home for prominent Hannibal businessman John Garth, the mansion was the focal point for notables passing through Hannibal.

Hometown boy Samuel Clemens (Mark Twain) spent several nights here in his lifelong friend's home in 1882 and also during his last visit to Hannibal in 1902.

Amazingly, the mansion contains mostly original furnishings; they are exquisite. The library, with its 9-foot-tall doors, is done in ele-gant walnut, with 1840 Empire furniture, marble fireplace with gold inlay, and a red-velvet Victorian reclining chair.

The dining room is graced with the original table and twelve chairs. Diane pointed to the hostess chair: "It was made extra wide to accommodate the full petticoats that were the style of the day." There's also an original painting done by Mrs. Garth in the family parlor.

We walked up the magnificent flying staircase that vaults three stories high with no visible means of support. It appears even more spectacular, hanging high in the air, because of the mansion's 14-foot-high ceiling.

Guest rooms are decorated in Victorian

splendor. On the second floor, the John Garth Room, occupying the old master bedroom, has a beautiful black walnut Victorian bed, with a 10-foot-tall headboard in grand Renaissance Revival style. The three-piece matching bedroom set is original to the home. Even the dresser stands nearly 10 feet high.

Diane said, however, that the Rosewood Room has become one of the inn's most popular lodgings. It's bright and airy, with long windows, great views of the grounds, lively "grapevine" Victorian print wallpaper, and a claw-footed bathtub painted by Diane's artist/daughter, Kari. (See for yourself; she signed the tub.)

It also boasts the "most expensive bed in Missouri," a walnut half-tester bed from the 1850s that's museum quality.

Also check out the Samuel Clemens Room, with its 12-foot-tall half-tester bed, a hand-carved rosewood beauty, to say the least.

Third-floor rooms are country beautiful, with wicker themes and great views of the grounds.

Breakfasts feature goodies like ham-and-cheese quiche, marmalade-filled muffins, rolls, and more. Iced tea is served on the spacious veranda during summer between 4:00 and 6:00 P.M. Hot mulled apple cider is the winter treat inside.

Newest inn treat: "Abigail's Secret," a new inn building in Hannibal's Historic District, with double whirlpool rooms renting for $95 to $115.

How to get there: From St. Louis, take I–70 west to Missouri 79 and go north into Hannibal. Turn west on Broadway, then south on U.S. 61. Turn east at Warren Barrett Drive (the first road south of the Holiday Inn) and follow signs to the inn.

Innkeepers: Irv and Diane Feinberg
Address/Telephone: R. R. 1; (314) 221–2789
URL: http://hanmo.com/twainweb/garth/garth.html
Rooms: 8; all with private bath and central air conditioning, phone on request.
Rates: $65 to $105, single or double, EPB.
Open: All year.
Facilities and activities: BYOB. Sitting rooms, parlors, wraparound porch. Acres of gardens, meadows, woodlands. Tours of the mansion given 11:30 A.M. to 3:00 P.M. daily. A short drive to restaurants, Mark Twain's boyhood house, Huckleberry Finn landmarks, Mississippi River paddle-wheel rides, caves, sightseeing tours, Mark Twain Outdoor Theater, specialty shops, and Great River Road that follows the Mississippi.
Recommended Country Inns® Travelers' Club Benefit: Super Tuesdays—stay Tuesday night free when staying three consecutive nights that include Tuesday, November–April.

Captain Wohlt Inn
HERMANN, MISSOURI 65041

This quaint inn sits high on a hill overlooking Third Street in the middle of ethnic Hermann's historic district, which is listed on the National Register of Historic Places for its architectural and historical significance. I immediately liked it, feeling as though I were visiting a favorite aunt's house; it had a comfortable, welcome-home kind of atmosphere.

That's in large part due to the reception I received from innkeeper Lee, who took me into her air-conditioned inn on a blistering hot and humid day. As we sat down in a charming dining room done in handsome slate blue, she told me that the home was built in 1886 by its namesake, a German riverboat captain who founded the Hermann ferry boat company.

She and her husband renovated the building in 1986, and they did a terrific job. A first-floor room (the only inn room in Hermann equipped for the handicapped) has bright country stylings and a four-poster bed.

As I walked up the staircase, I ran my hands over a walnut handrail that's original to the home. I found second-floor rooms equally appealing: pink-and-blue-bouquet country wallpapers, country ceiling borders, and handsome furnishings, including ceiling fans and a beechnut Jenny Lind bed that's been in Harry's family for years. It's also one of the prettiest I've seen in a long time.

Third-floor dormer rooms feature more pastel country prints, dormer windows, and, as in most rooms, lovely country quilts made by local artisans.

Lee prepares breakfast, serving filling egg casseroles, morning sausage, ham loaf and bacon, fresh fruit and juice, and delicious home-baked goodies. Her specialty is spinach–zucchini casserole, seasoned with cheese and onions. Yum!

Lee also pointed out a restored 1840 building next to the inn, which houses two additional guest suites. Country furnishings, wooden decks, and a garden with tables and benches make this house a comfortable retreat.

For dinner, try Taylor's Landing, which features hearty German ethnic foods like sauerbraten, bratwurst, and schnitzel; Vintage 1847 at Stone Hill Winery offers its own schnitzel, rainbow trout, and steak fillets in a romantic setting.

Then wander along Third Street, between Schiller and Market, which has remained largely as it appeared in the 1800s. Lots sold in 1839 for $50. The street was cut through a high knoll, hence the inn's "hillside" site.

How to get there: From St. Louis, take I–70 west to Missouri 19, then go south into Hermann. Turn east on Third Street to the inn. Private parking is between Second and Third streets, down an alley named Hollyhock Lane.

Innkeepers: Lee and Harry Sammons

Address/Telephone: 123 East Third Street; (314) 486–3357

URL: http://www.bbonline.com/mo/bbim/ or http://www.innsite.com/bbim

Rooms: 8, including 3 suites; all with private bath and air conditioning, 1 with wheel chair access.

Rates: $55 to $65, single or double; $85, suites; EPB. Two-night minimum during festival weekends (Maifest and Oktoberfest). Children under 12 free. Stay third night for half price.

Open: All year.

Facilities and activities: Short walk from restaurants, shops, and historic buildings of Hermann and the Missouri River. Short drive to area wineries and vineyards.

Recommended Country Inns® Travelers' Club Benefit: Stay two nights, get third night at half price, or 5 percent discount, Monday–Wednesday, if club is mentioned.

Southmoreland on-the-Plaza

KANSAS CITY, MISSOURI 64112

The minute we arrived, this elegant, sophisticated inn became one of my pa's top five places to stay. I couldn't agree more.

The superb 1913 Colonial Revival mansion boasts centuries-old shade trees, gracious lawns, rock walls, and formal gardens not often seen in the heart of the city. Inside, it has undergone a million-dollar restoration and renovation that includes some of the finest guest rooms in the Midwest.

Rooms are named for Kansas City notables. I stayed in Number 10—George Caleb Bingham (a mid-nineteenth-century painter whose works hang in the nearby Nelson-Atkins Museum of Art). It's graced with museum-quality prints of Bingham's portraits featuring Col. Napoleon Geddings, grandfather of the house's previous owner, and his wife. Other room treasures include a four-poster mahogany bed, a Chinese rosewood gossip bench, and bold wall coverings done in yellow, navy, and brick.

Pa drew number 4—Thomas Hart Benton, complete with Mission-style furnishings, an oak and copper four-poster bed, and a Tiffany-style lamp.

Each of our rooms had a private balcony, mine with a great view of the Plaza.

Attention baseball fans: Choose the Leroy "Satchell" Paige room during baseball season when the Royals are in town, and you will receive complimentary tickets to the ball game.

Susan and Penni were looking for a Maine coast inn when they stumbled across this treasure. "Welcome to Camden in Kansas City," Susan quipped.

They're also proud that the inn showcases the efforts of determined women to restore one of Kansas City's famed residences. "Since 1948 the house has had only women owners," Susan said.

The innkeepers want you to know that it's a business travelers' paradise, too. CEO-style perks include made-to-order breakfasts, round-the-clock reception and checkout, free local calls and fax, modem connections, and membership privileges (sports and dining) at a nearby historic private club.

All guests enjoy Penni's breakfasts on an 1860s harvest table in the informal dining room. Pa and I savored banana-apricot frappés, home-baked banana nut bread, and French toast stuffed with Lorraine Swiss cheese and dusted with powdered sugar and almonds.

If you're in a movie mood, repair to the living room. Inside an 1860s Austrian armoire, there's a television, VCR, and movie library with a hundred titles.

"All with happy endings," Penni said.

How to get there: From I–70, I–35, and I–29 in downtown Kansas City, take the Main Street exit. Go south to East 46th Street, turn east (left), and go about 1½ blocks to the inn, on the left side of the street.

Innkeepers: Penni Johnson and Susan Mochl
Address/Telephone: 116 East 46th Street; (816) 531–7979; fax (816) 531–2407
Rooms: 12; all with private bath and air conditioning. Wheelchair access. Free local phone calls.
Rates: $95 to $140, single; $105 to $150, double; EPB.
Open: All year.
Facilities and activities: Special dinners available in inn dining room. Library sitting room, wicker solarium, open-air balconies, courtyard, gardens, croquet lawn, off-street parking. Guests get free passes to Rockhill Tennis Club, a private facility. Nearby: walk to 300 specialty shops and restaurants of famed Country Club Plaza. Short drive to Nelson-Atkins Museum of Art, Henry Moore Sculpture Garden, Missouri Repertory Theater, Mill Run Creek, Crown Center, Harry Truman Sports Complex (home to Kansas City Chiefs and Royals).
Business travel: Located about 5 minutes from Crown Center and downtown. Corporate rates, meeting rooms, fax.

Wilderness Lodge
LESTERVILLE, MISSOURI 63654

I drove deep into the beautiful Ozark Mountain foothills to find this woodsy retreat. Located on 1,200 rolling acres near the bank of the crystal-clear Black River, the Wilderness Lodge offers some of the best country-style fun imaginable.

A group of young canoers were excitedly telling their parents about the afternoon's adventures as I entered the Main Lodge, the oldest and largest building on the property. The heavy log-beam construction and tan pitch made me feel like a pioneer in the wilderness.

The lodge's rough-hewn furniture is just what you'd expect. Especially interesting are American Indian–style rugs displayed on the walls, animal trophies, and the obligatory rifle hanging above a manteled hearth.

Later I sat in an open dining room with a giant picture window looking out over the grounds, watching more kids frolic in the pool. A game room, just off to the side, has card and game tables for all kinds of family fun. For romantics the lodge has a large fireplace room for snuggling on chilly evenings.

Family-style breakfasts and dinners are lodge specialties. Morning menus include eggs, pancakes, and beverages; dinner platters are heaped high with good country cooking such as fried chicken, fresh bread, and sweet pastries. After dinner you might sidle up to the bar for a nightcap.

I've rarely seen guest cabins so complement the beautiful Ozark countryside. Especially attractive is the use of native rock, peeled logs, pine siding, and porches built right into the landscape. Country-antique furniture and Indian artifacts add to the woodsy ambience; many rooms feature large fireplaces and high loft ceilings.

One of the most popular lodge treats: "City Slickers" trail rides. These week-long horsey treks for up to 200 riders follow local trails through the woods, along rivers, and over meadows. Held in April, June, July, September, and November, they cost $153 per person and include three meals daily and camping fees. Livery horses are $30 per day.

How to get there: From St. Louis, take I–270 south to Route 21 and continue south to Glover. Then head west on Route 21/49/72. Near Arcadia, take Route 21 south, then west for about 22 miles to Peola Road. Turn left and continue down the dirt and gravel path, following the signs to the lodge.

Innkeeper: Bob Schall
Address/Telephone: Box 90; (314) 637–2295, toll-free from St. Louis (800) 296–2011
Rooms: 26 units; all with private bath and air conditioning.
Rates: $60 per person, rooms and cottages; $75 per person, suites; MAP. Children's rates available. Two-night minimum required. Special package rates.
Open: All year.
Facilities and activities: Dining room, bar. Archery, shuffleboard, volleyball, horseshoes, Frisbee-golf course, walking trails, tennis courts, platform tennis. Also children's playground, swimming pool, hot tub (cold weather only), hayrides, canoeing, tube floats. Horseback riding.

School House Bed and Breakfast
ROCHEPORT, MISSOURI 65279

I walked into this 1914 three-story brick schoolhouse just as Vicki was beginning a tour of her inn and quickly discovered that it is a magnificent example of what restoration and renovation with a visionary eye can accomplish.

Guest rooms are very spacious, almost imperial, with their 13-foot-high ceilings, cheery ceiling and wall borders, schoolhouse-sized windows, shiny oak floors, and antique furnishings. I complimented Vicki on her handsome curtains; her talented hands made all the window treatments throughout the inn.

One guest room has a white iron-rail bed and cane-backed chairs; another is fashioned with a brass four-poster bed that's 7 feet tall. I also found delicately carved Victorian dressers, high-back chairs, pastel wall coverings, and even a trundle bed that adds a down-home feel.

I love the second floor's executive suite, with its mahogany four-poster bed, arched doorway, and three huge windows that spill light into this happy room. It boasts the schoolhouse's original fir floors, handsomely restored by Vicki and John.

For newlyweds and incurable romantics, the Bridal Suite is a must. Imagine a heart-shaped whirlpool tub, upholstered wall coverings, and more.

Vicki does all the breakfast cooking in an expansive second-floor kitchen that opens onto the inn's main common room. "Just seems like everyone follows me up here, and we end up talking as I prepare the food," Vicki said. Prepare yourself for her famous egg casserole, fresh fruit and juices, and homemade bran and cinnamon muffins.

Then browse among the hallway display case's historic town and school photos and memorabilia.

Rocheport itself is a "very Southern town," Vicki said. Its history stretches back to Indian times, as early journals noted primitive red-keel Indian paintings on limestone bluffs that edge out over the Missouri River near here. In fact, members of the Lewis and Clark expedition passed by in 1804, citing "uncouth paintings of animals."

At the height of ferryboat traffic, the town grew to more than 800 people. Today about 300 residents keep Rocheport's legacy alive; several historic structures still dot the landscape. You can pick up a walking-tour booklet at the inn.

How to get there: From Columbia, take I–70 west to Rocheport exit, then follow Highway BB 2 miles northwest into town. The inn is at Third and Clark streets (right on Highway BB).

Innkeepers: John and Vicki Ott, owners; Penny Province, manager

Address/Telephone: Third and Clark Streets; (314) 698–2022

Rooms: 10; all with private bath and air conditioning, 1 with wheelchair access. No smoking inn.

Rates: $85 to $150, single or double, EPB.

Open: All year except Christmas Day.

Facilities and activities: BYOB. Sitting rooms, outdoor garden, courtyard. Town on National Register of Historic Places, filled with nineteenth-century homes. Nearby: antiques stores and craft and pottery shops. Short drive to restaurants, local winery (Les Bourgeois) overlooking Missouri River and Boone Cave. Hiking and biking on renowned Missouri River State Trail.

Recommended Country Inns® Travelers' Club Benefit: Stay two nights, get third night free, subject to availability.

$\mathcal{B}$oone's $\mathcal{L}$ick $\mathcal{T}$rail $\mathcal{I}$nn
ST. CHARLES, MISSOURI 63301

I was intrigued by the numerous doors leading to rooms overlooking the gallery porch of the historic 1840 Carter–Rice building, now known as the Boone's Lick Trail Inn. It reminded me of a boarding house—but that wasn't quite it.

"Madame Duquette had her girls entertain patrons in those little rooms," V'Anne told me. "See, folklore tells us that in the 1820s, Duquette ran a brothel here. When I restored the building, those four doors still led to tiny, little cubbyhole stalls, big enough for only a cot and washstand."

The Boone's Lick Trail Inn, one of the oldest homes in town, is intertwined with all kinds of interesting history. Frenchtown is the site of many firsts, including the Lewis and Clark Rendezvous, the start of the Zebulon Pike expedition, and the beginnings of Daniel Boone's salt-lick trail. It's also where the Sante Fe Trail was planned and drafted.

The 1840 inn hosted hundreds of early adventurers and settlers passing through the town on their way west. V'Anne has restored second-floor guest rooms into country-charmed quarters. Some rooms have original plank floors, antique iron-rail beds, German lace curtains, and family antique heirlooms.

The newest room is the third-floor suite, with its hand-carved maple bed, antique slave's bed (daybed), and a private widow's walk overlooking the Missouri River.

I found the inn quiet and private, a welcome respite just a stone's throw from the hubbub that engulfed me on Main Street during this summer holiday weekend.

V'Anne prides herself on her never-ending breakfasts; no one will leave here hungry. Eggs Olé is a treat; so are her French crepes and special home-baked breads, homemade jams, yummy cinnamon rolls, and lemon biscuits. Then I'd suggest a walking tour that showcases the town's historic architecture (self-guided tour pamphlets can be obtained at the tourism department on Main Street).

If you work up a good appetite, I'd recommend the Mother-in-Law House on South Main for lunch, where I enjoyed their turkey-and-salad plate with a glass of white wine; Lewis and Clark's (also on South Main) arguably offers the town's finest evening dining. You'll also find restaurants specializing in local-flavored specialties like Crab Rangoon, beignets, catfish, and down-home barbecue.

And remember that this historic city is alive with festivals year-round, including May's Lewis and Clark Rendezvous; August's Festival of the Hills; and Oktoberfest.

How to get there: From St. Louis, take I–70 west to First Capitol Drive, exit, and continue to Main Street. Turn right; the inn is at Main and Boone's Lick Road.

Innkeeper: V'Anne Mydler

Address/Telephone: 1000 South Main Street; (314) 947–7000

Rooms: 4, including 1 suite; all with private bath. No smoking inn.

Rates: Sunday through Thrusday: $75 to $95, single or double; Friday and Saturday: $105 to $125, single or double; EPB. Slightly higher during Fête des Petites Côtes (Festival of the Hills) and holidays.

Open: All year except Christmas Eve and Day.

Facilities and activities: In the heart of Frenchtown, with restaurants, specialty shops, boutiques, and antiques stores. Overlooks Frontier Park, the Missouri River State Trail, and Lewis and Clark Trail. National Historic District.

St. Charles House
ST. CHARLES, MISSOURI 63301

I'm not sure anyone can prepare himself for the surprises awaiting discerning inngoers at St. Charles House.

Open the door to this re-created 1800s brick building within sight of the lazing Missouri River, and you step back into an air of Old World elegance and luxury.

The inn sits on Main Street of Missouri's first state capital, a street lined with more than one hundred historic brick buildings dating to the late nineteenth century (and today largely inhabited by arts and antiques shops).

It's a lovingly restored retreat from the bustle of visitors that can overwhelm the tiny hamlet. The replica house looks fit for a prosperous frontier businessman, sporting spacious rooms, fine antiques, and elegant surroundings.

"All of our antiques pre-date 1850," said Patti. Many were purchased in Denver, some right in town. Especially noteworthy is a massive Austrian buffet with intricate hand carving and a 9-foot-tall French walnut armoire.

The house's open floor plan includes a four-columned foyer and a bedchamber complete with oak hardwood floors, queen-sized canopy bed, and original Mary Gregory table lamp.

An elegant sitting area offers oriental-style rugs and a place to relax. There's even a mini-refrigerator in an antique side buffet along with a small wet bar.

Walk downstairs to reach the bath. Behind handsome double doors I found a claw-footed tub under a crystal chandelier in a huge room decorated in pink and blues. Just outside is another Victorian-style sitting room.

The innkeepers also own a guest cottage located a few doors down Main Street. This 1850s house is charming, outfitted in English country antiques that include a Welsh cupboard dating to 1813. Its two rooms offer pencil-post and four-poster cannonball beds, antique claw-footed tubs, and more fabulous antiques.

Hard to believe, but "it took only three days to buy all our pieces," Patti said. "We went on an antique-buying spree, and every place we stopped just happened to have exactly what we wanted."

How to get there: From St. Louis or Kansas City, exit I–70 at First Capital Drive, and follow that north, then east to Main Street; turn right and continue to the inn.

Innkeepers: Patricia and Lionel York

Address/Telephone: 338 South Main Street; (314) 946–6221 or (800) 366–2427 via town Tourism Center

Rooms: 1 suite with sitting room, porch overlooking Missouri River, and private bath. One 2-bedroom guest cottage with 2 baths, dining room, small porch. No smoking inn.

Rates: $95 weekdays, $130 Friday and Saturday for suite; $75 weekdays, $90 weekends for each room in cottage; deluxe continental breakfast.

Open: All year.

Facilities and activities: Walk to quaint shops, restaurants, riverboat cruises, tours of the first state capital. A short drive to downtown St. Louis and the Arch, St. Louis Art Museum, restored Union Station, Opera House, Powell Symphony Hall, and Fox Theatre.

The Inn St. Gemme Beauvais
STE. GENEVIEVE, MISSOURI 63670

This 1847 three-story, red-brick building is located in a town that's been called "the finest surviving example of French Colonial architecture in the country," with more than fifty historic buildings dating back to the 1700s, when the fur traders settled here.

Walls here are pioneer-tough—18 inches thick—and they're only one of the inn's unique features. In the foyer, I walked under a historic chandelier, dating from the early 1800s, that casts an amber glow over the hallway. Just to the right of the door is the inn desk, an old rolltop where you often can find manager Janet ready with a touring suggestion and a welcoming smile.

I enjoyed a French feast for breakfast, with hand-filled ham and cheese crepes an inn specialty. There are also tasty quiches, delicious homemade orange-pecan nut breads, fresh fruit cups, and more of Janet's delicious treats.

For dinner the innkeeper will suggest a spot to match your tastes. I like the Hotel Ste. Genevieve, just a short walk down the street, for scrumptious steaks, fish, and chops.

Eating in the inn's historic dining room is a treat in itself. It's cozy and quaint, with white walls, a white marble fireplace, and antique tables and chairs. I also felt a bit larger than life as I walked around this room. That's because its scaled-down dimensions are typical of the town's historic French-styled homes. And after all, this is the state's oldest inn.

There is also a common room in the cellar that at one time served as a "moonshine" tavern. It's a favorite gathering place for guests, offering books, magazines, games, and a continuously in-the-works jigsaw puzzle.

Owner Mike spent ten years operating a Florida inn. He's completely renovated and restored the inn, crafting five two-room suites (two with Jacuzzi tubs) and all with comfy king beds. He also put a hot tub in the backyard for outdoor relaxation.

Just a short walk away are all the town's fab-ulous architectural attractions. Especially interesting is the 1770 Bolduc House, a vertical-log "fort" regarded as the most authentically restored Colonial Creole house in the country.

This is also a great town for antique hunting; my favorite place is Le Souvenir, housed in the oldest brick building west of the Mississippi River.

How to get there: From St. Louis, take I–55 south to Route 32. Turn east and continue into Ste. Genevieve. Turn right on Market Street and continue for about 3 blocks to Main Street. Turn left on Main Street and continue to the inn.

Innkeepers: Mike Emerson, owner; Janet Joggerst, manager

Address/Telephone: 78 North Main Street (mailing address: Box 231); (314) 883–5744

Rooms: 7; all with private bath. No smoking inn.

Rates: $69 to $125, single or double; $15 extra person in room, $6 for child; EPB and afternoon tea; wine and cheese.

Open: All year.

Facilities and activities: Private dinners for 6 or more people by reservation. Dining and common rooms. Nearby: walk to antiques shops, galleries, and museums (many specializing in pre Civil War pieces). Historical town architecture includes some of the best examples of French Colonial homes in United States, including vertical-log homes. Annual Jour de Fête second full weekend of August.

Recommended Country Inns® Travelers' Club Benefit: 10 percent discount, Monday–Thursday.

The Southern Hotel
STE. GENEVIEVE, MISSOURI 63670

"Beginning in the 1820s, The Southern Hotel was known for the finest accommodations between St. Louis and Natchez, Tennessee," Barbara said as we walked through swinging doors into the hotel's old saloon, which now acts as a guest parlor. "The Mississippi was then about 4 blocks away, and the hotel employed a young slave to sit in the belvedere atop the house and watch for steamboats arriving at Ste. Genevieve's dock.

"Then he'd run across the street to the stables and get a wagon to meet hotel guests."

I never suspected that this grand old dame, built in Federal style with a graceful front porch around 1800, had become a deserted eyesore in the mid-1980s, "a dumping ground for everything people no longer wanted," Barbara said. It is a testament to the Hankinses' magnificent restoration work that The Southern once again exudes warmth, hospitality, and classical graciousness.

Guest rooms are charmers; much of the credit goes to Barbara, whose whimsical, artistic touches are evident everywhere. If you're one of the first guests, Barbara will let you wander among the eight rooms to choose your favorite. But let me warn you: The combination of country Victorian furnishings and fabulous folk art makes the selection a difficult task.

The Japonisme Room is tinged with oriental

influence, reflecting the Victorian fascination with the Far East, and includes Chinese silk prints in the bathroom as well as a claw-footed tub painted to match the room's decor.

The River Room features a headboard of "Old Man River" carved out of Missouri cedar logs by a local artist. Buttons and Bows boasts a linen-draped canopy bed. Cabbage Rose is quite romantic, with its carved Victorian headboard, white lace, and elegant wall coverings.

But one of my favorites is Wysocki's Room, with its three-dimensional folk-art headboard depicting a charming village. It's one of the most unusual beds I've ever seen.

Barbara cooks ups some fabulous breakfasts in her kitchen, which she decorated with handsome rosemaling, a Scandinavian folk art. I am fascinated by the unusual gourmet breakfast, which might include strawberry soup, banana bisque, mushroom quiche, freshly baked croissants, juices, and chocolate-tinged coffee. Six fine restaurants are within walking distance; Barbara will match one to your particular tastes for evening meals.

The innkeepers have restored the "summer kitchen" behind the hotel; it's now a gracious craft boutique featuring works of local artisans. And blossom-filled gardens surround the building and encourage visitors to stroll, sit, and enjoy.

How to get there: From St. Louis, take I–55 south to the Ste. Genevieve exit (Route 32). Continue into town and turn right at Market Street; go 1 block to Third Street; turn right to the hotel.

Innkeepers: Michael and Barbara Hankins
Address/Telephone: 146 South Third Street; (314) 883–3493 or (800) 275–1412
Rooms: 8; all with private bath and air conditioning.
Rates: $65, single; $80 to $95, double; $125 Buttons and Bows room; EPB.
Open: All year.
Facilities and activities: Billiard room, gracious common rooms, off-street parking. Located in heart of historic town, one of the oldest settlements west of the Mississippi River. Walking tours of French Colonial architecture, other historic buildings, quaint shops, boutiques, restaurants.
Recommended Country Inns® Travelers' Club Benefit: 10 percent discount, Monday–Thursday.

𝒲alnut Street Inn
SPRINGFIELD, MISSOURI 65806

"Is this a room or an apartment?" my pa kidded as we settled in at this gracious inn just a block from Southwest Missouri State University.

Our third-floor quarters, called The Loft, were spacious. *Huge* is probably a better word. The former attic sprawled along three rooms, graced with beautifully chosen furnishings that included two double beds, reading chair, sofa, writing desk, antique tables, chairs, chests, and more.

I also liked the interesting nooks and crannies, sun-filled skylights, and sounds of scurrying squirrels who often run over the rooftops in pursuit of falling pecans.

It's all part of the captivating atmosphere at this Victorian showplace, built in 1894 and now a designated State Historic Site.

Karol told us that the inn was Springfield's Designer Showcase house when it opened in 1988. "Noted artists designed each room," she said. Easy to see why it was a winner—the results are imbued with nineteenth-century grace but possess all the comforts of home.

Imagine oak floors, leaded-glass windows, Victorian sofas, soft lighting. In the Jewell Sitting Room there's even a square grand piano that predates the Civil War. But be forewarned—it looks better than it sounds.

Morning chimes summoned us to breakfast in the dining room, and Karol served up a mouth-watering feast of black walnut waffles, fresh fruit, and homemade breads. A nice touch: Nonguests can join you here for breakfast for $7 per person.

Of course, romantics might choose the breakfast-in-bed option.

After our meal my pa grabbed a cushy chair by the fireplace while I browsed through pictures of the inn's restoration in a scrapbook in the second-floor Gathering Room.

I also lined up dinner possibilities. The winner: Le Mirbelle. Entree choices include *filet de boeuf* Wellington with shallots and mushrooms;

Scotch-cured salmon; and *boule de neige*—a snowball of vanilla ice cream smothered in chocolate sauce and topped with coconut shavings.

Don't you love the Carriage House master suites with fireplace and whirlpool bath? Things just keep getting better here.

How to get there: From St. Louis, take I-44 west to Glenstone Road, then go south to Walnut; turn right and proceed to Hammons Parkway and the inn.

Innkeepers: Karol, Gary, and Nancy Brown
Address/Telephone: 900 East Walnut; (800) 593-6346 or (417) 864-6346
Rooms: 14, including 5 suites; all with private bath and air conditioning. Wheelchair access.
Rates: $84 to $139, single or double, EPB.
Open: All year.
Facilities and activities: Two sitting rooms, front porch, rear enclosed porch, deck, garden, goldfish pond. Nearby: Southwest Missouri State University campus, University Art Exhibition Center, Hammons Sports Center, Center for Performing Arts. A short drive to Springfield Art Museum, Landers Theatre, Bass Pro, Wilson's Creek National (Civil War) Battlefield.
Business travel: Located 5 minutes from Federal Building, Springfield City Hall, downtown. Corporate rates, meeting room, fax.

The Schwegmann House
WASHINGTON, MISSOURI 63090

The innkeepers have captured all the warmth and Old World hospitality of this historic German-influenced Missouri River town in this charming inn. I found it exciting to look out my window and see the waters of the Big Muddy and listen to the distant bellow of boat traffic on the river.

This stately pre–Civil War Georgian-style home was buzzing with activity upon my arrival. A family with three tow-headed kids was in the parlor looking over the dinner menus from area restaurants that are provided for guests. They couldn't decide if they wanted to "dude up" for supper or grab a hamburger and picnic next to the river.

Another young couple had bicycled to area wineries (this is the heart of Missouri Wine Country) and were showing off some of the bottles they'd purchased. They promised me samples later that evening. That's just typical of the inn's friendly atmosphere.

Most of the guest rooms are furnished with fine antiques and fun country accents. Some have river views; all have cute names. My favorites:

The Country Room, with its local handcrafts, high-back rocking chair, marble-topped lamp stand, tall armoire, and calico curtains on the window. I especially liked the hand-stitched star quilt on the bed.

The Eyelet Room, generously decorated with shockingly white lace. White eyelet curtains brighten three tall windows and sprinkle sunlight in all directions. A padded rocking chair is absolutely required for gazing out at the river. There's also a marble-topped dresser, writing desk, and a colorful hand-stitched quilt on the bed.

Breakfasts are a treat. There are plates of imported and domestic cheeses, sausages, and croissants. But save some room for homemade bread, muffins, thick fruity jams, and some fresh fruit to satisfy a morning sweet tooth.

Especially interesting are the historic town's many antiques shops and fine restaurants. The Basket Case Delicatessen (a big-city deli in a tiny town) serves terrific sandwiches. At the East End Tavern, you can grab a tasty burger while listening to colorful talk about "Mizzou's" college football teams. The Landing is an informal dinner spot for families, with pizza and great burgers that are favorites. Then there's Lehmann's and Creamery Hill for fine dining.

How to get there: From St. Louis, take I-44 southwest to Route 100 and go west until you reach Washington. Turn north on Jefferson, then turn west on Front Street (along the river). The inn is at the corner of Front and Olive.

Innkeepers: Bill and Cathy Nagel

Address/Telephone: 438 West Front Street; (314) 239–5025

Rooms: 10; 8 with private bath, all with air conditioning.

Rates: Sunday through Thursday: $75 to $120, single or double; Friday and Saturday: $85 to $120; EPB. Off-season rates available.

Open: All year.

Facilities and activities: Guest parlors, formal gardens. Across the street from Missouri River. Nearby: historic riverfront district and preserved 1800s architecture; restaurants; antiques and specialty shops. In the heart of Missouri's Wine Country; a short drive to winery tours.

Recommended Country Inns® Travelers' Club Benefit: **???** **wording**

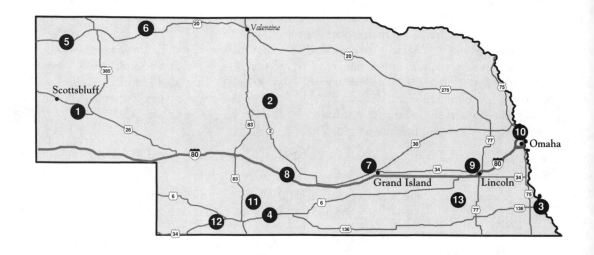

Nebraska

Nebraska

Numbers on map refer to towns numbered below.

Oregon Trail Wagon Train
BAYARD, NEBRASKA 69334

It's the quintessential Nebraska experience—riding a covered wagon through Little Monument Valley over the Oregon Trail.

That's right, the same Oregon Trail that brought more than 350,000 pioneers to the West between 1841 and 1869 on wagon trains that rallied at jumping-off points along the Missouri River. So before we talk about Kevin and Connie's efforts to re-create that westward trek in some small, exciting way, let's brush up on more history.

By the time immigrants reached Little Monument Valley (Scotts Bluff, or Chimney Rock, which is located about 35 miles east of here), they'd already been on the trail for nearly

two months. These landmarks signaled that almost one-third of the trail leading to Oregon had been traversed.

The immense sandstone-and-clay formations, about 14 million years old and nearly 5,000 feet high, were a startling change from the oceans of prairie grasses and monotonous flatlands that wagons had crossed for weeks. These High Plains remnants still startle visitors to the region. And it's through these very landforms, along the same pioneer trail, that Kevin and Connie's wagon trains move.

"We've had visitors from Russia, Israel, Australia, Japan, people from just about everywhere, on the wagon train," the "wagonmasters" said. "They all crave a little bit of the Old West, and that's what we give them."

Their covered wagons rumble over the Oregon Trail, past Scotts Bluff, Chimney Rock, and through the high plains prairie. One- to six-day treks re-create the life of an 1850 outfit. That means learning how to camp pioneer style, grease wagon wheels, pack trail bags and wagons, even fashion sun bonnets. Meals are taken at the wagon-train mess, and campfire history stories are shared after dinner—before you hit the hay by camping out under the stars.

If you'd rather take a morning tour of the trail and see where some of the old trail ruts cut into the prairie, sign up for the daily Old West trek, which leaves the ranch's base camp at 8:30 A.M. and returns before noon. Later you can go on a chuck wagon steak-dinner cookout and overnight in one of the ranch's three log cabins.

Let's face it. If you've ever wondered what it'd be like to pioneer across the Old West, this is your last best chance.

How to get there: From Ogallala, take U.S. 26 west; about 2 miles past Bayard, turn right on Oregon Trail Road; continue about 1½ miles to the Wagon Train Camp.

Innkeepers: Kevin and Connie Howard
Address/Telephone: Route 2, Box 502; (308) 586–1850
Rooms: 13 covered wagons; plus 3 log cabins, 2 with bath and shower, 1 primitive.
Rates: 24-hour wagon-train treks: $150 per adult, $125 each child under 12. Log cabins: $40 per night; discounts on 2 or more nights. Wagon trains, EPB; cabins, EP.
Open: April to November.
Facilities and activities: Ranch, picnic, and shelter areas. Chuck wagon cookouts, Old West tours, Sunday campfire breakfasts, canoe rentals. Nearby: Jail Rock and "Courthouse," Chimney Rock, Ash Hollow, Scotts Bluff National Monument.

Sandhills Country Cabin
BREWSTER, NEBRASKA 68821

Ask real estate agents about the value of a piece of property and they'll tell you that only three things really count: "Location, location, location."

If that's true, then Sandhills Country Cabin might be worth a million dollars. Just for its views.

It's located in the heart of Nebraska's Sandhills region, the world's largest vegetated sand dunes. Oceans of empty, hilly, sandy-soiled grasslands stretch from horizon to horizon, often with not so much as an outbuilding or barn desecrating the scenery. Just wandering cattle dot the landscape.

But the North Central Nebraska cabin has

even more going for it than that. It's surrounded by four beautiful rivers—the Dismal, Middle Loup, North Loup, and Calamus—and plunked down in the middle of a huge cow ranch.

In fact, the cabin nestles on the banks of the North Loup River, where you're more likely to see wandering deer, coyotes, and migrating sand-hill cranes than you are to see other people. It is rustic, with antique barnboard siding adding to its country decor. There's comfy furniture, a full kitchenette, and plenty of peace and quiet—except for the lowing of the cows.

When my brother Mark and I visited here, all was deserted, as the ranchers/innkeepers were out on the prairie doing chores. (Even their cabin brochure cautions that the "best time to call for reservations is between 6 A.M. and 8 A.M.") But that didn't stop us from enjoying the solitude of the open prairie, looking over cows, walking down to the river, and just plain having a good old country-boy time.

Beverly serves a full ranch breakfast to cabin guests. Then you can choose to wander around the ranch yourself, take a tour with the owners, or even help out with ranch duties during roundup and branding times.

The newest addition to this western outpost is another cabin, done in weathered barnboard to give it that Wild West feel. The three-bedroom, two-bath cabin also boasts a living and dining room. Yee-hah! Bring the entire family!

How to get there: From North Platte, take U.S. 83 north to Nebraska 2 (at Thedford); then go east about 27 miles to Dunning; continue east on Nebraska 91 to Brewster, then turn north on Nebraska 7, at the northeast edge of town; turn left on the first oiled country road, and proceed ½ mile to the cabin.

Innkeepers: Lee and Beverly DeGroff
Address/Telephone: HC 63 (mailing address: P. O. Box 13); (308) 547-2460
Rooms: 1 rustic cabin and 1 large cabin; each with private bath.
Rates: Rustic cabin: $50, single; $55, double; $12, each child under 12; large cabin: $200 per night; EPB. Horse and pet day charges available.
Open: All year.
Facilities and activities: Views of rivers, cattle ranch; horse barn available for your own animals. Fishing, canoeing, ranch trails, wildlife tours, cattle drives, branding, calving. Nearby: Halsey National Forest, Fort Hartsuff, Nebraska's Big Rodeo (Burwell), Calamus Dam and Fish Hatchery, National Country Music Festival (August in Ainsworth), Willow Lake, Sandhills scenic drives.

Thompson House
BROWNVILLE, NEBRASKA 68321

There's lots of history in Brownville. On July, 15 1804 at what is now the town park on the Missouri River, the fabled Lewis and Clark expedition came to shore, beaching their 55-foot keelboat, two pirogues, and dugout canoes. Meriwether Lewis noted the area's bounty of wild fruit in his journal—grapes, two kinds of wild cherries, gooseberries, hazelnuts, and more. Then the expedition continued on.

It took the 1854 Nebraska–Kansas Act to get Brownville started. Richard Brown became the first settler in the new territory, and soon the rivertown became a popular transfer point used by covered-wagon trains headed westward.

You'd be hard-pressed to guess correctly by looking around at today's tiny tranquil hamlet, but by the 1870s, Brownville's population soared to nearly 3,500. However, the town faltered when citizens passed a bond issue designed to attract the railroad to town; when a railroad company laid only 10 miles of track and then abandoned the project, the town went bankrupt—and settlers moved on.

Today, the hamlet supports a regionally renowned summer theater, attracting nationally known entertainers to its environs. It also boasts several historic buildings, the earliest dating to the 1859–1870 boom days.

One of these is the Thompson House, a handsome 1869 two-story brick home with five gables and two chimneys. It's located in a little hollow just past the town's main street.

Beautifully restored and transformed into a delightful bed and breakfast by Lorraine and Carl, the historic home boasts fine country Victorian furnishings, as well as a private walking bridge leading into the hollow that guarantees private times to enjoy natural surroundings.

All guest rooms are done in handsome Victorian antiques and include tall hardwood headboards, with beds graced by handmade quilts and coverlets. The master suite also offers a magnificent stained-glass window.

Common rooms include two parlors, one with a wood-burning stove. And Lorraine's

breakfasts might include egg soufflés, steam-sautéed turkey ham, homemade apple cinnamon and banana nut muffins, fresh fruits, juices and coffee.

Make sure you stroll around the town before you leave. And see if it isn't one of the friendliest little places this side of the Missouri.

How to get there: From Omaha, take U.S. 75 south to Auburn, then turn east on U.S. 136, and continue into Brownville; take a sharp left just before the bridge onto Main Street, continue to 4th Street, then turn left on College, go one block and turn right onto 5th Street; proceed for about half a block to the inn.

Innkeepers: Carl and Lorraine Rohman
Address/Telephone: Fifth and College Streets; (402) 825–6551
Rooms: 5; 3 with private bath, all with air conditioning.
Rates: $45 to $70, single or double, EPB.
Open: All year.
Facilities and activities: Patio/porch, large yard with walking bridge crossing creek. Nearby: is town art gallery and gift shops, summer theater, Missouri River cruises on *Spirit of Brownville*, two restaurants, old-fashioned soda fountain, Capt. Meriwether Lewis Museum of Missouri River History, Brownville Historical Society Museum. A short drive to Indian Cave State Park.

The Cambridge Inn
CAMBRIDGE, NEBRASKA 69022

"We always said it'd take a lot to get us out of Colorado," noted Elaine. "But once we stepped inside this house, we knew it had to be ours."

"It" is The Cambridge Inn, a historic 1907 Neoclassical Revival house that's been a landmark in Cambridge for as long as anyone can remember. Built by W. H. and Anna Faling (he helped incorporate the town), the magnificent house retains the elegant features of an era long past.

These include luxurious cherry, oak, and pine woodwork; stained and beveled glass; and hand-grained walls and ceilings created by Danish craftsmen.

Actually, it was Mike who first spotted the house, then for sale, on a return trip from visiting his son's college in Galesburg, Illinois. He drove around the block a few times, then told Elaine about it on his return home to Colorado. They made the five-hour drive from Loveland on a pleasant day in October, walked inside the house . . . , "And that was it," Elaine said.

The innkeepers have fashioned an elegant inn full of Victorian charm. An entrance hall showcases a magnificent oak staircase leading to second-floor guest rooms; above the landing is an incredible stained-glass window original to the house. Memorable breakfasts in the dining room, itself a showplace, with its 10-foot-tall built-in fruitwood and leaded-glass sideboard, might include French toast stuffed with cream cheese and walnuts, fruit plates, and more. And the parlor features twin oak columns at least 10 feet high.

Among the guest rooms, Ivy Court is my favorite. Originally the home's master bedroom, it retains a high Victorian ambience. Its antique furnishings include a writing desk. There's a sitting room and a bay window gussied up with lace curtains. Its private bath also claims the home's original "water closet"—a claw-footed tub, pedestal sink, and unusual foot bath.

Choose Morningside and you'll get a quilt-covered bed and antique oak armoire (see if you can find the signatures of those Danish workmen who crafted all the house's wood-grain appear-

ances out of common oak). Or opt for the more simple Goldenrod, once the maid's room but now a bright, cozy retreat decorated with patterns of wildflowers.

And make sure to get out and explore the region during your stay here. The inn is located in the heart of the Republican River Valley (in fact, most of the river's bends take a hard right . . . just kidding!) of the Prairie Lakes region in Southwest Nebraska—a spot noted for great fishing, boating, and biking across its gently rolling hills.

How to get there: Take U.S. 6/34 into Cambridge (whose name changes to Nasby Street in town). Follow the road to the intersection of Nasby and Parker; the inn sits on the corner.

Innkeepers: Mike and Elaine Calabro
Address/Telephone: 606 Parker (mailing address: P. O. Box 239); (308) 697–3220
Rooms: 5; 3 with private bath. No smoking inn.
Rates: $35 to $65, single; $50 to $75, double; EPB.
Open: All year.
Facilities and activities: Lunch and dinner available by arrangement. Parlor, library, dining room, front porch. Nearby: golf, museums, antiques stores, Medicine Creek State Recreation Area, hunting, fishing, boating, biking.

Fort Robinson State Park

CRAWFORD, NEBRASKA 69339

Any enthusiast of the Wild West has to love a stay at historic Fort Robinson. Established in 1874 near the site of the troubled Red Cloud Indian Agency, which handed out supplies to 13,000 hostile Sioux as mandated by a "peace treaty," Fort Robinson was one of the most troubled spots on the Plains and "witness to the last tragic days of the Plains Indian wars."

It was the scene of the Battle of Warbonnet Creek in 1876, when Indians from Red Cloud attempted to flee and join legendary Sioux warrior Crazy Horse after the Battle of Little Big Horn; where Crazy Horse was killed "while trying to escape imprisonment"—actually, he was bayoneted in the back by a fort soldier; and it saw the epic 1879 Cheyenne Outbreak, led by Dull Knife, when Cheyenne warriors escaped from barracks at the fort, only to be killed or captured two weeks later.

Wander around the grounds to see original buildings, which tell the story of the fort's storied past. Visit the Post Headquarters, now a museum filled with artifacts from Indian Wars days; tour Adobe Officers' Quarters, some of the fort's oldest buildings, dating to 1874; stop by the Blacksmith Shop, where a muscled smithy will tell you how busy he was in the days of the U.S. Cavalry.

Guest rooms are snapshots of history. You can overnight in one of those original adobe officers' quarters; take a modest room at the Lodge, originally the Enlisted Men's Barracks; or rule the Peterson Ranch, a home on a designated wildlife preserve 3 miles west of the lodge that includes use of the barn and corral.

Kids love a ride in an original stagecoach, just like the ones that crossed the plains. Jeep rides tour surrounding landscapes of buttes and grasslands and include a visit to the grounds of the infamous Red Cloud Agency; and buffalo treks offer up-close peeks at the American bison.

And tell me how anyone could resist a delicious buffalo-stew campfire cookout, with a sing-along under the stars.

How to get there: From Chadron, take U.S. 20 west; 2 miles past Crawford, you'll come to park headquarters; turn toward the parade grounds and you're there.

Innkeeper: Jim Lemmon, park superintendent

Address/Telephone: 3200 Highway 20 (mailing address: P. O. Box 392); (308) 665–2900, fax (308) 665–2901

Rooms: 22 lodge rooms, 24 cabins and adobes, 7 multiple-bedroom units, and 1 ranch house; all with private bath. Wheelchair access.

Rates: lodge rooms: $26 to $51, single or double; cabin/adobes: $52 to $83; multiple-bed room units: $125 to $151; ranch house: $130; EP.

Open: Park open all year; lodging open April through late November; activities open Memorial Day through Labor Day.

Facilities and activities: On the grounds of historic Fort Robinson. Full-service restaurant, museum, restored-buildings tour, activities center, sutler's store, swimming pool, horseback riding, jeep rides, train tour, buffalo tours, stagecoach rides, biking, hay wagon rides, chuck wagon cookout, campfire programs, rodeo, Post Playhouse (live theater), picnic shelter, campgrounds. Nearby: golf at Legends Butte, hiking at Soldier Creek Wilderness Area.

Meadow View Ranch Bed & Breakfast Bunkhouse
GORDON, NEBRASKA 69343

"You'll have to excuse me," Billie said as she dusted herself off. "I just got in from a day of branding and I can still feel the sand in my boots."

Billie and Clyde's cattle ranch stretches across 5,000 acres of Nebraska's Sandhills region, noted for sprawling prairie grasses and craggy, pine-dotted canyons. The original ranch bunkhouse, where guests overnight, is smack dab in the middle of these sandhills and lush meadows.

Along with 400 head of breeding cattle and "too many horses to count."

The amiable ranchers remind visitors that this is a working cattle ranch—you can help out with the chores during your stay. Sign up for the ranch's annual cattle drives and branding round-ups. Or simply enjoy this scenic, quiet retreat deep in the country.

Billie explained that the ranch has been in the family since 1906, when their ancestors homesteaded here from Texas. The bunkhouse has two bedrooms, sitting room, full kitchen, full bath and shower, and more. In the Waddill Room, you'll find antique furniture that belonged to the ranch's first settlers.

Ranch breakfasts include a guest favorite, Billie's blueberry cakes, as well as fruit-filled French toast, pancakes, eggs, sausage, juices, and coffee. If you want a memorable ranch evening, try Meadow View's steak or hamburger cookouts.

You'll feel like real cowboys and cowgirls out on the lonesome prairie.

How to get there: From Chadron, take U.S. 20 east past Gordon to Irwin Road, a dirt road just before mile marker 121 (if you pass this marker, you've gone too far). Follow Irwin 6 miles north, then go 2 miles west and continue to the ranch.

Innkeepers: Clyde and Billie Lefler
Address/Telephone: HC 91, Box 29; (308) 282–0679 or (308) 282–1359
Rooms: 2-bedroom ranch bunkhouse, with private bath and kitchen. No smoking inn.
Rates: $45, single; $60 double; $17 for each additional family member; $8 for children under 12; free for kids under 6; EPB.
Open: All year.
Facilities and activities: Horseback riding, Sandhills scenic jeep tour, wagon rides, satellite TV, VCR, hiking, nature photography. Nearby: Old-Time Cowboy Museum, Sandoz Museum, rodeos, canoeing on the Niobara River, Chadron State Park, Fort Robinson, Fur Trade Museum, Bowring Ranch, LaCreek National Wildlife Refuge, gateway to Black Hills of South Dakota.

The Kirschke House

GRAND ISLAND, NEBRASKA 68801

The feature I remember most about this handsome bed-and-breakfast inn is the magnificent stained-glass windows (original to the house) standing sentinel over the open, quarter-sawn oak staircase leading to second-floor guest rooms.

It's just one of the elegant touches that's convinced me to rate The Kirschke House as one of the prettiest little inns in all of Nebraska.

Lois and Kiffani have fashioned a country Victorian showplace in this historic 1902 two-story house, built by prominent contractor Otto Kirschke as his family home. (In case you're wondering why the house was made of brick— Kirschke owned the Grand Island Brick Works.

In fact, his firm also constructed the ornate Hall County Court House and other prominent business blocks and private homes.)

The house's original features include a windowed cupola, turret tower, and beveled and stained glass. In the sitting room, guests can enjoy a tiled fireplace, oriental rugs, and fine antiques. The innkeepers have added other Victorian antiques, delicate lace, and other period furnishings that translate into a terrific retreat. French doors lead to the dining room, where guests might take breakfasts of fresh fruit, egg and cheese casseroles with Canadian bacon, homemade blueberry muffins, and more.

My favorite guest room might be the

Morning Glory Vine Room, with its 6-foot-high oak headboard, bed adorned with an antique star quilt, and Victorian dresser with 6-foot-long mirror. But the most romantic probably is the Roses Room, with its lace-canopied four-poster bed and seven vine-dappled windows that let the sunlight stream in.

There's plenty to see in the area, including the Stuhr Museum of the Plains Pioneers, which even boasts Henry Fonda's birthplace home. But many guests are here to relax and would just as soon soak in the inn's wooden hot tub located in the lantern-lit brick washhouse, perfect for a late-night rendezvous with that special someone.

How to get there: From I–80, take Grand Island's west exit 312 and continue north 9 miles on Nebraska 281; at the Nebraska 30 exit, turn east, over an overpass into the city of Grand Island. Follow Highway 30 east to a traffic light at Broadwell Street; continue 4 blocks past this light, then turn north on Washington Street and go 1 more block. The Kirschke House is located across the street, north of the Edith Abbott Memorial Library.

Innkeepers: Lois Hank and Kiffani Smith
Address/Telephone: 1124 West 3rd Street; (308) 381–6851
Rooms: 5; 1 with private bath, 3 with sink in room. No smoking inn.
Rates: $45, single; $55 to $70, double; EPB.
Open: All year.
Facilities and activities: Can arrange for dinners. Sitting room, hot tub. Nearby: Fonner Park thoroughbred racing, sandhill-crane and whooping-crane migrations, Stuhr Museum of the Plains Pioneers, Piccadilly Dinner Theater, three public golf courses, L. E. Ray Beach and Park.

Memories Historic Bed and Breakfast
LEXINGTON, NEBRASKA 68850

This sprawling 1903 Victorian, built by Lexington's first jeweler, is a good spot to overnight while spending the day browsing in the numerous antiques shops in a town called "the antiques capital of Nebraska."

Even Marv and Pat's inn has its own antiques store, specializing in toys, dolls, teddy bears, folk primitives, and holiday items.

Holidays are well represented at Memories, since each of the inn's five guest rooms is named for a seasonal celebration. The Thanksgiving Room is adorned with an antique 1840s hanging quilt on one wall; coverlets on the bed date to the 1800s; and primitive folk art is everywhere.

Fourth of July will get every morning off to a star-spangled start. It has another antique quilt wall hanging, and there are a Victorian dresser and lots of folk art in red-white-and-blue motifs. The Christmas Room is most heavily Victorian of all the guest rooms, with antiques and folk art crammed into every nook and cranny.

Breakfasts in the dining room, complete with its own set of French doors opening to the patio and original oak woodwork, are sumptuous affairs. Consider fresh juices; raspberries and cream; ham, bacon, and egg casseroles; home-baked muffins, and more.

After eating, relax by the inn's patio fountain or walk off your feast by browsing through some of the town's antiques shops. Among my favorites are Richardson's Bargain Shed, for Depression glass; J R Antiques, with an intriguing variety of primitives, tins, and linens; and Bargain John and Sons Antiques, which specializes in primitive and antique furniture.

How to get there: From I–80, get off at the Lexington exit and take U.S. 283 into town; turn left (west) on 6th Street, go 2 blocks to Washington, then turn north on Washington and proceed to the inn (located at Washington and 9th streets).

Innkeepers: Marv and Pat Goldsmith
Address/Telephone: 900 North Washington; (308) 324–3290
Rooms: 3; all with private bath. No smoking inn.
Rates: $45 to $50, single; $50 to $60, double; EPB.
Open: All year.
Facilities and activities: Sitting room, parlor, dining room, 2 porches, patio, fountain. Nearby: 10 antiques shops, Dawson County Fairgrounds; "Annual Antiques Extravaganza" on Labor Day weekend.

The Rogers House
LINCOLN, NEBRASKA 68502

This 1914 Jacobean Revival house sits in the Historic Near South neighborhood of Lincoln, a quiet tree-lined respite off the beaten path from the city's University of Nebraska campus hubbub.

Built for its namesake banker, who hailed from Minden, The Rogers House, a local historic landmark, features leaded and beveled glass, French doors, polished hardwood floors, and antiques-filled guest rooms. It's hard to believe these elegant furnishings weren't destroyed during the home's ten-year stint as a fraternity house. "We have some frat brothers who return here on business," said Blake, an assistant innkeeper who led us on a guided tour of the inn.

"They tell us some pretty wild stories."

I especially liked the inn's common sunroom, which faces east and gets plenty of morning rays—a cheerful way to start any new day.

If you overnight in the Hillsdale Room, you'll be staying in the mansion's original guest room; it has a four-poster bed and great views of the historic neighborhood. The Doctor's Retreat, originally the summer master bedroom, is adorned with a four-poster lace canopy bed and its own private sunroom. Or perhaps you'd like to climb to third-floor tranquillity in the Jacobean Room, with its queen-sized antique bed, claw-footed bathtub, and window seat (where dancers used to sit awaiting appropriate suitors during mansion soirées in the house's ballroom (which originally took up the entire third floor).

Home-cooked breakfasts might include such specialties as German baked eggs, just-made muffins, fruit dishes, and juices.

Nora also has four guest rooms in a historic 1909 home next door; some of these feature whirlpool tubs. It's simply called the West House.

How to get there: From I-80, take the downtown O Street exit and continue to 9th Street; turn south (right), then proceed to A Street; turn left and continue to 22nd Street; turn left again and go 1 block to B. The inn is on the corner of 22nd and B.

Innkeeper: Nora Houtsma
Address/Telephone: 2145 B Street; (402) 476–6961
Rooms: 12; all with private bath.
Rates: $54 to $110, single; $59 to $115, double; EPB.
Open: All year.
Facilities and activities: Library, sitting room with fireplace, sunrooms. Nearby: downtown Lincoln, University of Nebraska campus, Historic Haymarket District shops, New State Museum, State Capitol, University of Nebraska Museum, Antelope Park sunken gardens, Christlieb Western Art Collection, National Museum of Roller Skating. Short drive to 7 Salt Valley State Recreation Areas, golf, swimming. Homestead National Monument about 50 miles south.

The Offutt House
OMAHA, NEBRASKA 68131

Jeannie was preparing the inn for a wedding reception upon our arrival. "It's beautiful weather for a bride," Jeannie said, referring to the bright sun and 84-degree temperature.

And it also was a great day to visit The Offutt House, a fourteen-room 1894 mansion built for its namesake legislator in elegant Château style. It became an Omaha landmark immediately upon completion.

Walk through a double set of double doors adorned with beveled glass to a greeting room with quarter-sawn oak woodwork. There are more fine woods in the rest of the house—rich mahogany graces the library (be sure to note the

10-foot-long fireplace mantel), and walnut fancies up the dining room.

Guest rooms offer several interesting features. The Fireside Room has its own fireplace, canopy iron-rail bed, and a deep claw-footed tub perfect for soaking away any worries. The Porch Suite has its own sleeping porch (of course!) surrounded by seven tall windows; it's a great place to cool off during hot Omaha summer nights. And the third-floor Honeymoon Suite is a remote getaway in this big house, ensuring privacy for newlyweds.

Jeannie's Sunday breakfasts might include sausage and egg *strata*, homemade sweet rolls, and juices and other beverages. Maybe that's when you can get the innkeeper to fill you in on the house's most enduring legend. Okay, I'll do it myself.

During the infamous Easter Sunday Tornado of 1913, when the Offutt House was one of only a handful of graceful homes that survived the terrible winds, a local source reported that "an open decanter of sherry was carried 35 feet from the dining room sideboard to the living room without spilling a drop."

Believe it or not!

How to get there: From downtown Omaha, take Dodge Street west to 39th Street, turn north, and proceed to the end of the block and the inn.

Innkeeper: Jeannie Swoboda

Address/Telephone: 140 North 39th Street; (402) 553–0951

Rooms: 8, including 2 suites; 6 with private bath.

Rates: $55 to $95, single or double, EPB Sunday only, continental breakfast all other days.

Open: All year.

Facilities and activities: Sitting room, library, bar room, screened sun porch. Located in Historic Gold Coast neighborhood; a short drive to Old Market Area, Western Heritage Museum, Strategic Air Command Museum, Joslyn Art Museum, General Crook House, Omaha Playhouse, Fontenelle Forest, Pappillion Creek Dam Sites.

Dancing Leaf Earth Lodge
STOCKVILLE, NEBRASKA 69042

The wind was blowing ferociously at about forty-five miles per hour when we arrived at Dancing Leaf, located on the banks of Medicine Creek, in a setting of rolling hills that once hosted farming ancestors of the Pawnee Tribe.

And the surrounding cottonwoods were really dancing, raising the noise level from their usual polite ballet to that of a stampeding crowd.

Les took us to one of the earth lodges, which appear much as they would have more than 1,000 years ago, built by the Upper Republican Culture in this region's prehistoric times. He explained that it took about 400 hours to construct the dwelling.

"First, you have to cut the timber, in this case about 300 ash, cedar, and hackleberry trees, and cure it months before you start to build," he explained. "Then we excavate a 20-foot-by-20-foot living floor and set native trees in holes to provide support for the walls and roof." These are made from more than 200 rafter poles, which are layered with sandbar willows and prairie hay to provide protection from the elements for this igloo-shaped dwelling.

My brother, Mark, was especially fascinated by these Native American earth lodges, perhaps because he'd recently finished a few college courses in prehistoric archaeology and the sociology of indigenous peoples.

Another unique characteristic of the lodge

is its long, low entryway. Mark and I had to bend almost in half to traverse the walkway.

"This acts as a chimney for the cold and heat," Les said. In fact, if you keep the lodge flap down, temperatures inside stay at 75 degrees during summer. Heat from the central fire hearth (with smoke escaping through a smokehole) keeps things toasty enough in winter.

But Dancing Leaf is much more than an opportunity to experience a facet of prehistoric culture. "Guests tell us that this place often prompts a personal spiritual reawakening, a chance to get in touch with the renewing power of nature and to learn more about themselves," Les said.

Such profound experiences occur most often after introduction to the sweat lodge, Les explained.

How to get there: From North Platte, exit I–80 and go south on U.S. 83; turn left (east) on Nebraska 23/18 at Maywood, and proceed to Curtis; then follow Nebraska 18 east into Stockville. Go into town; at the intersection with the county fairgrounds on the corner, turn left (there is a sign here), go past the fairgrounds, past the brick schoolhouse, and over the switchback bridge crossing Medicine Creek to the earth-lodge office. It's about 1½ miles north of Stockville.

Innkeepers: Les and Jan Hosick

Address/Telephone: Box 121; (308) 367–4233

Rooms: 2 authentic Native American earth lodges; portable bathroom provided.

Rates: $25 per adult, $17 per child; EP. $40 per adult, $27 per child; AP (may include some nontraditional meals).

Open: All year.

Facilities and activities: Native American sweat lodge, nature trails, primitive living skills classes, calendar pole and medicine wheel, prehistoric garden, spiritual-bonding points, council areas, Medicine Creek mud slides (swimming), canoeing, fishing. Also explore lodge's archaeological sites, museum, gift shop. Less than 1 hour's drive to Lexington antiques shops and Buffalo Bill's Scout's Rest Ranch in North Platte.

The Blue Colonial
TRENTON, NEBRASKA 69044

My brother, Mark, and I arrived at the Blue Colonial just past 8:00 P.M. Peter answered the door dressed in a Scottish clan kilt and its accoutrements.

We were slightly nonplussed, to say the least. After all, we were in the middle of Nebraska, miles from anywhere, and didn't expect to run into a traditionally garbed Highlander out on a llama ranch.

But proud Scotsman Peter explained that he and Marita were serving a formal dinner to guests, and though quite unexpected, we were more than welcome to explore the inn as we wished.

Marita soon joined us and conducted a whirlwind tour of this cozy inn. Rather than a ranch house, this bed and breakfast feels more like an elegant little country house. Marita showed off the lovely Gathering Room, which is beautifully decorated with many of Peter's British antiques, including Scottish clan swords and coats of arms, and a magnificent 1820s English desk.

As you've probably already guessed, Peter, a retired clergyman, was born in Scotland.

Despite Highlander influences, other gathering rooms and guest rooms have a more Western ambience to them. The Round-Up Room (see what I mean?) offers a television and is crammed with Western art and curios. And the library is another pleasant retreat, with its handsome brass chandelier and huge collection of books, seemingly covering every subject.

Of the guest rooms, Prairie Wolf might be the most impressive. That's because of its folk-art wolf headboard, which is just about life-sized. The Bison Room is another charmer, with its buffalo art, bronzes, and a buffalo-gun wall decoration. Even the shared bathroom is country cool, with its barnboard paneling, claw-footed tub, and mirror fashioned from a horse collar.

Breakfast can be enjoyed in your room, in the formal dining room, or (my favorite) in the small country dining room decorated with early nineteenth-century Scandinavian furniture.

Later on take a hike with the mama llama, who'll pack a mean picnic lunch while you hike over the grasslands. Just watch out; those llamas can spit better than most big-league ballplayers.

How to get there: From Culbertson, take U.S. 34 west 6 miles past Trenton, then turn right on a ranch road (there's a small BLUE COLONIAL sign, but you've got to look hard for it), and continue about 2 miles to the inn.

Innkeepers: Peter and Marita Todd
Address/Telephone: HC2, Box 120; (308) 276–2535
Rooms: 3, with 1 two-bedroom suite, share 2 baths. No smoking inn.
Rates: $48 to $68, single; $58 to $78, double; EPB. Packages available.
Open: All year.
Facilities and activities: Dinner and chuck wagon dinners available. Round-Up Room for television viewing, library, antiques store. Antiques and art collecting classes available. Hay rides. Hiking and picnicking can be arranged. Nearby: a short drive to Swanson Lake for swimming, fishing, boating. Golf course 6 miles away. Turkey, deer, pheasant, quail, geese, and duck hunting among the finest in state.

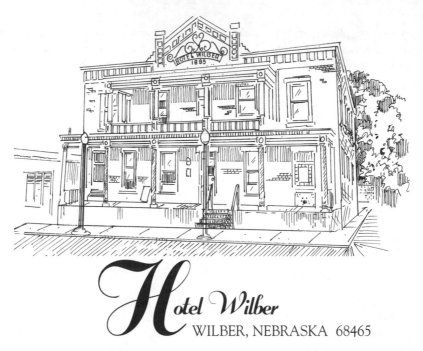

*H*otel *W*ilber

WILBER, NEBRASKA 68465

One glance at the dinner menu made my mouth water. *Pecena kachna*—roast duck served with *knedliky* (potato dumplings) and *zeli* (Czech-style kraut). Czech sausage. And Pilsner Urquell, a gourmet Czech beer rated "Europe's Finest."

Oh, yes. There's a hotel here, too.

Actually, the Hotel Wilber is an award-winning restoration of the town's historic 1895 hostelry that sits on the corner of Second and Wilson streets in the heart of Wilber, self-proclaimed "Czech Capital of the USA." Frances said that the entire town pitched in to raise funds for its phoenixlike rise to prominence; in fact, several of the antiques featured in guest rooms are heirlooms that belonged to families who helped transform the hotel into a deluxe inn.

One of my favorite hotel antiques sits in the lobby/sitting room: That handsome pump organ was brought to the region from Ohio by covered wagon in the 1800s.

Guest rooms are named for primary restoration contributors. Among my favorites is the Ourecky Room, with its brass bed, country-blue quilt, and lovely view of the courtyard through three tall windows; that's Grandma and Grandpa Ourecky in the photo hanging on the wall. The Herman Room features a handsome sleigh bed. And the Fiala-Cech Room offers a wicker bed and ceiling fan.

Eating is part of the experience at this hotel. Frances's breakfasts include homemade fruit-filled *kolaches*, baked eggs, French toast, waffles, hash browns—good country cooking with a European twist. And I already mentioned those terrific dinners.

Explore the little town during daytime strolls. Founded in 1873, Wilber boasts a fascinating array of historical treasures brought over from Slovakia, Moravia, and Bohemia. Decorative folk art adorns the business district. Festive Old World music fills the air. Merchants offer baked goodies, deli meats, and sausages made according to traditional Czech recipes. And quaint shops sell everything from hand-crafted furniture, rugs, and quilts to Bohemian crystal, lace, and collectibles.

At night relax at the inn's Old World–style basement pub for some conversation with fellow guests, locals, and other friendly sorts. Or sit under the stars in the hotel courtyard.

As one of Frances's brochures says, "The Hotel Wilber is *more* than a hotel. It's like staying at Grandmother's house. (Only we have a bar in the basement.)" Good to see that some people still have a sense of humor.

How to get there: From I–80, take Wilber exit 388 and proceed south on Nebraska 103 into Wilber. At Wilson Street, turn right to Second Street. The inn sits at this intersection.

Innkeeper: Frances Erb

Address/Telephone: 203 South Wilson (mailing address: P. O. Box 641); (402) 821–2020 or (800) 609–4663

Rooms: 10; share separate men's and women's baths, showers; all with air conditioning, cable TV by request.

Rates: $42 to $65, single or double, EPB.

Open: All year.

Facilities and activities: Lunch and dinner available in Old-World dining room, lobby sitting room, basement pub, garden patio. Can arrange walking tours of Wilber. Wilber Czech Museum, Czech Village, swimming pool nearby.

Recommended Country Inns® Travelers' Club Benefit: 10 percent discount, subject to availability, excluding the Wilber Czech Festival weekend in August.

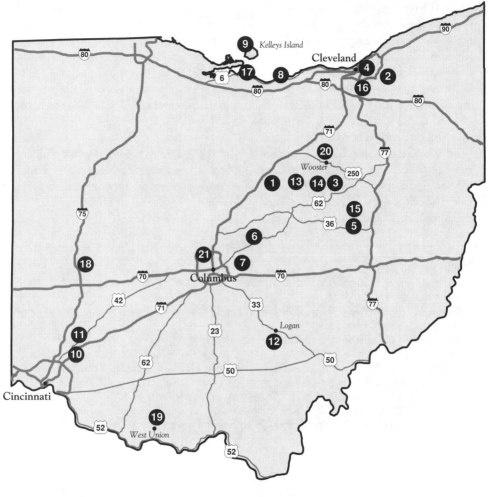

Kelleys Island

Cleveland

Wooster

Logan

Columbus

Cincinnati

West Union

Ohio

Ohio

Numbers on map refer to towns numbered below.

The Frederick Fitting House
BELLVILLE, OHIO 44813

Baby Kate originally discovered The Frederick Fitting House. It had been time for my then two-month-old daughter's midday feeding, so I drove down a quiet side street on this hot spring day looking for a parking spot bathed in shade. We stopped in front of a beautiful 1863 Italianate home and immediately were drawn inside.

It's absolutely beautiful, completely furnished in American folk art and Ohio antiques; many are family heirlooms with interesting stories behind them, so be sure to get Ramon and Suzanne to weave their magic tales.

The sight of the dining room almost took my breath away. Wonderful stencilwork has been done everywhere; it covers even the original yellow-pine plank floor.

Breakfasts are served on a big square table that invites conversation. (In summer, breakfast is outside in the gazebo.) Specialties include crepes, home-baked breads, and Dutch pastries, served along with Richland County honey, fresh fruit, and juice. There's even a choice of specially blended coffee and herbal teas. Ramon and Suzanne recommend Lola's in Marshfield or The Brass Plate in Loudonville for fine dining, or the nearby San-Dar restaurant for smorgasbord-style dining. They can also arrange candlelight dinners at the inn for guests.

Walking up a magnificent freestanding spiral staircase of walnut, butternut, and oak, I found three charming guest rooms. The Colonial Room, with a canopy bed covered in lace, is perfect for romantics. Especially noteworthy among its many fine antique furnishings is a primitive pioneer coverlet.

But my favorite is the Shaker Room, with its simple twin beds, antique writing desk, straight-back rocking chair, and wall pegs from which hang antique Shaker work utensils.

During the holiday season, the inn's two 10- foot Christmas trees are decorated with hand-crafted ornaments, and luminarias glow along the outside walkway.

How to get there: Bellville is directly between Cleveland and Columbus. Leave I–71 at exit 165 and proceed east on State Route 97 into the village. Turn left onto Fitting Avenue. The inn is the last home on the left at the intersection of Fitting Avenue and Ogle Street.

Innkeepers: Ramon and Suzanne Wilson
Address/Telephone: 72 Fitting Avenue; (419) 886–2863
Rooms: 3; all with private bath.
Rates: $48 to $62, single; $58 to $72, double; EPB.
Open: All year except Thanksgiving Day and Christmas Day.
Facilities and activities: Picnic-basket lunch; candlelight dinner with wine, fresh flowers, music. Golf course, tennis courts nearby. Little shops and jogging trails in all directions. Canoeing and skiing (in season) within a few minutes' drive. Two state parks a short drive away. The Renaissance Theatre, the Mansfield Art Center, and the Kingwood Gardens within a half hour's drive. Mid-Ohio Raceway in Lexington is site of major sports-car races.
Recommended Country Inns® Travelers' Club Benefit: Stay two nights, get third night free, Sunday–Thursday, May–October; or Monday–Sunday, November–April.

The Inn at Chagrin Falls
CHAGRIN FALLS, OHIO 44022

Driving into Chagrin Falls, I thought I'd entered a cinema time warp and arrived at Bedford Falls, home to Jimmy Stewart in the movie *It's a Wonderful Life*. See if you don't get the same feeling when you first arrive.

The inn is an elegant retreat fashioned from the historic Crane's Canary Cottage. Built in 1927, it still sports canary-colored clapboards that give a light and airy touch to the surroundings.

Inside, guests first reach the Gathering Room. It boasts English-style antiques, including my favorite—a plump, King George wing chair. There's also a Victorian round-back sofa fronting the large hearth, whose fire always seems to be going.

Guest rooms are exquisitely fashioned with antique reproductions of fine furniture houses such as Colonial Williamsburg, Drexel, and Baker. Among my favorites is the Crane Suite, with its king-sized bed, Jacuzzi, and a (now gas-burning) fireplace, original to the home, that has a massive hearth; it must measure at least 6 feet long and 4 feet high.

The Philomethian Suite is another beauty, offering a four-poster mahogany bed, plantation-shuttered windows, corner fireplace, and whirlpool. And my traveling companions, daughters Kate and Dayne, seemed partial to the Mill Room, named after the old paper mill powered by the falls. They liked the draped, four-poster canopy bed and fireplace, whose antique marble is imported from Italy.

You can enjoy breakfast in a handsome pine-paneled dining room that features oak refectory tables and highbacked Windsor chairs. Morning fare usually consists of cereals, seasonal fruits, English muffins with fresh jams, and the inn's specialty—sour cream coffee cake.

Do try dinner at Gamekeeper's Taverne, attached to the inn. Where else might you sample char-grilled blackwing ostrich fillet, black buck antelope, or sautéed elk tenderloin? Other delicious entrees include herb-crusted rib pork chop, cedar-planked salmon, and penne pasta with smoked venison sausage.

Of course, no visit to the inn would be complete without browsing among the boutiques of this quaint, picture-perfect village. And why not partake in a village tradition on your visit: Buy and ice cream cone and relax by the falls!

How to get there: From Cleveland, take I-77 south to I-480 east, then follow U.S. 271 north. The first exit on 271 is Chagrin Boulevard; get off and go east 9 miles to reach Chagrin Falls. As you come into town there will be a large hill; before reaching the stoplight at the bottom of the hill, turn right on West Street to the inn. If you pass the stoplight, turn around.

Innkeeper: Mary Beth O'Donnell
Address/Telephone: 87 West Street; (216) 247–1200, fax (216) 247–2122
Rooms: 15, with 4 suites; all with private bath, several with fireplace and whirlpool. No smoking in rooms.
Rates: $105 to $195, double; subtract $10 for single; continental breakfast.
Open: All year.
Facilities and activities: Gathering room with fireplace; Gamekeeper's Taverne for fine dining. Nearby: walk to falls, browse quaint village shops, hike in Western Reserve surroundings. Eastern suburb of Cleveland only a short ride to Rock 'n' Roll Hall of Fame, Jacob's Field, home of the Cleveland Indians; Severance Center, home to Cleveland Orchestra; The Flats, Cleveland's riverfront nightlife; and Sea World.

The Charm Countryview Inn
CHARM, OHIO 44617

"Papa, this is one of the most beautiful places I've ever seen," said Dayne.

It was mighty impressive, a huge country house perched atop a hill with an expansive front lawn that overwhelms the eye. The scene reminded me more of a country manor house than simply a handsome inn in the heart of Ohio's Amish country.

We drove up the winding driveway (actually, it's more like a road, it stretches on for so long) over a bridge that fords a bubbling creek and parked in front of the inn, which sits on the edge of peaceful woods amid a patchwork of Amish fields and pasturelands.

Even the air smelled country fresh and new.

The girls immediately started a game of tag on the lawn, while my wife, Debbie, and I went to introduce ourselves. A note taped to the door, however, told us that Naomi and Paul were at Sunday services and wouldn't be back for some time.

We were disappointed because our travel schedule wouldn't allow us to wait for them. But we sneaked a peek on our own.

What a place! Guest rooms are handsome, each individually decorated and featuring Amish-handcrafted oak furniture and handmade quilts on double beds. The living room has a fireplace, a perfect spot to curl up in front of with a book or magazine from the inn's "library." Kate, of lately a checkers fiend, pointed out a set that could occupy hours of our time.

Country breakfasts are taken on long harvest-style tables in the dining room. They will satiate any size of appetite and might include a concoction of fruit pizzas, scrambled eggs, hash browns, biscuits and gravy, home-baked muffins, and juices and other beverages; Sundays feature a continental breakfast.

By this time, daughters Kate and Dayne had settled into comfy rocking chairs on the inn's front porch, returning birdcalls from the feathery creatures that they had befriended during our short visit. We must come back again, sometime soon, and enjoy the tranquil setting.

How to get there: From Cleveland/Akron, take I–77 south to the Dover exit; turn west on Ohio 39 to Ohio 93 at Sugarcreek; turn south (left) on Route 93 and follow it 3 miles to Ohio 557. Turn west (right) and drive about 4½ miles through Farmerstown to the inn, which is on the left side of the road.

Innkeepers: Paul and Naomi Miller
Address/Telephone: State Road 557 (mailing address: P .O. Box 100); (216) 893–3003
Rooms: 15; all with private bath. No smoking inn.
Rates: $65 to $95, single or double, EPB, Monday through Saturday; continental breakfast on Sunday.
Open: All year except Christmas.
Facilities and activities: Sitting room, dining room, porch, gardens, woods, trails. Nearby: Ole Mill Furniture Store, antiques stores, Amish craft shops. A short drive to Amish home-cooking restaurants and eateries featuring ethnic Swiss cuisine.

$\mathcal{G}$lidden $\mathcal{H}$ouse
CLEVELAND, OHIO 44106

"Papa, are you sure this isn't some fancy mansion instead of a B&B?" asked my daughter, Kate.

Well, it is both. It is a 1910 mansion, built in distinctive French Gothic style by Francis Kavanaugh Glidden, son of the founder of the Glidden Paint Company (it was occupied by Glidden family members until 1953).

But now the landmark building serves as a historic (and classy) bed-and-breakfast inn, painstakingly restored to its original grandeur and Old World ambience.

The lobby itself is elegant and posh, with distinctive Victorian flourishes. But we got ahead of ourselves during our stay and couldn't resist a peek at the manse's original parlor, which now serves as the inn dining room. We marvelled at the great stone fireplace, a fire blazing in the hearth. Floral wall coverings gave a high Victorian feel to the room. So did the dark wainscoting and ceiling beams—all handsome hand-carved oak.

Our room was in the new wing, added in 1988 but designed to complement the house's historical significance and architectural integrity. Dayne, Kate's sister, especially liked the country Victorian decor.

"This antique pine is a lot like our house," she said. "It makes me feel sort of like I'm at home."

Sort of.

Glidden House suites are on the upper floors; a few even retain the original ornately carved fireplaces.

The next morning we were back in the parlor for a sprawling breakfast buffet of fresh fruits, juices, cereals, fresh-baked breads, muffins, croissants, preserves, and sweet rolls.

Kate and Dayne decided that it'd be "okay" to come back here someday.

How to get there: From I-90, exit at Dr. Martin Luther King Drive and go south to East Boulevard; follow the circle to Ford Drive and the inn.

Innkeeper: Sharon Chapman, general manager

Address/Telephone: 1901 Ford Drive; (216) 231–8900, fax (216) 231–2130

Rooms: 60, including 8 suites; all with private bath, TV, radio, and air conditioning. Wheelchair access.

Rates: $140, single; $150, double; $160 to $185, suites; continental breakfast.

Open: All year.

Facilities and activities: Dining room, sitting room. Stroll to Wade Oval. A short drive to Case Western Reserve University, Cleveland Garden Center, Little Italy, Museum of Natural History, Severance Hall, Institutes for Music and Art.

Recommended Country Inns® Travelers' Club Benefit: 25 percent discount, subject to availability.

Roscoe Village Inn
COSHOCTON, OHIO 43812

I became curious about the Roscoe Village Inn's King Charlie's Tavern. Turns out it is named after Charlie, the first white settler in these parts. Legend has it that an heir to the throne of England stopped in the village tavern on his way across the country and made quite a fuss about how towns were so much more interesting in Europe. Charlie made things a lot more interesting for him right then and there, hiking him up by the seat of his pants and throwing him out the door.

The inn's choppy brick exterior design borrows heavily from other Greek Revival canal-era structures in the village. Inside, the second-floor parlor is a favorite with guests. It's easy to see why: It has exposed wood beams, a huge fireplace fronted by high-back sofas, a beautiful wrought-iron chandelier, and tall windows. Wonderful crafts are sprinkled throughout the inn (including hand-stitched quilts)—native Ohio folk art reflecting the village's canal-era heritage.

Rooms have sturdy, handcrafted wood furniture made by Amish craftsmen in nearby Holmes County. Four-poster beds, high-back chairs, and more tall windows add to the charm.

A full-service dining room, complete with china and silver, offers meals to guests in an atmosphere of Early American elegance. The inn's master chef prepares the most exciting culinary delights, which have been featured in many magazines; selections might include veal, sea scallops, and roast duckling. Breakfasts offer terrific choices as well, including whole-wheat griddle cakes and hazelnut whole-wheat waffles, served along with farm-fresh eggs, honey, and sweet butter.

Later I walked along the historic Ohio & Erie towpath north from the village to where the *Monticello III*, a reconstructed canal boat, floats passengers to Mudport Basin. And don't miss all the antiques and specialty stores along Whitewoman Street, which gets its name from the Walhonding River—*walhonding* is the Delaware Indian word for "white woman."

The inn also custom-tailors your schedule for your complete relaxation and enjoyment; the innkeeper will set up one- to three-day itineraries to suit your level of fun.

How to get there: From Cleveland to the north, take I–77 south to exit 65. Follow Route 36/16 west into Coshocton. Turn west on Ohio 541, then north on Whitewoman Street to the inn. From Columbus and Indianapolis to the southwest, take I–70 and exit north on Route 60. Then turn east on Route 16 and follow into Coshocton. Next follow the directions listed above.

Innkeeper: John Carpenter, manager
Address/Telephone: 200 North Whitewoman Street; (614) 622–2222 or (800) 237–7397
Rooms: 50; all with private bath, air conditioning, phone, and TV. Wheelchair access.
Rates: $79, single or double, Sunday through Thursday; $89, single or double, Friday and Saturday; continental breakfast. Several seasonal weekend packages.
Open: All year.
Facilities and activities: Full-service restaurant, tavern, sitting rooms. Nearby: Roscoe Village, 1830 canal town, includes canal boat rides, 21 craft shops, 5 exhibit-museum buildings, 4 restaurants, horse-drawn trolley, Johnson-Humrickhouse Museum. Amish country nearby. Pro Football Hall of Fame in Canton. Scenic countryside of Ohio River Valley.
Business travel: Located about 75 miles from downtown Columbus. Corporate rates, meeting rooms, fax.

The White Oak Inn
DANVILLE, OHIO 43014

Ian and Yvonne are from Ontario, Canada, and their inn is already renowned for dinner menus reflecting their Canadian-Scottish heritage. In fact, the White Oak has made newspaper headlines as "the country inn that fosters foreign tastes."

Yvonne, the inn's superb chef, is a native of Scotland. She's not bashful in blending the best of her native and Canadian gustatory specialties into deliciously pleasing, almost exotic, dining experiences. Consider a few of her Euro-styled country-gourmet delights: Mulligatawny Soup, a curried chicken soup; French Canadian *Tourtière*, a double-crusted meat pie laced with spices and served with sweet chutney or chunky tomato

sauce; and for sweet tooths, Canadian Nanaimo Bars, a tortelike obsession of chocolate, custard, coconut, and walnuts.

Yvonne's also been chosen as one of only fifty country-inn chefs in the United States to be on the DuPont Corporation's Country Inn Chefs Advisory Panel, an honor based on her superior cuisine and hospitality.

Ian is the inn's primary decorator/contractor/landscaper and all-around good guy. Seemingly always looking for ways to improve the inn, he's most recently succeeded in acquiring an antique pump-organ case refinished and fitted as a front desk. "It makes a statement," he said.

So do the inn's guest rooms. Those in the

main building, complete with everything from antique headboards to hand-carved washstands, boast all kinds of hardwoods, including oak, maple, walnut, cherry and poplar. In fact, I defy you to find a more beautiful shade of red maple than in the Maple Room.

Downstairs in common rooms, all the magnificent woodwork is white oak; the floor, red oak. It was fashioned from timber on this very land, cut just across the road, Ian said.

Additional rooms in the Guest House, just a short walk from the main building, offer spacious bedchambers closer to the woods; these include queen-sized beds and cozy fireplaces, perfect for romantics of the inn-wandering crowd. And all guests can enjoy Ian's screened porch, a perfect way to take advantage of summer's cool breezes without becoming mosquito fodder.

And here's an honor for the inn. It has been chosen to be featured on the PBS series *Country Inn Cooking with Gail Greco*. One of Yvonne's recipes that is highlighted: French Canadian pork *tourtière*. Yummm!

Another interesting White Oak attraction: Several Indian artifacts have been unearthed on inn property. Perhaps you'd like to be in on one of Ian's "digs" during "archaeology weekends." Led by a Kenyon College archaeology professor, you'll help with everything from digging up the ground to washing artifacts and labeling them.

How to get there: The inn is closer to Millwood than Danville. From Columbus, take U.S. 62 northeast to the junction of U.S. 36 and U.S. 62. Go east on U.S. 36 for 1 mile to Ohio 715, then 3 miles east to the inn.

Innkeepers: Ian and Yvonne Martin
Address/Telephone: 29683 Walhonding Road; (614) 599–6107
Rooms: 10; all with private bath and air conditioning, 3 with fireplace. No smoking inn.
Rates: $75 to $90, single or double; $85 to $130 for fireplace rooms; EBP. $25 for additional person or bed in room. Two-night minimum on weekends in May and October, and all holiday weekends. Archaeology, wildlife, theater, and murder-mystery packages available.
Open: All year.
Facilities and activities: Dinner available; cost is $19 to $27 per person for 4-course gourmet meals. BYOB. Expansive grounds, lawn games, screen house. Nearby: good antiques in area stores. Kokosing River offers some of best smallmouth-bass fishing in Ohio; also canoe livery. Thirty minutes from Millersburg, center of Amish culture in the United States; 35 minutes from Malabar Farm State Park; 25 minutes from Roscoe Village in Coshocton, restored canal-era town with own canal boat and towpath, specialty shops, and craft stores.
Recommended Country Inns® Travelers' Club Benefit: Stay one night, get 50 percent off second night, Sunday–Thursday.

The Buxton Inn
GRANVILLE, OHIO 43023

Cecil and I sat in the charming basement dining room of The Buxton Inn, built in 1812 as a tavern by a pioneer from Granville, Massachusetts. "Stagecoach drivers would stop at the tavern during their journey across the frontier and would sleep down here on beds of straw," he said. He pointed out original rough-hewn beams and stone walls that are still sturdy after all these years. And I saw the great open hearth where the drivers cooked their meals.

The Buxton is Ohio's oldest continuously operating inn, and it's a treasure. Look closely and you'll see that the pegged walnut floors were laid with hand-forged nails. "Those windows were laid into foot-thick walls for protection from Indians," Cecil said. Black-walnut beams and timbers frame walls and ceilings; fireplaces are scattered throughout the house.

The main inn building has four guest rooms. The Eastlake and Victorian rooms are two-room suites. One features nineteenth-century Eastlake antiques; the other has elegant Victorian beds, an exquisite settee, and an antique crystal chandelier. The Empire Room is my favorite because of its large sleigh beds and fine silver chandelier.

Did you know that President William Henry Harrison supposedly rode a horse up the inn stairs to the second-floor ballroom during some spirited nighttime revelry?

Down the block, on the corner, stands the

1815 Warner House, with eleven more rooms similarly decorated. And nearby is Ty-Fy (Welsh for "my mother"), with four more guest quarters and Founder's Hall, with six bedchambers.

Delicious dining fare at the Buxton includes wholesome breakfasts with farm-fresh eggs, sausage, and flapjacks; lunch specialties lean toward Colonial-style fare; old-fashioned beef potpie topped with a flaky crust; and Osie Robinson's Chicken Supreme—a puff pastry filled with chicken in mushroom and pimiento sauce.

Loosen up your belt before you get to the dinner table. Inn favorites include French pepper steak with brandy, Louisiana chicken with artichoke hearts, and calf sweetbreads with Burgundy-mushroom sauce.

Cecil even makes dessert a difficult decision. Shall I choose Daisy Hunter's hot walnut-fudge cake a la mode, gingerbread with hot lemon sauce, homemade pecan pie topped with whipped cream, or "olde tyme" vanilla-velvet ice cream?

Oh yes. Ask Cecil about the inn ghost who was once a light-opera star.

How to get there: From Columbus, take I–70 to Ohio 37. Then go north to Ohio 661 and proceed into Granville. From Cleveland, take I–71 to Route 13 through Mansfield. Go south on Route 13 until you reach Ohio 661 just outside Mansfield. Head south on Ohio 661 into Granville and the inn.

Innkeepers: Audrey and Orville Orr, owners; Cecil Snow, manager
Address/Telephone: 313 East Broadway; (614) 587–0001
Rooms: 25, including 3 suites; all with private bath, air conditioning, phone, and TV. Wheelchair access.
Rates: $65.40 to $92.65, single or double, continental breakfast or discount on full breakfast. Children under 5 free.
Open: All year except Christmas Day and New Year's Day.
Facilities and activities: Full-service restaurant with 9 dining rooms; full-service bar. Nearby: tennis, golf, biking, swimming, horseback riding, art galleries, antiques shops, specialty boutiques, museums, historic sites. Also near Ye Olde Mill of 1817 and Hopewell Indians' Newark earthworks.

Captain Montague's
HURON, OHIO 44839

My ten-year-old daughter, Kate, an award-winning Irish dancer herself, noticed lots of Celtic "stuff" at the Captain's. "I married an Irishman," chuckled Judy. "And he's very proud of his roots."

Judy noted that there's usually Irish music playing throughout the inn. "If it was on now, I'd ask to see a little bit of your dancing, Kate."

That's all the encouragement Kate needed. She took her pose and pranced though parts of a jig and reel.

"Mighty impressive," Judy said and gave Kate a big hug.

The inn is mighty impressive, too. Built around 1878 by the town's shipbuilder and owner of the local lumberyard, the stately home boasts exquisite woods. Consider that the mantels in the parlor and dining room, as well as the intricately carved front staircase, are solid black walnut.

Yet the inn takes its name from the home's second owner—a Great Lakes sea captain who hauled ore and coal over its treacherous waters.

Kate's eight-year-old sister, Dayne, visited the Captain's with us, too. She loved the antiques and period reproductions, especially two rockers in the parlor. After a long day's drive through Ohio, Dayne relished the chance to stretch out on the comfy chair.

The girls adored the guest rooms. Me, too. I

especially liked the room named for the captain, a manly retreat with four-poster bed, sea chest at the foot of the bed, one of the home's original gas lamps, and pictures of sailing ships everywhere.

Kate and Dayne were taken by Sarah, the room named for the captain's wife. I think it was the brass bed with the frilly Battenburg lace canopy that got them. Or maybe it was the Victorian sitting couch. I liked the original coal grate over the fireplace hearth.

But I would have missed angel figurines sitting atop the mantel if the girls hadn't pointed them out.

You can enjoy breakfast in a huge Victorian dining room served at a ten-chair harvest table. Or opt for summer breakfast in the charming gazebo, converted from the home's carriage house. Judy's morning treats might include cinnamon coffee, Irish Cottage scones (the inn specialty), egg bakes, baked French toast, and more.

As we were saying our goodbyes, Judy pointed out the inn's original "ruby" glass on the front doors. "These were the forerunners of one-way glass," she explained. "Especially when it gets darker outside, you can see out perfectly well, but it's almost impossible to see anything inside the house."

"Cool," said Kate and Dayne. And it was!

How to get there: From Sandusky, take U.S. 6 east to Huron, then continue straight ahead on Cleveland Street as U.S. 6 jogs right. Follow Cleveland to Center Street and the inn.

Innkeepers: Judy and Mike Tann
Address/Telephone: 229 Center Street; (419) 433–4756 or (800) 276–4756
Rooms: 7; all with private bath and air conditioning. No smoking inn.
Rates: $68 to $135, single or double, EPB. Seasonal rates available. Two-night minimum on summer weekends.
Open: All year.
Facilities and activities: Outdoor in-ground swimming pool, gazebo/carriage house, manicured gardens. Nearby: short walk to Lakefront Park, beach on Lake Erie, Huron's famous mile-long pier. Browse historic architecture of Old Plat neighborhood. Cedar Point amusement park 7 miles away. Golf, tennis, wildlife estuaries, summer stock theater close by. Boat transportation to Lake Erie Islands 8 miles away.
Recommended Country Inns® Travelers' Club Benefit: 10 percent discount, Monday–Thursday, subject to availability.

Sweet Valley Inn
KELLEYS ISLAND, OHIO 43438

After just one day at this charming 1892 Victorian home on Kelleys Island (whose entire 2,800 acres are listed on the National Register of Historic Places), I realized that this was one of the Midwest's best inns.

But first, some history. Here's how the inn got started: Bev noticed a FOR SALE sign on the house when she returned to the island more than 30 years after she'd attended 4-H camp here. Paul had only been to the island once in his entire life.

"It'd make a perfect bed and breakfast," she told him.

The rest, as they say, is history.

Paul and Beverly have fashioned a turn-of-

the-century showplace at their pretty yellow house. Grand double front doors with original stained glass open to an elegant foyer. Tour the house and you'll discover that it has beautiful woodwork: cedar (from the island) in the dining room, butternut in hallways, oak in the kitchen, and pine on the second floor.

There are four working fireplaces. And a handsome butternut stairway, leading to upstairs guest rooms, is lighted by more original stained-glass treatments.

Every guest room features fine antiques, transporting guests back into a long-ago period of elegance. Our bedchambers offered antique pine plank floors, floral Victorian-style wall treatments, and beautiful window views of the property. "I feel really special here," our daughter Dayne said.

That's probably because, earlier in the evening, Paul had hitched up Firmy to the inn's Amish-custom-made surrey for an afternoon ride along the Lake Erie shoreline. (He'll even pick up guests at the ferry docks, if requested.) When we returned to the inn, Dayne and her sister Kate fed apples to the horse, vowing that they'd never forget him.

We spent some evening time in the Sun Room, which enjoys views of Bev's beautiful gardens, talking with the innkeepers while the girls played out on the lawn. Morning took us into the dining room, itself a showplace with its Empire buffet, black-marble fireplace, and plank floors.

Only breakfast surpassed the fine surround-ings. First we delighted in a fruit dish dappled with sour cream and brown-sugar sauce. Next came hot apple cinnamon muffins—nobody could get enough of these delicious treats. Then deviled eggs with mushroom sauce.

And for the final course: homemade waffles smothered with berries, walnuts, powdered sugar, and whipped cream.

"Whipped cream for breakfast!" Kate exclaimed. "This really is a great place."

I'll second that notion.

How to get there: From the ferry docks, "follow the traffic into town" (it's not hard to find, believe me) and look for Division Street. Turn north and continue about 1 mile down the road until reaching the inn, which is on the left side of the road.

Innkeepers: Paul and Beverly Johnson
Address/Telephone: 715 Division Street (mailing address: P. O. Box 733); (419) 746–2750
Rooms: 4 share 2 baths. No smoking inn.
Rates: $85, single; $95, double; EPB. Special packages available.
Open: All year.
Facilities and activities: Dining room, formal parlor, family room, enclosed sun porch, garden with pond, lawn with tree swings, horse barn and corral. Carriage rides and bike rentals available. Swimming, picnics, fishing, sailing, hiking, biking. A short drive to Glacial Grooves, ferry ride to Cedar Point Amusement Park.

Kings Manor Inn
KINGS MILLS, OHIO 45034

It wouldn't be an exaggeration to say that my daughters Kate and Dayne rated this handsome inn as one of their very favorites.

That's because it felt more like the country house of a beloved aunt. And the innkeepers' country-style hospitality had us feeling as if we were staying in our home-away-from-home.

Kings Manor Inn, built in 1903 by Col. George King, is nestled in the quaint village of Kings Mills. This was a company town created before the turn of the century to house employees of the King Powder Company and Peters Cartridge Company. Today all that remains of this once-proud industrial hamlet on the banks of the Little Miami River are a few historic buildings.

Including Kings Manor. It's a spacious manor-style house, graced with original hand-rubbed hardwood moldings, leaded-glass windows, and antique furnishings that include family heirlooms and pieces from the original King estate.

The girls had their favorite inn spots. One was the grand wraparound porch, where Kate and Dayne spent much time daydreaming, reading books, and watching evening rainshowers.

Another was the Sun Room, just across the hall from our bedchambers. Surrounded by tall windows, we plopped down into wicker chairs and sofas to share Kings Island stories. We lingered here for two straight days. Kate arranged for all of us to enjoy cool glasses of iced tea; her reward was another game of checkers, followed by a Monopoly marathon.

And when my wife, Debbie, and Dayne retired for the evening, Kate wrangled more Sun Room time by flipping on my favorite late-night entertainment, David Letterman, on the Sun Room television. That guaranteed another half-hour before hitting the hay.

Guest rooms are delightful. Ours was the Audrenia Suite, with hand-carved manteled fireplace and antique mahogany furnishings. Another favorite is the Scarlet Room, with its own whirlpool bath.

Kings Manor breakfasts are fancy affairs, with fine china, silver table service, and fabulous meals. We loved the heaping helpings of egg and cheese casseroles, crisp slices of bacon, home-baked muffins, fresh fruit plates, juices, milk, and more.

It was really hard for the girls to leave, since they'd made friends with Emily (Sue's daughter) and Maria (Sue's sister-in-law's daughter). They all posed for pictures while sitting on the porch, frolicking on the lawn, making funny faces . . .

We really miss this place.

How to get there: From Cincinnati, take I–71 north to Exit 25 (Kings Mills Road); get off and proceed east on Kings Mills Road into the village. Turn south (right) on Walnut and go to Church Street. Then turn left and continue to the inn.

Innkeepers: Dan and Sue Koterba, Adele Molinaro, Bob Molinaro
Address/Telephone: 1826 Church Street; (513) 459-9959
Rooms: 4, including 1 suite; all with private bath and air conditioning.
Rates: $65 to $75, single; $75 to $85, double; EPB.
Open: All year.
Facilities and activities: Sitting and dining rooms, library sun room, porch. Nearby: minutes from Paramount's Kings Island, one of Ohio's premier theme/amusement parks; The Beach waterpark; Jack Nicklaus's Golden Bear Sports Center (golf). A short drive to Lebanon and Waynesville antique shops. Bike the Little Miami Scenic Bike Trail, starting in town. Cincinnati is about 30 minutes away.
Recommended Country Inns® Travelers' Club Benefit: Multiple-night discounts available.

The Golden Lamb
LEBANON, OHIO 45036

Early 1800s stagecoach drivers and travelers (many of whom couldn't read) were simply told to drive to the sign of The Golden Lamb for a warm bed and a good meal. I saw the large wooden sign depicting a golden lamb still hanging in front of this charming and historic inn.

"It's a real friendly place," the innkeeper said, "the kind of place people like to come back to again and again."

I heartily agree with him. From its beginning in 1803, The Golden Lamb has offered warm hospitality to its guests. Samuel L. Clemens paced through its hallways while in rehearsal for a performance at the Lebanon Opera House. Charles Dickens eloquently com-

plained about the "lack of spirits" at the then-temperate hotel, circa 1842. Benjamin Harrison, Ulysses S. Grant, and eight other presidents stayed here.

The inn is famous for both its Midwestern cooking prepared by its European-trained chef and antiques-laden guest rooms named for illustrious visitors. I walked up creaking stairs and along squeaking hallway floorboards to marvel at the antique furniture gracing the second- and third-floor rooms.

Anyone can do the same; the doors to all unoccupied rooms are kept open. "We want people just coming to dinner to enjoy the antiques collection of our inn, too," he said. "We encourage them to walk through the halls and look inside."

I couldn't resist bouncing up and down on the replica of the massive Lincoln bed in the Charles Dickens Room, resplendent in its Victorian finery. Another favorite was the huge four-poster Boyd bed in the DeWitt Clinton Room.

All the rooms are spacious. Besides a rocking chair, a tall secretary stuffed with books, and other antique furnishings, mine had two four-poster beds.

My family dined in the Shaker Room, with wall pegs holding all kinds of antique kitchen gadgets, pots, and pans. I thought that the roast Butler County turkey with dressing and giblet gravy was almost like Mom's—a special treat. My

wife was delighted by another inn favorite, pan-fried Kentucky ham steak (specially cured and aged) glazed with bourbon. Baby Kate was fed well, too—with all the cooing and attention she received from the friendly waitresses.

The inn's display of authentic antique Shaker furniture is said to be one of the largest private collections of its kind. On the fourth floor are glass-enclosed display rooms featuring many fine pieces.

How to get there: Lebanon is midway between Cincinnati and Dayton. From I–75, take Ohio 63 east 6 miles to Lebanon. From I–71, take Ohio 123 west 3 miles to Lebanon. The inn is at the juncture of Ohio State Routes 63 and 123.

Innkeeper: Paul Resetar
Address/Telephone: 27 South Broadway; (513) 932–5065
Rooms: 18, with 1 suite; all with private bath.
Rates: $65, single; $75 to $95, double; $120 weekends, $110 weekdays for suite; EP.
Open: All year.
Facilities and activities: Full-service restaurant with wheelchair access, 9 dining areas, and tavern. Upstairs museum with Shaker furniture collection. Large gift and crafts shop. Nearby: Lebanon Antique Center featuring 150 dealers. A short drive to Warren County Museum, Kings Island amusement park, Jack Nicklaus golf center, town of Waynesville (more than 40 antiques shops).

The Inn at Cedar Falls
LOGAN, OHIO 43138

Southern Ohio's Hocking Hills offer some of the most spectacular vistas in the Appalachian foothills. And sitting squarely in the center of this magnificent landscape is The Inn at Cedar Falls.

Surrounded on three sides by Hocking State Park, the inn is a nature retreat—a wonderland of eighty acres filled with wildlife and whispering trees. Mink, red fox, and white-tailed deer abound. Woodpeckers and wild turkeys thrive in the dense forest. Spring brings a splash of colorful wildflower blossoms. Autumn hues are astounding.

I could stand on the south porch all day and look out over the hills. Or sit alongside the log house's potbellied stove on a cool autumn evening and enjoy a good book. Maybe just gaze out of my guest-room window at more fabulous scenery.

One of the inn's log houses dates from 1840. Ellen pointed out the 18-inch-wide logs and original plank floors. "When my mother first purchased this cabin, we discovered the original mud and horsehair chinking between the logs," she said, "so we had some work to do."

The log houses have common rooms and porches filled with rockers, mountain-style folk furniture, game tables, and a special room stuffed with books.

Meals often are served on the patio, where

gourmet-style food vies with the scenery for guests' attention. Visit during a "guest chef" weekend and you might be treated to everything from ratatouille in eggplant shells and grilled garlic shrimp to a chocolate torte with hazelnuts.

And where else can you find a cabin in the woods featuring such delicacies as apple-smoked pork loin, bean soup, bread pudding with whiskey sauce, and homemade breads, muffins, and desserts?

Guest rooms, located in the recently added "barn," are country cozy, furnished with antiques, rag rugs on plank floors, and rocking chairs. Windows offer scenic views, and fragrant wildflower bouquets are placed in each room. It's no surprise that the governor of Ohio has already stayed here.

Cabins are restored 1800s structures; one has a fireplace, and two have full decks. Each has a distinct personality—Colonial, Shaker, or antique.

Breakfasts might include a fruit compote and country ham with red-pepper relish and chutney. After your meal you can browse among locally made crafts in the inn's small gift boutique.

How to get there: From Columbus, take U.S. 33 south through Lancaster to the Logan–Bremen exit, which is State Route 664; turn right, go about 9½ miles to State Route 374, then turn left and continue 1 mile to the inn, located on the right side of the road (parking on the left).

Innkeeper: Ellen Grinsfelder
Address/Telephone: 21190 State Route 374; (614) 385-7489
Rooms: 9, plus 6 cabins; all with private bath and air conditioning, 1 with wheelchair access.
Rates: $55 to $70, single; $75 to $90, double; $140 to $150, Sunday through Thursday; $185, Friday and Saturday, for cabins; EPB.
Open: All year.
Facilities and activities: Dinner. Log-house common room, corner library, porch, log and patio dining areas. Gift shop. Special-activity weekends. Nearby: wildlife watching, hiking, cross-country skiing, photography. A short drive to canoeing and fishing on the Hocking River; geologic marvels including Cedar Falls, Ash Cave, Cantwell Cliffs, Conkle's Hollow, Rock House, Hocking Valley Scenic Railway, Lake Logan.

The Blackfork Inn
LOUDONVILLE, OHIO 44842

Sue will show you the handsome secretary that was brought to Ohio from Connecticut in a covered wagon by her great-great-grandfather. "He thought he'd be living in the wilderness with the Indians," Sue said, "so he was determined to bring at least one piece of fine furniture along with him."

In fact, there are several beautiful antique pieces that can be traced to Sue's family back East, including a Pembroke table that dates back to 1760 in the parlor. And the lovely Victorian walnut bedroom suite in the Josephine Room was made in Painesville, Ohio. It's a family heirloom. "My great-grandmother was born in that bed," Sue said. A photograph of her great-grand-

mother hangs on the wall.

The house itself dates back to 1865, when it was built by Phillip Black, a Civil War merchant who brought the railroad to town. That family used the house until the mid-1940s.

The inn's downstairs common rooms almost resemble a museum, so stunning are the antique furnishings. Guest rooms are more informal and are named for members of the Black family. Several have big brass beds and Victorian-style trappings, except for the whimsical Margaret Room—with its tropical feel contributed by an antique wardrobe displaying a Tahitian princess stencil.

There's another building at the Blackfork.

It's called the Landmark, built in 1847 by the namesake feed people. Two suites are the attraction here, boasting fireplaces and large baths.

Sue offers a hearty breakfast with some unusual choices. There are blueberry pancakes, apple fritters, cinnamon rolls, home-grown raspberries with Swiss cream, and Amish products such as trail bologna and specially made cheeses. She can also arrange evening meals at the inn, prepared by one of the fine local chefs.

Or sample elegant fare at the Brass Plate, a sophisticated restaurant for discriminating tastes. Herb-tinged vegetables and delicately prepared potato pancakes, veal dishes, and seafood all offer interesting tastes and sauces you wouldn't expect to find in a town with a population of less than 2,000.

And don't forget to browse through the Blackfork's rare-book shop—the only one in Loudonville.

How to get there: From Columbus, take I–71 north and exit on U.S. 30 east. Then take Ohio 60 south into Loudonville (it turns into Main Street). Turn north on North Water Street and continue a few blocks to the inn.

Innkeepers: Sue and Al Gorisek
Address/Telephone: 303 North Water Street; (419) 994–3252
Rooms: 8, with 2 suites; all with private bath and air conditioning.
Rates: $65 to $80, single or double for rooms; $100 to $125 for suites; continental breakfast.
Open: All year.
Facilities and activities: In Ohio Amish country. Nearby: Mohican State Park, historic Malabar Farm. A short drive to restaurants and Snow Trails ski area.

The Inn at Honey Run
MILLERSBURG, OHIO 44654

"Just look at that," Marge said, pointing to a black Amish carriage clip-clopping down a winding country road just below a room deck of The Inn at Honey Run. "That's why I love spring, fall, and winter here. You can still see sights like that through the trees. It takes you back to the 1800s."

To get here I had driven down a hilly, twisting road that I thought would never end. "We're hard to find," Marge admitted. Her graceful inn is situated on sixty hilly, wooded acres in the middle of Ohio Amish country. Its wood and stone construction blends magnificently with the gorgeous landscape.

"Birding here is great," Marge said, as she pointed to countless feeders surrounding the inn. "Visitors have recorded about thirty different species."

I was eager to see the rooms, and I wasn't disappointed. They're done in a potpourri of styles: early American; contemporary with slanted ceilings and skylights; and Shaker—my favorite—with many pegs on the walls to hang everything from clothes to furniture.

Marge uses Holmes County folk art to highlight each room; handmade quilts adorn walls and beds (which are extra long); and there are comfy chairs with reading lamps.

"I love books," Marge said, "so I made certain each room has a reading light and a chair that rocks or swivels, where you can put your feet up on the windowsill and read, or just stare out at the birds."

More surprises: Twelve "Honeycomb Rooms" are the "world's first commercial earth-shelter rooms," built under and into Holmes County hills. "It's the perfect place for over-stressed executives," Marge said of these almost cavelike retreats, which feature wood-burning fireplace, whirlpool bath, and breakfast delivered to the door. And there're two wonderful cabins perched high on a hill, with panoramic views of Holmes County landscapes.

Inn food is made from scratch, with pan-fried trout from Holmes County waters a dinner specialty. Marge's full country breakfast features juice, eggs and bacon, French toast with real maple syrup, and homemade breads.

Then you might take a hike on the grounds, perhaps followed by Luke, the inn's coon hound, or by Sandy, the beagle. And Willy (a white cat) can be borrowed for room visits!

How to get there: From Millersburg it is 3³⁄₁₀ miles to the inn. Go east on East Jackson Street in Millersburg (Routes 39 and 62). Pass the court-house and gas station on the right. At the next corner, turn left onto Route 241, which makes several turns as it twists out of town. Nearly 2 miles down the road, while proceeding down a long, steep hill, you'll cross a bridge over Honey Run. Turn right immediately around another small hill onto County Road 203, which is not well marked. After 1 mile, turn right at the small inn sign. Go up the hill to the inn.

Innkeeper: Marge Stock

Address/Telephone: 6920 County Road 203; (216) 674–0011; toll-free in Ohio (800) 468–6639

Rooms: 39, with 1 suite and 2 guest houses; all with private bath and air conditioning, most with TV.

Rates: $80 to $150, rooms; $150 to $280, cabins; single or double; continental breakfast. Two-night minimum Friday and Saturday. Special winter rates.

Open: All year.

Facilities and activities: Full-service dining room (closed Sunday) with wheelchair access. BYOB. Meeting rooms host movies and table tennis on weekends, library, game room, gift shop. Hiking trails, sheep and goats in pastures, nature lecture and walks most weekends, horseshoes, croquet, volleyball. Nearby: Holmes County antiques and specialty stores, cheese factories, quilt shops, 9-hole golf course. A short drive to Roscoe Village canal-era town and Warther Wood Carving Museum.

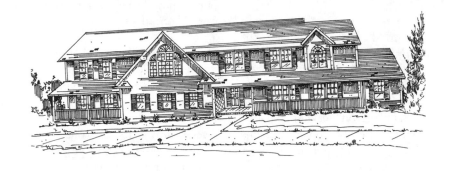

$\mathcal{V}$alley $\mathcal{V}$iew $\mathcal{I}$nn
NEW BEDFORD, OHIO 43824

"Look, Papa," Kate shouted. "Horses!"

A team of Percherons was hitched up to a plow tilling the fields under the steady hand of an Amish farmer, the broad brim of his straw hat billowing in the wind. Kate and her sister, Dayne, waved to the plowman, and he tipped his hat to them.

For the girls that was quite a start for our visit to the Valley View Inn. Nestled in the midst of Ohio Amish country (and one of the most tranquil areas of the state), the Valley View Inn is true to its name. It overlooks a far-reaching valley crisscrossed by tidy Amish farm fields, pastures, and woodlands. The vistas from its porch are among the Midwest's most beautiful.

Inside, there's more country-perfect peacefulness. Guest rooms have furniture handmade by local Amish craftsmen. And each bed is adorned with a hand-pieced quilt made by one of the inn's Amish neighbors. In fact, rooms are named for the pattern of quilt displayed on the bed.

We stayed in the Country Song Bird, a delightful retreat with two double beds and roomy quarters. After unpacking we headed out to the inn's corral, where innkeepers Dan and Nancy keep a number of their horses.

Kate and Dayne made sure that we revisited the porch to watch a terrific sunset; then we came back inside, sat down with a checkerboard, and played a few games. Dayne opted for looking at magazines found in the living room, curled up in front of the fireplace. Evening snacks included homemade cookies, juices and milk. And we couldn't go to sleep without a trip to the family room, where an old-fashioned player piano produced a toe-tapping melody.

Breakfast time is another eye-opener. Nobody can go away hungry, that's for sure—a full family-style breakfast is prepared by the inn's Amish cook. Goodies might include fresh fruit salad, ham puffs (a meat, cheese, and egg casserole dish), hash-brown casserole, homemade muffins, lemon bread, juices, and other beverages, and more. (Sunday, a time of worship and rest, offers a continental breakfast.)

It's also fun to drive along the country roads in search of Amish specialties. Homemade pies in little shops hidden in the driveways of Amish farms are worth the search. And if you've got room in your vehicle for an authentic, handmade Amish rocking chair, buy one. They can't be matched for comfort.

How to get there: From Cleveland, take I–77 south to the Dover exit, then turn west (right) onto Ohio 39; go about 9 miles to Ohio 93 at Sugarcreek and turn south (right). Continue 3 miles to Ohio 643/557. Stay on Ohio 643 to New Bedford; proceed south on Ohio 643 for about 3 miles to the inn, which is on the right.

Innkeepers: Dan and Nancy Lembke
Address/Telephone: 32327 State Road 643; (216) 897–3232 or (800) 331–8439
Rooms: 10; all with private bath and air conditioning. No smoking inn.
Rates: $75 to $105, single or double, EPB Monday through Saturday; EP Sunday.
Open: All year.
Facilities and activities: Sitting room, dining room, game room, large porch overlooking valley. Nearby: Amish crafts shops, food stores and restaurants; cheese factories; antiques stores; hiking, biking; wildlife tours.

The Inn at Brandywine Falls

SAGAMORE HILLS, OHIO 44067

"Look at the wonderful waterfall, Pa," said Dayne. "It's got to be 100 feet high."

My daughter was close—Brandywine Falls check in at 67 feet. But the hike on the boardwalk to the falls, and then down deep into the gorge itself, seems much greater.

Maybe that's because Dayne, Kate (my other daughter), and I were so taken by the grandeur of nature at Brandywine Falls, part of the massive Cuyahoga Valley National Park. We had been marveling at the natural beauty for miles before we came upon this handsome inn.

The Inn at Brandywine Falls turned out to be among my girls' favorite on our swing through eastern Ohio. Not only does it boast a waterfall,

hiking and biking trails, and expansive grounds perfect for running, jumping, and rolling about —it also has horses and goats!

"A perfect combination," opined Kate.

The inn, a Greek Revival beauty built in 1848 by James Wallace, was the centerpiece of a once-thriving pioneer community with a sawmill and gristmill, thriving businesses along the falls.

Today, all that is left of that village are some mill foundations and the inn. But the inn (and the falls) are more than enough!

Inn suites are among *my* favorites on the Midwest country inn landscape. The Granary offers towering windows overlooking a hemlock grove and rustic, wide-plank pine floors and hand-hewn wooden beams. Then there are the king-sized bed, wood-burning stove, two-person whirlpool, microwave, and fridge.

The Loft, which began as a small barn in the 1800s, has been transformed into another rustic wonder. It also features a wall of windows overlooking that hemlock grove, as well as a romantic loft area with bed and oversized whirlpool. Downstairs, you can marvel at all the country geegaws decorating the suite. There's even a model train that circles the ceiling—something kids especially love.

In the main house, the James Wallace Parlor has an elegant double sleigh bed luxuriating on Axminster carpeting, English armoire, hand-painted lamp shades, and an antique chair (oldest original piece of furniture in the house) that came from 1820s Maryland.

But I might opt for Adeline's Retreat, a charming and romantic second-floor room with double sleigh bed, claw-footed tub and the only guest quarters with glimpses of the falls.

Guests take breakfast in the dining room, where a portrait of James Wallace gazes down over the festivities. Goodies might include fruited oatmeal soup, fresh juices, homebaked breads, and hot beverages.

Did I mention that it's a candlelight breakfast?

Most important, however, is that a visit to Brandywine Falls offers you a chance to walk, listen, and marvel at nature. Relax. Visit the falls. Doze in the sun. Breathe in the aroma of wildflowers and the forest.

Just be.

How to get there: From the Ohio Turnpike, take exit 12, then continue on Highway 8 for 1½ miles to Twinsburg Road. Turn west (left) and drive another 1½ miles to a dead end at Brandywine Road. Turn right and cross the bridge. The inn is on the left.

Innkeepers: George and Katie Hoy
Address/Telephone: 8230 Brandywine Road; (216) 467–1812 or 650–4965
Rooms: 6, with 3 suites; all with private bath. No smoking inn. Wheelchair access.
Rates: $94 to $185, double; for single, subtract $5; EPB.
Open: All year.
Facilities and activities: Located on 33,000 acres of parkland known as Cuyahoga Valley National Park. Porch swings, chairs overlooking gorge. Short hike to boardwalk to falls and down into gorge. Bike and hike trails yards away.

The Tea Rose

SANDUSKY, OHIO 44870

What attracted us to the Tea Rose was its Victorian Tea Room. It's very English: Imported china rests upon fine table linens, classical music wafts through the room, and the choice of "tea and crumpets" seems endless.

There are black teas such as Russian Caravan, a blend of Darjeeling, Assam, and Ceylon—a rich combination. Or try a pot of Oolong, a gentle, peachy-tasting tea.

Dragon Well is a green tea with an herbaceous aroma. Prince of Wales remains one of my favorite blends, a classical "Burgundy" of teas. And my choice for breakfast tea? Why the Irish, of course, a strong, full-bodied, pungent, and robust burst of flavor.

Did I mention the Tea Room's other goodies such as English scones, crumpets, homebaked muffins, and a strawberry cake that's divine? Okay, I just did.

The house itself dates to 1890, when it served as rectory of the Grace Episcopal Church. The innkeeper (and her husband and son, the "two Andys"), spend countless hours restoring the home, especially working to bring back the beauty of the home's woodwork.

Upstairs, two guest rooms provide a welcome retreat. One, nicknamed the "Peacock Room," boasts a Victorian bed board dating to 1870.

"But I have to ask any gentleman wishing to

stay here how tall they are," said Ellen. "Because if they're over 6'1", they'll have to scrunch down in order to fit on the antique bed."

This room also has a sitting area in the "tower" of the handsome house.

Of course, this 6'2" writer would head to the inn's other room, where he wouldn't have to scrunch down under the covers to fit on the bed. This guest chamber is very English and also includes a sitting area.

Ellen serves breakfast down in the Tea Room. It might include a fruit plate, juices, egg dishes, breakfast meats, pancakes, French toast, and more. No one is going to go away hungry, that's for sure.

This innkeeper also is an interesting person-

ality in her own right. Licensed by the state to perform marriages, she has officiated at more than 300 weddings at the inn during the last fours years. She even writes her own marriage ceremonies.

If that isn't enough, Ellen is a psychic counselor who gives seminars and lectures on metaphysics and practices hypnotherapy. She gave my daughters crystals as a remembrance of their visit here. It's an experience they won't soon forget.

How to get there: Follow U.S. 6 into Sandusky. In town, the road turns into Washington Street. Follow to East Washington, in the Old Plat area, and the inn.

Innkeeper: Ellen L. Kraus
Address/Telephone: 218 East Washington Street; (419) 627–2773
Rooms: 2 share 1 bath
Rates: $55 with continental breakfast; $65 EPB. Off-season rates available.
Open: All year.
Facilities and activities: Tearoom. Located in downtown Sandusky in historic Old Plat area. Nearby: browse historic architecture in neighborhood. Walk to Cedar Point amusement park ferry dock; excursion boats to Lake Erie Islands.

The H. W. Allen Villa

TROY, OHIO 45373

June's villa brochure carries a translation of "bed and breakfast" in Japanese. That surprised me, but she explained that the nearby Panasonic plant regularly sends visiting Japanese executives here while taking care of business. In fact, two Japanese businessmen were checking in during my visit. In heavily accented English, they marveled at the "big, beautiful house."

It is very big and extremely beautiful. Built in 1874 by Henry Ware Allen, part owner of the largest flour mill in the county, the three-story Victorian mansion has fourteen rooms, 12-foot ceilings, seven fireplaces, and white- and black-walnut woodwork throughout.

The Smiths opened the inn to travelers in 1986, filled with their bounty of twenty years of antiques collecting. The furnishings are remarkably distinctive; the home seems more museum than wayfarer station.

Walk into the dining room to see June's extensive set of LaBelle Blue Flower china. I also like the flamboyantly colored porcelain mantel clocks that sit in seemingly every nook and cranny.

Also note hand stenciling done in 1874 that has been restored in the library and sitting room, a handsome design that rests above 11-inch walnut baseboards.

Now for the guest rooms: They may all be bathed in Victorian antiques, but I can't help marveling at the Allen Room, with its four-poster Gamblers brass bed and extremely unusual gold Hindu-style domed lamps that would seem at home in a maharajah's palace.

A breakfast of cinnamon French toast, vegetable omelets, or bacon, tomato, and egg dishes is served on a 15-foot-long antique table.

How to get there: From Dayton, take I–75 north to the Troy exit (exit 73, which is Ohio 55), and proceed 1 mile east, then 2 blocks north on South Market Street to the inn.

Innkeepers: Bob and June Smith

Address/Telephone: 434 South Market Street; (513) 335–1181

Rooms: 6, with 1 suite; all with private bath, air conditioning, TV, and phone.

Rates: $59, single; $74, double; suite, $64 single, $79 double; EPB. Cribs and baby beds available.

Open: All year.

Facilities and activities: Double parlor, dining room, and library. Nearby: Hayner Cultural Center, Historical Courthouse, Overfield Tavern, Museum of Troy History. A short drive to golf course, Dayton Art Institute, U.S. Air Force Museum.

Murphin Ridge Inn
WEST UNION, OHIO 45693

It didn't take a New York minute for my pa and me to fall in love with the Murphin Ridge Inn. Located in the heart of Adams County and tucked in the foothills of the Appalachian Mountains, Bob and Mary's handsome and historic homestead has everything most country inns only dream of:

History: It's located on the 600-acre site of a Virginia land grant awarded to a Revolutionary War soldier.

Scenery: The inn sits high on a ridge overlooking Peach Mountain at the edge of Appalachia's quiet woodlands and sweeping valleys.

Local color: Adams County is also the heart of Amish country, where horse-drawn buggies clip-clop along rural lanes.

Great food: Sumptuous gourmet meals in the 1810 farmhouse, original to the homestead, are prepared by chef Natasha Shiskevish, trained at the acclaimed Culinary Arts Institute of America in New York. Dinners might include everything from artichoke heart pâté and raspberry chicken sautéed in brandy and white wine to Cedar Run Salmon, Blue Creek rib eye, and desserts extraordinaire. A couple of inn favorites: homemade bread pudding with Michigan sour cherries and heavenly cobblers brimming with fruits and nuts.

My obsession: Kentucky fudge cake!

Great accommodations: The ten-room inn boasts handmade Shaker reproduction furnishings that are nearly museum quality. Two rooms feature fireplaces; two offer private balconies overlooking the Appalachian hills.

Wonderful innkeepers: Bob and Mary are among the most gracious hosts I've ever met, and as treasured as their historic inn. Ask Bob to tell you how Morgan's Raiders swept down Wheat Ridge Road during the Civil War in retaliation for its abolitionist activities, including its part in the Underground Railroad, which helped runaway slaves escape to the north.

A day after we left Murphin Ridge, my pa and I already missed the place badly.

How to get there: From Cincinnati, take Ohio 32 east to Unity Road. Turn right on Unity and follow to the stop sign; turn left onto Wheat Ridge Road for 3 miles, then turn left onto Murphin Ridge Road and continue to the inn.

Innkeepers: Bob and Mary Crosset

Address/Telephone: 750 Murphin Ridge Road; (513) 544–2263

Rooms: 10; all with private bath and air conditioning. Wheelchair access. No smoking inn.

Rates: $84, single or double, Wednesday and Thursday; $94, single or double, Friday through Sunday; EPB. $15 third person. No credit cards.

Open: All year except January; closed Mondays and Tuesdays.

Facilities and activities: Three-room 1810 farmhouse converted into full-service dining rooms, inn common room with cable television, VCR, books, and magazines; porch with rockers; heated swimming pool; horseshoe pit; outdoor basketball and tennis courts; 10 miles of hiking trails. Nearby: Serpent Mound and remote forest preserves for hiking; biking on backcountry roads; Amish stores.

The Wooster Inn
WOOSTER, OHIO 44691

Imagine an evening of professional light opera, maybe Offenbach's *La Belle Hélène*—which might be described as a Woody Allen–type version of *Dynasty* with ravishing waltzes—and you'll get the idea of the flair of the Ohio Light Opera. Now imagine following your musical evening with a scrumptious meal featuring champagne and a juicy steak served in a Colonial-style dining room.

That's just some of the fun you'll have at the wonderful Wooster Inn. Owned and operated by the College of Wooster, and located right on its beautiful campus, the inn is surrounded by tall trees and green fields. In fact, I watched a little friendly competition on the college's golf course right from the dining-room window.

The inn has an English-country feel to it. The lobby is spacious and casually gracious, with a large sitting area of high-back chairs and sofas. A stately grandfather's clock softly chimes on the hour. French doors open onto the Colonial-style dining room and terrace, which overlook the aforementioned links.

Guests may also use many of the facilities at the college. These include tennis courts and a golf course just out the back door. You can even use the library.

I stayed here recently to attend an authors' book fair. My room was very spacious, comfortable, and cheery, with windows overlooking the inn grounds, muted flowered wallpaper, oak and cherry furniture, quaint bedspreads, and a couple of wing chairs. Be sure to make reservations well in advance. College guests (and many visiting moms and dads) adore the inn.

Breakfast specialties include blueberry pancakes with Ohio maple syrup. Dinner offers a wide selection of choices, including beef tenderloin in Burgundy wine and pepper sauce, sherry-basted pork chops with rosemary, fresh rainbow trout or salmon, and veal cutlets.

The dining room also offers an extensive selection of wines, imported beers, and sherry.

How to get there: Five principal highways run through Wooster: U.S. 30 and 250, and State Routes 3, 585, and 83. From Cleveland, exit the 250 bypass at Burbank Road and continue south to Wayne Avenue. Turn east on Wayne to the inn.

Innkeeper: Andrea Lazar

Address/Telephone: Wayne Avenue and Gasche Street; (216) 264-2341

Rooms: 16, with 2 suites; all with private bath, air conditioning, and phone. Pets welcome.

Rates: $65 to $75, single; $75 to $85, double; $80 to $125, suites. Special weekend packages available.

Open: All year except Christmas Day.

Facilities and activities: Wheelchair access to dining room. Sitting area, outside patio. Nearby: access to many Wooster College activities and sports facilities. Ohio Light Opera special on weekends.

The Worthington Inn
WORTHINGTON, OHIO 43085

Masterful Sheraton, Hepplewhite, and Victorian antiques, elegant stained glass and crystal, bath mirrors imported from France, triple sheeting on beds, turndown service, and a complimentary split of champagne transport you back to a more graceful style of traveling. I bet you never would have guessed that this magnificent inn, completed in 1831 and then known as the Central House, was originally a stagecoach stop.

A $4 million restoration in 1983 transformed what had become a white elephant into a luxurious and romantic turn-of-the-century–style getaway.

I found many of the antique pieces stunning. Every room's decor is different; some sport an early American motif, complete with hand stenciling on walls and ceilings and elegant pine period pieces, while others are Victorian, featuring fine walnut, mahogany, and cherry antique furnishings.

The Presidential Suite is a descent into pampered decadence. It offers more than 800 square feet of pomp and luxury. On one of the walls are framed papers that set the terms of an indentured servant. Those valuable documents were found within the walls during restoration.

Four more suites, located in the 1817 Snow House just across the street, offer more elegance. The center-hall staircase is black walnut, and you can notice unpeeled log joints in the cellar.

It was even a treat for me to quaff a beer in the Pub Room. The splendid marble-topped bar, with its leaded- and stained-glass accoutrements, seemingly stretches on forever. Made in Austria, it originally was used as a soda fountain in Baltimore at the turn of the century. The bartender also explained how the interesting Cruvinet wine decanter system works.

The third-floor Van Loon Ballroom has an exquisite Czechoslovakian crystal chandelier weighing nearly 500 pounds and a romantic balcony overlooking the old village.

The inn's menu reflects a regional American influence, with veal and beef specialties abounding. And don't hesitate to try one of the rich desserts prepared daily at the inn's own bakery.

How to get there: From Cleveland, take I–71 south to Ohio 161. Exit west to Worthington, then turn left on High Street and continue to New England Avenue and the inn.

Innkeeper: Steve Hanson, general manager

Address/Telephone: 649 High Street; (614) 885–7700

Rooms: 26, with 7 suites; all with private bath, air conditioning, TV, and phone.

Rates: $115 to $150, single or double; $215 to $260, suites; EPB. Also special "without breakfast" rates.

Open: All year.

Facilities and activities: Four dining rooms, pub, ballroom. Located in historic Old Worthington Village. Free maps for walking tours of area, which include several homes built as early as 1804. Nearby: antiques shops, specialty stores, and boutiques.

Business travel: Located about 20 miles north of downtown Columbus. Corporate rates, conference rooms, fax.

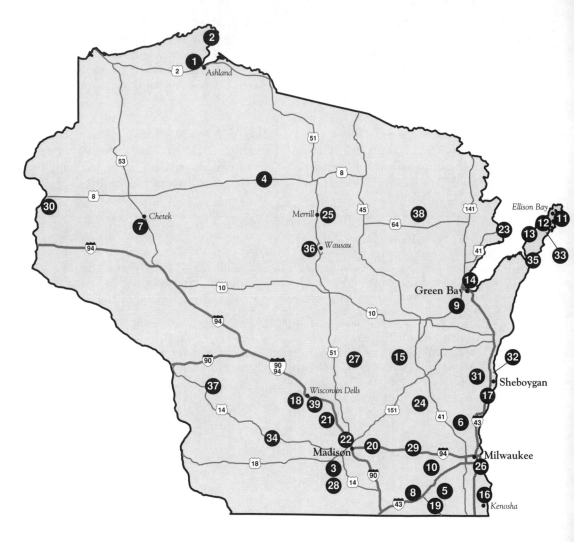

Wisconsin

Wisconsin

Numbers on map refer to towns numbered below.

Hotel Chequamegon
ASHLAND, WISCONSIN 54806

The Hotel Chequamegon resembles one of those grand resort hotels that sprang up on Great Lakes shorelines around the turn of the century.

Its massive white-clapboard styling harkens back to more elegant times. It is crowned on each end by rounded towers and capped out back by an expansive veranda with two cupola gazebos overlooking the water.

Inside, the warmth of the past enveloped me. Oak woodwork is everywhere, with posts and columns and high ceilings adding to the charm. Especially luxurious is the Northland Parlor Room, with its ornate, many-columned fireplace, brass chandelier, and high-back chairs; the room opens onto the huge veranda.

The Hotel Chequamegon is not a historic hotel, although it rests upon a historic site. Opened in 1985, and built at a cost of $12.5 million on the site of the first hotel of the same name (which burned down in 1908), it returns visitors to the days when Ashland was a booming lumber mecca. It derives its name from an Indian word, the Chippewa's *shuqauwaumekong*, which means "a narrow strip of land running into a body of water."

Simple but dramatic guest rooms are examples of understated elegance. Floral prints, fluffy quilts, comfortable sofas and chairs, and great views from lakeside rooms provide special touches. Executive suites have large whirlpool bath, wet bar, antique-style mahogany sleigh bed, balloon drapes, lace curtains, and more.

Fifield's, the inn's elegant restaurant, features such entrees as planked whitefish, fresh Lake Superior trout, blackened walleye, and an assortment of steaks and pastas. Molly Cooper's, fashioned to resemble a 1930s speakeasy, is an interesting spot for a nightcap.

How to get there: The hotel is located at the intersection of Highways 2 and 13, easily accessible from any direction.

Innkeeper: Mary Ellen Margetta, general manager
Address/Telephone: 101 West Front Street; (715) 682–9095
Rooms: 62, with 20 suites; all with private bath, air conditioning, TV, and phone.
Rates: $75 to $85, single or double, rooms; $85 to $140, single or double, suites; EP. Senior citizens' discount of 10 percent. Low-season rates from October 1 through May 1.
Open: All year.
Facilities and activities: Spa, indoor pool, restaurant, lounge. Overlooks waters of Lake Superior and 25-slip marina. Nearby: historic fishing village of Bayfield, with specialty and antiques shops; historic-home tours; ferry to Madeline Island, part of Apostle Islands National Lakeshore. Several downhill ski hills a short drive away, including Blackjack, Big Powderhorn, Indianhead, and Telemark.
Business travel: Corporate rates, meeting rooms, fax.

Old Rittenhouse Inn
BAYFIELD, WISCONSIN 54814

I sat in an elegant Victorian dining room in the early morning as an immaculately dressed Jerry, resplendent in a black velvet vest—with a long gold watch fob and a wide bow tie—served me an exquisite breakfast.

After sipping freshly pressed apple cider, I started on brandied peaches and blueberries in sour cream. Next came delicious New Orleans–style cinnamon French toast.

The sound of soft classical music wafted through the room, which was adorned with rich Victorian-print wallpaper, brass chandeliers, and antique oak and mahogany tables and chairs. I pulled my seat closer to the roaring fire in the hearth.

"I think it's important that the feeling inside a home fits the personality of the house," Jerry said as we talked about what made a good country inn, "and it must deliver personal service that makes it a special place to stay."

The Old Rittenhouse Inn scores well on both points. It's an opulent 1890 Victorian red-brick and wood-shingle mansion, not far from the spectacular shoreline of Lake Superior, with historic islands nearby to explore—an almost perfect destination. It has a long wraparound veranda and gabled roof; elegant dining rooms and sitting areas are done in formal prints, with fine Victorian furnishings and all kinds of period lamps.

Jerry's guest rooms are immaculate; many have four-poster beds, marble-topped dressers and vanities, and some have a fireplace to take the chill off cold winter days. Several boast tall windows looking out toward blustery Lake Superior. And there's complimentary champagne in each room in the evening.

Recently added inn rooms are incredibly spacious; I don't think it would be an exaggeration to say that they're the largest I've ever seen in any country inn. Big brass, iron-rail, and walnut beds are inviting. Then there are pretty stained-glass windows depicting Bayfield lakeshore scenes. All the new rooms have their own fireplace.

The inn also offers delicious multicourse gourmet meals. Here Mary is the genius. Her specialties include steak *Bercy* stuffed with oysters, fresh trout poached in champagne, and pork ragout. Homemade breads are served steaming in heaping baskets. Save room for some incredible desserts, such as Jerry's white-chocolate cheesecake.

Check out the Phillipses' other two Bayfield Inns. The elegant Le Chateau Boutin, a 1907 Queen Anne mansion, boasts fabulous appointments with seven guest rooms. The 1888 Grey Oak Guest House, a Gothic Victorian, offers four more bedchambers.

What an elegant "hat trick!"

How to get there: From Minneapolis–St. Paul, take I–94 east to U.S. 63. Take 63 north to State Route 2 and go east to Route 13. Take 13 north to Bayfield. The inn is on the corner of Rittenhouse and Third.

Innkeepers: Jerry and Mary Phillips
Address/Telephone: 301 Rittenhouse Avenue (mailing address: Box 584); (715) 779–5765
Rooms: 9, including 1 suite; all with private bath, 9 with fireplace, 5 with whirlpool, some with wheelchair access.
Rates: $99 to $159, single or double; $229, suite; continental breakfast. Special off-season packages.
Open: All year.
Facilities and activities: Three romantic dining rooms. Recreational activities of all kinds available: fishing, sailing, Apostle Islands National Lakeshore; fur-trading museum and other attractions on Madeline Island; canoeing on Brule River; annual festivals; cross-country skiing.

Cameo Rose Bed and Breakfast
BELLEVILLE, WISCONSIN 53508

If there is a more attractive Victorian-style inn than this one, let me know about it. But I'll put my money on the Cameo Rose, a hostelry that's blossoming into one of the finest little getaways in the Midwest.

"We built the house specifically for a bed and breakfast," Dawn told me. They adapted plans from a "House of the Week" design in the local paper. It was completed in 1991, though it has the Victorian-era complement of ornate gingerbread, slashing gables, and an imposing tower.

Inside, you'll find modern elegance. The foyer is two stories high, incredibly decorated to the season, with stairs leading to second-floor guest rooms. But first enjoy the guest parlor, with skylights gracing a cathedral ceiling and looking as if a *House Beautiful* layout has come alive.

Dawn does all the decorating—and it is exquisite. Of course, roses are everywhere, especially in the Tower Room, graced with Cameo Rose wall coverings, Battenburg lace, handsome quilts, and a double whirlpool whose window looks out over the surrounding valley.

I also loved the Rose Arbor room, with its rococo reproductions (such as that antique fainting couch). And all guest rooms have TVs and VCRs; the inn's film library contains more than 700 titles.

Dawn's breakfasts are tops, too. Served in the formal dining room on antique china with crystal goblets, consider hot breakfast fruit compote, eggs Benedict, berry struesel muffins ("Wild berries grow everywhere around here," Dawn said), and homemade cinnamon rolls—a house specialty.

The inn is located on 120 acres of hills and trees. Part of the renowned Ice Age Trail edges across the property. There are also miles of hiking paths that loop to hilltops, through maple and oak groves, and into the valley. Or relax among Dawn's rose and flower gardens, a blaze of colors in the growing season.

The Cameo Rose is a special place. But don't take my word. See for yourself.

How to get there: The inn is located 5 miles south of Verona, 3 miles north of Belleville (and about 12 miles southwest of Madison) in unincorporated Basco. From madison, take Highway 151 (Verona Road) west and use the Paoli exit. Basco, the town, is basically a sign and a small group of houses at Henry Road along Highway 69 about 1 mile past Paoli, on the way to Belleville. You'll see the Cameo Rose to the left on a hill, a bit more than 1 mile down Henry Road.

Innkeepers: Dawn, Gary, and Jennifer Bahr
Address/Telephone: 1090 Severson Road; (608) 424–6340
Rooms: 5; all with private bath. No smoking inn.
Rates: $79 to $129, single or double, EPB.
Open: All year.
Facilities and activities: Cathedral great room, porches, rose gazebo, flower gardens, 120 acres of hills, woods, hiking trails. Nearby: fifteen minutes from Madison, the University of Wisconsin, the State Capitol, State Street (shops and specialty stores), Dane County Coliseum, golf courses, water sports on Lakes Medota and Monona.

Palmquist's The Farm
BRANTWOOD, WISCONSIN 54513

"Are you Finnish?" asked Jim, whose grandfather came to the United States from that country. "Puhala is a pretty common Finnish name, you know."

I'm going to have to get busy on that family tree. This is the umpteenth time I've been told my name is Finnish. Even when I visited Helsinki a few years ago, the director of that city's folk museum introduced me to a group of people as "a Finn who has returned home."

Maybe. My mother's family came from Armagh, Northern Ireland. But we hit a dead end for my pa's relatives as soon as we reach Austria. Could the Puhalas have migrated from Finland to Austria on the way to America?

Enough about me. Jim and Helen boast a premier bed-and-breakfast experience on their 800-acre cattle ranch. You can hike its nature trails through maple groves and up hardwood ridges. Or help your kids with farm chores such as feeding the calves, chickens, horses—and spend some time with Barney, one of the friendliest yellow Labs you'll ever meet.

Perhaps the ranch's most spectacular digs are in the White Pine Inn, a massive log building built by Jim and a noted local log builder. A huge great room is the place to relax, then enjoy the porch and gaze up at the stars before retiring to your handsome suite.

I also like the Sauna House (just like a

Finn), a two-bedroom building with its own private sauna. And the River Cabin sits on the edge of the Somo.

Helen's food is legend in these parts and includes Finnish dishes such as creamed rice with raspberry sauce, oven pancakes with real maple syrup, and Finnish whole-wheat bread. It will be difficult to leave this place, so I'm warning you ahead of time.

How to get there: From the east or west, take U.S. 8. The ranch is located 12 miles east of Prentice and 20 miles west of Tomahawk off U.S. 8; look for the Palmquists' THE FARM sign at the intersection of U.S. 8 and River Road; turn on River Road and continue 1 mile to the inn.

Innkeepers: Jim, Helen, Anna, Toinie, and Art Palmquist

Address/Telephone: N5136 River Road; (715) 564-2558 or (800) 519-2558

Rooms: 8 in 2 buildings, with 4 suites; suites with private bath. Four other buildings for couples or families; all with private bath No smoking inn.

Rates: Weekends, daily: $60 adults, $30 children 5–11, $24 children 3–4; weekdays: $55, $27, and $22, respectively; AP. Bed and breakfast only: adults $70; children 3–12, $35.

Open: All year.

Facilities and activities: Sauna house, warming house with ski rentals, hiking on private nature trails, fishing in farm ponds and in the Somo River, children's farm activities, log cabin–building seminars, hayrides, sleigh rides. Nearby: bike the Bearskin Trail, hike the Ice Age Trail, visit Timm's Hill County Park (highest point in Wisconsin).

The Hillcrest Inn and Carriage House
BURLINGTON, WISCONSIN 53105

Like they say in real estate, the key to everything is location, location, location.

And the Hillcrest Inn has plenty of it.

Situated high on a hill overlooking the water, this four-acre estate has a very English feel to it. Even as we drove up the driveway, Debbie mentioned that the stone pillars at the entry gate recalled baronial country houses in Great Britain.

Later, Karen told us that those stone pillars along the curving driveway leading to the main house are original to the estate.

Dick and Karen decided on Hillcrest after visiting bed-and-breakfast inns all over the United States. "It was very Edwardian," Karen said. "Just what we were looking for."

Karen has fashioned guest rooms that are a little piece of jolly old England. The Kensington Room, with its green, burgundy, and gold, feels like quarters at an exclusive English gentlemen's club. There's a large double whirlpool that's great for relaxing with that special someone while watching the fireplace blaze away.

And a weekend in the Windmere Suite means you have the entire second floor of the Carriage House to yourselves. Of course, there's a large whirlpool for your ultimate soaking pleasure.

A favorite guest activity is to relax on the

inn's upper or lower porches. We walked through the garden down to the water, just across the street. If there's a prettier spot for a city inn in all the Midwest, I'd like to know about it.

How to get there: From downtown Burlington, take Highway 11 about 7 blocks to Pleasant Avenue. Turn south on Pleasant and continue for 2 blocks; then turn right on Storle Avenue and the inn.

Innkeepers: Dick and Karen Granholm
Address/Telephone: 540 Storle Avenue; (414) 763–4706
Rooms: 6; 4 with private bath.
Rates: $60 to $140, single or double, EPB.
Open: All year.
Facilities and activities: Magnificent parlor with panoramic water views, flower gardens, walking path to water, private shoreline. Nearby: watersports on Echo Lake and the Fox and White Rivers; antiques shops, boutiques, and art galleries in town.

Stagecoach Inn
CEDARBURG, WISCONSIN 53012

Stagecoach drivers slept on the basement's dirt floor in bunks made of stone rubble and straw. The chimney that took the flue for the driver's potbellied stove still stands.

The stagecoach-stop charm carries over to the guest rooms, which are decorated with period antiques. "We wanted to keep the inn authentic," Liz said. "This community is restoration-minded."

That's an understatement. The Stagecoach Inn is in the heart of the historic downtown district, which was anchored by the Wittenburg Woolen Mills, now restored and called the Cedar Creek Settlement. (The mill provided wool uniforms for soldiers during the Civil War.)

More than 150 rare "cream city" brick and stone buildings stand throughout town, many dating back to the mid-1800s.

Everything at the inn is cozy and cheery, with many special touches. Liz created the pretty stencils on the walls and reconditioned the original pinewood plank floors. Her antique four-poster and brass beds are covered with Laura Ashley comforters. Suites are decorated with more antiques, wicker, and Laura Ashley fabrics, and have two-person whirlpool tubs.

The Stagecoach Pub is located on the inn's first floor. I had an imported beer from a massive antique oak cooler at a century-old bar. The tin ceiling adds to the frontier charm. Folksingers entertain here on evenings twice a month. Liz serves breakfast here, too, at antique tavern tables. (Or you can take your breakfast on the back deck.) She offers hot croissants, juice, cereal, fresh fruit, bran muffins, coffee, and herbal teas, and she'll recommend a good spot for dinner in the historic town. You can play games and cards here at night, in a warm coffeehouse atmosphere. Late-night sweet tooths can find a candy shop on the first floor.

Look for these inn originals: The heavy front door dates from 1853; the intricate woodwork on the door and window frames, as well as the crown molding above the front door, is made of single pieces of wood carved to look multilayered; and the handsome cherry staircase

banister is authentic and impressive.

And the newest addition—a historical annex to the main inn. Called the Weber Haus, the 1847 frame building (just across the street) is one of the oldest operating structures in Cedarburg. Honeymoon couples love the privacy, and its three suites are decorated with four-poster beds, wicker, and antiques. It also has a garden and picnic area.

How to get there: From Chicago, take I–94 to I–43 and get off at exit 17 (Cedarburg). Take Pioneer Road 3 miles to Washington Avenue and turn right into Cedarburg. The inn is located on the right side of the street.

Innkeepers: Liz and Brook Brown
Address/Telephone: W61 N520 Washington Avenue; (414) 375-0208 or 375-3035
Rooms: 12, including 6 suites; all with private bath and air conditioning; suites with double whirlpool bath and TV. No smoking inn.
Rates: $70, single or double; $105, suites; continental breakfast.
Open: All year.
Facilities and activities: Stagecoach Pub, candy store. In heart of historic Cedarburg. Nearby: walk to Cedar Creek Settlement; the old Woolen Mill; Stone Mill Winery; antiques, craft, and specialty shops; restaurants and art galleries. Also nearby: bike trails, golf, fishing, cross-country skiing, River Edge Nature Center, museum, Ozaukee Pioneer Village, Ozaukee Covered Bridge (last covered bridge in Wisconsin).

The Washington House Inn
CEDARBURG, WISCONSIN 53012

Cedarburg is an historic woolen-mill town, with many rare "cream city" brick and stone buildings dating from the mid-1800s. In fact, the downtown area alone contains more historic structures than any other city west of Philadelphia!

One of these is The Washington House Inn, a country-Victorian "cream city" brick building completed in 1886. The tall front doors and authentic frontier ambience are softened by a long lobby sprinkled with Victorian furnishings, rich parquet floors, brass chandeliers, and a marble fireplace.

I looked at the original hotel register, which recorded visitors during the months of 1895. How did anyone ever have the time to write in that fancy scroll? I also noticed an unusual display: a "wedding brick" discovered during restoration with the date "1886" and the names of the happy couple scratched on it.

The guest rooms are named for leading citizens of historic Cedarburg. The country-Victorian decorations are absolutely charming, with floral wallpapers, fancy armoires, cozy down quilts, fresh flowers, and more. I really like the leaded-glass transom windows of some rooms.

In the newly restored rooms, there's more of a plain country feeling, but there's nothing plain about the decor. The exposed brick walls and beamed ceilings are spectacular.

Then there are some very deluxe quarters; my favorite has country-style antiques, loft beds cozied by their own fireplace, and another loft area that boasts a 200-gallon spa tub warmed by a second fireplace.

Or perhaps you'd like a room at the inn's other building, the 1868 Schroeder House, located about four doors down from the main inn; cozy fireplaces are part of the romance here.

It's fun to eat breakfast in a dining room with white pressed-tin ceilings, oak tables and chairs, and tall windows that wash the room in light. (Of course, you may have breakfast in bed, too.) Home-baked breads, cakes, and rolls are made from recipes found in an authentic turn-of-the-century Cedarburg cookbook. Cereal, fresh fruit, and beverages also are offered.

One of Wendy's favorite times of the day is the afternoon social hour in the dining room, with an opportunity to share with guests her love of this historic town. A manteled fireplace with Victorian sofas and chairs just off the main dining area makes things more cozy.

How to get there: From Chicago, take I–94 to I–43, just north of Milwaukee, and get off at the Cedarburg exit. This road eventually changes to Wisconsin 57; follow it into town (where it becomes Washington Avenue). At Center Street, turn left and park in the lot behind the hotel.

Innkeeper: Wendy Porterfield, manager
Address/Telephone: W62 N573 Washington Avenue; (414) 375–3550
Rooms: 34, including 15 suites; all with private bath, air conditioning, TV, and phone; 31 rooms with whirlpool bath. Wheelchair access.
Rates: $59 to $119, single or double; $129 to $179, suites; continental breakfast. Special packages available.
Open: All year.
Facilities and activities: Situated in heart of historic Cedarburg. Nearby: walk to restaurants and Cedar Creek Settlement: old Woolen Mill; Stone Mill Winery; antiques, craft, specialty shops. A short drive to Ozaukee Pioneer Village, Ozaukee Covered Bridge (last remaining covered bridge in Wisconsin).
Recommended Country Inns® Travelers' Club Benefit: 50 percent discount, for rooms $109–$189 only, Sunday–Thursday, excluding holidays.

Canoe Bay
CHETEK, WISCONSIN 54728

Dan and Lisa's inn, already one of the "Top Three" country inns in the Midwest, just keeps getting better. I know that's hard to believe, but take a look for yourself.

They've added four new luxurious cottage suites, featuring Frank Lloyd Wright's signature Prairie-style architecture along with "every possible creature comfort with the ultimate in privacy." Even Canoe Bay's exterior spaces have received what Wright called "organic architecture" treatment, with natural prairie, woodland grasses, and wildflowers designed and installed by a nationally renowned consulting ecologist.

The innkeepers spared no expense in recreating the great architect's distinctive style.

For example, the Oak Park Suite boasts a 14-foot wall of casement windows overlooking a lake; the Wood Grove Suite allows guests to observe natural surroundings from their platform two-person Jacuzzi through wraparound windows. Also count on river-rock fireplace, stereo TV/VCR/CD, wet bar with refrigerator and microwave oven, huge private deck, and more.

Or how about a dream cottage with a see-through fireplace next to the whirlpool plus lake views?

The main building centerpiece is a great room, with soaring natural-cedar cathedral ceilings, a wall of windows, and a 30-foot-tall, hand-constructed fieldstone fireplace.

Dan (former TV weatherman for WFLD-Channel 32 in Chicago) and Lisa built their inn on the shore of crystal-clear Lake Wahdoon, a fifty-acre spring-fed body of water surrounded by 280 acres of private oak, aspen, and maple forests. The inn provides breathtaking views, incomparable service, and complete privacy besides the many opportunities for outdoor recreation and relaxation, including wildlife watching.

Mornings bring pampering, with breakfast baskets delivered to your room or brought out to the patio overlooking the lake, where you can enjoy scores of chirping songbirds. Canoe Bay also offers dinner featuring gourmet cuisine to guests that would be difficult to beat even when considering Chicago or Minneapolis's best restaurants, thanks to CIA-trained Chef Bruno.

The inn's standout season could be autumn, with its incomparable colors, but holidays receive special treatment, too. Thanksgiving and New Year's Day guests can enjoy guided cross-country ski tours, ice skating, ice fishing, and a 14-foot-tall Christmas tree with all the trimmings. Not to mention a free, personal weather forecast from prognosticator Dan, who's often heard to say, "If there's a better place on Earth, I don't know it."

Forget Earth. This is heaven.

How to get there: Once in Chetek, Highway 53 is named Second Street. Follow that through town, over a bridge, and turn right on County D (there's a cemetery at this intersection); go about 1½ miles to Hogback Road (look for a CANOE BAY sign here); turn left and continue for about 7 miles to the inn.

Innkeepers: Dan and Lisa Dobrowolski
Address/Telephone: W16065 Hogback Road; (715) 924-4594 or (800) 568-1995
E-mail/URL: canoebay@discover-net.net / http://discover-net.net/canoebay
Rooms: 12, including 4 main lodge luxury suites and 4 luxury cottage suites; 3 luxury lodge suites, and 1 "dream cottage"; all with private bath, whirlpool bath, and air conditioning. No smoking inn.
Rates: $160 to $180, single or double, inn; $135 to $165, lodge; $175 to $205, cottages; $245, "dream cottage"; EPB. Gourmet dinners $50 per couple.
Open: All year.
Facilities and activities: Located on private 280 acres: 2 private lakes, hiking paths, nature trails, cross-country ski trails, cross-country rentals, bike rentals, fishing, swimming, canoes, rowboats, and more. Sitting room, video room, library. About 45 minutes west of St. Paul, Minnesota.
Recommended Country Inns® Travelers' Club Benefit: 10 percent discount, subject to availability.

Allyn Mansion Inn

DELAVAN, WISCONSIN 53115

This 1885 Queen Anne mansion has one of the most elaborate restorations of "high Victorian" style in the Midwest. Walnut woodwork, frescoed 13-foot ceilings, and ten Italian marble fireplaces will delight inn lovers and house preservationists alike.

Eye-catching stained, leaded, and etched glass, parquet floors, and brass chandeliers add even more elegant touches. And I felt like royalty when ascending a magnificent three-story walnut staircase that rises to a stunning horseshoe window.

Marvelous antique furnishings predate 1900, the bounty of Joe and Ron's multiyear collection. I especially liked the Wave Crest glass (New England, circa 1890s); it's one of the finest sets of its kind in the Heartland.

In spite of the inn's opulent stylings, Joe likes to point out Victorian-era curiosities. "Who else but those Victorians would think of making a cow's hoof into an inkwell?" he said, holding up the antique for inspection.

Guest rooms are spectacular re-creations of Victorian splendor. Besides a photograph of the home's matriarch "trying to smile," according to Joe, Mrs. Allyn's Room features a piece original to the house (and my favorite Victorian gadget to date), a Murphy-type bed that resembles a fine walnut wardrobe, finials and all.

Mr. Allyn's Room has black print Victorian

wallpaper, besides a marble fireplace and a mahogany canopy bed. "People gave me funny looks when I chose this pattern," Joe said. "But I thought it would match the house's architectural character." It sure does.

Hallways are some of the widest I've ever seen, so rooms seem private and quiet. And even the halls are finely furnished. Joe pointed out that the third floor's antique Victorian sofa was ticketed for the Iowa governor's mansion before the innkeepers decided that more people would see it here. "It doesn't look as though it's ever been used," I said. "It's so uncomfortable, it should last a thousand years," he retorted.

The most recent restoration is a 60-foot-high Eastlake tower built to the original architectural plans, which the innkeepers found in an old basement safe. Guests may climb up the open tower, accompanied by the innkeepers.

Joe and Ron make all their jams and jellies, perfect for smothering homemade muffins and breads that are served at breakfast along with fresh fruit, bacon, egg casseroles, and more.

P.S. Ron used to sing in the Chicago Symphony Chorus; maybe you can convince him to croon a few bars from the musical *Les Misérables*.

How to get there: From Milwaukee, take Wisconsin 50 west into Delavan and continue west on Wisconsin 11 to the inn.

Innkeepers: Joe Johnson and Ron Markwell
Address/Telephone: 511 East Walworth Avenue; (414) 728 9090
Rooms: 8 share 7 baths; all with air conditioning. No smoking inn.
Rates: $60, single or double, Sunday through Thursday; $90 to $100, single or double, weekends; EPB. Midweek discounts and corporate rates available. Two-night minimum, end of May through Columbus Day.
Open: All year.
Facilities and activities: Evening social hour on weekends. Three formal parlors, library reading room. Patio, Victorian rose and herb garden. Nearby: restaurants, Circus Hall of Fame. A short drive to Lake Geneva resort, Kettle Moraine State Park, Alpine Valley Music Center, skiing, antiquing.

James St. Inn
DEPERE, WISCONSIN 54115

Don't let the generally nondescript appearance of this riverside inn fool you.

The historic four-story 1892 Columbian Mills, originally built by prominent Wisconsin John Dousman, didn't close until 1982. Today, a restoration company has transformed the old mill into a luxurious bed-and-breakfast inn, with brick walls and archways, beamed ceilings, antique brass light fixtures, and other elegant amenities.

All guest rooms are comfortable, mostly done in elegant Shaker-style appointments.

But check out the suites. Some boast whirl-pools, fireplaces, private balconies, and views of the Fox River. Like Suite 106, a favorite of mine, with its mahogany and walnut furniture—and riverside location.

I like some of the "extras," too. Morning newspapers are free at the front desk—including Sundays; fresh-perked coffee is always ready for guests in the lobby; and wine and cheese are served every afternoon from 4:00 to 9:00 P.M.

There's another interesting aspect to the James St. Inn. Did you notice it?

Okay, I'll tell you.

The river flows under the inn!

So, when they tell you here that your "room is on the water," they really mean it.

How to get there: From Green Bay, take Wisconsin 57 south into DePere. At James Street, turn right and continue to the river and the inn.

Innkeepers: Kevin C. Flatley, manager
Address/Telephone: 201 James Street; (414) 337–0111, fax (414) 337–6135
Rooms: 30; all with private bath.
Rates: $69 to $119, single; $79 to $129, double; continental breakfast.
Open: All year.
Facilities and activities: Fireplace in gathering room, library, river promenade. Nearby: minutes from St. Norbert College, National Railroad Museum, Heritage Hill State Park, Hazelwood, Lambeau Field (home of the Green Bay Packers), Green Bay Packer Hall of Fame.
Business travelers: Data ports in rooms, fax machine, conference room, corporate rates.
Recommended Country Inns® Travelers' Club Benefit: 10 percent discount, Monday–Thursday. $199 package for two nights in a whirlpool suite with complimentary evening wine and cheese and "continental plus" breakfast.

$\mathcal{E}$agle $\mathcal{C}$entre $\mathcal{H}$ouse
EAGLE, WISCONSIN 53119

When Riene and Dean, local historians and preservationists, began talking about moving from their 1880s farmhouse, Riene said, "I won't move into a new home unless it's like Hawks Inn."

No problem. Dean, a sixth-generation master carpenter whose family emigrated to Wisconsin from Germany in the 1840s, drew up plans to replicate Hawks Inn, an authentic 1846 stagecoach stop located in nearby Delafield.

What a job they've done. Their classic Greek Revival house is built atop a hill overlooking sixteen acres of prairie plants and meadow. Dean used nineteenth-century building methods to fashion period architectural details such as hand-built window sashes, eyebrow windows, and pine plank floors, along with other labors of love.

"People don't realize that Wisconsin once had six hundred stagecoach inns," Dean said. "We wanted today's travelers to experience what staying at a stagecoach house was really like."

Riene personally greeted us at the door. Inside we felt heat from two wood-burning stoves that warm double parlors on the first floor: The Tap Room offers tavern tables for card games, books and magazines, and part of the antique collection that Riene has collected for more than twenty years; the formal parlor boasts a straw-filled Victorian couch and other handsome period furnishings.

Our third-floor room was huge, with pine plank floor, an 1840s rope bed (well strung, so I did "sleep tight"), and beautiful rag rugs made by Dean's grandmother.

Other guest rooms are equally handsome and spacious, including two suites offering something that nineteenth-century travelers never knew—whirlpool tubs.

For breakfast we feasted on Dean's cranberry and walnut pancakes, homemade raisin and cranberry breads, fresh fruits and yogurt. The meal is served on Riene's antique English stoneware—part of a 700-piece collection—in the inn's dining room.

Hear the tick-tock of the clock in the dining room? That's coming from a pre–Civil War timepiece that still tells accurate time. And here's more pioneer-style fun: Riene's special 1800s weekends, with innkeepers (and guests) in period costumes and a six-course dinner that includes everything from quail with forcemeat stuffing to rabbit pie.

How to get there: From Milwaukee, take I–94 west to Wisconsin 67, then go south through Eagle to the inn, located about ½ mile north of Old World Wisconsin.

Innkeepers: Riene Wells-Herriges and Dean Herriges

Address/Telephone: W370 S9590 Highway 67; (414) 363-4700

Rooms: 5, including 2 suites; all with private bath and air conditioning, suites with whirlpool tub. No smoking inn.

Rates: $85 to $95, single or double; $145, suites; EPB.

Open: All year.

Facilities and activities: Parlor, taproom, front and side porches overlooking hills and meadows, hiking trails. Nearby: Old World Wisconsin, nationally acclaimed pioneer living-history museum; Kettle Moraine State Forest South, with Ice Age landforms, lakes, hiking and cross-country ski trails; riding stables; sleigh rides. A short drive to downhill skiing, antiques shops, golf course.

Recommended Country Inns® Travelers' Club Benefit: 10 percent discount, Monday–Thursday, November–April, excluding holidays.

The Griffin Inn
ELLISON BAY, WISCONSIN 54210

Here's a little bit of New England on the rugged Door County peninsula. Owner Paul has done lots of restoration work on the charming white clapboard inn, built in 1921, which rests among nine quiet acres that include an apple orchard and lovely gazebo.

I like the cozy country feeling of the main floor, with its library and large stone fireplace surrounded by high-back Queen Anne chairs that make it a popular spot for night talkers. And for guests enjoying the innkeeper's nightly popcorn parties.

The dining room is all rich wood tones with lots of antiques, and a decorative wood-burning stove in the corner brings back memo-

ries of North Woods winter adventures.

Ten quaint rooms line the hallway of the second floor. Each has country prints and is decorated in antique and country-style reproductions. All have an antique double bed adorned with handmade quilt. You'll also find Victorian dressers, tall armoires, and comfy rockers in your room.

Paul offers a huge country breakfast, prepared fresh in the kitchen daily. Treats may include fresh seasonal fruit, German apple pancakes or a soufflé, freshly baked breads and muffins, homemade coffee cake, and coffee, teas, and cocoa.

For cottage guests Paul presents a breakfast

basket with the day's freshly baked selections, juice, and coffee.

Bring your bicycles to explore the backroad beauty of "The Door's" rugged countryside or the spectacular shoreline of Green Bay and Lake Michigan. Or drive to the many art galleries and specialty shops that line the streets of tiny lakeshore villages that dot the peninsula.

Maybe you'll even want to take a ferry across Death's Door, a sometimes turbulent channel of water, to Washington Island—itself a great getaway.

How to get there: Take Route 42 to Ellison Bay and turn east on Mink River Road. The inn is about 2 blocks up the road.

Innkeeper: Paul Ennis

Address/Telephone: 11976 Mink River Road; (414) 854–4306

Rooms: 10 share 2½ baths; 4 cottages with private bath; all with air conditioning. No smoking inn.

Rates: Rooms, $75, single; $79 double; EPB. Cottages, $86, continental breakfast basket. Winter weekend packages available.

Open: All year.

Facilities and activities: Sitting room, sports court, and gazebo on grounds. Fishing, boating, and swimming within walking distance. Golf, horseback riding, tennis, art galleries, potters, antiques shops, restaurants, and the Peninsula Players theater group within a short drive.

The Ephraim Inn
EPHRAIM, WISCONSIN 54211

I believe Ephraim has the most beautiful harbor in all Door County. And the Ephraim Inn, located in the heart of this charming village's historic district, faces that harbor, affording guests one of the finest vistas around.

The inn itself, despite its conspicuous setting right next to the always packed Wilson's Ice Cream Parlor, is a haven for relaxed hospitality. Not quite a decade old, it exudes the warmth of a fine country home, and its wood beams, exposed brick, and country antique reproductions add to the charm.

More than half of the guest rooms provide a magnificent view of the harbor and the tiered green bluffs that rise above it. Each is identified by a hand-carved and hand-painted wooden plaque affixed to the door.

Tulip Heart is one of my favorites, with its four-poster pine bed, fluffy bed quilt, and country cupboard for clothes. I especially liked the Shaker-style wall pegs that circle the room. An antique jelly cupboard keeps modern conveniences like the television out of sight.

Forget-Me-Not has more of the same, including an iron-and-brass-rail daybed and hand stenciling; and Tulip Star, on the second floor, boasts a four-poster English bed and an alcove window that affords more great harbor views.

For breakfast, count on fresh fruit and

juices, Colombian coffee, homemade granola, freshly baked muffins, egg dishes, and more, all served in cozy dining areas. Perhaps you'd enjoy a table across from a crackling fire on a brisk fall morning.

The inn common room also faces the harbor and exudes a very masculine feeling. It's all oak paneling and exposed brick, with another fireplace and soft sofas for night talk.

Then get set for some wandering. Start next door at Wilson's Ice Cream Parlor, a Door County landmark since 1906, and where I first caught a glimpse of my wife-to-be. We were each staying at different country inns at the time.

How to get there: From Sturgeon Bay, take Wisconsin 42 into Ephraim. The inn is just after Wilson's Ice Cream Parlor.

Innkeepers: Nancy and Tim Christofferson
Address/Telephone: Route 42 (mailing address: P. O. Box 247); (414) 854-4515
Rooms: 17; all with private bath, air conditioning, and TV.
Rates: $79 to $145, single or double, EPB. Two-night minimum throughout year with advanced reservations.
Open: April through October; weekends during winter.
Facilities and activities: Across the street from bay and beach. Next to Wilson's Ice Cream Parlor. Nearby: a short walk to specialty shops and studios, sports facilities and activities (boating, sailboarding). A short drive to restaurants, golf, hiking trails, ski trails, Peninsula Players Theater, and Birch Creek Music Center.

White Gull Inn
FISH CREEK, WISCONSIN 54212

Russ Ostrand, the inn's "Master Boiler," is a bear of a man. He sits perched on a small chair in the dining room, pumping his concertina and singing "oom-pah" songs to guests as they devour his latest fish boil—whitefish, potatoes, and a secret recipe boiled outside in a huge caldron with flames darting toward the sky. Served with hot loaves of bread, homemade coleslaw, and mugs of ice-cold beer, it's a Door County institution. A tasty extra is home-baked cherry pie for dessert.

I like the casual atmosphere of the White Gull Inn; it makes me feel right at home. The landmark 1896 white clapboard inn also looks New England picture-perfect.

Local legend says that the inn originally sat on the other side of Green Bay, 18 miles away, in Marinette, Wisconsin. During a frigid Door County winter around the turn of the century, it was dragged on a crudely fashioned log sled by draft horses across the frozen waters to its present location. Sort of a Victorian mobile home. Andy, however, says that he believes the White Gull, unlike its sister inn, The Whistling Swan, was built where it stands today.

Some guest rooms are cozy, comfortably furnished with country-Victorian antiques that create an intimate, romantic retreat. I loved the iron-rail beds that Andy has painted a cheery white. There are also high ceilings and plank floors covered with braided scatter rugs. Other cottages and houses call to mind family times.

The inn lobby has a large fireplace, often with a blazing fire to take the chill off a typically nippy Door County morning. There's also a new inn common room with gas fireplace and color television.

Besides Russ's famous fish boils, the dining room also serves feasts like beef Wellington, baked whitefish (a local favorite), and chicken piccata.

But don't miss the fish boil, especially you first-timers. It's not just a dinner; it's a real happening.

Also check out the Whistling Swan, a sister inn across the street. I love the quaint rooms and the enclosed porch overlooking Main Street.

How to get there: From Milwaukee, take Wisconsin 43 north. Near Manitowoc, take Wisconsin 42 north past Sturgeon Bay into Door County. In Fish Creek, turn left at the stop sign at the bottom of a hill along the twisting road and proceed about 3 blocks to the inn.

Innkeepers: Andy and Jan Coulson

Address/Telephone: 4225 Main Street (mailing address: P. O. Box 160-C); (414) 868–3517; fax (414) 868–2367

Rooms: 9, plus 3 cottages and 2 buildings for multiple couples; all with private bath and air conditioning. No smoking inn.

Rates: Main Lodge, Cliff House: $119 to $175, single or double; cottages: $149 to $198 for 4 to 6 people; houses: $178 to $240 for 4 to 8 people; EP. Midweek winter packages. Two-night minimum on high-season weekends, 3-night minimum on some holidays.

Open: All year.

Facilities and activities: Wheelchair access to dining room; famous Door County fish boil featured on Wednesday, Friday, Saturday, and Sunday nights. Situated in the heart of historic Fish Creek: Walk to art galleries and specialty and antiques shops. State parks and golf nearby.

Recommended Country Inns® Travelers' Club Benefit: 10 percent discount, Sunday–Thursday, November–April, excluding Christmas–New Year's period, not valid with other packages.

The Astor House
GREEN BAY, WISCONSIN 54301

Green Bay's only bed-and-breakfast inn boasts a tony three-diamond rating. Not hard to understand once you've visited this gracious 1888 Victorian beauty.

Just look at the craftsmanship: the exterior boasts fishscale shingles, vertical boards, sunbursts, and circle motifs—all decidedly Victorian; inside, there are leaded glass, 9-foot oak pocket doors, original silver crystal chandelier, and a grand staircase with octagonal-carved spindles.

Doug took me on an inn tour. The Marseilles Garden suite, he says, is like a Monet flower garden come to life and perfect for lovers. Consider its ivy-laced headboard, arbor trellis, gas-log fireplace, and double whirlpool room.

The Hong Kong Retreat is nearly 4,000 square feet of space, reached by a spiral staircase leading to the third floor. Luxuriate in the double jade whirlpool; the black tile fireplace is guaranteed to keep things cozy.

And the Vienna Balconies is a two-level suite with another double whirlpool in its bedroom and a private third-floor balcony overlooking inn gardens.

Breakfasts are delivered to your room or may be taken in the guest parlor. It might include scones, apple tortes, baked apples and pears, and other goodies. Recipes are taken from renowned bed-and-breakfast cookbooks.

There's even turndown service at the Astor

House. Finally, a reason for this rabid Chicago Bears fan to think of Green Bay and not envision those evil Packers.

How to get there: Located at the junction of Highways 54 and 57, 8 blocks from Green Bay's City Centre. From Milwaukee (Port Washington), take Wisconsin 57 north into Green Bay; it turns into Monroe Street in town; watch for Wisconsin 54, and the inn.

Innkeepers: Doug Landwehr and Nan Nelson
Address/Telephone: 637 South Monroe Avenue; (414) 432–3585
Rooms: 5 suites; all with private bath. No smoking inn.
Rates: Weekend: $109 to $149, single or double; weekdays: $79 to $99, single or double; continental breakfast.
Open: All year.
Facilities and activities: Guest parlor, wraparound veranda. Located in Astor Historic District—take self-guided walking tour of notable homes. Short drive to Lambeau Field, Green Bay Packer Hall of Fame, Heritage Hill State Park, Oneida Casino, Weidner Center for the Performing Arts. Bay Beach Wildlife Sanctuary, Arena Expo Center.

Schneider's Oakwood Lodge

GREEN LAKE, WISCONSIN 54941

The huge white cottage with the arched second-floor balcony jumped out at me as I approached the bend in the country road. It was surrounded by tall trees, perched lakeside in a perfect getaway setting.

I discovered that this is one of only a few buildings that remain of the original massive Oakwood Hotel complex built in the 1860s. Now it's a charming inn with "the best view of Green Lake."

I sat outside on the back-porch dining terrace, just a stone's throw from the lake, devouring some excellent breakfast specialties: homemade buttermilk pancakes. There were also hearty helpings of homemade breads and rolls, and cakes and sweet rolls for morning sweet tooths. What a fabulous way to enjoy the day's first meal—lakeside alfresco. In cold weather breakfast in the dining room is also delightful.

There are twelve charming rooms in this historic building; my favorites are upstairs facing the lake. I like just to sit and watch all the colorful sails bob along the waters. Some of the rooms have high walnut headboards and brass beds.

Oakwood Lodge doesn't serve dinner, but the romantic Grey Rock Mansion of the Heidel House resort is a one-minute drive down the road. I also recommend Norton's, a nearby seafood restaurant right on the lake—a local favorite. And I like Carver's on the Lake (open only in summer), specializing in French cuisine, and Alfred's.

How to get there: Travel Wisconsin 23 west to Business 23 and then turn left on South Street. Take South to Lake Street and turn right. Oakwood Lodge is at the intersection (bend of the road) of Lake Street and Illinois Avenue.

Innkeeper: Mary Schneider

Address/Telephone: 365 Lake Street; (414) 294–6580

Rooms: 12; 9 with private bath, some with balcony.

Rates: $80 to $98, single; $90 to $108, double, on weekends; weekday rates available; EPB. Children, cribs, $10 extra per night. Two-night minimum on weekends; 3-night minimum on holiday weekends. Off-season rates available.

Open: All year except November and March.

Facilities and activities: Family room, room balconies, patio, private lake pier and raft. Water sports and activities. Will arrange midweek golf packages. Nearby: three golf courses, including renowned Lawsonia, nearby; horseback riding; specialty shops in town; cross-country skiing.

The Manor House
KENOSHA, WISCONSIN 53140

If you consider a stately, historic Georgian mansion overlooking Lake Michigan to be the perfect getaway, get into your car immediately and proceed to The Manor House.

This magnificent home, the largest in Kenosha, was built in the mid-1920s for a vice president of Nash Motor Company, forerunner to the American Motors Corporation. The house has been tastefully restored to elegance with English antiques and furnishings from the 1800s; you'll lounge on Chippendale, Queen Anne, and even a smattering of furnishings from the Rothschilds' Mentmore Manor in Buckinghamshire, England.

Rich oak paneling, glistening crystal chandeliers, arched hallways, and marble fireplaces add to the splendor. I was overwhelmed by the grand oak staircase that greets visitors as they step into the home's entryway. And the formal dining room, sparkling with antique crystal, is an especially handsome room in which to eat breakfast and get acquainted with other guests.

The Purple Room is the manor's largest; a unique touch is the small nurse's bed at the foot of a massive antique hand-carved four-poster bed made in 1870. A tall Victorian dressing mirror adds another touch of elegance, as do the room's small chandelier and manteled working fireplace. It also has separate men's and women's dressing rooms and a lake view.

I especially liked the Rose Room. With brass chandelier, a connecting dressing room, and a view of the manor's formal rose garden, it provides an especially romantic ambience for couples celebrating a special day. (In fact, it's the inn's honeymoon suite.)

And two new suites have lake views. My favorite is Grand Suite, with a 6-foot whirlpool, fieldstone fireplace, and private balcony.

Several common rooms, and the grounds themselves, hold their own excitement. A grand sitting room features wonderful Chippendale sofas and a Steinway grand piano. The second-floor foyer is an antique lover's paradise. And the manicured lawns, gardens, and fountains invite romantic hand-in-hand walks in a colorful and fragrant haven.

Breakfasts of home-baked goods, fruits, tea, egg dishes, pancakes, juices, and special-blend coffees are served in the elegant dining room. Then stroll across the street to an unspoiled eleven-acre lakeside park and enjoy breathtaking sunscapes.

How to get there: From Chicago or Milwaukee, take I–94 to Wisconsin 50 and turn east. Follow to Third Avenue and turn left, continuing to the inn.

Innkeeper: Laurie Novak-Simmons, manager
Address/Telephone: 6536 Third Avenue; (414) 658–0014
Rooms: 6; all with private bath, air conditioning, and TV.
Rates: $100 to $199, single or double, EPB.
Open: All year.
Facilities and activities: Formal parlor, sitting room. Formal gardens, sunken lily pool, water fountain, and gazebo. Walk across street to lakeside park. Walking tours of Kenosha Lakeshore historic places. A short drive to restaurants; Lake Michigan charter fishing, boating, beaches; bike trails, golf, downhill and cross-country skiing. Lakeside Players theater, Chiwaukee Prairie conservation area, Palumbo Civil War exhibit.

The American Club
KOHLER, WISCONSIN 53044

Just 4 miles from the shoreline of Lake Michigan, amid tall pines, patches of white birch, scrubbed farmhouses, and black soil, is one of Wisconsin's best-kept secrets. It's The American Club, a uniquely gracious guest house.

I found an uncommonly European ambience at this elegant inn. With its Tudor-style appointments of gleaming brass, custom-crafted oak furniture, crystal chandeliers, and quality antique furnishings, The American Club looks like a finely manicured baronial estate. It's also the only five-diamond resort hotel in the Midwest.

Built in 1918 as a temporary home for immigrant workers of the Kohler Company (a renowned plumbing manufacturer, still located across the street), the "boarding house" served as a meeting place where English and citizenship classes were taught—a genuine American Club.

Some rooms feature a four-poster canopied brass bed and huge marble-lined whirlpool bath. Special suites contain a saunalike environmental enclosure with a push-button choice of weather—from bright sun and gentle breezes to misty rain showers. And consider these guestroom amenities: fluffy bathrobes, scales, twice-daily maid service, daily newspapers—the list goes on!

West-wing rooms are equally gracious. And the Club's Inn at Woodlake offers sixty additional moderately priced rooms ($89 to $139, single; $109 to $159, double) that include continental breakfast and privileges at the Sports Core and Blackwolf Run.

The inn's showcase restaurant is The Immigrant, where I dined on a gourmet meal of smoked Irish salmon. The wine list was impressive, too. For dessert I walked to the Greenhouse, in the courtyard. This antique English solarium is a perfect spot for chocolate torte and other Viennese delights.

The hotel's Pete Dye–designed Blackwolf Run golf course, comprising two very distinct eighteen-hole courses, is one of the most dramatic links around. Upon its opening in 1988, it was named the "Best New Public Course in the Nation" by *Golf Digest*. Of course, it's now rated one of the top three courses in the nation! I cannot get there often enough.

How to get there: From Chicago, take I–94 north and continue north on I–43, just outside of Milwaukee. Exit on Wisconsin 23 west (exit 53B). Take 23 to County Trunk Y and continue south into Kohler. The inn is on the right. From the west, take I–94 south to Wisconsin 21 and go east to U.S. 41. Go south on 41 to Wisconsin 23; then head east into Kohler.

Innkeepers: Susan Porter Green, vice-president; Alice Hubbard, general manager
Address/Telephone: Highland Drive; (414) 457–8000 or (800) 344–2838, fax (414) 457–0299
Rooms: 236; all with private whirlpool bath, air conditioning, TV, and phone. Wheelchair access.
Rates: Novermber through April: $130 to $585, single; $160 to $585, double; summer season rates slightly higher. Each child over 10, $15 extra; children 10 and younger free. Two-night minimum on weekends from July through September. Several packages available.
Open: All year.
Facilities and activities: Nine restaurants and full-service dining rooms. Renowned for extravagant buffets, special-event and holiday feasts; large Sunday brunch. Ballroom. Sports Core, a world-class health club. River Wildlife, 500 acres of private woods for hiking, horseback riding, hunting, fishing, trapshooting, canoeing. Cross-country skiing and ice skating. Also Kohler Design Center, shops at Woodlake, Kohler Arts Center, Waelderhaus. Nearby: antiquing, lake charter fishing, Kettle Moraine State Forest, Road America (auto racing).
Business travel: Located 5 minutes from downtown Sheboygan. Corporate rates, conference rooms, fax services.

Frank Lloyd Wright's Seth Peterson Cottage
LAKE DELTON, WISCONSIN 53940

Here's your only chance to overnight in a Frank Lloyd Wright original!

First, you've got to find the secluded masterpiece. I traveled over twisting backroads in the Baraboo Mountains (one of the oldest mountain ranges in the country), through heavily wooded terrain before coming to the entrance—a humble dirt-road driveway that is guarded by a swing gate to ensure the privacy of cottage guests.

The cottage sits on a wooded bluff overlooking Mirror Lake. It is much smaller than it looks in photos. But its austere Prairie stylings are unmistakably Frank Lloyd Wright.

In 1958, Seth Peterson, a lifelong Badger State resident and enthusiast of the master architect, convinced the ninety-year-old Wright to design a cottage. The famed architect designed a tremendous amount of space into the limited area available.

The floor plan follows Wright's architectural philosophy, which he enunciated in 1954: "Organic architecture must come from the ground up into the light by gradual growth. It will itself be the ground of a better way of life."

And the result: an elegant and simple building, often described as containing "more architecture per square foot than any other building he ever designed."

The cottage, perched atop that wooded

bluff, is made of native sandstone. It boasts a dramatic sandstone floor that "mirrors the craggy cliffs of the lake and surrounding terrain."

A wall of windows allows natural light to suffuse the interior while allowing a constant awareness of the closeness of nature—trees virtually surround the structure. And it contains the Wright signature—a massive sandstone fireplace in the living room.

There are also French doors opening onto a terrace that allows breathtaking views of the water below.

An overnight here is something that won't soon be forgotten. It's like participating in history.

How to get there: From Chicago, Milwaukee, or Madison, take I–94 north to Wisconsin 23; go south to Shady Lane Road and turn left (east); proceed to Mirror Lake Road and turn left (north); then follow as the road turns into Fern Dell and proceeds east; watch for the inn on the left side of the road. (If you come to Mirror Lake State Park headquarters, go back—you've gone too far east.)

Innkeeper: Audrey Laatch, Preservation Board Chairperson
Address/Telephone: Fern Dell Road (write c/o Sand County Service Company, Box 409, Lake Delton 53940); (608) 254–6551, fax (608) 254–4440
Rooms: 1 cottage, with living room, dining room, kitchen, bedroom, bath. No smoking inn.
Rates: $195, single or double; $995 weekly; EP.
Open: All year.
Facilities and activities: Located deep in the woods, high on a bluff overlooking Mirror Lake. Short ride to Mirror Lake State Park, waterparks and attractions of Wisconsin Dells, Ho Chunk Casino, Mid-Continent Railway Steam Train. Nearby: skiing, fishing, hiking, biking, boating.

French Country Inn
LAKE GENEVA, WISCONSIN 53147

What looks like a modest lakeside retreat from the outside reveals itself to be a magnificent showplace. I marveled at the lobby's intricate parquet floors, hand-carved solid-oak staircase, and rich chandeliers—all shining and sparkling from rays of the sun sprinkling in through a large skylight.

The inn's main house, including that magnificent staircase, was completely hand built by master craftsmen in Denmark in the 1880s. Later it was dismantled in piecemeal fashion, shipped by boat and rail to Chicago, and reassembled as the Danish Pavilion for the 1893 Columbian Exposition. After that the building was purchased and moved to its present site.

Note that the inn's colorful past includes a stint as a speakeasy and gambling casino during Prohibition.

Eager to see the guest rooms, I wasn't disappointed. Located in annexes just steps from the main building, the rooms are gracefully done in country-French styles, with brass beds, high-back chairs, balloon drapes, and more. Some have cathedral ceilings and skylights; all have their own gas fireplaces and private balconies overlooking Como Lake. In fact, the balconies are only 25 feet from the shoreline.

Late-afternoon tea, featuring samples from the inn kitchen, is served in the parlor, itself a warm retreat dominated by a fireplace and more country-French furnishings. A full breakfast of cheese and sausage omelets, fresh fruit, juice, and homemade croissants should leave no one hungry.

The inn restaurant, boasting a graceful panorama of the shoreline, delights in French-American specialties. Or you might wander through Lake Geneva, which boasts some fine dining. The innkeepers can recommend a spot to fit your appetite.

How to get there: From Chicago, take I–94 to Wisconsin 50 west and proceed about 3 miles out of Lake Geneva. Then turn north at the inn sign off Highway 50 and proceed down the winding road to the inn.

Innkeeper: John Cole

Address/Telephone: Highway 50 West, Route 4, Box 690; (414) 245–5220

Rooms: 24, including 1 suite; all with private bath, air conditioning, TV, and phone.

Rates: Sunday through Thursday: $105 to $115, single or double; Friday and Saturday: $135 to $155, single or double; EPB. Two-night minimum on weekends. Special holiday and low-season rates.

Open: All year.

Facilities and activities: Full-service restaurant and bar, afternoon tea, outdoor swimming pool. Nearby: golf, horseback riding, and winter ski areas. A short drive to Lake Geneva specialty shops, boat tours, water activities.

The Geneva Inn
LAKE GENEVA, WISCONSIN 53147

When the inn's pianist played Disney's "Beauty and the Beast" and "A Whole New World" for daughters Kate and Dayne, their candlelight dinner was complete.

Prettied up in fancy dresses, the girls beamed, softly sang along with the music, and blushed as the musician nodded a smile their way.

But this pampering was only the beginning of personal touches and extras served up by this elegant retreat on the shores of Lake Geneva. In fact, the Geneva Inn might be the best-kept secret in this old resort town. Resonating with the peaceful atmosphere and luxurious decor of an English inn, the thirty-seven-room hotel most closely resembles a dignified British gentlemen's club.

The hotel gleams with mahogany, oak, and other fine woods; Waverly wall coverings add rich textures; and hunter green dominates the color scheme. The centerpiece of the common rooms is a three-story, glass-topped atrium dominated by a massive brick fireplace.

Our girls loved their guest room, with its English pencil-post beds, brass lamps, refrigerator, wet bar, and more. But it was the oversized double whirlpool bath that got most of their attention, its bubbly waters providing almost as much fun as a Wisconsin Dells water park.

We were delighted by the inn's Grandview

Restaurant (which certainly lives up to its name, overlooking Lake Geneva). My wife, Debbie, chose swordfish Negril, while I opted for angel-hair pasta primavera; there's also a kids' menu, featuring everything from grilled chicken and shrimp to that old standby—a hot dog with French fries.

After dinner we walked out to the inn's marina docks, but chilly weather drove us back into our rooms. I'll take credit for the perfect timing—we got back just in time for a sunset exploding in fiery orange colors that we watched from our private balcony.

The pampering includes turndown service with complimentary cognac and chocolates; thick, fluffy bathrobes; specially made quilts adorning beds; a refrigerator fully stocked with all kinds of late-night treats; and a free newspaper waiting outside the door in the morning.

The inn's breakfast buffet reminded us of morning meals in Europe: mounds of fresh fruits and melons, croissants, morning meats and cheeses, and fragrant teas that start the day off right.

Two in-town recommendations: Our girls love the "ice-cream social" boat float, offered by the Geneva Lake Cruise Line, located at the Riviera docks on Wrigley Drive; the seventy-five-minute cruise offers Lake Geneva history narration and Wisconsin-made ice cream.

Or take a float on the mail boat, one of the few remaining marine mail deliveries in the United States. What make this so interesting? Well, the boat never actually stops—the mail carrier must jump off the boat, deposit mail in boxes on the dock, and leap back onto the boat without ending up in the drink!

How to get there: From I–94, exit at Wisconsin 50 and go west to Lake Geneva. At the intersection of Wisconsin 50 and 120, turn south on 120 and continue 2 miles to the inn.

Innkeeper: Richard Treptow, general manager
Address/Telephone: N2009 State Road 120; (800) 441–5881
Rooms: 37, including with 4 suites. Wheelchair access.
Rates: $145 to $185, single or double; $215 to $350, lakeside suites; continental breakfast.
Open: All year.
Facilities and activities: Full-service restaurant, lounge, sitting room with fireplace, dock and marina. Nearby: a short drive to Geneva Lake Cruise Line docks; K. J. Flemings, Ltd. (Irish imports); Yerkes Observatory; Uncle John's Fun Park; downtown shops; golf courses, public beach, fishing. Hike the 26-mile path around the lake for up-close glimpses of multimillion dollar mansions. Alpine Valley downhill ski area, horseback riding, dog track, Green Meadow Farm.

Fargo Mansion Inn
LAKE MILLS, WISCONSIN 53551

I arrived on a warm spring day to find the grounds of the inn masked by a cover of bright-blue flowers. "Mr. Fargo planted the scilla more than one hundred years ago," Tom said. "They only last about two weeks, but they continue to come up every year."

Tom and Barry have done a masterful job restoring this 1881 mansion built by Enoch J. Fargo, a local entrepreneur and descendant of the famed Wells Fargo family. The foyer alone is a stunning masterpiece of Queen Anne architecture, with a 30-foot-high ceiling and handsome winding staircase of quarter-sawn oak.

Guest rooms, named for Fargo relatives and friends, are elegant and comfortable. The Elijah Harvey Suite celebrates that period when Victorians became fascinated with Turkish stylings. Earthy colors, Turkish rugs, an ornate Victorian double bed with marble-topped washstand, and a reading nook are inviting enough. But the bathroom includes a whirlpool surrounded by hand-cut Italian marble done in earth-tone colors that carry out the Turkish theme to the hilt. It's addictive, so don't be surprised if you begin to utter remarks such as, "Take me to the Casbah." You'll also enjoy its private balcony. It's one of my favorite getaway spots.

Tom and Barry call the E. J. Fargo Suite their "grandest." It has an 8½-foot Victorian queen-sized bed, a working marble fireplace warming a cozy sitting area, ceiling-to-floor bay windows providing a panorama of the grounds, and a private porch done up in wicker furniture during summer weather, perfect for sunset watching and relaxing.

Where's the bathroom? Go to the bookcase and "remove" a title called *The Secret Passage*. The bookcase swings open to reveal a secret passageway and a bathroom done entirely in Italian marble, with a whirlpool bath built for two and an oversized glass-enclosed shower. The effect is memorable.

Breakfast—which includes egg casseroles, morning meats, croissants, juice, and coffee—is often taken in the music room; the massive table can seat twenty. For dinner there are several restaurants nearby; the innkeepers will recommend one to suit your tastes.

On a walk after our meal, Barry said that the sidewalks surrounding the inn were the first in the state of Wisconsin. Fargo himself went to Germany to learn how to mix the concrete for them.

And here's a news flash: Coming soon— five new luxury rooms on the inn's third floor.

How to get there: From Milwaukee, take I–94 west to Lake Mills exit (Wisconsin 89). Go through town to Madison Street, turn left, then turn left on Mulberry Street and proceed to the inn.

Innkeepers: Tom Boycks and Barry Luce
Address/Telephone: 406 Mulberry Street; (414) 648–3654
Rooms: 5, including 2 suites; all with private bath and air conditioning; phone and TV on request.
Rates: $79 to $160, single or double, EPB.
Open: All year.
Facilities and activities: Parlor, sitting room. Perennial flower garden. Bicycles-built-for-two available to guests. Nearby: Rock Lake beaches, boating, swimming. A short drive to restaurants, hiking trails, Indian burial grounds, Aztalan State Park, Drumlin Bike Trail, golf, tennis, trapshooting.

Victorian Treasure Bed and Breakfast

LODI, WISCONSIN 53555

It's hard to imagine that this rambling Victorian, with its expansive wraparound veranda, was built for only $3,000 in 1897 by lumber baron and Wisconsin state senator William G. Bissell. Snooping traced a great-granddaughter to Rockford, Illinois, and she gave the innkeepers some early-1800s photos of the house. These now hang on the inn walls.

Many original chandeliers, brass door fittings, and woodwork hearken back to fine Victorian-era craftsmanship. The tulip-drop brass chandelier in the sitting room, which casts a warm glow over Victorian high-back chairs and sofa, is one of the home's original gas fixtures.

I walked up a grand staircase, coming to a wide hallway that leads to guest rooms. The handsome Queen Anne's Lace Room has a queen-sized four-poster canopy bed in front of three floor-to-ceiling windows draped with antique lace panels for privacy. It also has an expansive bath featuring a two-person whirlpool.

In the Primrose Room, a queen-sized bed with antique Eastlake headboard and footboard is set amid a blaze of bold Victorian printed wall coverings. The effect is light and airy, with three huge windows that allow sunlight to filter into the room.

And the Wild Ginger Room has handsome

furnishings (especially the hand-carved walnut bed and bureau) and a porch perfect for star-gazing.

All beds have down comforters, four pillows, luxurious linens—real European style.

Kimberly's five-course gourmet breakfast might include fresh fruit with ginger syrup, home-baked nut breads and cinnamon rolls, vegetable frittata, omelets, locally "grown" sausages, and more. The "house" specialty: pecan cream-cheese stuffed French toast topped with fresh (seasonal) fruit sauces.

Another choice—stay at the inn's other property, the Palmer House; it's an 1893 Queen Anne Victorian with four luxury suites that include whirlpool bath, fireplace, stereo, and wet bar.

Perhaps the Angelica suite is the inn's finest. It boasts three rooms, a mahogany tester bed, double whirlpool—even a private front porch. Things can't get much better than this.

How to get there: From Chicago and Milwaukee, take I–90/94 to Wisconsin 60 and go west into Lodi. In town take Route 60 (now called Lodi Street) 1 block west, then turn right on Prairie Street. It's the first house on the left.

Innkeepers: Kimberly and Todd Seidl

Address/Telephone: 115 Prairie Street; (608) 592–5199

Rooms: 8, including 4 suites; all with private bath and air conditioning. No smoking inn.

Rates: $65 to $169, single or double, EPB, afternoon wine, cheese, and fruit.

Open: All year.

Facilities and activities: Sitting rooms, porch. Nearby: water activities on Wisconsin River and Lake Wisconsin. Hiking, rock climbing, bird-watching on Baraboo Range. Also nearby: restaurants; downhill and cross-country skiing; Devil's Lake State Park, with 500-foot bluffs; American Players (Shakespearean) Theater in outdoor amphitheater; Taliesin, home of Frank Lloyd Wright; golf; bald eagle watching.

Business travel: Located about 20 miles north of Madison, 20 miles south of Baraboo. Corporate rates, meeting room, fax.

Recommended Country Inns® Travelers' Club Benefit: 20 percent discount, Monday–Thursday.

Canterbury Inn

MADISON, WISCONSIN 53703

"You spend so much time in bookstores, you should live in one."

This is an oft-repeated refrain in the Puhala household. So we did the next best thing. We spent the weekend in one.

Officially called a bed, book, and breakfast, the Canterbury Inn boasts a decidedly English ambience. Its handsome bookstore, with arched interior doorways and comfy chairs for serious book browsings, rambles into several rooms, with stacks of tomes almost reaching the ceiling. And something's always happening on the other side of the store, home to Canterbury's coffeehouse.

Guest rooms are exquisite, each named for a traveler to Canterbury (from Chaucer's *Canterbury Tales,* of course). All boast hand-crafted stencils that elaborate on their character's stories. I like the Merchant's Room especially for an entrance into the bath—its fanciful whimsy bespeaks of medieval artistry.

Can you sleep in the bed of the Knight's Room while Palamon and Arcite look longingly at you from their prison tower?

Maybe the Miller's Room is more your style, which has a painting of the poor lad known as Nicolas the Gallant, "and making love was his secret talent."

How to get there: From John Nolan Drive in Madison, take Broom Street west past Gotham (it's one-way the wrong way) to Gilman; turn right and got to Henry; turn right and proceed to Gorham; turn right to the inn.

Innkeepers: Jeffrey Gardner, manager

Address/Telephone: 315 West Gorham; (608) 258–8899 or (800) 838–3850

Rooms: 6; all with private bath; wheelchair access. No smoking inn.

Rates: Weekday, $117 to $237; weekends, $145 to $255; special events (UW home football weekends, graduation weekends, holidays, art fair, etc.), $164 to $290; single rates $20 less; continental breakfast.

Open: All year.

Facilities and activities: Bookstore, coffeehouse, coffeehouse jazz sessions, author readings, afternoon teas, chamber music, chess club, kids' reading. Nearby: walk to State Street, State Capitol. Short drive to Dane County Coliseum.

Mansion Hill Inn

MADISON, WISCONSIN 53703

An extraordinary inn! I knew it would be special as soon as a tuxedo-clad manservant opened a tall door, graced with elegantly stenciled glass, to greet me officially.

This 1858 building is an architectural showplace. Its fine construction materials include white sandstone from the cliffs of the Mississippi, Carrara marble from Italy, and ornamental cast iron from Sweden. The original owner imported Old World artisans to do all the construction work. It shows.

Nearly $2 million has been spent to restore the mansion to its former magnificence. I loved the handsome arched windows and French doors that let the sunlight spill in. Hand-carved

white-marble fireplaces blaze with warmth, and a spectacular spiral staircase winds four floors up to the belvedere, which provides a panoramic view of the city.

All the rooms are exquisitely furnished in beautiful antiques—some of the finest I have ever seen. I stayed in the McDonnell Room, which evokes a bold Empire atmosphere. I felt like royalty in these surroundings: arched windows, French doors, a large crystal chandelier, and an incredible 10-foot-tall tester (canopy) bed that one might find in the sleeping quarters of the Prince of Wales.

It also had an oval whirlpool tub, where I soaked in the swirling hot waters with a set of tubside stereo headphones clamped on my ears.

Another extraordinary room has floor-to-ceiling bookcases with a hidden door opening into an incredible bathroom with arched windows, classical Greek Revival columns, and a huge marble tub.

And a deliriously romantic retreat is the Turkish Nook, swathed in Victorian silks, strewn with pillows and ottomans, and featuring a tented sultan's bed—all evoking the sensual delights and intrigues of the mysterious Middle East.

It's easy to understand why "Too much is not enough" is the inn maxim.

You can dine on gourmet meals, which are specially arranged on request. Or explore Madison's gustatory delights on your own, perhaps at L'Etoile, L'Escargot, or The White Horse Inn.

How to get there: From Milwaukee, take I-94 west to Madison. Exit west on Wisconsin 30 to Wisconsin 113. Go south to Johnson; then west to Baldwin. Turn south on Baldwin to East Washington, and then turn west toward the capitol building. At Pinckney Street, turn north. The inn is on the corner of Pinckney and Gilman.

Innkeeper: Janna Wojtal

Address/Telephone: 424 North Pinckney Street; (608) 255-3999

Rooms: 11, including 2 suites; all with private bath, air conditioning, cable TV, stereo, VCR, and minibar.

Rates: Weekdays: $80 to $230, single; $100 to $250, double. Weekends: $100 to $250, single; $120 to $270, double. Continental breakfast

Open: All year.

Facilities and activities: Victorian parlor, dining room (with catered dinners available), belvedere, private wine cellar, garden. Access to health spa, private dining club. Mansion Hill Historic District invites touring, especially Period Garden Park. Madison is state capital; many fine ethnic restaurants, specialty shops, art galleries, recitals, theaters, nightclubs. Nearby: University of Wisconsin main campus; swimming, fishing, boating in surrounding lakes.

Recommended Country Inns® Travelers' Club Benefit: Stay two nights, get third night free, Monday–Thursday.

Lauerman Guest House Inn
MARINETTE, WISCONSIN 54143

This stately mansion is a traffic-stopper.

With towering Corinthian pillars, a commanding white-rail balcony overlooking the Menominee River, and an ornate portico that once welcomed horse-drawn coaches containing formally attired gentlemen and their handsomely dressed ladies, the Lauerman Guest House Inn was hailed as one of the most outstanding examples of Colonial Revival architecture in this part of the Midwest.

Built in 1910 by its namesake—a local businessman who was grossing more than $1 million a year from his department store—the inn exhibits all the special touches of turn-of-the-century elegance.

I was immediately drawn to beautiful Art Deco lamp figurines that grace staircase posts on the main floor. (These exquisite pieces, fashioned after Greek goddesses, were named *Naiade* and *Diane* by the artist.)

Oak and black walnut shine throughout the rich interior, and the commanding brass chandelier, leaded-prism windows, and timbered ceilings are original to the home.

Guest rooms are charming. One of my favorites is the Bow Room, with its hand-silk-screened wallpaper done in an English garden floral pattern. Through the huge window I could gaze at the stately black walnut trees that dot the grounds. I even liked the bath, with its original soaking tub, pedestal sink, and cameo window.

Other rooms are equally comfortable. Cecilia's features a ceramic-tiled fireplace with an ornate cast-iron screen and the home's original wall safe; Freda's Room has handsome mahogany woodwork as well as a whirlpool bath; and the Master Suite offers more mahogany and bird's-eye maple woodwork and French doors that open to an expansive private porch overlooking the Menominee River.

For breakfast consider waffles, eggs, sausage, juice, and coffee. Then just get out and enjoy the countryside.

How to get there: From Green Bay, take U.S. 41 north into Menominee. Turn left on Riverside Avenue and continue 1½ blocks to the inn.

Innkeepers: Sherry and Steve Homa, Tony and Doris Spaude
Address/Telephone: 1975 Riverside Avenue; (715) 732–7800
Rooms: 7; all with private bath, air conditioning, TV, and phone.
Rates: $49, single; $68, double; EPB.
Open: All year.
Facilities and activities: Menominee River marina 2 blocks away. Two golf courses within 2 miles. Restaurants, Theater on the Bay, University of Wisconsin at Marinette a short drive away.

The Audubon Inn
MAYVILLE, WISCONSIN 53050

It's difficult to articulate the scope of this elegant renovation. An 1896 hotel that had fallen into disrepair now sparkles as a community showplace thanks to Wisconsin country inn king Rip O'Dwanny.

Rip and his partners invested more than $500,000 in handsome woodwork alone, then imported hand-dyed carpets from Great Britain, commissioned fourteen fabulous stained-glass windows that adorn the dining room and bar, and also commissioned a master craftsman from Wisconsin to create marvelous handmade etched-glass panels that decorate the inn. Did I say decorate? These are not mere decorations, but fine works of art.

Guest rooms are superbly crafted, boasting four-poster canopy beds handmade in New Hampshire and adorned by hand-crafted quilts, Victorian-inspired wall coverings "imported" from California, double whirlpool Kohler tubs, Shaker-inspired writing desks, brass lamps, wooden window blinds, and more.

"I feel that this is the ultimate country inn," Rip said. "Not only does the inn offer luxurious comfort and privacy but also a great restaurant that employs four master chefs and a pastry chef."

In fact, my gourmet dinner rivaled anything I've ever tasted in a fancy New York restaurant. The menu changes monthly, but when offered, I highly recommend the swordfish *moutarde* (a charbroiled steak served atop a mustard cream sauce, and wonderfully presented).

Also impressive: grilled barbarie breast of duck, served with raspberry sauce, and New York strip steak *au poivre*, adorned with cracked-peppercorn sauce.

And you'll be sorry if you don't sample an incredible strawberry dessert tart.

The bar is quite special. Consider that Rip had the second and third floors above the bar removed to the ceiling; then he fashioned skylights on the third-floor roof and opened the second floor completely so that natural light could fall on a massive, hand-etched glass depiction of geese in flight over the marsh (the hallmark of this wetland bordertown) that is the lounge's incredible centerpiece and ceiling. It's already been called the most beautiful bar in Wisconsin.

Simply put, it would be difficult to discover a full-service Midwest country inn that could match the Audubon's class, style, and menu selections.

One final note: Located in the heart of Canada goose country, the inn is named in honor of famed naturalist John J. Audubon. A stained-glass window in the dining room depicts the renowned wildlife artist.

How to get there: From Milwaukee, take U.S. 45 north to Wisconsin 67; then go west into Mayville's downtown district and the inn.

Innkeeper: Anne Verwiebe, manager
Address/Telephone: 45 North Main Street; (414) 387–5858
Rooms: 17; all with private bath, air conditioning, TV, and phone. Pets OK.
Rates: Weekdays: $79 to $109, single or double; weekends: $89 to $119, single or double. EPB on weekends, continental breakfast weekdays.
Open: All year.
Facilities and activities: Lunch, dinner, Sunday brunch. Sitting rooms, bar with lounge. Nearby: Horicon Marsh, spring and fall geese migration; Kettle Moraine State Forest, hiking, biking, and backpacking; golfing; cross-country skiing; lake activities.
Recommended Country Inns® Travelers' Club Benefit: 15 percent discount, Sunday–Thursday.

The Brick House

MERRILL, WISCONSIN 54452

We came to thunder down the Underdown!

And after our mountain-biking adventure over rugged North Woods logging trails and unbroken tall-grass switchbacks, my brother, Mark, and I agreed that this slice of northern Wisconsin is in itself a kind of world-class off-road heaven.

The Underdown, located about 9 miles north of Merrill, is a 21-mile-long monster trail that lures mountain bikers from all over the country. It gets its moniker from namesake Bill, a moonshiner who based his still operations deep in these woods during Prohibition Days.

But these North Woods boast more than

that. Other world-class bike routes include Harrison Hills trails, the Hiawatha Trail, Parrish Highlands Trail, Augustyn Springs Trail, Jack Lake Trail, Bearskin State Trail—the list seems endless.

Mountain-bike rentals are available at Scotty's in nearby Tomahawk; you can rent twenty-one-speed, lightweight off-road bikes on a daily and weekly basis, with family packages available.

A great place to set up "base camp" for a mountain-biking getaway is The Brick House, located in the heart of Merrill, just a short drive to most of the best trails.

The handsome 1915 Prairie-style home is

country cozy, with everything from beveled glass doors to a little fireplace that's perfect for cool spring and autumn nights. Guest rooms are elegantly quaint. The Daly Room offers antique furnishings, an 1800s burled walnut bed, two wing chairs, and feather pillows that had me thinking of my grandpa's billowy feather bed. The cool pastel colors of the Veranda Room take the edge off summer's heat—the ceiling fan helps, too. So does the porch.

Through their membership in the North Woods Bed and Breakfast Association, Kris and Randy can arrange inn-to-inn mountain-biking tours. For a fee, they'll arrange transportation of your car, luggage, and extra gear to a target inn, so that everything will be waiting there upon your arrival.

Kris knows that you'll need lots of energy on the trails, and her breakfasts certainly do the job of providing it. Meals might include her specialty: puffy stuffed French toast (filled with cream cheese and walnuts), thinly sliced breakfast ham, fresh fruits, juices, and more.

Now, hit the road, pal.

How to get there: From Wausau, take U.S. 51 north to Merrill and take exit 208 (Highway 64); go west (left), and when you get to the stoplight where Highway 64 veers to the right, proceed straight; this takes you onto Main Street. Follow Main to Cleveland; the inn is on the corner.

Innkeepers: Randy and Kris Ullmer
Address/Telephone: 108 South Cleveland Street; (715) 536-3230
Rooms: 2 share 1 bath. No smoking inn.
Rates: $40 to $50, single; $45 to $60, double; EPB.
Open: All year.
Facilities and activities: Sitting room, dining room, porch. Nearby: mountain-biking trails, Boulder Lake Naturalist Walks, eagle watching, Wolf River rafting and floats, Nicolet National Forest, ghost-town touring, fishing (Wolf Hunting, Evergreen, Prairie, Occonto rivers), hiking the Ice Age Trail, touring rustic roads, crosscountry skiing, snowmobiling, hunting.

The Pfister
MILWAUKEE, WISCONSIN 53202

Elvis stayed here. So did Buffalo Bill, Jack London, and Arturo Toscanini. Ditto for nearly every president since William McKinley. Luciano Pavarotti was enamored of the towels. And it's one of the few places where Rodney Dangerfield *got* respect.

Seems just about anybody who's anybody stays at the Pfister, Milwaukee's grande dame hotel as well as one of the Midwest's most distinguished hostelries. What's the secret?

"People come to the Pfister to come to the Pfister," said Peter Mortensen, chief concierge.

That's true since a five-year, multimillion-dollar restoration has returned the 1893 hotel to its former grandeur. There are hand-painted

murals on the ceiling, terra-cotta angels guarding a turn-of-the-century fireplace, ornate marble columns, gold-leaf detailing, brass and gilt chandeliers—and that's just in the lobby.

Each of the 307 rooms has a marble bathroom, complete with hair dryer an mini-television. Brass and mahogany are everywhere. Many suites, including those in the historic wing, feature a whirlpool tub and three telephones—bedside, deskside, and in the bathroom.

Similar rooms in the twenty-three-story Pfister Tower, added to the original building in 1966, offer breathtaking views of Lake Michigan. (Its Presidential Suite, where I once spent a memorable weekend, resembles a posh penthouse apartment, complete with master bedroom and wet bar.) And guest-room furnishings include everything from Chinese Chippendale cabinets to elegant Renaissance chairs.

Of course, the rationale for going to an elegant hotel is to see and be seen. So get out of your room and head to the hotel's English Room, where you can dress to the nines for a "grand hotel" dining experience.

Winner of numerous culinary awards, this Milwaukee institution offers selections such as breast of pheasant prepared with a peppered game sauce and celery chips, and sautéed twin tenderloins of beef with roasted garlic potato puree and grand mustard sauce, all served by tuxedoed waiters. And who can pass up a dessert of bananas Foster or cherries jubilee?

Need some exercise after all that food? Walk around the lobby and second-floor mezzanine, graced with what's claimed to be the largest hotel collection of Victorian art in the world.

Or head to the glass-encased, twenty-third-floor swimming pool for laps and a sweeping panorama of the city. Forget about bringing towels—there're plenty of fluffy ones available.

Before leaving, lounge around the lobby's historic fireplace. Rediscovered during restoration, it's where hotel guests and full-time Milwaukeans used to gather in the hotel's grand turn-of-the-century days. "I like to think of it as Milwaukee's living room," Mortensen says.

How to get there: From Chicago, take I–94 (Tri-State Tollway) to Milwaukee; exit at I–794/Downtown Milwaukee (get in the right-hand lane). Follow that to the Van Buren/Jackson exit; get off and follow that exit (as it veers left) to Mason Street. Turn left and go 2 blocks to Jefferson; finally, turn left and continue to the hotel.

Innkeeper: Rosemary Steinfest, general manager
Address/Telephone: 424 East Wisconsin Avenue; (414) 273–8222 or (800) 678–8946, fax (414) 273–0747
Rooms: 307, including historic hotel rooms and suites; all with private bath, air conditioning, and phone. Wheelchair access.
Rates: Rooms: $135 to $155, single or double; suites and specialty rooms: $160 to $450; EP. Special packages available.
Open: All year.
Facilities and activities: The Greenery, a full-service restaurant, lunch buffet in Cafe Rouge, The English Room, 24-hour room service; swimming pool, massage therapy, hotel shops, famed fireplace room for drinks and gatherings. Nearby: Grand Avenue Mall, Bradley Center (Milwaukee Bucks NBA basketball games). A short drive to County Stadium (Milwaukee Brewers MLB baseball games).
Business travel: Located in the heart of downtown Milwaukee, a few minutes walk from City Hall, MECCA Convention Center. Corporate rates, conference rooms, fax.

$\mathcal{L}e$ Maison Granit
MONTELLO, WISCONSIN 53949

Just one glance at this handsome inn reveals it is something special.

Located on a hill overlooking Lake Montello, with scores of flower gardens blooming everywhere on the fabulously landscaped 2½-acre estate, the 1909 house is a testament to its builder, C. S. Richter.

Richter quarried the "world's hardest granite" right here in Montello. The richness of its quality made it a national favorite for memorials such as the sarcophagi of Grant's Tomb, Civil War monuments in Gettysburg, and the paean to General Custer in the Black Hills.

So it's little wonder that the inn house is a French translation of "the granite mansion."

Look at this beautiful stonework, with the facing of stately granite spauldings lending an aristocratic touch to this grandeur-filled home. Note the delicate ceiling moldings, custom-made French mirrored stained-glass windows, hand-carved stair banister—and Richter's own personal billiard table, graced with pearl inlays. You can play on that table even today.

Guest rooms boast furniture gathered from around the world. I like the walnut Room whose namesake wood envelops the entire room; the Oak Room, with its deep claw-foot bathtub; and the Cherry Suite, which takes up the entire third floor and offers both a whirlpool tub and hand-painted private staircase.

The breakfast room is bright and airy, graced with a hand-painted version of *The Garden of Eden* on its walls; it's all flowers and vines. But I like to head down to the ornate walkway along the lake, a great place to contemplate all the beauty surrounding you here.

How to get there: From east or west, enter Montello on Wisconsin 23, which turns into Underwood Avenue in town. Follow to the inn, which is located along the lakeshore.

Innkeeper: Shirley J. Mast
Address/Telephone: 55 Underwood Avenue; (608) 297–9078, fax (608) 297–2939
Rooms: 4, with 1 suite; all with private bath. No smoking inn.
Rates: $85 to $169, single or double, EPB.
Open: All year.
Facilities and activities: Tea garden, walking paths through 20 different flower gardens, patio, terrace with benches on shore of Montello Lake. Take a canoe or hop aboard the inn's private pontoon boat. Fishing off boat or shore. Rent inn Mercedes for touring. Nearby: twenty minutes to world-class golf at Lawsonia, Tuscumbia, in Green Lake.
Business travelers: Kickapoo Meeting Room, 100 yards from main house, seats 12, fax and computer equipment, links to Internet.

The Linden Inn
NEW GLARUS, WISCONSIN 53574

We stood in front of the Bank of New Glarus drive-up building, which resembles one of those quaint, timbered chalets found in Swiss villages.

But what makes this chalet special is its 14-bell glockenspiel. Debbie and daughter, Kate and Dayne, waited patiently for the music, expecting to hear "The Happy Wanderer" or some familiar Swiss tune.

Finally, the bells began to clang, and we strained to catch the melody. Kate was the first to recognize it.

"Hey Pa," she said. "Isn't that the Notre Dame fight song?"

Indeed, it appears the Fightin' Irish are a favorite even in "America's Little Switzerland."

That's the appellation given to this charming Old World village of New Glarus. On August 15, 1845, 108 Swiss immigrants from the Canton of Glarus arrived here after a four-month, 5,000-mile journey (including visits to Missouri and Illinois), searching under strict orders for land similar to the rolling hills of the old country.

One glance at the Euro-style picture-postcard landscape of the surrounding Little Sugar River Valley confirms their choice. Add to it the irresistible charms of Swiss hospitality, red-and-white Swiss flags, colorful canton shields, and ubiquitous flower boxes filled with red, white, and pink geraniums, and you'll realize that Europe is only a 3½ hour drive from Chicago.

To experience the full measure of New Glarus's Swiss *gemütlicheit*, eat at Hans Lenzlinger's 1853 New Glarus Hotel. Hans, a Swiss-born entrepreneur, boasts the best authentic Swiss cuisine in the village.

Even my daughters, ever the fussy eaters, raved about the *kaesechuechli*, a baked cheese pie with delicate crust and served with fresh fruit, a perfect luncheon treat.

For dinner, savor the piccata schnitzel, a specialty from the Italian Swiss canton of Ticino. Pork tenderloin fillets are dipped in a delicate cheese batter, pan fried in butter, and smothered in fresh sautéed mushrooms; the result is heavenly.

Don't worry about calories. On Friday and Saturday evenings, the Roger Bright Band dishes up nonstop polka music. So you can polka, polka, polka, until you drop those pounds.

Overnight at the Linden Inn, a restored 1867 home situated on original village platt land surveyed in 1851. The inn, reflecting the owners' interest in Shaker history, is simple and elegant. I like the Enfield suite, which has its own sitting room. And the inn's Simple Gifts Gallery offers fabulous Shaker reproduction handicrafts.

How to get there: From Wisconsin Highway 69, take Wisconsin 39 west into New Glarus. Follow it through the center of town to the inn.

Innkeepers: Rachel and Richard Schmied
Address/Telephone: 219 Fifth Avenue; (608) 527–2675
Rooms: 3; all with private bath. No smoking inn.
Rates: $60 to $80, single or double, EPB.
Open: All year.
Facilities and activities: Large wraparound sitting porch, gallery store. Walk to Swiss shops, restaurants, attractions. Short drive to Chalet of the Golden Fleece (museum), Swiss Historical Village, New Glarus Woods State Park, Sugar River State Bicycle Trail (rentals available), Tyrol Ski Basin, and Norwegian village of Mt. Horeb.

Inn at Pine Terrace

OCONOMOWOC, WISCONSIN 53066

Cary O'Dwanny and his wife, Christine, two of the inn's principal owners, greeted me outside their inn, an impressive three-story Victorian mansion built in 1884 by the Schuttler family, well-known wagon makers from Chicago. In fact, two Schuttler sons married girls whose families used those wagons to haul barrels of beer for their breweries; one was an Anheuser, another a Busch.

As soon as I stepped inside the massive double doors of the tiled foyer, accented with stained and etched glass, I knew the inn would be quite special.

The restoration, which took more than two years to complete, is an accomplished one. Cary spent more than $750,000 in millwork alone to bring back the elaborate butternut and walnut moldings that are everywhere. Furniture, done in antique Eastlake style, was custom made especially for the inn. A curving walnut handrail that crowns the three-story staircase is valued at $55,000. Most bathrooms have a marble-lined two-person whirlpool bath; guest-room doors have brass hinges and hand-carved wooden doorknobs; custom wall coverings and brooding Victorian paint colors evoke the period as almost no other inn has before.

Once the town was an exclusive vacation spot for wealthy Southern families escaping the summer heat. "The mansion was the 'in' place to be," Cary said. "Five U.S. presidents were guests here, beginning with Taft." Other notables included the likes of Mark Twain and Montgomery Ward.

Elegant guest rooms are named for historic residents of Oconomowoc. Most are huge by inn standards, with the first-floor beauty perhaps the showpiece. It features a massive bedroom area with a crowning touch: marble steps leading to a marble platform, upon which sits a white-enamel, brass-claw-footed bathtub illuminated by a bank of three ceiling-to-floor windows—shuttered for privacy, of course.

Rooms on the third floor are smaller, since these are the old servant's quarters; however, they are no less attractive. My room, named for Captain Gustav Pabst, was a charming hide-

away with slanting dormer ceilings that created a small sitting-room alcove; its brass lighting fixtures, rich woodwork, deep-green wall coverings, double whirlpool tub, and tiny window offering a view of Lac La Belle made it one of my favorites.

A breakfast buffet, served in the dining room on the lower level, means cereals, fresh fruits, home-baked muffins, and coffee. Later you can lounge at the inn's swimming pool, or take a dip in the refreshing water while already making plans for your return visit here.

How to get there: From Milwaukee, take I–94 west to U.S. 67. Exit north and continue through town to Lisbon Road. Turn right; the inn is just down the street.

Innkeepers: Shirley W. Hinds and Penny A. Yakes, managers
Address/Telephone: 371 Lisbon Road; (414) 567-7463
Rooms: 13; all with private bath, air conditioning, phone, and TV, 6 with double whirlpool bath. Wheelchair access. Well-behaved pets OK.
Rates: $59.50 to $119.50, single or double, continental breakfast.
Open: All year.
Facilities and activities: Sitting room, swimming pool, breakfast room, conference room. Nearby: short walk to Lac La Belle for swimming, fishing, boating, and 3 beaches. Restaurants and Olympia Ski Area, with downhill and cross-country skiing, a short drive away.

St. Croix River Inn
OSCEOLA, WISCONSIN 54020

This eighty-plus-year-old stone house is poised high on a bluff overlooking the scenic St. Croix River. It allows unsurpassed, breathtaking views while providing one of the most elegant lodgings in the entire Midwest.

I'm especially fond of a suite with a huge whirlpool bath set in front of windows, allowing you to float visually down the water while pampering yourself in a bubble bath.

"The house was built from limestone quarried near here," Bev said. "It belonged to the owner of the town's pharmacy and remained in his family until a few years ago."

Now let's get right to the rooms (suites, really), which are named for riverboats built in Osceola. Perhaps (and this is a *big* perhaps) Jennie Hays is my all-time favorite inn room. It is simply exquisite, with appointments that remind me of exclusive European hotels. I continue to rave about a magnificent four-poster canopy bed that feels as good as it looks and a decorative tile fireplace that soothes the psyche as well as chilly limbs on crackling-cool autumn or frigid winter nights.

Then there is the view! I'm almost at a loss for words. A huge Palladian window, stretching from floor to ceiling, overlooks the river from the inn's bluff-top perch. It provides a romantic and rewarding setting that would be hard to surpass anywhere in the Midwest. The room has a whirlpool tub, and there's a private balcony with more great river views.

The G. B. Knapp Room is more of the same: a huge suite, with a four-poster canopy bed adorned with a floral quilt, tall armoire, its own working gas fireplace, and a whirlpool tub. Then walk through a door to the enclosed porch (more like a private sitting room), with windows overlooking the river. There are also exquisite stenciling, bull's-eye moldings, and private balconies.

Pampering continues at breakfast, which Bev serves in your room. It might include fresh fruit and juices, omelets, waffles, French toast, or puff pastries stuffed with ham and cheese, and home-baked French bread and pound cake.

Bev also delivers to your room a pot of steaming coffee and the morning paper a half hour before your morning meal. She can recommend a great place for dinner. But you simply may never want to leave your quarters.

Let's face it: This is one of the Midwest's most romantic retreats—pure grace and elegance.

How to get there: From downtown Osceola, turn west on Third Avenue and follow it past a hospital and historic Episcopal church (dating from 1854, with four turreted steeples). The inn is located on the river side of River Street.

Innkeeper: Bev Johnson
Address/Telephone: 305 River Street; (715) 294-4248
Rooms: 7; all with private bath and air conditioning, 2 with TV.
Rates: Friday and Saturday, $100 to $200; Sunday through Thursday, $85 to $150; single or double; EPB. Gift certificates available.
Open: All year.
Facilities and activities: Outdoor porch, sitting room overlooking St. Croix River. Nearby: several area antiques shops, canoeing, fishing, downhill and cross-country skiing at Wild Mountain or Trollhaugen. A short drive to restaurants and Taylors Falls, Minnesota—a lovely little river town with historic-homes tours and cruises on old-fashioned paddle wheelers.

52 *Stafford*
PLYMOUTH, WISCONSIN 53073

Cary, better known as Rip, has created a little bit o' Ireland in the middle of cheese country: 52 Stafford, an "authentic" Irish country house complete with imported European appointments, classy guest rooms, and Guinness Stout on tap.

"I wanted the feeling of casual elegance," Rip told me as we shared a pint of bitters, "where you could feel at home in blue jeans or a tuxedo.

"I also decided to use only the finest materials when decorating the inn," he said. First-floor hardwoods are all solid cherry, with crown moldings and solid-brass chandeliers (weighing eighty pounds apiece) adding classical touches.

He picked the yarn colors for the hand-made floral carpet imported from England that graces the inn. Much of the leaded glass came from Germany. Chinese silk adorns lobby wing chairs.

The bar is imposing. It's solid cherry, stretching almost to the ceiling. Green and white tiles cover the footrest. Then there's beautiful hand-sandblasted etched glass, with deep-relief designs of harps and wreaths done by a local craftsman. The glass gave off a lilting greenish glow. Just pull up a bar stool, order a Guinness on tap, and you'll be close to heaven.

All rooms are individually decorated. Mine had a handsome English four-poster bed and fox-hunt wall prints, tall shuttered windows, crown ceiling moldings, and an elegant brass chandelier.

Another special inn feature is a first-floor antique leaded-glass window—*above* a fireplace. It has more than 400 jewels and beads in it, while the fireplace flue must swing to the left, around the window.

Rip's breakfast, served in the inn's handsome dining room, offers huge omelets, French toast, homemade muffins, and much more.

But his dinner chefs have fashioned quite a gustatory reputation for 52 Stafford and one of its sister inns, The Audubon Inn, located in Mayville, Wisconsin. Consider Guinness brisket (a beef brisket simmered in Irish stout

and served with boiled carrots, Kilkenny potatoes, leeks, and cabbage). Or try the Stafford steak (a certified eight-ounce black Angus beef tenderloin served with a shiitake mushroom sauce). And how can you resist Bailey's Irish cheesecake for dessert?

A final note: 52 Stafford's Saint Patrick's Day celebrations have been known to last for an entire week before March 17 and culminate with a huge parade.

How to get there: From Milwaukee, take I-43 north, switching to Wisconsin 57 just past Grafton. At Wisconsin 23, turn west and drive into Plymouth. At Stafford Street, turn south. The inn is on the right side of the street.

Innkeeper: Cary O'Dwanny
Address/Telephone: 52 Stafford Street (mailing address: P. O. Box 565); (414) 893–0552
Rooms: 20; all with private bath, air conditioning, TV, and phone. Wheelchair access. Well-behaved pets OK.
Rates: $79.50 to $119.50, single or double, EPB on weekends, continental breakfast weekdays. Two- or 3-night minimums on Road America race weekends.
Open: All year.
Facilities and activities: Dinner. Sitting room, Irish folksinger/entertainment in bar. Nearby: Road America in Elkhart Lake, state parks with hiking, biking, nature trails, cross-country skiing (in season), Old Wade historic site, swimming and fishing at local lakes, charter fishing on Lake Michigan.

The Rochester Inn
SHEBOYGAN FALLS, WISCONSIN 53085

An elegant creation, this 1839 National Historic Landmark has been transformed from a pioneer general store into a den of opulence.

Lest my adjectives overwhelm my pen, suffice it to say that the Rochester Inn's cozy rooms are quite breathtaking. Imagine guest rooms, each with its own parlor, fashioned with quality antique reproductions that include wingback chairs, Chippendale-style sofas, and finely polished armoires.

Though each has its own distinctive look, they are similar in their Victorian-inspired stylings. For example, the Charles D. Cole Room (named after the Sheboygan Falls settler who built this structure) is swathed in hand-some wall coverings produced in California and features a pencil-post bed adorned with a hand-made quilt, its own wet bar, and a double whirlpool bath.

I also liked the triangular window just above the bed. Original to the house, it was discovered when the old clapboard was ripped off.

Breakfast treats, taken in a small dining room, include a choice of quiche, French toast or pancakes, scrambled eggs with ham or sausage, cinnamon and butter croissants, and fresh fruit. Jacquelyn also offers specialties such as poached pears, stuffed French toast, and pecan waffles. She can arrange a prebreakfast sip of juice or coffee in your room.

Also take a peek at the photo hanging above the dining-room table. It shows the building in its early days. Note that there seem to be no sidewalks—not even a road.

For dinner wander to Sean's father's flagship inn, 52 Stafford, for wonderful gourmet-style meals. Or just enjoy the Irish folk music performed by artists brought directly from the Auld Sod; might as well take a pull on a Guinness, since your stay at the Rochester entitles you to two complimentary drinks from the 52 Stafford bar.

(By the way, early settlers named this town Rochester, only to discover that a village in New York claimed the same name—so they changed it to Sheboygan Falls.)

Sean's father calls this "the classiest little inn in America." He may be right. And we may have the makings of a country-inn family dynasty.

How to get there: From Milwaukee, take I–94 to U.S. 43 north and continue to the Sheboygan Falls exit (exit 51); turn west and proceed about 8/10 mile to County A, turn north until reaching Wisconsin 28, and take Wisconsin 28 west into the town and to the inn.

Innkeepers: Sean and Jaquelyn O'Dwanny

Address/Telephone: 504 Water Street; (414) 467-3123

Rooms: 5, including 4 suites; all with private bath, air conditioning, TV, and phone. Well-behaved pets OK.

Rates: $79.50 to $119.50, single or double, Sunday through Thursday; $89.50 to $139.50, single or double, Friday and Saturday; EPB. Two-night minimum on special festival weekends.

Open: All year.

Facilities and activities: Nearby: a short drive to restaurants, Kettle Moraine State Forest for biking and hiking, Lake Michigan fishing and boating, Road America (automobile racing), Blackwolf Run for golfing, Kohler Design Center.

Church Hill Inn
SISTER BAY, WISCONSIN 54234

This inn sits high on a hill, glistening in the Door County sunlight like a regal jewel in the crown of the royal family.

It is designed and decorated in English country style, striving to blend the best of an elegant small hotel with the intimacy of a European bed-and-breakfast inn. I think it succeeds quite well.

Masterful guest rooms are beautifully done in antiques and reproductions. In fact, many of the antiques were purchased in England and brought back especially for the inn.

Each of the inn's stately wings features its own separate sitting areas, complete with fireplace, high-back chairs, and books and magazines; there are also a wet bar and a porch. These areas feel much like the library of an English country estate and are nice places to unwind and relax.

That is, if you ever leave your room. They are handsome; many feature a four-poster canopy bed done in rich mahogany, queen-sized mattress, Empire-style dresser, and private balcony.

For total luxury enjoy a room with double whirlpool bath, fireplace, refrigerator, and huge bay windows with quaint bench seats that might offer a view of the flower-filled terrace.

Or maybe you'd like a room that has delicate French doors opening directly onto the inn's swimming pool and its elegant sunbathing deck.

You'll breakfast on tasty treats like cherry crisp, poppyseed bread, sausage-and-egg soufflés, French toast, and more.

And don't forget that complimentary snacks or hors d'oeuvres are served in the lobby sitting room every day from 4:00 to 6:00 P.M. It's a great way to unwind and swap Door County stories at the same time.

How to get there: From Sturgeon Bay, go north on Wisconsin 42 and continue into Sister Bay. The inn is on a hill near the intersection of Wisconsin 42 and 57.

Innkeepers: Paul and Joyce Crittenden
Address/Telephone: 425 Gateway Drive; (414) 854-4885
Rooms: 34; all with private bath. Wheelchair access.
Rates: Weekdays: $124 to $164, single or double; weekends: $134 to $174, single or double; EPB. Three-night minimum on summer weekends. Special packages available.
Open: All year.
Facilities and activities: Sauna, whirlpool, exercise room, heated outdoor pool. Located in heart of Door County peninsula, one of the Midwest's premier vacation spots. Nearby: golf courses, water sports, shopping, antiques, orchards, shoreline. Country Walk specialty stores steps away. Town's beach, dock, and downtown 2 blocks away.

The Springs
SPRING GREEN, WISCONSIN 53588

The Springs is a luxurious Frank Lloyd Wright–inspired resort nestled among the rolling wooded hills of the picturesque Jones Valley on land once owned by the famed architect.

Faithful to Wright's vision of organic architecture, the resort neatly blends in with the verdant countryside, full of low-to-the-ground horizontal lines, inspiring vistas through long rows of windows, and massive terraces of natural stone.

Inside, the resort boasts more Wright-inspired surprises. Cherokee reds and other earth tones add touches of understated elegance. Furnishings might have come directly from Wright's own studio, full of unexpected lines and angles. And guest suites offer equal graciousness.

Our suite was a handsome paean to Wright's genius as well as a luxurious oasis. My wife, Debbie, loved the original art adorning the walls. Our daughters, Kate and Dayne, couldn't wait to test the whirlpool bath. I was drawn to the balcony, which overlooks the beautiful award-winning Robert Trent Jones Golf Course.

The girls lobbied for a quick swim, so we headed to the pool. They were thrilled to discover a massive pool shaped by three intersecting circles, along with a huge lap pool and spa tub. I went to the fitness room for a quick workout on fabulous equipment. Then we hiked around the golf course, planning my future assault on these nationally renowned links.

Dinners are exquisite culinary events, thanks to chef Scott Finley. His mushroom strudel (wild mushrooms sautéed in white wine and heavy cream and nestled in a pastry puff shell) is heavenly. A favorite entree is grilled filet mignon topped with a small pat of blue-cheese butter and a tarragon-rich béarnaise sauce. And desserts of chocolate chambord or crème caramel can excite the palate of anyone.

It's almost impossible to visit the Springs without challenging the links. I took on the resort's newest nine, designed by PGA golfer Andy North, himself a Wisconsin native. He envisions this layout as the "Pinehurst of the Midwest."

Could be. I got bitten by the narrow fairways and big-hitter challenges (not to mention mosquitoes—bring insect repellent). In fact, I probably left more balls in the woods than on the greens. And the par-four, 371-yard number six offers one of the prettiest views in the state.

How to get there: From Madison/Middleton, take U.S. 14 west to Spring Green; just outside Spring Green, you'll see directional signs for THE SPRINGS; follow the signs to the resort.

Innkeeper: Tom van Duursen, general manager

Address/Telephone: 400 Springs Drive; (608) 588–7000 or (800) 822–7774, fax (608) 588–2269

Rooms: 80 suites; all with private bath, whirlpool, cable TV, balcony or patio. Wheelchair access.

Rates: $165 to $185, single or double, June through September; $110 to $165, off-season; continental breakfast. Special lodging and golf packages available.

Open: All year.

Facilities and activities: Full-service dining room, casual restaurant, snack bar, swimming pool, lap pool, spa tub, full-service health club, sitting area with fireplace facing woods, world-class golf course (27 holes), hiking trails, cross-country ski trails. Nearby: a short drive to Taliesin (Frank Lloyd Wright's home), American Players Theater (Shakespearean company), House on the Rock, Tower Hill State Park, Spring Green art galleries and crafts shops, horseback riding, biking, Wisconsin River canoe rides.

Business travel: Located about 45 minutes west of Madison, 3 minutes from downtown Spring Green. Corporate group rates, conference rooms, fax.

The Inn at Cedar Crossing
STURGEON BAY, WISCONSIN 54235

This handsome inn, housed in an 1884 merchant building modeled after European markets, is one of my Door County favorites. Debbie and I especially liked all the elegant guest rooms.

And they are exquisite—some of the most luxurious in the Midwest. Consider the Corner Suite, which reflects the inn's 1880s heritage in grand fashion. An ornately carved archway, with two tall columns, frames the handsome bedchamber, whose queen-sized bed is adorned with a down-filled European comforter. Golden-oak furniture surrounds a cozy fireplace in the "sitting room," a perfect spot for romantic whispers.

The Vintage Roses Room is awash in rose-tinted hues and includes a walnut four-poster bed, hand-carved Victorian walnut furnishings, romantic gas log fireplace, and double whirlpool tub.

For simpler tastes, try Country Pine; it has hand-stenciled walls and a four-poster bed trimmed in white cutwork linens. Of course, the marbled bath with double whirlpool is a favorite with guests.

There are at least two other rooms I must mention: the Anniversary Room offers a king-sized, hand-carved mahogany canopy bed, with period furnishings, fireplace, and whirlpool tub; and besides its pencil-post bed, massive whirlpool bath, fireplace, and hand-painted armoire, A Touch of Williamsburg features its own private porch.

Guests often meet in the Gathering Room for evenings, where they can curl up with a good book next to the fireplace, play parlor games, or munch on popcorn. But leave some room for mornings, because Terry's breakfasts are a real treat. Count on homemade muffins, scones, coffee cakes, maybe even some Scandinavian fruit soup.

No visit to the inn would be complete without dinner at its heralded restaurant, rated by *Milwaukee Journal* magazine as one of the twenty-five best in Wisconsin. Scrumptious dinners might include tart cherry-stuffed pork loin, whitefish baked in brown butter with capers and pine nuts, and grilled New York strip steak with pungent cherry chutney; among sinfully decadent desserts are double diablo chocolate tortes and the inn's famous "mile-high" cherry pie—it weighs seven pounds whole!

Of course, menus continue to change; no telling what kind of scrumptious meals you'll enjoy on your next visit.

How to get there: Go north on Wisconsin 42/57, around Sturgeon Bay, over the new bridge. Turn left on Michigan Street and go about 1 mile to the first stop sign. Then turn right on Fourth Avenue, go 1 block, then left on Louisiana. The inn is just before the stop sign, on the right.

Innkeeper: Terry Wulf
Address/Telephone: 336 Louisiana Street; (414) 743–4200
Rooms: 9; all with private bath and air conditioning, TV on request.
Rates: $85 to $145, single or double, continental breakfast. Two-night minimum on weekends when Saturday night is included. Three-night minimums on most holiday and peak fall weekends. Special winter/spring packages available November through April.
Open: All year.
Facilities and activities: Full-service restaurant, 2 dining rooms, pub with mahogany bar. About 3 blocks from waterfront. Nearby: walk to quaint shops, restaurants, Miller Art Museum, historic district, downtown area. Half-hour's drive to beaches, antiques shops, tip of Door County peninsula. Cross-country ski rentals available at inn through local outfitter.

White Lace Inn
STURGEON BAY, WISCONSIN 54235

Bonnie and Dennis Statz call their award-winning inn "a romantic fireside getaway." I can't think of a better place to spend a cozy, pampered weekend for two.

And things have only gotten better since my last visit. Now the White Lace Inn resembles a private Victorian-era park, with three handsome historic buildings connected by a red-brick pathway that winds through landscaped grounds filled with stately trees, wildflower gardens, and a rose garden featuring varieties dating from the 1700s. You will also enjoy the Vixen Hill gazebo, a great place to pause among the inn's many gardens; it is a beauty from Pennsylvania.

The Main House was built for a local lawyer in 1903; what's surprising is the extensive oak woodwork put in for a man of such modest means. Stepping into the entryway, I was surrounded by magnificent hand-carved oak paneling.

Bonnie has a degree in interior design and has created guest rooms with a warm feel, mixing Laura Ashley wallpaper and fabrics with imposing, yet comfortable, antique furnishings like rich oriental rugs and high-back walnut and canopied beds. Fluffy down pillows are provided, handmade comforters and quilts brighten large beds, and lacy curtains adorn tall windows.

The 1880s Garden House has rooms with their own fireplace. They're done in myriad styles, from country elegant to the grand bold-ness of oversized Empire furniture.

This time my wife and I stayed in the Washburn House, the third and newest "old" addition to the White Lace. All rooms here are luxurious; ours had a canopy brass bed with down comforter, fireplace, and two-person whirlpool. It was graced with soft pastel floral chintz fabric and white-on-white Carol Gresco fabrics that tell a story (in fact, some of her work is part of the Smithsonian Design Institution collection). The bath's Ralph Lauren towels are heavenly.

Next time, I want a room in the Hadley House—maybe one with a huge whirlpool, fire-place, and private balcony.

Back in the main house, Bonnie's home-made muffins are the breakfast treat, along with juice, coffee, and delicious Scandinavian fruit soup (a tasty concoction served cold) or old-fashioned rice pudding. Blueberry soup and apple crisps are summer specials. It's a great time to swap Door County stories.

For dinner the innkeepers will recommend a restaurant that suits your tastes. I'm always pleased with the Inn at Cedar Crossing. Or try Oliver Station, a restored railroad station con-verted into a casual restaurant and microbrew-ery. Great beer and beer/cheese soup.

How to get there: From Milwaukee, take U.S. 41 north to Wisconsin 42, toward Sturgeon Bay. Just outside the city, take Business 42/57 and fol-low it into town, cross the bridge, and you'll come to Michigan Street. Follow Michigan to Fifth Avenue and turn left. White Lace Inn is on the right side of the street. Or you can take the 42/51 bypass across the new bridge to Michigan Street. Turn left on Michigan, go to Fifth Avenue, and take a right on Fifth to the inn.

Innkeepers: Bonnie and Dennis Statz
Address/Telephone: 16 North Fifth Avenue; (414) 743–1105
Rooms: 19, in 4 historic houses; all with private bath and air conditioning, some with fireplace, whirlpool, TV, and wheelchair access.
Rates: $75 to $190, single or double, continental breakfast. Special winter or spring fire-side rates and packages available November through May.
Open: All year.
Facilities and activities: Five blocks to bay shore. Nearby: specialty and antiques shops, restaurants, Door County Museum, Miller Art Center; swimming, tennis, and horseback riding. A short drive to Whitefish Dunes and Potawatomi state parks, Peninsula Players Summer Theater, Birch Creek Music Festival. Cross-country skiing and ice skating in winter. Gateway to the peninsula.
Recommended Country Inns® Travelers' Club Benefit: 25 percent discount, Monday–Thursday, November–April, excluding holidays. Not valid with any other offers or reduced rates.

Rosenberry Inn
WAUSAU, WISCONSIN 54401

I have just arrived at the Rosenberry Inn early on a weekend morning. Inside on the guest-book stand rests a cowbell to alert the innkeepers of new arrivals.

It's library quiet in the house. I just know I'll wake the entire place if I ring that bell, and I don't want a guilty conscience—especially on Sunday.

Oh, what the heck. *Cllaaannnnggggg!*

Laurie and Fred continue to work endlessly to rescue this wonderful house from ruin and restore it to its early-1900s splendor. There's rich woodwork everywhere. Leaded and stained glass casts prisms of light on the stairwell. Antique photographs and prints add to the bygone-era feeling.

All the rooms are graced with Victorian antiques and some country primitives; four have a fireplace.

In the rose-colored room, I like the iron-rail beds and the working fireplace—good to take away the chill after skiing at nearby Rib Mountain. Another has antique Victorian bedspreads, homemade comforters, and a fireplace that transforms the room into a cozy retreat.

My favorite has a pressed-tin ceiling, fireplace, and a collection of cranberry glass.

The best place for games is the third-floor card room, with its long harvest table and stenciled vines.

I like eating breakfast (juice, Laurie's home-baked banana bread, muffins, and coffee) up in the old attic, now cheerily decorated with wall stencils of farm animals, along with antique tables and chairs. Or come to the dining room. Whatever, do not miss a chance to sample Laurie's cherry cheesecake muffins or Fred's berry-baked pancakes. The innkeepers can recommend a restaurant to suit your dinner tastes.

The Schmidts have an additional home, located in the Historic District just 1½ blocks away. Rooms in the DeVoe House have a fireplace and whirlpool bath. These are cozy retreats for big-city visitors.

How to get there: From Milwaukee, take I–94 west to U.S. 51 and head north until you reach Wausau. At Highway 52, go east to Franklin Street and turn left to the inn.

Innkeepers: Laurie and Fred Schmidt
Address/Telephone: 511 Franklin Street; (715) 842–5733
Rooms: 9, including 2 suites; all with private bath, air conditioning, TV, and phone.
Rates: $49 to $59, single; $65 to $88, double; $125, suites; continental breakfast.
Open: All year.
Facilities and activities: Gathering room, porch. Nearby: downtown Wausau and the Mall, Washington Square shopping complex, antiques shops, boutiques, restaurants, Leigh Yawkey Woodson Art Museum. A short drive to Dells of Eau Claire nature trails, rock climbing, rappelling, fishing, and canoeing. Rib Mountain skiing; cross-country ski trails.

Westby House
WESTBY, WISCONSIN 54667

This charming Queen Anne–style inn, located in a Norwegian community, is a Westby landmark. The eighteen-room mansion, built in the 1890s, has all the special Victorian touches: a tall tower, stained-glass windows, gingerbread finery, and elegant interior woodwork.

I saw a 1915 photograph of the house in the hallway. Doesn't look as though it's changed much since then. Lucky for me—and you, too.

Chandeliers with cranberry-colored shades cast a rose-tinted glow. The antique Amish quilts hanging on walls make an attractive backdrop.

To reach the second-floor guest rooms, I walked up a long staircase. Note the old butler's pantry. It's fun to imagine servants scurrying about up here, preparing breakfast for the turn-of-the-century household.

The guest rooms are small-town charming. The spacious Anniversary Suite has a large brass bed, lacy curtains on windows, and a Victorian love seat and chair; it's a guest favorite.

There are two white iron-rail beds in the Greenbriar Room. And the Squire Room has cheery country accents, such as eyelet lace curtains and a hand-painted queen-sized bed, which looks awfully inviting.

The inn's most recent addition is the Fireplace Room. This two-room suite has regal antiques (including a fainting couch), lots of lacy finery, a fireplace, and a cozy nook inside the home's tall tower—high Victorian and very romantic.

Downstairs, the busy Victorian dining room draws people from all over town for its delicious, hearty food. I sat in front of a manteled fireplace at an antique table complete with bentwood chairs and devoured my lunch: a hot crabmeat sandwich with tomato slices and jack cheese. Dinner also looked pretty inviting, with choices such as fresh trout or sautéed shrimp with mushrooms and onions. (Of course, everything at the inn is made from scratch, right down to the salad dressing.)

I suggest that you try the *torsk,* an inn spe-cialty. It's eight ounces of Norwegian cod baked in lemon butter and served with egg noodles. Then opt for a luscious dessert—the Victoriannie—a homemade brownie topped with ice cream, whipped cream, and a cherry.

Remember that Westby's Olympic-style ski jump draws top athletes to its winter competitions every year. It's a great time to enjoy the Westby House hospitality.

How to get there: The inn is located halfway between Chicago and the Twin Cities. From LaCrosse, take U.S. 14/61 southeast into Westby. Turn west onto West State Street and continue to the inn.

Innkeeper: Patricia Benjamin Smith

Address/Telephone: 200 West State Street; (608) 634-4112

Rooms: 6, including 1 suite; 3 with private bath, all with air conditioning, TV, and phone.

Rates: $65 to $80, single or double, continental breakfast.

Open: All year.

Facilities and activities: Full-service restaurant. Short walk to specialty stores and antiques shops. In Wisconsin Amish country, with quaint back-road exploring. Winter cross-country skiing, major ski-jump park and training site. Town celebrates many Norwegian holidays.

Recommended Country Inns® Travelers' Club Benefit: Stay two nights, get third night free, Sunday–Thursday.

Wolf River Lodge
WHITE LAKE, WISCONSIN 54491

Where can you find world-class white-water rapids, kayaking, and fly-cast trout fishing in a spot where eagle and osprey soar overhead and roadsides are smothered by early summer wildflowers? The Wolf River Lodge, of course.

This rustic lodge is a center for river rafting on the Wolf River. In the majestic Nicolet National Forest country, frothing white-water rapids tumble over boulders and ledges, dropping 12 feet per mile for 25 miles. The crystal-clear water is often icy cold.

The log building is surrounded by tall trees and teeming wilderness. A large, rustic dining room, with exposed logs and long oak dining and tavern tables, offers solid fare.

A cozy sitting room with a crazy-quilt arrangement of chairs and sofas is a favorite guest gathering spot—the large stone fireplace is the reason. Some relax here after a long day of cross-country skiing; others just watch the glow of the fire.

I browsed through piles of books sitting on a large coffee table. Naturally, lots of them give tips on white-water rafting, canoeing, and kayaking. The wackiest offering was a surfing handbook.

The guest rooms are small but cozy, with pine furniture and country finery. I like the brightly colored quilts and braided rugs that add color to the rustic charm. George Washington didn't sleep here, but a senator who became our thirty-fifth president did.

The food is simple but delicious. Breakfast means a morning treat: the lodge's renowned crepes. Most evening meals feature delectable trout; delicious roast duck; thick, juicy steaks; or baked stuffed pork chops with pine-nut dressing.

The lodge's newest wrinkle: a carriage-house loft (with its own private bath) that sleeps two to six people; this handsome log home should be a real family-pleaser.

How to get there: From Milwaukee, take I–43 north to Green Bay; then take U.S. 41/141 north to Wisconsin 64. Head west to White Lake. Turn north on Wisconsin 55 and then watch for the Wolf River Lodge signs that direct you there.

Innkeeper: Joan Jesse

Address/Telephone: White Lake; (715) 882–2182

Rooms: 9, plus 1 carriage house; 2 rooms and carriage house with private bath.

Rates: Weekends: $75, single; $95, double; weekdays: $60, single; $80, double. Carriage house $150 per night with four people. EPB. Most reservations are made at week long or weekend package rates. Special ski-season rates (Christmas season to mid-March).

Open: All year.

Facilities and activities: Full-service dining room, bar, wine cellar, parlor and game rooms, gift shop, outdoor hot tub. Located on Wolf River, with world-class white-water rapids during high-water periods. River is runnable April through October. Excellent trout fishing May and June. Ideal terrain for cross-country skiing, horse-back riding.

Recommended Country Inns® Travelers' Club Benefit: Stay two nights, get 50 percent off third night.

$\mathcal{T}$hunder $\mathcal{V}$alley $\mathcal{I}$nn

WISCONSIN DELLS, WISCONSIN 53965

This 130-year-old homestead, run by descendants of the original Norwegian immigrants who settled here, dishes out the finest home-cooked farm-style meals in the Dells.

Everything's organically grown, home-ground, and made from scratch, including the most delicious whole-grain griddle cakes (topped with lingonberries) this traveler has ever tasted. Also try scrambled eggs with Ole's Norwegian white sauce. Yum! And breakfast meats include scrumptious turkey ham.

Daughters Kate and Dayne ordered the "animal pancakes" offered for kids. They squealed with delight when everything from lions to rhinos appeared on their plates.

And massive cinnamon rolls—*Detergodt!* They are good! In fact, we ordered twice as many the next day.

During the meal owner Anita Nelson introduced daughters Sigrid and Kari, dressed in traditional folk costumes, who fiddled Norwegian folk tunes and pioneer songs. Their serenade was a lovely way to start the day.

After breakfast children can help "Farmer Benson" collect eggs in the hen house, feed goats, pet chicks, and watch peacocks fan their colorful feathers. Although Dayne did get a little nervous when asked to pick up some of the chicks and return them to the hen house.

"Would you please do it?" she asked Farmer

Benson. "After all, you're the farmer."

Besides a Friday-night fish fry, Thunder Valley also offers Saturday-evening dinners and chautauquas. Home-style food includes slow-cooked beef pot roast sautéed with onions, mashed potatoes, fresh garden vegetables, and more; entertainment might be anything from the Grieg Norwegian Men's Chorus to a quilt show or ice-cream social.

The Norwegian hospitality extends to charming guest rooms. The original Farm Hus has six of them: Lena's Room offers an antique iron double bed; Wildflower features two full-sized beds with goose-down comforters and a kitchenette; and the Norskevalley is a spacious bedchamber with California king bed, feather-filled comforter, antique Norwegian desk, and claw-footed bathtub. The Hus's gathering room boasts a Franklin stove, sitting room, and dining room.

Another inn building, the Guest Hus, features rustic knotty-pine interiors; it's espcially good for families. And the Wee Hus, a cottage that's perfect for romantic getaways and honeymooners, is adorned with colorful folk-art accents.

VELKOMMEN TO THUNDER VALLEY INN, say all the signs. Here, they really mean it!

How to get there: The inn is located just north of Wisconsin Dells on Highway 13. Best way there is to take Exit 87 (Highway 13) from I–90/94. Go east through downtown Wisconsin Dells to the stoplight (junction of Highways 16, 23, and 13); turn left on Highway 13 and go about 1 mile; watch for the inn's sign on the right.

Innkeepers: Anita Nelson, Kari and Sigrid Nelson
Address/Telephone: W15344 Waubeek Road; (608) 254-4145
Rooms: 10 rooms, plus 1 cottage; all with private bath. No smoking inn.
Rates: $45 to $85, single; $50 to $90, double; EPB.
Open: All year (inn), May to October (restaurant).
Facilities and activities: Full-service restaurant with folk-music performances, gift shop, children's farm tours. Nearby: a short drive to Noah's Ark Water Park, Country Legends Music Theater, Ripley's Believe It or Not Museum, Storybook Gardens, Biblical Gardens, Stand Rock Winnebago Indian Ceremonial, Wisconsin River boat cruises, the Ducks (amphibious World War II vehicles) Wisconsin River tours, gift shops, boutiques, golf, fishing, horseback riding, more.

Indexes

Alphabetical Index to Inns

Inns with Full-Service Restaurants

Bed-and-Breakfast Inns

(serve breakfast only)

Riverside Inns

Inns on Lakes

Inns with a Swimming Pool

Inns near Downhill or Cross-Country Skiing

Inns Especially Good for Kids

Historic Inns (Hotels)

Romantic Inns

No Smoking Inns

Inns with Wheelchair Access
(to at least one room)

Inns for Business Travelers

Inns Offering Travelers' Club Benefits